T0204569

THE RETREAT
TO COMMITMENT

THE RETREAT
TO COMMITMENT

WILLIAM WARREN BARTLEY, III

Second edition, revised and enlarged

OPEN COURT PUBLISHING COMPANY
La Salle   London
1984

Printed in the United States of America

OC842   10 9 8 7 6 5 4 3 2 1

ISBN 0-87548-420-4

Library of Congress Cataloging in Publication Data

Bartley, William Warren, 1934-
    The retreat to commitment.

    Includes bibliographies and indexes.
    1. Rationalism. 2. Protestantism. 3. Knowledge,
Theory of. 4. Criticism. I. Title.
B833.B37 1984   121   84-14862
ISBN 0-87548-420-4

To My Mother
Elvina Henry Bartley

There is nobody in the commonwealth of learning who does not profess himself a lover of truth; and there is not a rational creature that would not take it amiss to be thought otherwise of. And yet, for all this, one may truly say, there are very few lovers of truth for truth's sake, even amongst those who persuade themselves that they are so. How a man may know whether he be so in earnest, is worth enquiry.

—JOHN LOCKE, 1699

TABLE OF CONTENTS

INTRODUCTION TO THE SECOND ENGLISH EDITION, 1984, AND TO THE FRENCH, GERMAN, AND ITALIAN TRANSLATIONS

> The reasonable man adapts himself to the conditions which surround him. The unreasonable man persists in trying to adapt surrounding conditions to himself. . . . All progress depends on the unreasonable man.
>
> —George Bernard Shaw

1. What This Book Is About

This book explores the nature and limits of criticism. Thereby it explores the nature and limits of rationality. It contains a generalization of Sir Karl Popper's approach to philosophy.[1] By applying this generalization, it is able to solve a philosophical problem that has, since antiquity, been thought to be insoluble—that of the examination and justification of basic presuppositions. As an immediate result, the traditional arguments for both scepticism and fideism, and for most forms of relativism, are vanquished.

The book attempts to do what might be expected of an adequate presentation of any new approach. It delineates how it differs from earlier

---

[1]On the relation between my views and Popper's see my "Rationality, Criticism, and Logic", *Philosophia*, vol. 11, nos. 1-2 (February 1982), pp. 121–221; and also K. R. Popper, *Realism and the Aim of Science*, vol. 1 of the *Postscript to the Logic of Scientific Discovery*, ed. W. W. Bartley, III (London: Hutchinson, 1983), pp. 18-34.

answers to the problems of criticism and of rationality, and it explains why such attempts failed, and how it succeeds where they failed. To perform the latter task it uncovers the common, previously unrecognized "structure" that doomed previous answers, and then shows how to circumvent this structure. It explains how the character of past philosophical inquiry is due almost wholly to this structure, and goes on to suggest what new philosophical problems and lines of investigation open up once this structure is abandoned. The whole argument thus has sweeping ramifications for philosophy of science, epistemology, social and political philosophy, and ethics; and also for the understanding and interpretation of the history of philosophy. For the resolution of such a problem creates a new, unprecedented problem-situation within philosophy.

These implications were seen by many readers of the first edition (1962) of this book.[2] Yet others were misled by the subject matter or "case study" that dominates the first part of the book, and have supposed that this is a book in the philosophy of religion—a book, in particular, about Protestantism. So it is. But virtually everything said here about religious thought can also be said, *pari passu,* about contemporary secular philosophy of science and epistemology—or even, for that matter, about philosophy of mathematics.[3] The argument affects, and is intended to affect, fideism, relativism, and scepticism not only in Protestantism, but *wherever they arise.* Thus—to the extent that it works at all—the argument affects such diverse thinkers (thinkers who have nothing to do with Protestantism) as Wittgenstein, Michel Foucault, Quine, and Heidegger, and is directed at the urbane transatlantic pragmatism of Richard Rorty as much as at the Edinburgh school of sociology of knowledge.[4] The book is, in short, directed at all those thinkers whose work depends on the assumption that the problem of

[2]For examples, see Walter B. Weimer, *Notes on the Methodology of Scientific Research* (New York: Lawrence Erlbaum Associates, 1979); Michael J. Mahoney, *Scientist as Subject: The Psychological Imperative* (Cambridge, Mass.: Ballinger, 1976), pp. 140–51; Joseph Agassi, "Rationality and the *Tu Quoque* Argument", *Inquiry,* vol. 16, pp. 395–406; Joseph Agassi, *Science in Flux* (Boston: D. Reidel, 1975), esp. pp. 149–50, 363–64, 365–401, 422–23, 511–12; Gerard Radnitzky, *Continental Schools of Metascience* (Göteborg, 1968), pp. 177–78; Gerard Radnitzky, "Are Comprehensive Theories of Rationality Self-Referentially Inconsistent?", in *Proceedings of the 7th International Wittgenstein Symposium* (Vienna: Hölder-Pichler-Tempsky, 1983), pp. 262–65; Gerard Radnitzky, "In Defense of Self-Applicable Critical Rationalism", *Proceedings of the 11th International Conference on the Unity of the Sciences* (New York: ICF Press, 1983), pp. 1025–69; Renford Bambrough, "Unanswerable Questions", *Proceedings of the Aristotelian Society, Supplementary Volume,* 1966, pp. 151–72; Wolfhart Pannenberg, *Theology and the Philosophy of Science* (London: Darton, Longman & Todd, 1976); Max Schoch, "Vom Protestantismus zum Kritizismus und weiter", *Neue Zürcher Zeitung,* June 24, 1965; Paul Holmer, *Journal of Religion,* April 1964, pp. 161–63; Neil Cooper, *Philosophical Quarterly,* January 1965.

[3]See Imre Lakatos, "Infinite Regress and Foundations of Mathematics", in *Proceedings of the Aristotelian Society,* Supplementary Volume, 1962, pp. 155–84; and "Proofs and Refutations", *British Journal for the Philosophy of Science,* nos. 53, 54, 55, 56 (1963–64). These papers are reprinted, with pertinent alterations, in his *Proofs and Refutations* (Cambridge: Cambridge University Press, 1976), and in *Mathematics, Science, and Epistemology* (Cambridge: Cambridge University Press, 1978).

[4]See my "A Popperian Harvest", in Paul Levinson, ed., *In Pursuit of Truth* (New York: Humanities Press, 1982); "Philosophy of Science", in *New Trends in Philosophy,* ed. A. Kasher and S. Lappin (New York: Humanities Press, 1984); "On the Differences between Popperian and Wittgensteinian Approaches", in

the limits of criticism and rationality *cannot* be solved. For in this book that problem is solved.

To combat such misinterpretations of the message and import of the book—to help the reader to see how the argument applies in areas other than religion and Protestant thought—I have added to this edition six appendices, developing my argument in a more general way, and illustrating how it applies in philosophy of science, logic, ethics, metaphysics, and elsewhere. While the book as a whole is directed to the general reader, some of the appendices are somewhat technical.

2. What This Book Is Not About

It is possible for rationality to be unlimited in some respects and limited in others. This book concerns the alleged limits of rationality *with regard to criticism*, and does not concern, except incidentally, other ways in which rationality may be limited. While I shall argue that rationality is indeed unlimited with regard to criticism, I also believe that in many other respects rationality—or at least what some people *call* rationality—is severely limited.

It is useful to recall some of the different kinds of limitation that relate to rationality. For there are, in the philosophical literature, a number of different problems of rationality, relating to these different types of limitation.

One of these has to do with *the limits of explanation* or *the limits of knowledge achievement*. Thus some writers maintain that certain limitations arise from the psychological and biological structures of the human mind. Less controversial is the contention that certain physical conditions in nature—e.g., the existence of radiation chaos and the velocity of light—limit research in parts of the universe. Again, we can sometimes attain the principle on which phenomena of a certain class operate without being able to explain more concrete detail. For instance, while knowing the mechanics whereby waves are formed on the surface of the water, we are unlikely ever to be able to predict the shape and movements of particular waves. This type of limitation on prediction, owing in part to indeterminacy and feedback, arises in economics as much as in physics, and forces one to reject those

Proceedings of the 10th International Conference on the Unity of the Sciences (New York: ICF Press, 1982); "Non-Justificationism: Popper *versus* Wittgenstein", in *Proceedings of the 7th International Wittgenstein Symposium* (Vienna: Hölder-Pichler-Tempsky, 1983), pp. 255–61; "The Challenge of Evolutionary Epistemology", in *Proceedings of the 11th International Conference on the Unity of the Sciences* (New York: ICF Press, 1983), pp. 835–80; and "Philosophy of Biology *versus* Philosophy of Physics", in *Fundamenta Scientiae*, vol. 3, no. 1 (1982), pp. 55–78.

forms of "constructivist rationalism" that underly most programs of economic and social planning.[5] Quite closely related limitations arise from our historical existence and the impossibility of predicting the historical future due to there being at least one factor in its shaping that we demonstrably cannot predict: namely, the future growth of human knowledge.[6] We predict by reference to our present theories; we learn by refuting our present theories, by deriving predictions from them and trying to falsify those predictions. But we cannot derive or predict a refutation of these theories *from* these theories (provided they are consistent). Hence we cannot predict what we shall learn. Yet other limitations are connected with the necessarily selective character of description; related limitations arise from the character of the vehicle by means of which the description is being made. Then there are practical limitations, such as those explored by Freud and Jung, due to human weakness, physical frailty, humanity. Another sort of limitation is stressed by F. A. von Hayek,[7] who argues that any apparatus of classification must possess a structure of a higher order of complexity than that possessed by those objects which it is to classify; hence no examining agent can ever explain objects of its own kind or degree of complexity.[8]

I see no point in construing these limitations on explanation, prediction, and knowledge achievement as limitations on *rationality*. Yet whatever one *calls* them, the limitations themselves are, in my opinion, quite real and inescapable. Any theory of rationality, or rationalism, that tries to avoid these limitations (and most do) is doomed to failure.

In this book, however, I am not concerned with these limitations. This is not because these limitations on explanation, knowledge achievement, prediction, and cybernetic operation are unimportant or fail to relate to my other concerns. Quite the contrary, I pass over these questions here for two reasons. First, these questions are already far better and more widely understood than are the questions discussed in this book. Second, my own

---

[5]For the critique of "constructivist rationalism", see the works of F. A. von Hayek, especially: *The Counter-Revolution of Science: Studies on the Abuse of Reason* (New York: Free Press, 1955); *The Constitution of Liberty* (Chicago: University of Chicago Press, 1960); *Individualism and Economic Order* (London: Routledge and Kegan Paul, 1949); *Law, Legislation and Liberty*, vols. 1-3 (Chicago: University of Chicago Press, 1973, 1976, 1979); *Studies in Philosophy, Politics, and Economics* (Chicago: University of Chicago Press, 1967); *New Studies in Philosophy, Politics, Economics and the History of Ideas* (Chicago: University of Chicago Press, 1978); and *Freiburger Studien* (Tübingen: J.C.B. Mohr Verlag, 1969).

[6]See K. R. Popper, *The Poverty of Historicism* (Boston: Beacon Press, 1957), pp. ix-xi; and *The Open Universe: An Argument for Indeterminism*, vol. 2 of the *Postscript to the Logic of Scientific Discovery*, 1982, esp. sec. 22. See also my "Knowledge Is a Product Not Fully Known to Its Producer", in Kurt Leube and A. Zlabinger, eds., *The Political Economy of Freedom* (Munich: Philosophia Verlag, 1984).

[7]See *The Sensory Order* (Chicago: University of Chicago Press, 1952), pp. 184ff.

[8]In some philosophical discussions, the limitations just mentioned—some of which have more to do with the limitation of knowledge than the limitation of rationality—have often been fused and confused with the particular limitations that *do* concern me here. Some writers who have advocated fideistic irrationalism, such as Pascal, have blended together many different kinds of rationality limitations in their writings—in order, for instance, to stress the weakness and misery of any man who insists on relying on his pitiful reason "without God".

primary concern is to deal with a so-called *logical* limitation on criticism and rationality which is sufficient, without aid from other limitations, to create and perpetuate the sceptical, fideistic, and relativist positions which this book attempts to refute.

Although something of what I mean when I speak of rationality and its limits may now be clearer, the word "rationality" may nonetheless still create some initial barriers between author and reader. I must ask the kind reader not to assume too quickly that what he or she means, and what I mean, are the same, but rather to explore the matter with me, and to discover what understanding of rationality emerges from the discussion. In encouragement, I can report my own experience: I first began to work on problems of rationality, and to lay the groundwork for this book, when I realized that my own initial understanding of rationality—as well as traditional and contemporary conceptions thereof—was hopelessly defective.

In any case, matters of importance almost never hang on terminology alone, and this is particularly true here. To suggest how little it does matter, I ask that readers refer back to the quotation from George Bernard Shaw with which this Introduction begins. Generally, I mean by "reasonable" what Shaw means by "unreasonable"; *and I agree with what Shaw says.* I do not think of reasonableness as "cooperativeness" or "submissiveness" to circumstances. (And this example alone indicates the inadequacy of any attempt to "relativize" reason to the expectations of a particular community.)

Indeed, it is regrettable that common practice inclines one to call the problems of this book problems of rationality, rather than, simply, of the limits of criticism and argument, and of the conditions furthering the growth of knowledge, awareness, and discovery. The term "rational*ist*", in particular, has been purloined by some thinkers who are foreign to my way of thinking: uncritical thinkers who are as imbued with dogmatism, partisanship, and rigidity as any of whom one might think. On the other hand, other thinkers who, because of their stance regarding the problem of the limits of rationality, may be called "irrationalists"—Karl Barth for instance—are on the whole wide-ranging, flexible, and critical individuals. I ask the reader kindly to bear these provisos in mind as he or she reads my later remarks about various kinds of rational*ist* and rational*ism*.

In sum, I am concerned in this book with real problems of the limits of criticism and argument, and the way in which individuals have conceived of themselves and their lives in terms of such supposed limits. I am *not* particularly interested in advancing the claims of any particular group of individuals that may style itself rationalist.

3. *The Morbidity of Theories and the Birth of Ideologies*

Let our theories die in our stead.
—KARL POPPER

While systems of belief are born pretty much in the same way, they die differently.

This is apparent in the distinction that Karl Popper makes between two different kinds of belief system: scientific theories and ideologies.[9] Scientific theories, he says, are—from a biological point of view—attempted mutations or adaptations that are deliberately subjected to selection. That is, the scientist deliberately tries to refute them—to eliminate them—by finding facts which they do not fit. Whereas ideologies are retained regardless of the facts; they are not abandoned when they clash with the facts; rather, they die out or are eliminated only, if at all, together with their carriers—together with the community of dogmatic believers.

Popper intends his contrast between theories and ideologies to mark the difference between critical and dogmatic thinking, illustrating it with the touching story of an Indian community whose elimination came about because of its members' belief in the holiness of life, including the life of tigers.

This is helpful as a rough-and-ready distinction, and can easily be expanded to treat Protestantism and its history. For while Protestantism has obviously never been a science, it is deeply permeated by critical thinking, and its history is a kind of battlefield between critical and ideological thought. Although there has always been a strong streak of irrationalism and anti-intellectualism in Protestantism, its history and modes of thinking have, nonetheless, also always been deeply entangled with modern science and the scientific revolution. The real clash between religion and science, in all its poignancy, with all its fateful consequences, is more sharply and clearly focused in the history of Protestantism than anywhere else. Its growth and decline are properly part of the larger history of science—which includes, of course, the story of the alterations that science has wrought in our understanding of ourselves and the world.

It is distinctive of Protestant Christianity that, through most of its history, many of its most important thinkers have assumed that it was—despite

---

[9]See his "The Death of Theories and of Ideologies", in *La réflexion sur la mort*, 2e symposium international de philosophie, Ecole libre de philosophie "Plethon" (Athens, 1977), pp. 296–329; and "The Rationality of Scientific Revolutions", in Rom Harré, ed., *Problems of Scientific Revolution. Progress and Obstacles to Progress in the Sciences* (Oxford: Oxford University Press, 1975), pp. 72–101.

periodic crises and the ongoing "warfare" between science and religion—ultimately fully compatible with science and the scientific outlook and represented a *reasonable* form of religion. But in the twentieth century, Protestantism abandoned its association with science and rationality and *became* an ideology. Thus, as treated in this book, Protestantism is a system of beliefs that was never a science and became an ideology. Why did it become an ideology? It became an ideology as an alternative to dying.

Such a fate is not at all peculiar to Protestantism, or even unusual: it often overtakes systems of beliefs, quite apart from any question of their scientific status. A religion, such as Protestantism, may be held for a time critically, and then turn into a dogmatic ideology.[10] An obsolete science, after being refuted, also may live on as ideology. Approaches that originate in an attempt to think critically and scientifically—Freudian psyschology and behaviorism, to take two examples—may turn into dogmatically held ideologies.[11] They, too, may prefer to become ideologies rather than to die.[12]

This book uses Protestantism as a case study to investigate this kind of transition or development, and is hence concerned with the *morbidity* of critical belief. It investigates what can happen to an objective system of belief to lead it, after being held for a time quite critically, to be gradually or abruptly, as the case may be, transformed into a dogmatically held ideology. Thus I am interested in systems of belief and how they are held; what may be done to them, how one can tinker with them, to enhance or reduce their criticizability. In particular, the book is concerned with how men use ideas to protect ideas from competition, to remove them from the selective process that is the heart of criticism. If it is ironic that an *argument* should be used to protect an idea from the competition of argument, it is also particularly effective that this should be so. For ideologies are often under attack from those who take argument seriously; and there is no better defense against such persons—persons who are moved by argument—than a good argument.

While the book thus concerns the morbidity of *beliefs*, it is not much concerned with the morbidity of *believers or of communities of believers*. This would involve a different manner of investigation. Thus I am concerned only peripherally with details about Protestant churches and their membership: I am, for example, not concerned with membership statistics, with

---

[10]See also Robert M. Young, "Natural Theology, Victorian Periodicals and the Fragmentation of a Common Context", in *Darwin's Metaphor and Other Studies of Nature's Place in Victorian Society* (Cambridge: Cambridge University Press, 1980); reprinted in *Darwin to Einstein: Historical Studies on Science and Belief*, ed. Colin Chant and John Fauvel (London: Longman, 1980); pp. 69–107.

[11]On the case of Freudianism, see K. R. Popper, *Realism and the Aim of Science*, vol. 1 of the *Postscript to the Logic of Scientific Discovery*, part 1, sec. 18; Seymour Fisher and Roger P. Greenberg, *The Scientific Credibility of Freud's Theories and Therapy* (New York: Basic Books, 1977); and Janet Malcolm, "Annals of Scholarship", *New Yorker*, December 5 and 12, 1983.

[12]On the ideological transformations of obsolete scientific theories, see my "The Challenge of Evolutionary Epistemology", esp. p. 845.

growth or decline in numbers, with growing or declining political and social influence, or with the distribution of Protestants among the various social and ethnic groups and classes.

4. Competition and Rationality

The most important logical feature of contemporary Protestant thought is the use of an ancient argument—one that appears already in the work of Sextus Empiricus—concerning the limits of justification and criticism.[13] The use Protestant thinkers make of this argument suffices to render Protestantism uncritical and to turn it into an ideology.

This argument is that the most important ideas—presuppositions, first principles—cannot be justified or criticized, and are hence beyond rational evaluation; moreover, that all individuals must, for logical reasons, hold such ideas; and that, as a consequence, anyone has a sound excuse for being uncritically committed to some such first principle or dogma.

This argument, itself an idea about rational argumentation, has the effect of protecting certain other ideas from rational argumentation by removing them from competition. In effect, the argument decrees that our most fundamental ideas are not and need not be in argumentative competition with other ideas (i.e., are beyond criticism) due to an intrinsic logical feature of argumentation.

This book is devoted to the examination and rebuttal of this argument.

I have just mentioned competition, for there is an intimate connection between competition and rationality.

No reference to Max Weber is needed to remind the reader of the historical association between Protestantism and the rise of capitalism.[14] The connection of either with rationality may be less obvious. Yet if one fails to make this connection, or to mark the change that Protestantism has more recently undergone with regard to rationality, one can hardly understand the close association that much Protestant thought and many Protestant groups now have with socialism rather than with capitalism. What is this link between competition and rationality?

---

[13]Sextus Empiricus, *Works*, 4 vols. (Cambridge, Mass: Harvard University Press). See also R. H. Popkin: *The History of Scepticism from Erasmus to Spinoza* (Berkeley: University of California Press, 1979); and *The High Road to Pyrrhonism* (San Diego: Austin Hill Press, 1980). See also my "Approaches to Science and Scepticism", *Philosophical Forum*, vol. 1, no. 3 (Spring 1969), pp. 318–31.

[14]See Max Weber, *The Protestant Ethic and the Spirit of Capitalism* (New York: Charles Scribner's Sons, 1958). See also R. H. Tawney, *Religion and the Rise of Capitalism* (New York: Harcourt Brace and World, 1926); Reinhard Bendix, *Max Weber: An Intellectual Portrait* (New York: Doubleday, 1960); and R. K. Merton, "Science, Technology and Society in Seventeenth Century England", *Osiris*, no. 4 (1938).

Although some forms of competition are stupidly irrational, competition tends to engender rationality. How does this happen?

I do not for a moment believe that man is a rational animal, let alone that men are born with a "faculty" of reason. Rather, rationality, like consciousness itself,[15] is a comparatively late, and still rather rare, and, where it exists, fragile development. Most individuals exist in a troubled, slumbering fantasy world, and, when most awake, are bound by rigid habits and unconscious patterns of behavior.[16] Comparatively few persons enjoy the give-and-take of criticism or think to any purpose other than to dominate.

Nonetheless, science—which is utterly dependent on criticism and detachment, and on thinking for the sake of the truth rather than for the sake of domination—has come into being, and has flourished, during the past four hundred years. How has this happened?

We owe this, *for better and for worse,* to competition.

Although we are not born with a faculty of reason, we are born, like monkeys, with a good ability to imitate.

This ability to imitate is highly adaptive; it comes in handy in mimicking successful strategies on the part of others when we want to be as successful ourselves. In an authoritarian age or setting, subservience, obeisance, flattery, and behavior aping that of those in power may aid advancement. It may serve survival to be *like* others, and *not* to be daring, probing, critical. Of course such behavior is also often comical or pathetic, for people ape according to their lights, and may give crude imitative renderings of the behavior of those whom they are trying to flatter but whose behavior they really do not comprehend at all.

Imitation continues to come in handy when the influence of such older authorities begins to break down. For example, with the rise of capitalism, a probing, entrepreneurial, inquisitive, exploratory attitude toward the world, and a reflective critical (flexible rather than rigid) attitude toward one's beliefs and behavior, began to offer an advantage to those who were probing and critical. The very expression "to allow one's theories to perish in one's stead" marks the potential survival value of such a policy to those who could acquire knowledge, attend to facts and information, adjust their ideas rapidly in changing market situations, move in quickly to take advantage of *unexpected* opportunities (i.e., opportunities that might not entirely square with current beliefs, and hence might also be unanticipated by most of one's competitors), and perform some task better or more efficiently than was possible in the customary manner.

Such behavior also can be imitated—although perhaps more painfully.

[15]See Julian Jaynes, *The Origin of Consciousness in the Breakdown of the Bicameral Mind* (Boston: Houghton Mifflin Company, 1976).

[16]See my *Morality and Religion* (London: Macmillian, 1971), esp. chap. 4; and my *Werner Erhard: The Transformation of a Man* (New York: Clarkson Potter, 1978).

Those whose way of life is threatened by the enterprising behavior of entrepreneurs may be *driven* to become more imaginative, reflective, and self-critical themselves. To compete more successfully, they may be forced to imitate and emulate their probing, inquisitive, and self-reflective competitors, and thus to become more rational. When critical, rational behavior confers an advantage, rational methods, by the usual selective processes of evolution, will be developed and will spread by imitation.[17] Of course people also imitate rationality according to their lights; and what will spread much faster than rational behavior itself will, once again, be crude "do it yourself" accounts of what imitators suppose it must be like to be rational or scientific. Most contemporary methodologies of science, particularly those popular in the behavioral sciences, are examples of such aping and imitation.

I italicized the word "driven" above. For people do not generally *like* to think or to change their minds; it is not comfortable to do so. Why, then, do so—unless it be to some advantage? Competition is "a process in which a small number makes it necessary for larger numbers to do what they do not like, be it to work harder, to change habits, or to devote a degree of attention, continuous application, or regularity to their work which without competition would not be needed."[18]

This process is at the heart of the historical relationship between science and Protestant Christianity and also of their present situation.

By resorting to the argument about the limits of justification and criticism, and of rationality, Protestantism in a sense gives up the battle; it removes its basic principles from the competitive arena, and engages in a sort of intellectual counterpart of economic protectionism. This is sufficient, as we shall see, to render it an ideology. And it presents an interesting problem to the historian of ideas. There has never been any doubt that the use of criticism can be hampered by power: by the power of censorship, for example. But here is a case where criticism is hampered not by any sort of force, but solely through the power of reason itself: a reasonable argument about the limits of reason is used convincingly—reasonably—to restrict reason.

In attempting to refute this argument, I am concerned about its use not only in Protestantism, but elsewhere, too, in perhaps more important, and hence more dangerous, areas. The use of this argument continues to be widespread;[19] and wherever used, it provides the custodians of ideas with a rational excuse that permits them to protect their own principles from competition—whether these be claimed to be the principles of science (for

---

[17]See Hayek, *Law, Legislation and Liberty,* vol. 3, pp. 75–77.
[18]Ibid., p. 77. Cf. Weber, *The Protestant Ethic and the Spirit of Capitalism,* pp. 67–68.
[19]See my "Non-Justificationism: Popper *versus* Wittgenstein".

there are also many ideologists of science), or political principles, or whatever. This argument transforms *whatever* it touches into pseudo-science and ideology.

In preparing this new edition of *The Retreat to Commitment,* I have corrected, expanded, and improved various passages and sections throughout. In particular, I have expanded chapter 3, section 2; I have added a new section (6) to the same chapter; I have rewritten chapter 4, sections 1 and 5, as well as chapter 5, sections 2 and 3; in chapter 6, I have deleted section 3, which is now dated. Throughout the text I have added new footnotes; and I have added six new appendices. Apart from such changes, the text follows the original American edition, published by Alfred A. Knopf in 1962.

—W.W.B.

The Hoover Institution
on War, Revolution and Peace
Stanford University
August, 1984

PREFACE

This is an essay in the theory of the open mind. Through a study of the conflict between the rationalist and Protestant traditions it tries to solve what has been called "the central problem that confronts moral philosophers in our time".[1] This problem, which lies at the core of that conflict, is whether some form of relativism is inescapable because rationality is so limited, logically as well as practically, that the choice between ultimately competing religious, moral, and philosophical positions is, in the last resort, *arbitrary*. For example, is an individual's decision to become a *rationalist—* even from a rationalist point of view—any less subjective, relative, arbitrary, irrational than an individual's decision to become a Christian?

Not surprisingly, concern with this problem, and with the clash between competing traditions, often arises out of personal conflict. Bertrand Russell, one of the most ardent twentieth-century apostles of the Enlightenment, seems to provide a case in point. Reflecting on the implications of moral relativism, he wrote:

> I am not, myself, satisfied with what I have read or said on the philosophical basis of ethics. I cannot see how to refute the arguments for the subjectivity of ethical values, but I find myself incapable of believing that all that is wrong with wanton cruelty is that I don't like it. . . . when it comes to the philosophy of moral judgments, I am impelled in two opposite directions and remain perplexed. I should deeply rejoice, if I could find or be shown a way to resolve this perplexity, but as yet I remain dissatisfied.[2]

The answer to the problem of this essay—I shall refer to it alternatively as the dilemma of ultimate commitment and as the problem of the limits of rationality—is of fundamental importance in any attempt to resolve such perplexity. For if relativism is inescapable, then a consistent rationalism becomes intellectually impossible.

Throughout his life, Kierkegaard sought to answer the question: How can

---

[1] D. H. Munro, "Russell's Moral Theories", *Philosophy,* January 1960, p. 50
[2] Bertrand Russell, "Notes on *Philosophy,* January 1960", *Philosophy,* April 1960.

I become a Christian? Barely two generations later, Nietzsche sought to learn how men could live as atheists in a world where God was dead. There is something of both these questions in the following pages. But the main question, a question that expresses the principal philosophical interest of many persons today, is this: How is it possible any longer for a man to remain a consistent rationalist? The Enlightenment seems to have come to that.[3]

In the following pages I intend to show that it is *untrue* that the choice between competing moral, religious, political, or philosophical creeds— such as Christianity, communism, and empiricism—must be fundamentally arbitrary. My conclusions involve a proposal about the nature not of Christianity but of rationality, or the tradition of rational discussion; a proposal that rejects most traditional and contemporary characterizations.

A word about the essay's many limitations. Since my main efforts have been to understand a philosophical problem, to present the outline of its solution, and to indicate some of the consequences of the belief that the problem could not be solved, my historical and social observations are used only as examples and illustrations which are intended to lend context and clarity to the main argument. I do not pretend to give an exhaustive critique of the thinkers or the systems of thought which I discuss and criticize. The published work of the most important Protestant theologian, Karl Barth, alone runs to over 15,000 printed pages of rather small type—even though he once described much of his work as a "footnote" to theology. I have tried to aim my criticisms at only the most basic assumptions of these systems of thought, their feet as it were, without which they cannot stand.

St. John's Wood   W.W.B.
London
1961

---

[3]Several senses of the word "rationalism" are in common circulation. In one sense it is used to refer to the predominantly seventeenth-century rationalist (as opposed to empiricist) thought of philosophers like Descartes, Spinoza, and Leibniz. In another sense, introduced by F. A. von Hayek, the word may refer to the "constructivist rationalism" of those who believe in historical prediction and social and economic planning. I am not a rationalist in either of these senses: I follow many writers in using the term "intellectualism" for the first sense; and I agree with Hayek's arguments against constructivist rationalism. But the term may also be used to refer, in the most general way, to the tradition whose members are dedicated to the task of trying to learn more about the world through the practice of critical argument. I shall use the term in this sense throughout this essay, one of my main aims being to make this sense clearer (see Introduction, above). None of these senses of rationalism needs to involve another view that is sometimes called "rationalism", the undoubtedly false view that men are able to act self-critically or rationally most or all of the time. W. D. Hudson fails to take this into account when he accuses me of the probably false opinion that it is *psychologically* possible for men to hold their deepest convictions with detachment. See his "Professor Bartley's Theory of Rationality and Religious Belief", *Religious Studies*, 9 (September 1973), pp. 339–50, esp. p. 340.

ACKNOWLEDGMENTS

I have been grappling for a long time with the issues treated in this essay, and am indebted to many persons.

Most of all I am indebted to Sir Karl Popper, my great teacher, friend, and former colleague at the London School of Economics and Political Science, University of London. I believe that Popper succeeded, whereas Kant failed, in solving Kant's problem—to reconcile and explain the valid elements of both intellectualism and empiricism while avoiding the mistakes of each. More important, I believe that he presented, in his account of empirical falsification within science, the first example in the history of philosophy of what I shall later call a "nonjustificational" form of criticism. The main contribution of this book is to generalize and to interpret this type of criticism and to apply it both inside and outside of science—and even to the rational or critical tradition itself. Although I have various points of disagreement with Popper, some of which are mentioned on the pages that follow, I would be proud to think that the impact of his thought has influenced every page of this essay.

It is a pleasure to thank Joseph Agassi, the late Nels F. S. Ferré, W. B. Gallie, I. C. Jarvie, the late Walter Kaufmann, H. Hugh Van Dusen, the late Henry Pitney Van Dusen, J.W.N. Watkins, and J. O. Wisdom, all of whom criticized an earlier draft or commented extensively on previous editions. Although their comments have helped me to make major improvements, they are of course in no way responsible for the mistakes that remain; in several cases they have disagreed emphatically with me. I am particularly indebted to Professors Kaufmann, Watkins, and Wisdom, whose painstaking criticisms have saved me from a number of blunders and forced me to rewrite several parts of the essay.

I also want to thank Hans Albert, Gunnar Andersson, Jeffrey A. Barach, Peter L. Button, Werner Erhard, Gerd Fleischmann, Sir Ernst Gombrich, Brian Gomes da Costa, Jagdish Hattiangadi, F. A. von Hayek, W. D. Hudson, Noretta Koertge, Stephen Kresge, the late Imre Lakatos, Hans

Lenk, D. M. MacKinnon, the late Reinhold Messner, Simon Moser, Peter Munz, Klaus Pähler, Wolfhart Pannenberg, R. H. Popkin, John F. Post, Gerard Radnitzky, J. C. Peter Richardson, D. P. Walker, Walter B. Weimer, and Paul Weingartner for the benefit of personal conversations and correspondence about some of the topics discussed here.

For the republication of this book not only in English but in French, German, and Italian translations, I am indebted to the interest and enthusiasm of Dr. André Carus, Mme Renée Bouveresse, Professor Hans Albert, and Signor Angelo Petroni.

I wish as well to thank my students at various institutions, particularly those at the London School of Economic and Political Science, the Warburg Institute of the University of London, the Royal Institute of Philosophy, and the Austrian College, Alpbach, Tirol, where these ideas were first developed and presented, for their keen interest and questions.

For fellowships and grants which enabled me at various times to work on the problems of this book, I am grateful to Harvard University; the United States Educational (Fulbright) Commission in the United Kingdom; the Danforth Foundation; Gonville and Caius College, Cambridge University; the Deutscher Akademischer Austauschdienst; the American Council of Learned Societies; the *est* Foundation; the American Philosophical Society; the Fritz Thyssen Stiftung; the Walter and Vera Morris Foundation, the Institute for Humane Studies; and the Hoover Institution, Stanford University.

THE RETREAT
TO COMMITMENT

1
IDENTITY, INTEGRITY, AND COMMITMENT TO CONFUSION

> Whoever is hard put to feel identical with one set of people and ideas must that much more violently repudiate another set; and whenever an identity, once established, meets further crises, the danger of irrational repudiation of otherness and temporarily even of one's own identity increases.
>
> —ERIK H. ERIKSON, 1958[1]

> I must earnestly beg the kind reader always to bear in mind that the thought behind the whole work is: what it means to become a Christian . . . the truth and inwardness of the reflective expression for becoming a Christian is measured by the value of the thing which reflection is bound to reject . . . one does not reflect oneself into being a Christian, but out of another thing in order to become a Christian. . . . The nature of the other thing decides how deep, how significant, the movement of reflection is. . . . The reflection is defined by the difficulty, which is greater just in proportion to the value of the thing left behind.
>
> —SØREN KIERKEGAARD, 1848[2]

One of the commonest complaints about the present might be expressed in this way: ours is a time when the rebel without a cause has succeeded the rebel without an effect. Whereas our ancestors, even when they strove in vain, seemed to know what they were against and what they were for, we see good and bad in everything and rebel against our state of indecision. Unable to find purpose in our lives, we hold symposia on "national purpose". Our literature and social commentary and even our manners are composed out of the vocabulary of alienation: "indifference", "withdrawal", "disenchantment", "non-involvement", and "No, thanks" spell the distance between contemporary men and future ideals as well as old loyalties.

---

[1]Erik H. Erikson, *Young Man Luther* (New York: W. W. Norton & Company, 1958), p. 259.

[2]Søren Kierkegaard. *The Point of View for My Work as an Author*, written in 1848 and first published posthumously in 1859, four years after the author's death.

3

Like most such chronic complaints, this one varies in intensity from year to year; and it denigrates the present at the expense of idealizing the past. Yet despite this, and despite its hackneyed character, it is both apt and timely. For people are not yet alienated from the problem of alienation, or indifferent to the hope of overcoming indifference. Although one social analyst has claimed that "the *direction* of cultural change is from commitment and enthusiasm to alienation and apathy",[3] alienation is still treated as an urgent *problem,* to be ameliorated if not overcome, not as something like death which must be helplessly accepted. This very involvement with indifference perhaps explains in part why the phenomena and mood of alienation uneasily coexist with an obsession—in religion, politics, literature, philosophy—with those things that once were thought to diminish alienation: ideology and commitment. "Obsession" is not too strong a word. For even in academic philosophy, often proudly claimed by its practitioners to be one of the most abstract and impractical of subjects, the related notions of "commitment", "choice", and "decision" have forced their way to the center of discussion—and this on both sides of the Atlantic, in movements as differently rooted as the British philosophy of linguistic analysis and contemporary American pragmatism.[4] In French and German philosophies, similar notions provide motifs in phenomenology, in hermeneutics, and in the various existentialisms.

Ardor for commitment, however, rarely seems to be adequate by itself to overcome alienation. It is true that many people, baffled about who they are and what they might be or should be, and incapable of forging acceptable personalities for themselves, still try to bring order into their lives by choosing ready-made characters and causes—by identifying, sometimes through what is called a "free commitment", with some established cultural tradition. Regardless of the country or philosophical tradition in which they are made, these commitments have a way of waning—particularly among those who seem most in need of them. Migration from one "absolute" commitment to another, although occasionally constricted by social sanction, is largely unrestricted. Divorcing one's commitment—apart from the comparatively rare political case—rarely requires legal proceedings, even when it is attended with as much psychological turmoil as divorcing one's

[3]See Kenneth Kenniston's discussion, "Alienation and the Decline of Utopia", *American Scholar,* Spring 1960, p. 162.

[4]For examples out of an extensive literature, see these essays and books: Stuart Hampshire, "Identification and Existence", in *Contemporary British Philosophy,* ed. H. D. Lewis (New York: Macmillan, 1956), and *Thought and Action* (London: Chatto and Windus, 1959); Morton White, *Toward Reunion in Philosophy* (Cambridge, Mass: Harvard University Press, 1956), pp. 231 ff., 272 ff., and chap. 16; and *Religion, Politics, and the Higher Learning* (Cambridge, Mass: Harvard University Press, 1959), chap. 4 (sec. 2) and chap. 10.

See also the works of Michael Polanyi, esp. *Personal Knowledge* (London: Routledge & Kegan Paul, 1958); Thomas S. Kuhn, *The Structure of Scientific Revolutions* (Chicago: University of Chicago Press, 1962); Richard Rorty, *Philosophy and the Mirror of Nature* (Princeton: Princeton University Press, 1979); and "Two Perspectives on Richard Rorty", *Radical Philosophy,* Autumn 1982, pp. 1–7.

spouse. The ideological divorcing and remarrying; the uneasiness of many who remain "settled down"; and the tensions of those who never wed again or at all—all are themselves part of the situation. If the estrangement from cause and commitment helps to explain the fruitless yet fervid experimentation in just such cause and commitment, what explains the alienation in the first place? It is difficult to say. The situation is probably too complex to lend itself to a compact or simple explanation.

Nonetheless, I believe that one important source of the situation, and—more particularly—of the seemingly endemic frustration that meets those "cultural physicians" who attempt to correct it, has been almost entirely unexplored. What I have in mind is this. We are faced today by a circumstance that radically limits the effectiveness of any personal or social cause, aim, identification, or commitment from the very start. Namely, *the most important of the traditions in which identity, purpose, and commitment have been sought themselves partake in the general confusion.* Traditions, too, appear not only to have been evolving but to have been going through agonizing self-analysis and to have emerged lacking an inner core. Thus the man who tries to acquire a character or a cause by identifying himself, through commitment, with a particular tradition often exchanges his "I am confused" for an "I am a member of a confused tradition". Doubtless he may gain thereby, at least temporarily: now he has a name; he can at least say what he is. But he cannot so easily explain what it is to be what he is, not so much because he does not know as because no one knows, or else because everyone has a different answer.[5] This is one reason why mystification accompanies so many commitments.[6]

This situation of internal confusion in those traditions within whose resources we might have expected to find identity has sometimes been obscured, partly because traditions are often wrongly represented as blocklike social entities, secure against change; partly because the demand for suitable characters has sometimes outstripped the supply of available traditions, with the result that simple substitutes have appeared, complete with brand names and labeled contents, to entice speculators in commitment. The situation looks different, however, as soon as we turn from such manufactured items—particularly from those like Nazism[7] which make little pretense of being rationally defensible—to the older, intellectually and morally more serious traditions, such as rationalistic humanism, Christianity, or Marxism. Few of those who are spiritually committed to Christianity, for instance, could describe its "essence", let alone defend it. "Who can tell

---

[5]For an interesting discussion of some related questions, see Van A. Harvey, "On Believing What Is Difficult to Understand", *Journal of Religion*, October 1959.

[6]On such mystification see my "Wittgenstein and Homosexuality", in George Steiner and Robert Boyers, eds., *Homosexuality: Sacrilege, Vision, Politics* (*Salmagundi*, Fall 1982-Winter 1983), pp. 166–96.

[7]Or anti-Semitism. See Jean-Paul Sartre, "Portrait of the Anti-Semite", *Partisan Review*, Spring 1946.

what vagary or what compromise may not be calling itself Christianity?" asked Santayana more than fifty years ago. "A bishop may be a modernist, a chemist may be a mystical theologian, a psychologist may be a believer in ghosts."[8] Santanyana was observing, not complaining. After all, he described himself as both an atheist and a Roman Catholic. What Santayana believes, someone jibed, is that "there is no God, and Mary is His Mother".

When Santayana wrote this passage, the papal encyclical *Pascendi dominici gregis,* of September 8, 1907—which had exorcised Catholic modernism while assigning the blame for it to "curiosity and pride"—was still controversial. Today the modernism movement in Catholicism has in a sense triumphed. And with its triumph the problem of identity within Roman Catholicism has increased. As Paul VI remarked: "Today we Roman Catholics have doubts about who we are. We no longer know catechism or church history."[9] Yet, despite this, the limits of modernism are more sharply defined than ever: to be a Catholic Christian is, at the very least, to accept the authority of the pope in certain matters of faith and morals.[10] Lacking these limits, the situation in Protestantism is murkier. If, indeed, as has been suggested, a *tradition,* which is marked by a relative uniformity of attitudes, ways of behavior, aims, and values, may be distinguished from an *institution,* which merely fulfills certain social functions for shifting groups of very different people,[11] then Protestantism is becoming less a tradition than an institution. For being a Protestant now seems to require little more than calling oneself a Protestant, and finding it helpful, spiritually, socially, or in some other way, to do so. What is "generally lacking", as Kierkegaard insisted more than a hundred years ago, is a "decisive categorical definition" for a situation in which "one does not know and cannot make out whether one is situated in paganism, whether the parson is a missionary in that sense, or whereabouts one is."[12]

Today, Kierkegaard's question of what it is to be a Christian has become an almost obsessive preoccupation of Protestant Christians. For during the last sixty years, Protestant thought, both rejecting and rejected by the groups and traditions with which it had been allied and from which it had drawn nourishment throughout its history, has had to face the choice of either forging for itself a newly independent identity, more secure against the betrayal of unreliable allies, or else of abdicating the claim to authority and even to leadership in intellectual or spiritual matters. For Protestantism, this was tantamount to a choice between irrationalism and suicide.

---

[8]George Santayana, *Winds of Doctrine* (New York: Harper and Brothers, 1957), p. 4.

[9]*National Catholic Reporter,* October 22, 1976, p. 6.

[10]On the question of Christian identity for Roman Catholics, see Hans Küng, *Christ Sein* (Munich: Piper, 1974); Karl Rahner, "Die anonymen Christen", in *Schriften zur Theologie,* vol. 6 (1965), pp. 545–54; and *Schriften zur Theologie,* vol. 5 (1962), pp. 136–58; and "Atheismus und implizites Christentum, in *Schriften zur Theologie,* vol. 8 (1967), pp. 187–212.

[11]K. R. Popper, "Towards a Rational Theory of Tradition", *Conjectures and Refutations* (London: Routledge & Kegan Paul, 1963).

[12]Kierkegaard, *Point of View for My Work as an Author.*

This essay is a study of problems of self-identity and integrity in the Protestant and rationalist traditions. Probably the two most influential spiritual traditions of Western culture, both have helped provide involvement and purposive living in the past; and both still offer their services to help overcome present-day alienation. However, these two traditions not only are internally confused but are breeding confusion and alienation quite out of proportion to the internal confusion of either. Their identities are so intertwined historically that members of either (the rationalist as well as the Protestant Christian) must try to understand the nature of their own tradition partly by contrasting it with the identity of the other. So confusion in one engenders confusion in the other.

I shall approach these matters, and try to clarify them, in terms of a study of the relationship of the present *crisis of identity* in Protestantism to a long-standing *crisis of integrity* in the rationalist tradition.

Problems connected with identity and integrity are of course familiar. I intend to use these two ideas, and in particular the two phrases just italicized, in a sense I borrow from the sociologist and psychoanalyst Erik H. Erikson.[13] They refer to two characteristic turning points in the lives of most individuals, periods which, particularly in the life of the *homo religiosus,* be he priest or philosopher, are often fused.[14] The individual's problem of identity, encountered by most people in late adolescence and early adulthood—though it can occur at almost any time—is to shape, out of the elements provided by his heritage, his conception of himself, and his idea of what others see in him, an identity that he believes he will be able to live with in integrity. The problem of integrity is, given one's identity, purpose, and claims about oneself, how to live up to them.

Although these concepts are primarily intended to refer to periods in the lives of individual human beings, they can be applied to such things as traditions and societies. Since the application of such concepts to "social wholes" is fraught with danger, a word of caution is in order. When we transfer these concepts from individuals to traditions we must leave behind part of the original theory. In individual human beings, crises of identity typically occur in late adolescence. To traditions, however, which are not biological organisms, such concepts as adolescence do not apply.[15] I shall use these concepts only as shorthand devices for indicating that the individual thinkers and writers of the traditions in question, those who

---

[13]Erikson, *Childhood and Society* (London: Imago, 1950); *Young Man Luther* (New York: W. W. Norton, 1962), p. 14 and passim; *Identity and the Life Cycle (Psychological Issues,* Monogr. 1) (New York; International Universities Press, 1959); *Identity: Youth and Crisis* (New York: W. W. Norton, 1968); *Gandhi's Truth* (New York: W. W. Norton, 1969); and *Life History and the Historical Moment* (New York: W. W. Norton, 1975).

[14]See *Young Man Luther,* p. 261. For a different view of identity see my *Werner Erhard: The Transformation of a Man* (New York: Clarkson N. Potter, 1978), pp. 181–84; and appendix 1, below.

[15]Perhaps the main error of "sociological holism", which is a name for the application to social wholes, such as societies and civilizations, of concepts that originate in the description of human behavior, may be generalized, in a pun, as follows. The error of holism is the *wholesale* transfer of such concepts from human beings to social wholes. In fact, some may be transferred and some may not.

attempt to evaluate them and make articulate their fundamental characteristics, are baffled by their job, and that this bafflement extends to those who look to them as spiritual guides.

In outline my thesis is this. Despite a chronic crisis of identity, which has in this century become acute, it has still been possible to identify with the Protestant tradition while retaining intellectual integrity. However, this has been so only because of the existence of an unanswered philosophical argument that has made it impossible for adherents of the *rationalist* tradition to live in genuine integrity with their own self-image or identity. The same philosophical argument, in many respects a logical puzzle, provides at once a wanted refuge of safety for Protestants and a skeleton in the rationalists' intellectual closet. Rationalists are overcommitted to a notion of rationality that is impossible to attain; and the seemingly inevitable frustration of the effort to escape this overcommitment prevents them from achieving integrity.

The failure of rationalists to resolve their own crisis of integrity—a failure which, in turn, is rooted in their own problems of identity—has enabled Protestants to preserve their Protestant identity without loss of integrity.

However, if the rationalist crisis of integrity could be resolved—if it were possible to answer the philosophical argument in which it is rooted—then it would no longer be possible for a man to retain his Protestant identity with intellectual integrity. A Protestant could no longer contend that "since rationality, or critical activity, is fundamentally limited", Protestant Christian faith can legitimately come in when that limit is reached.

In the course of this essay I hope to explain my thesis, to probe the inner resources of the contemporary Protestant identity, and then to resolve the crisis of integrity of the rationalist tradition by solving the problem of the limits of rationality, thereby eliminating this rational excuse for Protestant commitment. To achieve these aims, we must begin by considering the background and the outcome of the search for identity in both Protestantism and rationalism. These two traditions interacted most significantly in recent history in the period of the breakdown of Protestant liberalism and the resultant shift to neo-orthodox thought.

2
THE SEARCH FOR IDENTITY IN PROTESTANTISM

During the last year or two, few weeks have gone by when some liberal chieftain has not passed down the national thoroughfare of one or another of our high-grade and more highly circulated periodicals noisily scourging his idol. . . . speculation grows on "after liberalism what?" A new idol is expected to appear presently and the curious are occupying themselves with imaginative anticipation.
—J. C. DANCEY, 1934[1]

Because I have been and am a modernist it is proper that I should confess that often the modernistic movement, adjusting itself to a man-centered culture, has . . . watered down the thought of the Divine and, may we be forgiven for this, left souls standing like the ancient Athenians, before an altar to an Unknown God! On that point the church must go beyond modernism. We have been all things to all men long enough. We have adapted and adjusted and accommodated and conceded long enough. We have at times gotten so low down that we talked as though the highest compliment that could be paid to Almighty God was that a few scientists believed in him. Yet all the time, by right, we had an independent standing ground and a message of our own in which alone is there hope for humankind.
—HARRY EMERSON FOSDICK, 1935[2]

1. The New Idol

In the autumn of 1935, when Harry Emerson Fosdick climbed to his pulpit in Riverside Church in New York City to denounce the excesses of modernist Protestant liberalism, much of the conflict, irony, and pathos of twentieth-century American religion came together. In this lopsided, "non-denominational Baptist", neo-Gothic cathedral overlooking Riverside Drive

---

[1]J. C. Dancey, "In Defense of Liberalism", *Christian Century*, December 12, 1934, pp. 1592–94.
[2]Sermon printed in the *Christian Century*, December 4, 1935.

on one side and Harlem on the other, buttressed from within by steel girders, paid for by the Rockefeller family, and echoing with the strains of old-fashioned hymns piped out by a kind of glorified music-hall organ, the leading preacher of Protestant liberalism—a man who had been attacked by many of his fellow Christians during half his life because of his "betrayal" of genuine Christianity—was about to confess to his prosperous congregation that his own brand of modernist liberalism had gone too far, that he was now joining those who required a more distinctly Christian gospel.

Fosdick's sermon in itself marked no watershed of thinking; it simply dramatized a trend. By the time he spoke out, the features of the new idol that was to replace Protestant liberalism in the New World as well as in the Old were becoming clear. Paul Tillich, who had arrived in New York City in November 1933, a refugee from Hitler's Germany, had begun to publish his first articles in English. Reinhold Niebuhr—like Tillich, a colleague of Fosdick's at Union Theological Seminary, on New York City's Morningside Heights—had published in quick succession his *Moral Man and Immoral Society* (1932), *Reflections on the End of an Era* (1934), and *An Interpretation of Christian Ethics* (1935),[3] three books that were to make Niebuhr's original reinterpretation and application of some ideas of Karl Barth and Emil Brunner familiar to the American public, and to help change the climate of religious thought in the United States. In 1925 Niebuhr had asked: "Shall we proclaim the truth or search for it?"[4] A decade later, he was enjoining Christians and liberals to "stop fooling themselves",[5] and proclaiming "the pathos of liberalism".[6]

The new idol that was to replace liberalism is referred to by names like "neo-orthodoxy", and "new Reformation theology". Although the emphases of this new theology have changed considerably since its birth, its main themes remain largely the same, and its leading names are still Barth, Brunner, Niebuhr, and Tillich. Since the death of these thinkers, not one figure who even approaches comparable stature has arisen. These themes are suggested both by the names of the movement and by Fosdick's address. The movement is new, and yet connected somehow with the orthodox Protestant theology of the Reformation. Opposed to liberalism and to the undignified "adjustment and accommodation" that attended liberal theology, it stresses the importance of an "independent standing ground" or "impregnable stronghold"[7] for Christianity. And it has been led not by thinkers with backgrounds in fundamentalism but by men like Fosdick,

---

[3]The first two were published by Charles Scribner's Sons, of New York; and the last by Harper & Brothers, of New York.

[4]*Christian Century,* March 12, 1925, pp. 344–46.

[5]"When Will Christians Stop Fooling Themselves?", *Christian Century,* May 16, 1934, pp. 658–60. See also "Let Liberal Churches Stop Fooling Themselves!", *Christian Century,* March 25, 1931.

[6]*Nation,* September 11, 1935, pp. 303–4.

[7]Karl Heim, *Christian Faith and Natural Science* (New York: Harper and Brothers, 1957), pp. 32–33.

liberal in tendency, alive to change. At the same time, Fosdick's address also suggests the variety of the opinions united under the anti-liberal banner. For example, although one of Barth's main theses was that the Christian God was indeed "Unknown",[8] Fosdick prayed for divine forgiveness for this very idea.

2. A Logical Development

This new Protestant thought is complicated. Yet accounts of it are often oversimplified, especially by those who try to explain it away as little more than a religious echo of the social, moral, and intellectual evils and upheavals of the twentieth century. There is more exaggeration than truth in such interpretations.

It is, to be sure, one of the ironies of modern thought that the existence of evil—the biggest problem and greatest embarrassment of the eighteenth-century natural theologians—has become one of the most persuasive argumentative assets of their twentieth-century successors. Contemporary religious apologia often begin by calling one's attention to the disunity and misery of the present world, continue by attacking for its superficiality some popular theory that does not emphasize the existence of such woe, and proceed to exult that Christianity (as if it were the only alternative) has always recognized the ambiguous nature of man and the existence of sin in the world. Acceptance of Christianity and abandonment of the alternative theory are urged as the answers to the evil—whatever the evil, the theory, or the interpretation of Christianity happens to be.

This strategy has great persuasive power and rhetorical effectiveness: there is nothing like evil, especially when described in a rather lurid way with statistics on suicides, war tolls, mental-hospital enrollment, and the destructive power of nuclear weapons, to set the mood for the acceptance of a *non sequitur*. It is not surprising, then, that many people have found the *non sequitur* more tolerable than the misery and meaninglessness. To accept a *non sequitur* is, of course, to contravene the logical rules of valid argument, and perhaps to try

> . . . *to arrange a private validity*
> *And make nature envious of what*
> *She so deplorably undervalues.*[9]

Is contemporary theology, then—like the products of many other *non*

[8]See also the final chapter of H. R. Niebuhr, *Christ and Culture* (New York: Harper and Brothers, 1956).
[9]Christopher Fry, *The Lady's Not for Burning* (London: Oxford University Press, 1949).

sequiturs—no more than an understandable neurosis, an imaginary foxhole dug in no man's land, something the theologians have invented in order to cope with the unbearable reality around them? I do not think so. The question of the origin of contemporary theology, as well as the question of its truth, must be separated from the question of its popularity. Although the basic defense of contemporary Protestant thought does ultimately rest on an appeal to irrationalism, many of the most significant features of its historical development are fairly logical products of certain long-standing theological assumptions, combined with those conclusions of late-nineteenth- and early-twentieth-century biblical criticism and social and political thinking which made Protestant liberalism untenable. Although these features are well suited to making capital out of contemporary world problems and individual anxieties, they were not deliberately invented for this purpose.

It would be surprising if the situation were otherwise. For one of the most important factors leading up to the twentieth-century crisis of Protestantism is just the fact that throughout most of its history Protestantism had been closely allied with the rationalist tradition. Although Luther, in a famous outburst, remarked that "reason is a whore", a *mésalliance* is an alliance for all that. Both Luther and his more fastidious disciple and colleague Melanchthon eagerly sought the aid of Renaissance humanism in order to justify and rationalize their own repudiation of Catholic authority.

The alliance was an on-again, off-again affair, but sufficed to permit scientists and Protestant theologians to mount a common front against Roman Catholic obscurantism on one hand and the fundamentalism of some of the working-class Protestant sects on the other hand.

In addition to the practical bonds provided by a common opposition to the intellectual and spiritual authority of Rome, Protestantism and rationalism shared an optimistic theory of knowledge which seemed theoretically to justify that rejection. The Protestant view that the Bible, the Word of God, was an open book which men, once they had cast off the shackles of tradition, could read and understand without the mediative interpretation of an authority, echoed in religious form the epistemology of the new science, which regarded Nature as an open book, directly accessible to man—either through his senses, as in Bacon's philosophy, or through his intellect, as in the methodology of Descartes—independently of the interpretation of the Church. As the *veracitas dei* made manifest the religious truth of the Book, when approached in the proper spirit, so the *veracitas naturae* made manifest the scientific truth of the Book of Nature when approached in the proper spirit.[10] The optimistic anti-authoritarian view that man was

---

[10]For the idea of the optimistic epistemology of manifest truth, see Popper, "On the Sources of Knowledge and of Ignorance", in *Conjectures and Refutations*. See also Barth, *From Rousseau to Ritschl* (London: SCM Press, 1959), p. 53.

able to apprehend the truth by his own efforts was influential in the sixteenth century both in the birth of Protestantism and in the rebirth of rationalism.

For this reason alone, none of the notorious clashes between science and religion—neither Luther's rejection of the ideas of "the fool" Copernicus, who "wants to turn the whole art of astronomy upside down" in defiance of the book of Joshua,[11] nor John Wesley's pronouncement, as late as 1768, that "the giving up of witchcraft is in effect the giving up of the Bible"[12]—should be allowed to obscure the fact that during most of Protestantism's history, its intellectual leaders, with a few exceptions, have tended to take for granted that the results of autonomous intellectual inquiry would be in ultimate harmony—whatever difficulties might turn up along the way—with Protestant religious thought.[13] The New England lightning-rod controversy of 1755 is a more representative case than those already cited. The Reverend Thomas Prince delivered a sermon at Boston's Old South Church in which he ascribed the frequency of earthquakes that year to the erection of "iron points invented by the sagacious Mr. Franklin". "In Boston", he pointed out, "are more erected than anywhere else in New England, and Boston seems to be more dreadfully shaken. Oh! there is no getting out of the mighty hand of God".[14] Professor John Winthrop, a Harvard theologian, promptly replied that it could hardly be impious to prevent thunder and lightning—both tokens of divine displeasure—from doing their proper work. "It is as much our duty to secure ourselves against the effects of lightning", Winthrop explained, "as against those of rain, snow, and wind by the means God has put into our hands".[15]

The importance of the celebrated controversies over geological discoveries and Darwinian theory should also not be exaggerated. In fact, the more eminent Protestant theologians discarded the Bible's cosmological and scientific statements relatively painlessly. For, by Darwin's time, they had grown used to the idea of a continually refurbished Christianity— independent of those features of traditional Christianity which, it was insisted, were transient, accidental accretions on true Christian doctrine.

Only in the present century has the assumption of ultimate harmony between reason and Protestant thought really broken down and the relationship been severed both in theory and in practice. Now, not in Luther's time, the whore is symbolic of Protestantism's relationship to

---

[11]See Luther, *Tischreden* (Weimar: Hermann Böhlau, 1916), vol. 4, p. 4638.

[12]Andrew D. White, *The Warfare of Science and Theology* (London: Macmillan, 1896), vol. 1, p. 363.

[13]James Luther Adams, "Tillich's Concept of the Protestant Era", printed in Paul Tillich, *The Protestant Era* (Chicago: University of Chicago Press, 1948), pp. 277 ff. See also Maurice Mandelbaum, "Philosophic Movements in the Nineteenth Century", in Colin Chant and John Fauvel, eds., *Darwin to Einstein: Historical Studies on Science & Belief,* and Mandelbaum's *History, Man and Reason: A Study in Nineteenth-Century Thought* (Baltimore: The Johns Hopkins University Press, 1971), esp. chap. 1.

[14]A. D. White, *Warfare*, vol. 1, p. 366.

[15]Ibid.

reason. Now reason is something to be indulged in from time to time with no sense of responsibility; previously it was a partner in a very stormy marriage. And this is the main cause of the present crisis of identity in Protestantism. Yet even here the retreat into irrationalism has been motivated by rational considerations, not simply by some irrational "spirit of the age". Moreover, the new Protestants believe they have a rational excuse, through the "problem of ultimate commitment", for an irrational commitment to their "independent standing ground".

These reservations about the common interpretation of contemporary Protestant thought as an irrationalist development themselves need to be examined carefully. That a way of thinking can be considered a reasonable, fairly logical development does not in itself make that thought acceptable: a logical development does not necessarily lead to true conclusions unless its premises are also true. And many of the premises of contemporary theology are false, as I shall attempt to show later. In addition, that the movement away from reason was sound does not mean that most people who participated, even most of the leaders, did so for sound reasons. Almost any widespread intellectual shift involves many different motivations. Some people move with the crowd; some simply take a fancy to a theory they do not understand at all; others revolt for "reasons" which are too irrational to describe. Finally, the fact that a shift in intellectual perspective has been carried out deliberately and logically, rather than arising from deep-seated passion, does not, even from a rationalist point of view, make it necessarily more admirable. Indeed, one of the least attractive features of the new Protestantism is the Machiavellian coldness and calculation with which it has been championed as the best means to insure the survival of institutional Protestantism. This mood appears even in Karl Barth (see chapter 3, section 2), whose earliest published complaint about Protestant liberalism was that it did not give him strong enough material for his sermons.[16] And it is echoed in the rather tiresome spirit of annoyance—the "we must stop letting ourselves be pushed around" attitude—which is suggested in Fosdick's sermon and which echoes throughout the new thinking. What is usually lacking in the new Protestantism's reasonable retreat from reason is just that passionate depth which makes certain other twentieth-century revolts against reason relatively attractive: for example, the rebellion against reason (involving an erroneous notion of reason) in the name of fundamental human relationships which Koestler recorded in *Darkness at Noon*, or the protest against the so-called scientific spirit of Marxism which Pasternak tried to live out in his oppressive society.[17]

---

[16]Barth, "Moderne Theologie und Reichgottesarbeit", *Zeitschrift für Theologie und Kirche*, 1909, pp. 317–21.
[17]See John Strachey, "The Strangled Cry", *Encounter*, November and December 1960; and Reinhold Niebuhr, "Strachey's Cry", *Encounter*, January 1961.

Nevertheless, I shall emphasize the considerations behind the shift which seem to me to be the most rational, in an effort to be as fair as possible. The account I am about to give is intended, first, as a partial reconstruction of the problem situation that thinking Protestants faced and to a large extent continue to face. Second, and more important, this analysis will serve as background for the philosophical problems I shall discuss.

3. The Rise of Protestant Liberalism

Problems of Christian identity are not new to Protestantism or to modern times. The seeds of what is sometimes described as the search for the substance or essence of Christianity were perhaps sown by Jesus himself, in his secretiveness about his belief that he was the Messiah. However this may be, the requirements of Christian faith and practice, as distinct from the question of Jesus' own identity, were already an important issue during the early life of the Church. This can be seen from a record in the Book of Acts (chapter 15) of an early debate among the disciples in Jerusalem. St. Paul, St. Peter, and St. James, among "great dissension", gathered to debate whether obedience to the laws of Moses, including the requirement of circumcision, was essential to Christian practice. Circumcision, they eventually decided, was nonessential; and early Christianity, profiting from the decision, spread among the Gentiles less painfully. In a perhaps perverted sense, this particular issue is still alive. In 1958 Reinhold Niebuhr argued that it is no longer essential for Christians to carry on evangelistic activity among the Jews.[18] The apostles in Jerusalem, who had in effect been debating whether Christian evangelism could rightly be carried on anywhere else, might have been surprised at Niebuhr's view.

In the nearly two thousand years of Christianity between St. Paul and Reinhold Niebuhr, there have been repeated controversies about the fundaments of Christianity—its cosmology, its philosophy, its claims about the scriptures, its ethics. The essentiality of each of these has been debated in turn. Indeed it might be said that issues of self-identity have provided the main intellectual problems of Christianity throughout its history.

Such problems have been most acute in the various Protestant branches of Christianity, which by their very structure and by their intellectual and political alliances and attitudes have been highly susceptible to erosion. To the extent that it is just another form of the debate about Christian identity, the new Protestant thought might be regarded as but the latest manifesta-

---

[18]See Reinhold Niebuhr, *Pious and Secular America* (New York: Charles Scribner's Sons, 1958); and my review of it in *Commentary*, March 1959.

tion of concern about these problems. Even so, the debate enters an entirely new plane with the appearance of the new thought. For the new Protestant thought is far less a response to disagreement about Christian identity than a response to a gnawing fear among Protestants of total loss of Christian identity.

Since this fear arose from the collapse of Protestant liberalism, it will be necessary to review this point of view briefly in order to put the new Protestant thought in context. Here it was that the search for identity in Christianity came to a climax; here the explosive force latent in the very presuppositions of such a search was finally ignited.

An eminent Protestant liberal, Theodore T. Munger, wrote in 1883: "If Christianity has any human basis, it is its entire reasonableness. It must not only sit easily on the mind, but it must ally itself with it in all its normal action."[19] This is a characteristic liberal utterance—not only in its conviction of the reasonableness of Christianity but in its assumption that Christianity has a "human basis". During the nineteenth century, certain philosophical, psychological, moral, and political assumptions—all reasonable within the context of nineteenth-century thought—so meshed with an equally reasonable interpretation of the message of the historical Jesus that liberal Protestantism, the fusion of those assumptions and that interpretation, seemed the most radically reasonable religious position. In this period it was not only possible but easy for a man, without tension or duplicity, to identify with both Protestant Christian and rationalist traditions, to be both Christo-centric and rationalist, both Christian and "modern man". If such a man could serve two masters, it was because those masters were partners.

There have been two main varieties of Protestant liberalism in America, and Munger spoke as a member of the later type. The earlier Protestant liberalism was itself divided, comprising both a Jeffersonian kind of Deism and the rather more conservative Unitarianism of the late eighteenth century. Both of these had been formed in opposition to the Calvinist doctrines of human depravity and divine election. And many of their intellectual leaders agreed in accepting the philosophical psychology of John Locke and in adhering—here also supported by Locke—to the eighteenth century's "natural religion", with its first-cause and design arguments for the existence of God, and its many other "proofs" and evidences for the main principles of religion.

Although most contemporary theologians are quite opposed to the earlier variety, it is the later style that they have usually had in mind in their polemics against Protestant liberalism. That is, their attacks are generally directed at the influential turn-of-the-century liberal systems of such men as

---

[19]See Herbert W. Schneider, *Religion in 20th Century America* (Cambridge, Mass.: Harvard University Press, 1952), p. 119.

Walter Rauschenbusch and Shailer Mathews in America, and Albrecht Ritschl and Adolf von Harnack in Germany. These later liberal systems sprang from an emphatic *rejection* of the Lockean tenets that had undergirded the earlier liberalism, and from a rather enthusiastic acceptance of the leading themes of Kantian and post-Kantian German "idealism".

This second type of Protestant liberalism first appeared in America early in the nineteenth century in the New England transcendentalist movement, a tiny "greater Boston" clique that successfully overthrew the early Lockean liberalism within the Unitarian Church. Although New England transcendentalism never became a national church movement, as did subsequent forms of this variety of Protestant liberalism, its members were probably more articulate than their successors. Perry Miller has judged it "the most energetic and extensive upsurge of the mind and spirit enacted in America until the intellectual crisis of the 1920's".[20]

The transcendentalist movement began in the middle 1820s, when some of the most talented of Boston's Unitarian young people began to feel that they, like Achilles in Zeno's story, were taking an infinitely long time to reach their goal, an earthly New Jerusalem. They began to wonder aloud whether Americans were not being held back by their own Unitarian Church, and to complain about the materialism, complacency, and "low commercial tone" of their prosperous native Boston, and about the lack of any real enthusiasm, fervor, or spiritual quality—ingredients they thought necessary to keep spiritual life progressing in pace with material conditions. Their churches they accused of offering only a "religion of pale negations", something "satisfactory to Boston merchants and Harvard professors, but not to those who still cherished the ancient fire of Puritan mysticism or sought to realize the New World dream of a regenerate humanity".[21] "Corpse-cold", concluded Emerson. "The heart is pulverized", echoed Ripley. Dissatisfied spiritually, the young transcendentalists sought to effect a "change of heart" among their compatriots.

They found a philosophy to nurse their dissatisfactions and spur their hopes in the pages of the new European periodicals that their Unitarian fathers and relatives had ordered for the Boston Athenaeum in order to keep in touch with the European Enlightenment. Although the light across the Atlantic had not been extinguished, Europe had been having an intellectual revolution of its own while the Unitarians were quarreling with the Calvinists. Locke's philosophy was now widely and authoritatively consid-

---

[20]Perry Miller, ed., *The Transcendentalists* (Cambridge, Mass.: Harvard University Press, 1950), pp. 14 ff. For material relating to the transcendentalist movement, see also G. H. Williams, ed., *The Harvard Divinity School* (Boston: Beacon Press, 1954); George F. Whicher, ed., *The Transcendentalist Revolt against Materialism* (Boston: D. C. Heath and Company, 1949); and Octavius Brooks Frothingham, *Transcendentalism in New England* (New York: Harper & Brothers, 1959). Miller's excellent anthology is especially valuable for a study of the religious aspects of the movement.

[21]Whicher, Introduction to *The Transcendentalist Revolt*, p. vi.

ered, among European thinkers, to have been refuted by the work of Hume
and Kant. After reading the accounts of this revolution in European
thought—first in the English writings of Carlyle, Coleridge, and Words-
worth, and later in the original German of thinkers such as Kant,
Schleiermacher, and Strauss—the young Unitarians drew their conclusions.
If Unitarianism as they knew it rested on Locke's philosophical psychology,
and if this had been refuted, Unitarianism was intellectually bankrupt. That
it was spiritually bankrupt they were already convinced. Moreover, the new
German philosophy seemed to provide just that enthusiasm, depth, and
moral fervor—in addition to the call for a "change of heart"—which was
needed to effect a revolution in human motivation to match the revolution
in man's material condition which the American republic had already begun
to achieve.

The transcendentalists later came into direct and often personal touch
with the new Continental thinking. In March 1836, for example, Ripley
published in the *Christian Examiner* a study and defense of Schleiermacher's theology, recommending it as a possible ground of synthesis and
reconciliation between the still-warring factions of Calvinism and Lockean
Unitarianism.[22] In May 1841 Theodore Parker delivered his famous "Discourse of the Transient and Permanent in Christianity"—following by only
two years the essay of the German theologian and historian David Strauss,
Vergängliches und Bleibendes in Christentum (The Transient and the
Permanent in Christianity).[23] "Christianity", Parker announced, "is a simple
thing, very simple. It is absolute, pure morality. . . . All this is very
simple—a little child can understand it. . . ."[24]

Despite considerable initial opposition, the transcendentalists eventually
won an effective victory within Unitarianism. Yet the entry of transcendentalist thought into the mainstream of American Protestantism, traditionally
suspicious of anything smacking of Unitarianism, was to be delayed until
the closing years of the nineteenth century, when, having been baptized by
the efforts of Horace Bushnell, it was popularly christened "Protestant
liberalism". Not until 1907 did the Baptist theologian Rauschenbusch, now
regarded as one of Protestant liberalism's more representative American
exponents, expound such views in his influential *Christianity and the Social
Crisis*. Even then, it was another decade before the movement gained any
really important following among the clergy.

Why, despite its early appearance in Boston, was this sort of Protestant
liberalism denied a wide hearing for so long? Although a sharp attack by

[22]George Ripley, "Schleiermacher as a Theologian", *Christian Examiner*, vol. 20, pp. 1–46; reprinted in
Miller's anthology, pp. 99–102.
[23]Parker's discourse is reprinted in Miller's anthology, pp. 259–83. Parker acknowledges his indebted-
ness to Strauss's historical work in his farewell letter to his congregation, "Theodore Parker's Experience as a
Minister", excerpts of which are reprinted in Miller, pp. 484–93.
[24]Miller, p. 277.

Calvinist thinkers certainly helped weaken its impact, most historians blame the "theological lassitude" that pervaded most American religious thought from the end of the eighteenth century until the last quarter of the nineteenth.[25] In those last and very revolutionary twenty-five years, however, Darwin's theories, the dramatic new evolutionary philosophies which provided easy-to-understand challenges to the story of creation as given in Genesis, combined with disgust at the excesses of Calvinist evangelistic revivalism, forced theologians to reconsider their assumptions. The industrial revolution forced them to review their social and ethical ideas as well: until the closing quarter of the nineteenth century, Protestant thought had tended to patronize the status quo.

Yet, even if Protestantism was now severely challenged both intellectually and socially, evolutionary theory and industrial unrest were not by themselves sufficient to push it into liberalism.[26] It was easy enough for a theologian to combine evolutionary views with Andrew Carnegie's Gospel of Wealth: "wealthy man equals fit man equals good man equals Christian man." In this equation God helps those who help themselves by living a hard-working Protestant Christian life, and heaps rewards upon them in this life. Poverty, said the great Civil War preacher Henry Ward Beecher, is the consequence of sin, even though he was later to show in his own personal life that one can sin without being impoverished. Christ's ethic became the practice of the "all-round-American boy" and the successful businessman. The late Episcopal Bishop William Lawrence of Massachusetts, a very rich man, suggested that one's wealth was an index to one's godliness. "Godliness is in league with riches", he affirmed. "In the long run, it is only to the man of morality that wealth comes."[27] Jesus, for many people, became a sort of bearded Dale Carnegie who did not charge for lessons.

Yet, although some thinkers could combine the evolutionist threat with a reaffirmation of Calvinist belief and Protestant identification with the social status quo, many others—though equally "evolutionist"—could not. The suffering and injustices resulting from industrialization seemed too blatant to be overlooked or explained away. Whatever might happen in the long run, in the visible short run any God who helped the robber barons seemed indeed to them to be helping those who helped themselves . . . to other people's money. Earlier transcendentalism had evolved as a literary and

---

[25]See Sidney E. Mead, "American Protestantism Since the Civil War: II" (*Journal of Religion*, April 1956, p. 75): "Since the end of the 18th century, the bulk of the Protestant denominations had cultivated scholastic orthodoxy, enlivened and more or less sentimentalized by pietistic revivalism and apart from the spirit and mind of modern civilization."

[26]See James R. Moore, *The Post-Darwinian Controversies: A Study of the Protestant Struggle to Come to Terms with Darwin in Great Britain and America, 1870–1900* (Cambridge: Cambridge University Press, 1979).

[27]Reprinted in *Democracy and the Gospel of Wealth*, ed. Gail Kennedy (Boston: D. C. Heath and Company, 1949), p. 69. Lawrence's address, "The Relation of Wealth to Morals", first appeared in the *World's Work*, January 1901.

philosophical movement, struck less by social injustice than by social "lack of depth", and had later added a social program to its program of "motivational" reform. Protestant liberalism now arose in response to social problems and seized on the already developed transcendentalist philosophy as a useful instrument to justify its social program. In it the social reformers found the two things they most needed: a basis for their social program, and an effective way to reconcile science and religion. The considered viewpoint resulting from this pragmatic wedding between Protestant social reformers and transcendentalist philosophy is what contemporary theologians usually have in mind when they speak of Protestant liberalism.

Perhaps this viewpoint can be best understood by reviewing some of the most important Protestant liberal beliefs about ethics, politics, and the historical Jesus.

4. The Liberal Understanding of Jesus

For most liberal Protestants, the historical Jesus was their strong ally in the battle against Calvinist orthodoxy and social injustice, and their great general in the fight for a regeneration of culture.

He was a strong ally because the Calvinists had assumed that the Christ of Christian dogma—the Jesus who had, at least since the early Chalcedon decision, been emphasized in the theological writings of the church—was the same as the Jesus of history. What better way to scatter the forces of Calvinism than to refute such assumptions by bringing back the Jesus of history to mock such misinterpretations of his message? If it could be shown through historical research that the historical Jesus had taught a message vastly different from that ascribed by the Calvinists to the Christ of dogma, the very core of Calvinism would be destroyed. Hence the liberal Protestants, first in Germany and later in America, enthusiastically undertook research in biblical criticism and began the famous quest for the historical Jesus. Jesus was also the great general of the liberal Protestants. Their leader, teacher, and guide in the fight for personal and social transformation, he had, they thought, given men the key for cultural reform in the guise of the most spiritual ethic the world had ever known. The crux of his message, they agreed, was the call for a *metanoia*, a conversion, repentance, or radical change of attitude toward life.[28]

Throughout their investigations, the liberals sought to give this picture of

---

[28]For a beautifully stated example of the "change-of-attitude" interpretation of Christ's message, see Vladimir G. Simkhovitch, *Toward the Understanding of Jesus* (New York: Macmillan, 1921).

the historical Christ a firm historical basis by means of scriptural study and independent research into the history of Jesus's time. At first, one of their more powerful aids was the belief that the Gospel of John presented the oldest and most accurate narrative of Christ's teaching and life, probably even the report of an eyewitness. It was in this Fourth Gospel that the idea of change of attitude was emphasized, here that the idea of the Kingdom of God on earth and the picture of Jesus as a great spiritual teacher were least ambiguous. The first three synoptic Gospels, on the other hand, in view of their many descriptions of miracles and claims about a supermundane kingdom, could be regarded as rather primitive distortions of Jesus's message on which the church had mistakenly fastened.[29] Under the penetrating searchlight of the liberals, the historical Jesus, long buried under misinterpretations and false dogma, seemed at first to come to life after centuries of misunderstanding, and eagerly to endorse and bless the liberals' own ideas.

This obliging agreement enabled the liberal Protestants to remain sincere Christians. On the other hand, many features of the modernity they had embraced seemed to lead away from Christianity: they were forced to reject its ancient metaphysics, its estimate of man, its authoritarian temper. But at the critical moment, when they otherwise would have had in sincerity to abandon Christianity, the latest results of their historical investigations presented them with a picture of Jesus to which they could assent after all. If they could in fact accept the message and person of the true Jesus of history, they had a right—indeed a stronger right than the Calvinists—to call themselves Christians.

That the message of a great religious teacher should be an ethical one accorded with the Kantian and post-Kantian belief that ethics is the core of religion—a significant agreement, considering the influence Kant's thought exerted on the liberals. Jesus now appeared as the greatest of religious teachers because the liberals found that he had lived in perfect accordance with whatever "facts of human consciousness" they judged to be basic to the moral life—whether *duty,* as in Kant, or "absolute dependence", as in Schleiermacher. To follow Jesus's example, they argued, would be to transform one's own life and to contribute to the ultimate transformation of cultural existence.

---

[29]"I take it as established that the Gospel of John is the narrative of an eyewitness and forms an organic whole", wrote Schleiermacher. Quoted by Albert Schweitzer in *The Quest of the Historical Jesus* (London: A. & C. Black, 1910), p. 66.

5. *Political and Psychological Assumptions of Protestant Liberalism*

Whereas liberal biblical scholarship indicated that Jesus *intended* his ethic as a practical social gospel, and that his ethical remarks had formed the core of his teaching, the chief politico-psychological assumption of Protestant liberalism was that Jesus's ethic was in fact practical.

The Protestant liberals considered a *revolution in human motivation* to be the chief political need of their time. This was Kant's suggestion in *Religion Within the Limits of Reason Alone*; and it was Rauschenbusch's conception in 1907. Even as late as 1933 the Federal Council of Churches proclaimed that "the Christian conscience can be satisfied with nothing less than the complete substitution of motives of mutual helpfulness and good will for the motive of private gain".[30]

The principal reason why the liberals centered their hopes on a change in human motivation is not difficult to find. As they analyzed the social order of their day, they concluded that many economic and social institutions worked against social justice. Yet, strongly influenced by Marxist analysis, they believed there was little hope of reforming these institutions from within, since the institutions themselves encouraged greed and selfishness and an economic individualism that was opposed in spirit to the imposition of the social controls the liberals thought were necessary. The social circle was a vicious one: the institutions encouraged wrong attitudes, and the wrong attitudes helped perpetuate unjust institutions. Since most liberal Protestants were, unlike Marx, opposed in principle to a *violent* social revolution aimed at changing social and economic institutions by force, they were compelled to focus their efforts on the task of changing human attitudes. Such an effort to revolutionize men's attitudes seemed to them a *Christian* program, since they believed that the change of motivation which was required would have to involve a shift from the profit motive to the selfless, "mutual service" motivation they considered part of the ethic of the Sermon on the Mount.

The vague liberal assumptions about man's "dignity", and their Kantian belief that the obligation to do one's duty was a universal human experience, led many of them to feel that such a change of attitude was possible on a large scale. Few of them were definite about just what kind of social institutions would accompany that change. But they agreed that in principle a set of practical social and economic institutions existed which would be

[30]See Schneider, p. 77.

compatible with the ethic of the Sermon. Human motivation and social justice could, in principle, be reconciled, however they might cancel each other out at the moment.

If the only solution to social problems lay in a widespread revolution in motivation, and if the Christian churches were the custodians of the only ethic based on the proper motivation, then the Christian churches had an all-important role in the social order. On them, literally, lay the task not only of regenerating society and eventually bringing in the Kingdom of God but of saving society from chaos and violent revolution. To some of the more liberal liberals, this was not only the present duty of Christians; the establishment of the Kingdom of God on earth was the ultimate goal of Christianity. The resulting feeling of ominous responsibility in the face of social crisis lent some excitement and fervor to the program.

The notion that it was feasible for the churchmen of America to effect a world-wide revolution in human motivation would probably have been impossible without a widespread *popular* belief that progress, however it might be delayed, was *inevitable*. The theology of progress—fostered in America by the Enlightenment philosophy, encouraged by long periods of peace and by relative economic progress, and endorsed by popular misinterpretations of evolutionary theory—allowed the ordinary liberal Protestant to embrace a utopianism that would have shocked the most optimistic Jeffersonian.

An optimism that seems unbelievable today was not, however, the unique property of the Protestant liberals; it underlay a surprisingly large part of late-nineteenth-century culture. Even an acute observer like George Santayana was able to write in his essay "The Intellectual Temper of the Age", published just before World War I:

> Our bodies in this generation are generally safe, and often comfortable; and for those who can suspend their irrational labours long enough to look about them, the spectacle of the world, if not particularly beautiful or touching, presents a rapid and crowded drama and (what here concerns me most) one usually intelligible. . . . We are not condemned, as most generations have been, to fight and believe without an inkling of the cause. . . . The whole drift of things presents a huge, good-natured comedy to the observer. It stirs not unpleasantly a certain sturdy animality and hearty selftrust which lie at the base of human nature.[31]

On a somewhat less sophisticated level—that of Edward Bellamy's famous prophecy, *Looking Backward*—a preacher in the year 2000 looks backward to the year 1887, forward to the future, and concludes his Sunday sermon with these words:

[31] *Winds of Doctrine*, pp. 2–3.

With a tear for the dark past, turn we then to the dazzling future, and, veiling our eyes, press forward. The long and weary winter of the race is ended. Its summer has begun. Humanity has burst the chrysalis. The heavens are before it.[32]

At least the advice to veil our eyes was sound.

6. The Decline of Protestant Liberalism

> "You forget", said the Devil with a
> chuckle,
> "that I have been evolving too".
>   —W. R. INGE

Thirteen years after the publication of the passage just quoted, Santayana prepared a new introduction for his *Winds of Doctrine*. He no longer felt so safe—not even about "our bodies in this generation". "That comfortable liberal world", he now wrote, "was like a great tree with the trunk already sawed quite through, but still standing with all its leaves quietly rustling, and with us dozing under its shade. We were inexpressibly surprised when it fell and half crushed us. . . ."[33]

Whereas the detached Santayana might be only inexpressibly surprised after being half crushed by a tree, many of his contemporaries blinked open their eyes with less equanimity to an unshaded and not very brave new world. Their attempts to understand what had happened triggered the feverish intellectual activity that is familiarly characteristic in this period. The studies, as well as the dance halls, were roaring in the twenties.

Most of the events and ideas that occasioned the lapse of confidence in liberalism generally, not just in Protestant liberalism, made vivid, if not wholly accurate, impressions on this generation. Buttressing a dramatically colorful and imaginative theory with clinical detail, Freud helped shatter popularly man's high estimate of his own selflessness and rationality, his belief that he was at least master of his own belfry. World War I, the rise of the secular authoritarianisms, and the failure of the League of Nations, all unintended developments, helped to topple the conceptions of personal and social progress and rational planning which had so comfortably undergirded liberalism and the Social Gospel. Though much naïve optimism survived World War I, within the United States if not elsewhere, the Depression muzzled much of that. The popular tune of the 1920s, "My God, How the Money Rolls In", gave way, after 1929, to "Brother, Can You Spare a

---

[32]Edward Bellamy, *Looking Backward: 2000–1887* (London: Alvin Redman, 1948), p. 208. First published in 1888.

[33]Santayana, Preface to the 1926 edition of *Winds of Doctrine* (New York: Charles Scribner's Sons), p. vi.

Dime?" and "Sing Me a Song of Social Significance". The promise of a chicken in every pot became a prayer for anything in the pot.

By World War II, which began with the whimper of the "phony war" and ended in the bang of Nagasaki, some men not only had begun to doubt human capacity to keep pace with science, and the "ultimate satisfactoriness" of scientific achievement, but even wondered whether the rise of science itself was not a cloud upon the future. The pietistic fallout of the nineteenth century gave way to a more menacing sort of rain; faith in the future was replaced by adulation of the passing moment. "Enjoy Yourself, It's Later Than You Think" now hit the Hit Parade. Concern about the struggle for the survival of the fittest was replaced by concern about the struggle for the survival of anyone.

On a more abstract level, the philosophical assumptions of liberalism were also crumbling. Its post-Kantian idealism was heavily attacked by a new wave of empiricism which arose during World War I and the 1920s, led by the onslaught of pragmatism and the new logical positivism. Moreover, most of Kant's categories, which had been thought to be necessary mental principles, had by now broken down—shattering one of the last defenses of the notion that we could at least be certain about our innate prejudices and about the way in which our minds "imposed their nature" on reality. Kant thought that an alternative to Euclidean geometry was inconceivable. But the invention of non-Euclidean geometry showed that this was not so. Kant thought that we had to see the world of nature in terms of Newton's dynamics, and that an alternative was inconceivable. But Einstein's theory of relativity showed that this was not true either.[34]

How did these events and discoveries affect *Protestant* liberalism in particular? Any causal analysis of the historical situation would probably lead to the conclusion that this succession of social and intellectual explosions was principally responsible for the shift from optimistic Protestant liberalism to the pessimistic mood of neo-orthodoxy, the "theology of crisis". Here I am primarily interested not in an exact causal analysis but in the question whether the shift was intellectually warranted. The answer must, I think, be affirmative.

Protestant liberalism could have survived most of these blows within the critical tradition. The Bible contains rich material for a more tragic and realistic analysis of human existence and a deeper interpretation of human nature, and it is hardly necessary for a liberal really to believe that men every day and in every way grow better and better. In fact, more sophisticat-

---

[34]Kant also thought that we must see nature in terms of the "law of causality", and that such a determinism was implied by Newtonian physics. More recently, Popper has argued that even classical physics—not to mention modern quantum physics—was indeterministic. See his "Indeterminism in Quantum Physics and in Classical Physics", *British Journal for the Philosophy of Science*, (1950–51). See also K. R. Popper, *The Open Universe*, vol. 2 of the *Postscript to the Logic of Scientific Discovery;* and *Quantum Theory and the Schism in Physics*, vol. 3 of the *Postscript*.

ed liberals such as Dewey, Shailer Mathews, and Ritschl did not feel as naïvely optimistic as is often stated: their progressivism was a *program* they were perhaps overly confident about, but rarely a *prediction*. Indeed, the idea of inevitable progress was not in fact part of evolutionary theory, but inevitable progress was itself a remnant of the anthropomorphic theism they had already abandoned, a remnant which looked at history as a play with a steady buildup to a happy ending.

Such considerations probably explain why one occasionally hears a neo-orthodox theologian claim, without any attempt to sound paradoxical, that his own viewpoint is at heart in the tradition of Protestant liberalism; that the Protestant liberals, stunned by the simultaneous collapse of so many of their assumptions, tended to cling to them desperately and *irrationally* and thereby to abandon *real* liberalism for the sake of an *arrested form* of liberalism, to identify the particular form and emphases of turn-of-the-century liberalism with the liberal spirit. There is a great deal of truth in such contentions. On a more fundamental level, however, the neo-orthodox claim to represent a more liberal Protestant liberalism is unwarranted. The collapse of at least one assumption of Protestant liberalism could hardly have been survived within the liberal rationalist tradition. This was the Protestant liberal interpretation of the historical Jesus. Without this, a Protestant Christianity in the rationalist tradition became impossible; and hence a shift away from Protestant liberalism—and not only from a particular historical form of it—became intellectually imperative.

To clarify this important point, we need to consider why the liberal interpretation of Jesus collapsed, and then to examine the formidable problems for Protestant liberalism which grew from the ruins.

7. The Liberal Jesus Vanishes

The Protestant liberals inaugurated the historical criticism of the New Testament and the quest for the historical Jesus in the hope that the Nazarene might rise up as their ally against Calvinists and others who, they believed, had dogmatically twisted his spiritual message into the call to obedience before "mystery, miracle, and authority". The early results of this criticism nourished this hope, increased the plausibility of their program, and encouraged them to continue.

Further research, however, revealed that the historical Jesus was far more intractable than a good liberal might have expected—particularly from another liberal. In so far as the historical personality, Jesus of Nazareth, could be restored to life at all, it tended to mock the liberals and to bless, even if reservedly, the Calvinists it had been expected to disown. By 1910 Francis Crawford Burkitt, introducing the first English translation of Albert Schweitzer's *The Quest of the Historical Jesus,* solemnly rebuked the liberals with these words:

> . . . when the alternative of "Jesus or Christ" is put forward, as it has been in a recent publication, or when we are bidden to choose between the Jesus of history and the Christ of dogma, few except professed students know what a protean and kaleidoscopic figure the "Jesus of history" is . . . we are beginning to see that the apocalyptic vision, the New Age which God is to bring in, is no mere embroidery of Christianity, but the heart of its enthusiasm. And therefore the expectation of vindication and judgment to come, the imagery of the Messianic Feast, the "other-worldiness" against which so many eloquent words were said in the nineteenth century, are not to be regarded as regrettable accretions foisted on by superstition to the pure morality of the original Gospel. These ideas are the Christian Hope . . . not to be given up so long as we remain Christians at all.[35]

What had happened, when described in detail, makes a complex and exciting story. Basically, however, the result was fairly simple: so many problems arose out of the attempt to find a liberal Jesus in the historical documents that eventually the entire program collapsed from within. Thereby the Protestant liberals suffered a most extraordinary and ironical reverse. The central historical problem which proved the undoing of the liberals concerned the eschatological content of Christ's message, that is, his view of the nature of the coming Kingdom of God. Did the historical Jesus build on the presuppositions of late Jewish eschatology concerning the coming of the Messiah and the supernatural Kingdom of God? Or did he build on a foundation that preached an ethic of love simply for the purpose of regenerating the culture of *this* world? The three synoptic Gospels, Matthew, Mark, and Luke, seemed to support the first view; the best evidence for the latter appeared to be in the Gospel of John. At first, attempts were made to reconcile the two interpretations, to coordinate the Christ of the synoptic Gospels and Jewish eschatology with the Jesus who was thought to have preached that his messiahship and the heavenly kingdom were purely spiritual. All attempts at reconciliation, however, broke down: it had to be one or the other.[36]

Eventually, through the work of such historians as Johannes Weiss and Schweitzer, the first view triumphed. The Pauline epistles and Mark's gospel became accepted as the earliest and most reliable historical documents; the Gospel of John was now regarded as a later literary and philosophical reinterpretation of Jesus' life, written for the apologetic purpose of explaining why Christ and the Kingdom of God had failed to come. It introduced

---

[35]F. C. Burkitt, in his Preface to the English edition of Schweitzer, *The Quest.*
[36]Schweitzer, Introduction to the third edition of *The Quest,* 1954.

the idea of a *spiritual Kingdom* within men and spiritualized the message and portrait of Jesus. In his great book by that name, Schweitzer magnificently chronicled and made generally available the results of this "quest of the historical Jesus", which lasted for four generations during the nineteenth century and commanded the efforts and attention of some of the most powerful minds in German historical scholarship.

After Schweitzer's report, it was no longer possible to claim that the historical Jesus was faithfully portrayed by the persuasive liberal picture of the moral teacher, the surpassingly good man who taught the fatherhood of God and the brotherhood of man without making any supernatural claims.[37] The real Jesus, as far as the most advanced branch of historical research into biblical foundations could tell, had preached an early supernatural return; his ideas had been thoroughly conditioned by the Jewish eschatology of his time. Later independent historical investigations into Jewish eschatological views corroborated these conclusions. From now on, anyone who was to be faithful to the historical Jesus would have to take into account that he was apparently convinced of his eschatological message and his divine mission. His purpose, as he had apparently conceived it, was to establish the Kingdom of God on the side of God and in tension with, if not simply against, the kingdom of this world. The message he preached was not intended as an ethical key for the transformation of the worldly kingdom. He was not a leader and teacher of culture, but an opponent of culture who *threatened* mankind with his promise to come to judge those who identified themselves with the hopes of this world's culture. Jesus appeared to be a forbidding, world-denying figure, hardly a nineteenth-century-style social reformer with whom Protestants could easily identify. Schweitzer writes:

> The spiritual life of our own time seems like to perish at His hands, for He leads to battle against our thought a host of dead ideas, a ghostly army upon which death has no power, and Himself destroys again the truth and goodness which His Spirit creates in us, so that it cannot rule the world.

In short, the liberal picture of Jesus had apparently been unhistorical.

This new view of the historical Jesus also forced the liberals to entertain more seriously an uncongenial view of the Christian Church. Partly because of a certain anticlericalism among some of the socialist movements that had

---

[37]This was written prior to the dissemination of information regarding the Nag Hammadi papyri. This new material radically affects all accounts of early Christianity—including Schweitzer's. Some of this material—although it in no way rehabilitates liberalism—contains material that would have pleased Protestant liberal theologians. See Elaine Pagels, *The Gnostic Gospels* (New York: Random House, 1979); James M. Robinson et al., *The Nag Hammadi Library* (New York: Harper & Row, 1977); J. M. Robinson, "The Jung Codex: The Rise and Fall of a Monopoly", *Religious Studies Review*, vol. 3, no. 1, January 1977. For an earlier argument for the diversity of Christian origins see Walter Bauer, *Rechtgläubigkeit und Ketzerei im ältesten Christentum*, 1934. See my discussion of these texts in appendix 1, sec. 3.

aligned themselves with Protestant liberalism, partly for their own reasons, the liberals had been fond of emphasizing the *individual* Christian and minimizing the role of the organized church in Christianity. Jesus himself, they argued, had not intended to found a church; the church was a later development, formed under pressure.

The eschatological theme, however, now brought into focus the New Testament emphasis on the role of the church, or community of believers; showed how important such a group would be for the fulfillment of Jesus's eschatological claims and expectations; and related it, further, to the famous Old Testament idea of the "remnant" of the faithful whence redemption would come to mankind. This reevaluation of the role and biblical basis of the church helped strengthen the already growing call for ecumenical unity among Protestant groups.

If the New Testament's apparent endorsement of the idea of an organized church was unwelcome to some liberals, the implications for the Christian ethic which the new understanding of the historical Jesus involved were far more disagreeable. The Sermon on the Mount, it appeared, had never been intended by Jesus as a practical ethics and politics of love for this world. To use Schweitzer's phrase, Jesus had advocated a temporary *interims Ethik* for his followers, to be used during the interim period between his crucifixion and the Last Judgment. These followers mistakenly expected, as did Jesus himself, that the coming of a *supernatural* Kingdom of God would quickly follow his crucifixion. If the supernatural Kingdom of God was about to come, those who expected to enter it hardly needed an applicable ethic in terms of *this* world's needs; the most prudent move for men holding such expectations was in fact the abandonment of the goods and attachments of this world, as indicated in the Sermon, in preparation for the expected spiritual apotheosis of the next.

However, since Jesus and his followers had been mistaken, and since there was no way of predicting when, if ever, the heavenly kingdom would arrive, any ethic founded on an expectation of its immediate advent could not be expected to be politically or personally practical as a guide for the establishment of a spiritualized kingdom of this world.

Of course, the fact that Jesus did not intend his ethic to be practical would not, by itself, exclude the possibility that the ethic might in fact be practical. He might have moralized more practically than he knew. However, the events of the twentieth century were illustrating dramatically that it was not in fact practical. The Protestant liberals had sought a change of attitude that would permit the ethic of the Sermon to be implemented in everyday political and economic experience, but Freud's observations about man's good will and rational capabilities made the possibility of such a widespread motivational transformation appear intellectually absurd. Liberalism was the bull in a bear market. As people began to realize, through trial and sometimes devastating error, that the direct application of such utopian ideas to practical politics could be foolish and self-defeating, liberalism also came to seem like the bull in the china shop.

The old utopianism—under which the slogan that World War I was a "war to end wars" or "to keep the world safe for democracy" was taken seriously enough to bring the churches to the support of the military program—was enervated by the war's far from utopian or democratic outcome. When some of the more callow assessments of the war began to appear, the sting of insult aggravated the hurt of failure. Once the war was over, the famous dean of London's St. Paul's Cathedral mocked the idealists. "During the war," Dean Inge wrote, "we said we were fighting to make the world safe for democracy. That was a lump of sugar for the American eagle, and fortunately for us, he swallowed it".[38] Hoover's pacifism, the studied attempts of America and the United Kingdom to pare down each other's navies during the 1920s and early 1930s while Hitler was marching to power, and the many other desperate, sometimes touching attempts to set things right all at once, contributed further to the coming bitter harvest of foolhardy utopianism. The ethic of the Sermon on the Mount was indeed impractical.

So the Protestant liberals, who had assumed that the Christian religion, even divested of its cosmological content, would preserve an important social message, and who had often retained their affiliation with Protestantism for the sake of this social program, now learned that no social ethic had been at the core of Jesus's message, and that even if one had been, the particular ethic ascribed to him was socially impractical. The obvious question could not help arising: For what purpose should those who were primarily interested in transforming culture continue their identification with Protestantism—particularly if they could not accept the ideas that appeared to be in fact at the basis of the Christian message? As Burkitt had written: "These ideas are the Christian hope . . . not to be given up so long as we remain Christians at all."

8. Were the Liberals to Blame for the Liberal Picture of Jesus?

The importance of these historical findings and the questions they engendered in confounding Protestant liberalism can hardly be overestimated. Yet some have evoked an even more sweeping criticism of the liberals. Not only were their facts wrong: their historical method was radically incorrect, if not sinfully perverse. The liberals, it is suggested, used Christ's person as a

---

[38]William Ralph Inge, in *Living Philosophies* (New York: Simon and Schuster, 1931), pp. 307–17.

peg on which to hang their prejudices and hopes. The resulting clotheshorse personality they used as a persuasive social tool to implement their dreams and to lend both rational plausibility and divine authority to their very human message.

This methodological complaint is basically just, but it needs to be applied with some restraint. If the liberals are guilty, they can hardly be blamed for it. They were, after all, unaware of the complexity of biblical research; and they themselves were largely responsible for inaugurating and continuing it, even after they had become conscious that they were conspiring in their own undoing. Schweitzer is too hard on them, even when he colors his severity with ambiguity. After praising the relentless honesty of the liberals, he goes on elsewhere to castigate them vigorously for not seeing the New Testament terrain as clearly as he himself had done. Twentieth-century New Testament historians like Schweitzer possess a sounder, more self-conscious methodology largely because they have been aware of and able to avoid the liberals' far from deliberate or obvious methodological errors.[39] The man who invented the electric light did not criticize the inventor of the candle.

The liberals gave to Jesus the kind of reverential yet unsatisfactory homage men have always paid to great personalities, great art, great literature—those phenomena, themselves ambiguous, which command the fealty of so many different people for so many different reasons. Most men like to think that anything of high repute contains at least a fragment of themselves; it is hard to worship something totally alien. "Critics who write about Shakespeare", according to W. H. Auden, "reveal more about themselves than about Shakespeare, but perhaps that is the great value of drama of the Shakespearean kind, namely, that whatever he may see taking place on stage, its final effect upon each spectator is a self-revelation".[40] Plato has repeatedly undergone the same treatment, as Werner Jaeger and others have pointed out. One example Jaeger gives, the interpretation of Plato presented by Schleiermacher, is interesting in itself, since Schleiermacher was also the first liberal theologian to begin a serious study of the historical Jesus.[41] Naming Schleiermacher as the initiator of the quest for an understanding of the true historical Plato, Jaeger writes: "The trend of this approach was towards seeing Plato, who had become a mighty figure detached from time and history, within his own social background, and making him a real, solid, historical character." The accomplishment and the

---

[39]Although I believe this practice was usually carried out unconsciously, there are occasional indications of a self-conscious awareness that the historical Jesus was being made a peg for modern ethical ideals. For example, in Samuel Butler's *Erewhon Revisited,* the Sunchild has some things to say which are explicitly intended to refer to developments in the Anglican theology of the nineteenth century. The Sunchild, having returned to Erewhon, urges his followers to use his figure unabashedly for their best ethical conceptions, so that "you will make me out to be much better and abler than I was, or ever shall be . . .". (London: Jonathan Cape, 1927), p. 267.

[40]W. H. Auden, "The Fallen City", *Encounter,* November 1959.

[41]See Jaeger, *Paideia,* vol. 2, p. 78, and Schweitzer, *Quest,* p. 62.

undoing of the liberal historians was to fit a long-idealized Jesus back into his own social and historical milieu.

Again, not only superficial liberal Protestants used Jesus for their own purposes. The great novelist Dostoevsky, who nowadays is often claimed as one of the early Christian existentialists and a forerunner of our neo-orthodox theologians, treated the historical Jesus in a typically liberal Protestant fashion. In the famous Grand Inquisitor scene of *The Brothers Karamazov*, Dostoevsky also conjured up an unhistorical Jesus to haunt the authoritarian Christians of his day. One of the novelist's greatest political phobias was that the Roman Catholic church he so detested would conspire with the growing socialist and communist movements of the late nineteenth century. These political premonitions Dostoevsky expressed in his little-known column "A Writer's Diary", published first while he was editor of the weekly *Grazhdanin,* and later independently. His accounts, according to one commentator, made "the flesh of his readers creep with the bogeys of Communism and Roman Catholicism (whose hidden hand he detected everywhere)".[42] In order to preserve his power in the face of the growing socialist movement, the Pope, wrote Dostoevsky, would have to be "prepared to deny Christ and believe in the human ant heap".[43] The Papists, he wrongly predicted, would unite with socialism to oppose freedom, Holy Russia, and the Orthodox faith. In fact, it turned out that socialism united with Holy Russia to oppose freedom, the Papists, and the Orthodox faith.[44]

In the Grand Inquisitor scene Dostoevsky brought to life his political hopes and fears. The Christ that appears in Seville is a symbol of freedom and anti-authoritarianism, starkly opposed to the Inquisitor's "benevolent" suppression of freedom. Although the implications of the scene are mani-foldly ambiguous, one of them is plain: in order to unite with socialism, the Roman Catholic church would have to abandon the historical Jesus. So even Dostoevsky, "forerunner of present-day Christian existentialism", invoked Jesus's aid in a cultural battle against socialism.

Although the Protestant liberals in America more often took Christ for an ally in their battle *for* a kind of socialism, their approach was, on a more fundamental level, the same as Dostoevsky's: Christ was to be man's helper and guide in his battle against social evil, however that evil might be conceived.

All interpretations—scientific, historical, or literary—are impregnated with theories and prejudices, very often unconsciously held. In order to be

---

[42]Gerald Abraham, *Dostoevsky* (London: Gerald Duckworth & Co., 1936), p. 118.
[43]Ibid., p. 126.
[44]In so far as noncommunist forms of socialism are concerned, it seems to have been the Protestants who eventually united with socialism. See, for example, the early writings of Reinhold Niebuhr and Paul Tillich, and Tillich's statement that "there can be nothing beyond religious socialism". See also the accounts in the Tillich and Niebuhr volumes of the Library of Living Theology.

criticized, or even to be open to criticism, these princples of interpretation must be brought to light. If the principles, once revealed, stand up to criticism, we may continue to use them, now consciously. If they break down, they should be abandoned or at least used more carefully. The achievement of Schweitzer and his predecessors was to display the unconscious principles on which the liberal interpretation of Jesus was based, and to show—in the light of advancing historical knowledge—that many of these were untenable. Schweitzer's own positive interpretation of the historical Jesus is of course also not final. Quite the contrary, it has itself been undermined during the past half-century. Yet this development offers little consolation or encouragement to recalcitrant Protestant liberals.[45] Rather, the most common contemporary scholarly conclusion about the historical Jesus is that *no* coherent picture of his life and message is possible: the evidence is too fragmentary and contradictory to support *either* the Protestant liberal picture or Schweitzer's alternative. Such a conclusion is compatible with the faith-demands of the neo-orthodox style of thinking and feeling, in so far as it demands an unquestioning commitment to Jesus regardless of what his character and message may have been. Such a conclusion is, however, hardly attractive to a Protestant liberal; the Protestant liberal has always wanted to know the nature of that to which he was committing himself.

---

[45]But see footnote 37 above, concerning the Nag Hammadi papyri; see also appendix 1, sec. 3.

3
THE NEW
PROTESTANT THOUGHT

O God, grant us the serenity to accept
What cannot be changed;
The courage to change what can be
changed;
And the wisdom to know one from the
other.
—REINHOLD NIEBUHR

For every evil under the sun,
There is a remedy, or there is none.
If there be one, try to find it;
If there be none, never mind it.
—MOTHER GOOSE

1. On the Border

When a position runs into recalcitrant facts, some adjustment needs to be made. Sometimes the simplest thing is to deny the facts, a policy for which theologians have traditionally shown some talent. Such a course was hardly open to the Protestant liberals, who had for many years been accusing anti-Darwinian fundamentalists of doing just that. Confronted with a historical Jesus whose person and message were, at least in any straightforward sense, both illiberal and irrational, the Protestant liberals had to face squarely a new and rather formidable question: *Was Jesus himself one of those nonessential historical shells one could in principle discard during the search for the essence of the Christian message?*

A negative answer to this question had of course been tacitly assumed all along. But now, for the first time, Protestant theologians became consciously aware that the various attempts to state the *essence of the Christian message* were subordinate to the question of the *essence of being a Christian*. And a truly Christian identity, it was plausibly argued, demanded assent to the person of the historical Jesus—as he actually had been, not as one might have liked him to be. To the extent that honest identification with the rationalist tradition required that one withhold assent from the newly discovered historical Jesus, it became impossible for a man to be, in good conscience, both a Protestant Christian and a rationalist.

So, contrary to a familiar interpretation of the shift away from Protestant liberalism, the choice was not between Protestant liberalism and neo-orthodoxy. Protestant Christian liberalism had become intellectually impossible. Rather, the choice that confronted Protestant thinkers who were aware of what was at stake was between (1) a non-Christian rationalism, which lacked the essential characteristic of Christian identity, assent to the person of the historical Jesus, and (2) a newly self-conscious Christian Protestantism resolved to hold fast to Jesus no matter how irrational a policy that might turn out to be.

This is one of the most important reasons for the intellectual and numerical strength of irrationalist forces within Protestantism today. Since it was almost impossible to put up a serious case for thoroughgoing rationalism *within* Protestant Christianity, those liberal rationalists who wished to be able to discard anything that conflicted with rational principles had to abandon Christianity. And those who held fast to Jesus had to be illiberal or uncritical at least about Jesus, however critical they might be on other matters. This development, although its significance may not have been fully appreciated at the time it occurred, may prove to have been the most decisive turning point in the intellectual history of Protestantism.

With the breakdown of Protestant liberalism, then, the long marriage of the rationalist tradition and Protestantism came to an end. Some marriages end in death or separation; this one ended in a carefully documented divorce: The essence of being a Christian was written into the constitution of the new ecumenical movement, whose members were required to agree that "Jesus Christ is Lord". Leonard Hodgson has chronicled in his Gifford Lectures one important episode of the court proceedings:

> In the summer of 1937 the World Conference on Faith and Order and the Universal Christian Council for Life and Work had agreed to unite in forming the World Council of Churches. In May 1938 there was a meeting at Utrecht in Holland for the purpose of drawing up a constitution for the proposed Council. The Faith and Order Movement had always been a Conference of churches "which accept our Lord Jesus Christ as God and Saviour", . . . The Life and Work Movement had never had this restriction, and I was expecting the Council to be constituted on its wider scale, with the narrower basis written into its constitution as a requirement for its Faith and Order activities. But speaker after speaker, representing a wide variety of churches from America, Great Britain, Germany, Scandinavia and elsewhere, demanded the acceptance of the Nicene Faith as the basis of the Council itself. I took care to point out that this was not demanded by the Movement I represented as the price of our adherence. It became abundantly clear that this basis would be adopted, not because of any desire to conciliate the stalwarts of the Faith and Order Movement, but because it was the almost unanimous demand of all those present. One speaker voiced the mind of the meeting when he said that if it was intended to have a Council of Christian

Churches they must be Christian churches, and Christian churches are churches which accept the Nicene Faith.

The prevailing impression made on my mind was that the debate registered the change that had come over the theological world since I had begun my theological studies in 1913. There was no one present to voice the modernist liberalism which would almost certainly have been a prominent, if not the dominant, force in any similar gathering held a quarter of a century earlier.[1]

If the voice of liberalism had stopped speaking out at the church's conferences, it had not yet stopped pestering the consciences of the church's theologians. For the choice between rationalism and Protestant Christianity was not easy or pleasant for most of those compelled to make it. If, on one hand, the new Protestant position offered considerable relief, on the other hand it opened new and agonizing dilemmas.

Some relief came from the new definiteness it provided. A basically negative and eliminative spirit like that of Protestant liberalism was bound to leave a religion in a weakened position. For example, its refusal to take up a dogmatic position that could be easily understood and followed by the masses—at a time of rapid industrial growth in mass society—placed Protestant liberalism in danger of committing suicide. Among the critics of Protestantism who noticed this kind of weakness was John Henry Cardinal Newman, the great nineteenth-century British convert to Roman Catholicism. In his "Discourses to Mixed Congregations", he described the Protestants as "children tossed to and fro, and carried about by every gale of doctrine". He added: "If they had faith, they would not change."

Another, more ominous complaint came from Karl Barth. Deploring the practical difficulties graduates of liberal theological faculties faced in conducting their ministries, Barth attributed the trouble to religious individualism, to the Kantian and liberal idea of relying on the internal admonitions of conscience, rather than on external authority, for moral and spiritual guidance.

> Whosoever keeps himself to "modern" theology [wrote Barth] must know that the question is: to be or not to be. For science deprives him of that entire historical outfit of ideas and concepts which were the "motive and quietive" of the religion of the past. . . . For whosoever wants to speak to others only of that which in his own life has become cause or effect of faith, is confronted by the Scylla of clericalism which offers more than it has, and by the Charybdis of agnosticism, which offers nothing at all. But both stand threateningly before us younger theologians, and to this I attribute our immaturity, our surprisingly small enthusiasm for religious activism.[2]

---

[1]Hodgson, *For Faith and Freedom* (Oxford: Basil Blackwell, 1956), vol. 1, pp. 13 ff. For New Testament support for the position, see Romans 10:9; I Corinthians 8:6, 12:3; II Corinthians 4:5; Philippians 2:11; Colossians 2:6–8.
[2]Barth, "Moderne Theologie und Reichgottesarbeit".

Writing about "Modernism and Christianity", George Santayana observed:

> What would make the preaching of the gospel utterly impossible would be the admission that it had no authority to proclaim what has happened or what is going to happen, either in this world or in another.[3]

Protestant liberalism in effect had given up all claim to such authority. The new thought, by drawing a limit to change, tried to regain some of its lost authority.

But the new thought also deeply troubled many of its leaders; and their writings record the intensity of their personal struggles over the matter. Paul Tillich strikes a representative tone when he writes of those who "have found that they were not what they believed themselves to be, even after a deeper level had appeared to them below the vanishing surface. That deeper level itself became surface, when a still deeper level was discovered".[4] The "concept of the border", Tillich has written elsewhere, is the "fitting symbol for the whole of my personal and intellectual development. It has been my fate, however, in almost every direction, to stand between alternative possibilities of existence, to be completely at home in neither, to take no definitive stand against either".[5]

In Tillich, as in most other eminent Protestants, and indeed as in any *homo religiosus* or *philosophicus,* the problems of self-identity and integrity are fused and chronic. "The chosen young man", Erikson has written:

> extends the problem of his identity to the borders of existence in the known universe; other human beings bend all their efforts to adopt and fulfill the departmentalized identities which they find prepared in their communities. He can permit himself to face as permanent the trust problem which drives others in whom it remains or becomes dominant into denial, despair, and psychosis. . . . others hide in the folds of whatever tradition they are part of because of membership, occupation, or special interests. . . . others must look to their memories, to legends, or to books to find models for the present and the future in what their predecessors have said and done. No wonder that he is something of an old man (a *philosophus,* and a sad one) when his age-mates are young, or that he remains something of a child when they age with finality.[6]

Torn as they were between Christian allegiance and allegiance to reason, it is not surprising that most of the theologians who like Tillich remained Christians attempted to develop a compromise Christian theology that, although basically irrational, would nevertheless be as rational a form of irrationalism as possible.

---

[3]*Winds of Doctrine,* p. 32.
[4]Tillich, *The Shaking of the Foundations* (New York: Charles Scribner's Sons, 1948), p. 56.
[5]Tillich, *The Interpretation of History* (New York: Charles Scribner's Sons, 1936), p. 3; see also pp. 40 ff.
[6]Erikson, *Young Man Luther,* pp. 261 ff.

Although these attempts differ widely, a certain pattern is common to most of them. On the one hand, they show a dramatic flexibility: any statement of the essence of the Christian *message* is taken to be *in principle* revisable. There is never again to be any fundamentalist adherence to a fixed interpretation of the Christian message, whether Protestant liberal or old Calvinist. Neo-orthodoxy is by no means neo-rigidity. On the other hand, there is an equally dramatic definition of the *limits* of this far-ranging flexibility within a basic inflexibility: whatever his message might turn out to be, assent to Jesus is required. It is a tribute, however, to the real flexibility of the reaction to Protestant liberalism that almost the *only* thing its members are generally agreed on is this assent to Jesus Christ. Many doors are opened; one door is closed. Christian identity is defined in terms of commitment to the messenger, not to some interpretation of his message. Claims to knowledge about God are exchanged for faith in Christ.

2. Enter Karl Barth: And Back to Kierkegaard

The brilliant Swiss theologian Karl Barth forged the basic ideas undergirding the ingenious compromises that enabled some liberally inclined people to remain Protestant. Many other important contemporary theologians, from Emil Brunner at one extreme to Tillich at the other, are in rather serious disagreement with Barth—not always to the credit of their intellectual and strategical sensitivity. Yet even where they differ from him most radically, they usually owe to his writings their principal concepts and the way they state their problems.

Barth wove into a web of amazing complexity of detail, yet beautiful simplicity of structure, an acute denunciation of the basic errors of liberalism and an elegantly appealing alternative approach. Given his intentions and his commitments, it is hard to imagine a more skillful intellectual solution. He is one of the most interesting, as well as one of the most learned, self-critical, and bold writers in the history of Christian thought.

To understand Barth's thinking, one must first recall the life and work of a nineteenth-century thinker to whom I have referred only once or twice so far, though he overshadows the entire discussion. I mean, of course, Søren Kierkegaard (1813–55), the Danish theologian who is commonly presented today simply as a forerunner of existentialism.

Kierkegaard stood quite apart from most religious thought of his own time. Until the second decade of the twentieth century, his influence was marginal. Chiefly responsible for bringing Kierkegaard's thought to public notice then were three writers: the Danish philosopher, Harold Höffding;[7] the German writer Theodor Haecker, whose work on Kierkegaard (1913) influenced Karl Kraus and Martin Buber in Vienna and certain members of the Brenner Kreis around Ludwig von Ficker in Innsbruck;[8] and most important, Karl Barth.

In *Römerbrief,* first published in 1918[9]—the book that made his reputation and is often credited with having started the neo-orthodox movement in Protestantism—Barth quoted Kierkegaard generously; and for the following eight years—until Kierkegaard's ideas began to be put to uses of which Barth did not approve[10]—he made no secret of his debt to him as a predecessor and ally. Kierkegaard had already avoided, in the 1840s, the main snare in which liberal Protestants found themselves caught by the beginning of the World War; and he had taken the alternative approach to theological questions which their main opponents and successors, led by Barth, were to follow.

Kierkegaard's work was written in reaction to early Protestant liberalism as shaped by Kant and Hegel. After having shattered traditional theology and metaphysics with his critique of metaphysics and of the traditional proofs for the existence of God, Kant had aligned himself with those who located the essence of Christianity in its morality. Particularly important to the liberal Protestant ethic which grew out of Kant's work is his *universalizability principle.* According to this principle, an argument against an act such as murder might go as follows: "One ought not to do that, for if everybody were to do that the results would be catastrophic. Therefore no one should do that." A reasonable objection to a moral proposal (or maxim) would, then, be that it could not be universalized. Many nineteenth-century Protestant thinkers supposed such an approach to be implicit in Christianity. Could not the Sermon on the Mount, with its injunction: "Do unto others as ye would have them do unto you", be read as a kind of anticipation of Kant's universalizability principle? Hegel appears to have toyed with this very idea in his early essay, "The Life of Jesus" (1795).

Thinking along such lines, liberal Protestants, as we have seen, took the historical Jesus to be a paradigm example of a good rational social manager or reformer; and they took Protestant liberalism itself to be the most reasonable form of belief just because interpretations of its personal and

---

[7]Through Höffding, Kierkegaard also influenced the physicist Niels Bohr. See Max Jammer, *The Conceptual Development of Quantum Mechanics* (New York: McGraw-Hill, 1966), pp. 172–73.

[8]See my *Wittgenstein* (New York: Lippincott, 1973; Rome: Armando, 1975; Madrid: Ediciones Catedra, 1982; Brussels: Editions Complexe, 1978; Munich: Matthes & Seitz, 1983).

[9]Karl Barth, *Römerbrief* (1918), and subsequent editions.

[10]Around 1927 Barth abruptly dropped Kierkegaard: in his enormous twelve-volume *Church Dogmatics* (Edinburgh: T. & T. Clark), Barth mentions Kierkegaard about twenty times, often in small type and in passing, and usually to criticize one or another of his minor ideas. In a brief autobiography which appeared in 1945, Barth does not even list Kierkegaard among those thinkers who shaped his doctrinal standpoint. See my essay, "Everybody's Kierkegaard", in the *New York Review of Books,* April 28, 1966, pp. 11–15.

social ethics (presumably based on those of Jesus) seemed to them to be in harmony with the rationalist ethics of Kant, Hegel, and their followers. Kierkegaard, standing apart from his contemporaries, wrote scathing denunciations of this-worldly "ethical" Christianity and the presumed marriage between rationalism and Protestantism which he thought responsible for it. The theme that Christianity lacks character recurs throughout his writing. It is easy to be a Christian: so-called Christians neither accept nor reject Christianity seriously—and thus do not take it seriously. If some tenet were attacked by reason, the tenet would be rejected or reinterpreted. Reason marched forward conquering new ground; Christendom followed dutifully after. If this were to continue, Kierkegaard warned, Christianity stood in danger of losing its claim to distinctiveness. In *Fear and Trembling* Kierkegaard allows his pseudonymous author, Johannes de Silentio, to comment that the Greeks could have done just as much as far as reasonable ethics was concerned. No revelation, nothing special was required. For this reason, such a limited form of Christianity stood in danger of losing its identity. Kierkegaard thought that the picture of Jesus as a great practical moral teacher—even if correct—would have been both insufficient and inappropriate as a defense of Christianity. *But what if it were undermined by historical scholarship instead of reinforced by it?* What would be left? Kierkegaard's question was terribly prescient. For by the first decade of the present century, as we have seen, this picture of the historical Jesus had come to grief.

What had been called the Christian ethic by many Christians during the nineteenth century was—just as Kierkegaard had warned—not Christian. The Christian ethic was no more essential to Christianity than was the Christian cosmology. To be sure, Kierkegaard himself rarely discussed nineteenth-century, ethics-oriented biblical criticism directly; and from the few comments he did make one can tell that he hardly anticipated all the results which Schweitzer records—not to mention later twentieth-century research. Nonetheless, passages in *Fear and Trembling* are clearly meant to mock the *Leben Jesu* of David Strauss. And in *Training in Christianity* and *The Philosophical Fragments,* Kierkegaard clearly denies the apologetic effectiveness of such historical research. "History", Kierkegaard writes, "makes out Christ to be another than he truly is". Although Kierkegaard scoffed at the effectiveness of such historical research, his own picture of the historical Jesus differed sharply from that of the liberals.

Kierkegaard buttressed his attack on rational, ethics-centered Christianity with a direct defense of the "absurd". Using the fideistic-sceptical arguments concerning the limits of rationality that one can find in Sextus Empiricus, in Pascal, or in Bayle, Kierkegaard emphasized the essential incompleteness of any rationalistic system such as Hegel's. In his *Concluding Unscientific Postscript, Philosophical Fragments, De omnibus dubitandum est, Fear and*

Trembling, Training in Christianity, and elsewhere, he argued that rationality is necessarily limited, that the correctness of any system or way of life can never be proved. Any attempt to do so generates an infinite regress of proving; and thus a dogmatic presupposition is necessary. To adopt any particular way of life one *has to* make an irrational choice of some "absolute presupposition" or revelation. This act of choice will not be determined by any "rational criterion"—such as the "universalizability principle". In effect, Kierkegaard argued that there is an excuse for irrationalism against which a rationalist has no defense, since it is valid from his own point of view.

The resulting conflict between reason and religion is brilliantly dramatized by Kierkegaard. If there is indeed such a limit to rationality, why should God not countermand a reasonable ethic? For instance, God could even demand murder through what Kierkegaard calls a "teleological suspension of the ethical". This possibility Kierkegaard explores in *Fear and Trembling,* where Abraham demonstrates his *absurd* faith in God first by believing, contrary to familiar biological laws, that his wife Sarah would bear him a son in her old age; and then by his readiness to kill his beloved son Isaac at God's command in spite of the absurd violation of reasonable ethics which such an act would involve.

Kierkegaard concentrated on the Abraham story for many reasons. First, he probably knew that Kant had criticized Abraham's behavior as unreasonable in *The Quarrel among the Faculties* (1798). Secondly, one might have expected a Christian writer of Kierkegaard's time to have chosen Jesus as his example of the man of faith. By contrast to such writers, Kierkegaard avoided pinning the essence of Christian action on the imitation of the historical Jesus. To be a man of faith was for him *to obey* God blindly, absurdly, without recourse to reason—one's model of the man of faith was more Abraham than Jesus.

This is not to say that Kierkegaard entirely avoided speaking of the imitation of Christ. In some of his papers he does write, rather vaguely, of the imitation of Christ, usually stressing solitude, suffering, and renunciation of this world. This may well have been due to his eventual reconciliation to the fact that he was not to marry or have a conventional career. But even here Kierkegaard does not use the imitation of Christ for an apologetic purpose, and he elaborately qualifies his use of the word "imitate". Moreover, his conception of a world-renouncing historical Jesus, although erroneous in detail, is close to those of Schweitzer, Barth, and the neo-orthodox thinkers, and far removed from the liberal portrait.

Consequently, those investigations into the character of the historical Jesus which eventually destroyed the liberal portraits of Jesus as a great practical moral teacher hardly affected Kierkegaard's characterization of the essence of being a Christian. Having avoided the traps of late-nineteenth-century theology and biblical scholarship which eventually shattered Protestant liberalism, Kierkegaard suddenly became relevant, and loomed at the end of World War I as one of the few significant Christian thinkers of the nineteenth century who not only had not succumbed to Protestant liberalism but also had attacked it in its heyday. Kierkegaard's appeal to the early Barth and his followers needs no further explanation. Kierkegaard stresses not simply the existence but even the necessity of a conflict between reason and religion. His religious hero, Abraham, serves, within the Judeo-Christian tradition, as a paradigm example of the man *obedient* to God. When a conflict arises between, on the one hand, his allegiance to the moral code—indeed to what is understood to be God's own moral code, forbidding murder—and, on the other hand, to a religious commandment which stands in stark disagreement with the moral code, his choice is clear. In the Old Testament the agony of that choice is plainly illustrated; but just as plain is its inevitability. For Abraham there is an "either/or". Rational morality would bring him to one decision; obedience to God would bring him to another. As the man of faith he had to obey God.

Whatever Barth's later reservations about Kierkegaard or his influence may have been, Barth remains the contemporary theologian most emphatic in stressing the same difference between—and the possible conflict between —the Word of God and the Word of Man. In his later years, surveying the growing weakness of the Protestant churches, Barth wrote increasingly of the solitude and isolation of the theologian. Yet if he ever wavered in his own absolute commitment to what he called the Word of God, he did not—unlike Tillich—parade his doubting. "There is no justification for doubt itself", he insisted. "No one should flirt with his unbelief or with his doubt. The theologian should only be sincerely *ashamed* of it".[11] The italics are Barth's.

Yet it is not the familiar irrationally committed neo-Calvinist "dogmatist" that I wish to emphasize. I wish to recall a side of Barth that is almost never mentioned. In fact, he was one of the most brilliant strategists of theological survival in the history of the Christian church. Far from being dogmatic in the ordinary sense of that word, he was remarkably flexible, a most rational irrationalist. What makes it possible to say this of him is precisely his treatment of what he saw as the inescapable necessity for commitment.

A man of regular habits, Barth listened to the music of Mozart for one half-hour each morning. Writing of Mozart, he characterized himself: "This man was creative, even and precisely while he was imitating. Verily, he did not only imitate. From the beginning he moved freely within the frame of

---

[11]Karl Barth, *Evangelical Theology* (New York: Holt, Rinehart & Winston, 1963), p. 131. Or as N.H.G. Robinson has expressed the matter, Christian theology operates under "obedience, from first to last, to divine revelation". See his "Faith and Truth", *Scottish Journal of Theology*, June 1966, p. 145.

the rules of the art of his time, and later more and more freely. But he did not revolt against these rules, nor break them. He sought and found his greatness in remaining himself precisely while binding himself to these rules. One must see both his freedom and his restraint, side by side, and seek his singular quality behind this very riddle."[12] Moving creatively within the rules was the problem, and the riddle, of Barth's own life.

His solution to this riddle set the strategy for religious defense and renewal within Protestantism from the early 1920s until the late 1950s. Having first outlined his main ideas in his commentary on Paul's Epistle to the Romans, Barth expanded, developed, changed, and corrected them in his later works, particularly in his massive, multivolume *Church Dogmatics*. Here I can review briefly only a few of his main ideas and point to some difficulties in them; but this will suffice at least to show what is meant by calling his view "as rational a form of irrationalism as possible". My basic objection to Barth's thought, which involves the absolute irrational commitment on which he—like Kierkegaard—bases his approach, is a matter to discuss later.

Beginning with the assumption or commitment that revelation "happened" in Jesus, Barth resolves to take the assumption seriously in order to trace its implications. Some of the more important of these implications are:

(1) Traditional apologetic theology—i.e., *argument on behalf of* the Word of God—must be rejected as both useless and irreverent. It is *useless* because if the Word of God has really been accepted as such it is superfluous to offer reasons for so doing. Moreover, neither those who are forever damned nor those who are to be redeemed could arrive at commitment to the Word of God, as revealed in Jesus, either by themselves or through the effort of all the apologetic theologians in the world. One might say that Barth believes some men are boxes, forever sealed unto themselves, and that others are cameras, able in principle to receive God's light. But even in the latter cases only God can open the shutter. The gift of faith is a miracle that is entirely in God's hands.

Apologetic theology is *irreverent* because the only proper attitude toward what one has accepted as the Word of God is awe, trust, and obedience. One should accept the Word as the command of God, not try to apologize for it on the dubious liberal grounds that it "works" or agrees with human nature. If it is *God's* word, one does not compliment it by saying, as the liberals did, that it agrees with mere *human* nature.

(2) But if the theologian is not to argue on behalf of Christian commitment, what is his task? Barth thinks he has two main jobs, either of which can begin only when commitment to the Word of God has already been

---

[12]Karl Barth, "Wolfgang Amadeus Mozart", in *Religion and Culture*, ed. Walter Leibrecht (London: SCM Press, 1959), pp. 72–73. See also my "Karl Barth: The Last of the Protestants", in *Encounter*, March 1970.

made.[13] These are the *description* or exposition of the Word to which he is committed, and the *criticism and testing* of his own and other descriptions, past and current. Thus *argument, creative discussion and disagreement about the content* of the Word of God is to be expected, even to be required. *Argument about the truth* of the Word of God is, however, forbidden. Thus Barth bound himself, and yet remained creative.

(3) This is no return to fundamentalism. By "Word of God" Barth does not simply mean "the Bible". The Word of God denotes the revelatory *historical event* to which the Bible and other documents and utterances of the church bear witness. The locus of religious authority, to which commitment is made, is removed from the Bible to the historical event behind it to which it purports to bear witness.[14]

(4) Hence the Bible itself is only a report about and testimony to the Word of God, as revealed through Christ. It is a fallible human report, interpretation, and witness. Like all human reports, it is subject to error. Not only may *we* misunderstand the Bible; even those who wrote it may have misinterpreted the revelatory event which they had observed.

(5) Thus all theological statements—that is, statements *about* the Word of God—including those in the Bible, those in the Creeds, those spoken in the pulpits of the churches, and those articulated in theological systems about the essence of Christianity, from the church fathers to the Protestant liberals, are subject to constant revision and testing against the Word of God.

All theological statements are forever *conjectures* about the Word of God.[15] We can never know whether or not our statements do in fact express the truth about the Word of God or whether they are mixed with error stemming from our misinterpretations, or from our conscious or unconscious imposition of our own presuppositions on the historical event. "As a theological discipline", Barth writes on the first page of his *Church Dogmatics,* "Dogmatics is the scientific test to which the Christian Church puts herself regarding the language about God which is peculiar to her". Theology has a continuing critical task; revision and correction of dogma is to be expected.

Thus the Christian must commit himself to the Word of God. But the theologian ought not to commit himself to any particular interpretation of the Word of God, to any particular cultural morality or ideology; the church must not be permitted to become a mere reflection of social and cultural conditions, and it certainly is no servant of secular morality.

Since such talk often bewilders people, it may be helpful to try to explain

---

[13]Barth, *Church Dogmatics,* vol. 1, part 1.

[14]See ibid., vol. 1, part 2, for a discussion by Barth of his disagreements with the fundamentalists.

[15]Barth also uses the words "essay" and "hypothesis" to describe theological statements and the character of dogma. See ibid., vol. 1, part 2.

it by mapping these expressions approximately into ordinary secular language. Take the case of the natural scientist: he is presumably committed to the truth about the natural world, but is not committed to the truth of any particular hypothesis about the nature of that natural world. Substitute "theologian" for "natural scientist", "Word of God" for "natural world", and "interpretation" for "hypothesis", and you have the crux of Barth's position.

(6) The Word of God is the *only* criterion to which theological statements need conform, the only standard in respect to which they may be criticized. Although all of us, to be sure, approach any document with a store of interpretative principles, in a clash it is *our* principles which must yield.[16] God's Word and Commandment to men "stands in judgment" on their prideful speculations and is to be accepted and obeyed, whatever the devilish promptings of contemporary thought. "It cannot be otherwise than that Dogmatics runs counter to every philosophy no matter what form it may have assumed", Barth warned in his *Credo*.[17]

In other words, argues Barth, if it is improper to challenge a scientific statement on the ground that it does not conform with the Word of God, it is also improper to challenge a theological statement on the ground that it does not conform to scientific demands.[18]

Thus, Barth's methodology helps explain the breakdown of past statements about the true identity or essence of Christianity and allows for the possibility that all such statements will eventually be revised. It does this by removing the locus of faith from any particular statement of the essence to the historical fact that lies behind all such statements. "The question of truth", he writes, "with which theology is throughout concerned, is the question as to the agreement between the language about God peculiar to the Church and the essence of the Church . . . which is Jesus Christ".[19] The essence of being a Christian is submission to the essence of the Church, which is Jesus Christ.

To sum up, Barth gave an answer to the question of what are the boundaries of change and belief and of criticism within Christianity. His answer is that a Christian may abandon any statement about the *content* of the Christian message—on the ground that it is an inadequate statement of what the message really is—but he may not, *as a Christian,* abandon the Christian identity, the essence of being a Christian, which is submission to the authority of the Word of God, whatever its content may turn out to be. Christians, for Barth, are those people who interpret the Word of God and

---

[16]Ibid., vol. 1, part 2, pp. 728–33.

[17]*Credo,* p. 186. See also *Church Dogmatics,* vol. 1, part 2, p. 730, and vol. 3, part 1, pp. 343 ff.

[18]Yet Barth does not believe that science and theology ever in fact conflict. It is, he implies, only a *philosophy* of science which can conflict with theology. See *Church Dogmatics,* vol. 3, part 2. See my comments on the instrumentalist view of science, which makes this view possible, in sec. 5 of this chapter.

[19]*Church Dogmatics,* vol. 1, part 1, p. 3.

do not ask whether It is true, but only whether any statement about It is a true statement about the Word of God. For anyone who begins with the assumption—or the commitment—that final revelation happened in a particular historical event, Barth's is the best theory I know about how to approach the task of determining the content of that revelation.

But for many the difficulty lies in the initial irrational assumption or commitment. We wish to question the truth of the Word of God. And that in itself puts us outside Barth's Church. We are either sealed boxes or cameras as yet unused; there is no way to tell which.

To exclude argument about the truth of the Word of God is to adopt a minimal but nonetheless absolute concession to irrationalism. Asking not, "What is the essence of Christianity?" but "What is essential to being a Christian?", Barth demanded of Christians nothing more, or less, than absolute commitment to the Word of God as revealed by Jesus. The required commitment proved to be vague in a rather precise and quite convenient way. It was sufficiently vague to allow a flexibility among Protestant theologians surpassing even that of many of the old liberals. Never again was any identification of Christian doctrine with a fixed cultural viewpoint or ideology, whether liberal or Calvinist, to be permitted. On the other hand, the limits of this flexibility were defined, in that commitment to the Word of God was not itself subject to reconsideration.

The flexibility of Barth's formula enabled the ecumenical movement for union among Protestant churches to minimize the importance of the denominations' differing interpretations of Christian doctrine and to emphasize their common commitment to the Word of God.[20] Since even the formula was open to different interpretations, the resulting flexibility was wide. In any case, Barth's formula was written into the constitutions of the new ecumenical organizations as the price of admission; and at the same time, by exacting this price, Protestants gained at least the illusion of taking a new tough-minded line. Their formula might indeed be so vague as to be virtually empty: but it was not susceptible to erosion by the latest findings of science or by cultural fads.

Moreover, Barth's emphasis on *searching* for the Word of God propped up the Protestants' sagging morale by explaining the collapse of earlier statements about the true essence of Christianity, and by providing explicitly for the possibility that even more radical revisions would take place in the future.

Barth's formula was of course not without its own dangers, ones with

[20]See William Hamilton, "On Doing Without Knowledge of God", *Journal of Religion*, January 1957. Hamilton argues that Christians can only speak of the "minimum that is left" by telling the stories of their lives to one another.

which he never satisfactorily dealt: if the character of the Jesus or the Word of God to whom assent was required was indefinite, and if such commitment was required *no matter what* Jesus was and did, at best the subjective commitment itself would be definite. Its object would be an "I know not what and I care not what"—perhaps a less than satisfactory object of worship.

Related to this is the formidable problem of how far it is possible to test conjectures, especially genuinely new ones, about an event that has disappeared into the irrecoverable past. Barth's difficulty here has wrongly been compared with that of naïve empiricism. Empiricists have believed that the experiential reports sought in order to test scientific theories and eradicate prejudices of scientists could themselves be free from prejudice and theory, so that they could read Nature straight, as it were. This mistake Barth avoids: he acknowledges that even his best experiential reports about the Word of God—those found in the New Testament—are themselves impregnated with interpretation, theory, and prejudice.

On the other hand, the natural experimenter who abandons the notion that his sense experiences are given and incorrigible can go on to test his sense experiences themselves by further tests. But the only sense experiences that could have helped criticize our reports of the historical event which Barth calls the Word of God—those of other contemporaries of Jesus— appear now to be as far beyond recall as the event itself.

In view of Barth's critique of Protestant liberalism and his religious conservativism, one might expect him to have been politically reactionary. On the contrary, he was a socialist, and had once seriously contemplated devoting his life to the trade-union movement. In this regard, Protestant liberalism lives on in his work. His politics vividly illustrates his attitude toward the conflict between secular moralities, ideologies, and political powers on the one hand—and the Word of God on the other.

A vociferous anti-Nazi, Barth was expelled by Hitler from his chair in Bonn, and forced in 1935 to return to his native Switzerland. By contrast, he never showed any particular hostility to communist forms of totalitarianism, and even refused—despite hundreds of indignant protests—to condemn such acts as the Russian invasion of Hungary in 1956. He did, however, sharply scold Western cold-war ideologists who advocated that Christianity be championed as a spiritual alternative to communism.

That Barth's political positions would arouse disagreement is easy to understand; that they cause bewilderment is puzzling, for Barth's politics are closely connected with his theological position.

Barth never would have *symphathized* with Hitler, but one rather doubts that Barth would have gained any notoriety as an anti-Nazi had Hitler not attempted to interfere with the doctrine of the Protestant churches in

Germany. Indeed, had Hitler left the churches to go their own ways, at least doctrinally—had he not imposed his new order on the old religion—it is not inconceivable that Barth would have behaved in a way which would have permitted him even to retain his chair. But toying with the intellectual tradition of de Lagarde, Langbehn, and Moeller van den Bruck,[21] Hitler attempted for a time to use the churches as vehicles of a "German-Christian" Nazi ideology. It was principally *this* Nazi policy that Barth opposed, and for essentially the *same* reasons that he opposed Protestant liberalism in 1918 and the idea of the "Christian West" after World War II. According to Barth, it is contrary to the basic commitment of the theologian to the Word of God to allow *any* cultural ideology or morality, *good or bad,* to be incorporated into, or blended with, Christian doctrine. *Autonomous,* Christianity stands alone, in judgment on culture. The communists, unlike the Nazis, did not attempt to commit this particular sin: frankly atheistic, they were ready to destroy the churches if the opportunity presented itself, but were rarely disposed to create a "Marxist Christianity". Barth anticipated that through skillful diplomacy and tact the churches could achieve a viable "live and let live" accommodation with the communists. In this he may well have been politically naïve, but he was utterly consistent—even if one may sense a kind of madness about that very consistent order of priorities.

3. Gestalt Theology

Many of Barth's fellow theologians—Brunner, Bultmann, Niebuhr, Tillich —were unable to follow him all the way into the extreme theological purism of describing what the Word of God says without trying to relate it to contemporary philosophical and scientific thinking or to contemporary political affairs. In the face of the breakdown of rationalizing and accommodating Protestant liberalism, these men found themselves in a situation rather analogous to that of the post-Humean empiricists who in the search for material substance stripped away all the perceivable properties of material objects only to find—to their surprise!—that nothing perceivable remained. After the Christian ethic and the liberal picture of Jesus had been discarded, no obvious rationally defensible candidate was left in terms of which Christian commitment might be explained.

Even when it had been agreed to identify Christianity by a formula—that is, to accept that the essence of being a Christian was assent to Christ—there

---

[21]See Fritz Stern, *The Politics of Cultural Despair* (Berkeley: University of California Press, 1961).

remained the question of what assenting to Christ amounted to. Was there in the Bible no unique and reasonable message that could be called, even in a conjectural way, the message of Christianity, despite the breakdown of all the obvious candidates for such a keystone position? If such a message did exist, the formula could at least be explicated in terms of it.

And if no such message existed, what would remain of Protestant Christianity beyond a highly confused, loosely knit political alliance of traditional organizations whose members grasped at shadows of shadows— a world as confused and chaotic as that of the empirical philosophers, with their bundles and jumbles of sense impressions?

If the character of the Jesus to whom assent was required was indefinite, and if commitment to Jesus was required *no matter what* Jesus was and did, then, as we have just seen, the threat was that only the subjective Protestant commitment would be definite. Its object would be an "I know not what and I care not what"—hardly a satisfactory object of worship for anyone who regards religion as more than a series of bows and ceremonies, who seeks a personal identity in the Protestant tradition.

For example, H. R. Niebuhr, after defining a Christian in a typical neo-orthodox way as "one who counts himself as belonging to that community of men for whom Jesus Christ—his life, words, deeds, and destiny—is of supreme importance as the key to the understanding of themselves and their world", goes on wistfully to remark that the variety of personal and communal beliefs in Jesus Christ is so great, and the interpretation of his essential nature so manifold, "that the question must arise whether the Christ of Christianity is indeed one Lord".[22]

When Peer Gynt asked: "What is this question of being one's self?" the Button Molder replied that it was to "follow the Master's intention". When Peer insisted: "But suppose one was never told what the Master's intention was?" the Button Molder answered: "One must have insight."[23] Many contemporary theologians have tried to provide such insight through a kind of Gestalt approach: if one stands back from the details of the text, takes the Bible as a whole, and reads beneath the surface, one finds remaining a "Christian vision of man", a "Christian interpretation of history", a "biblical *Weltanschauung*", "permanent symbols", a "Christian epistemology", or something of the sort. All these ideas are materials for a rationally defensible content for Protestant commitment. They are not themselves put forth as essential; if *they* broke down, they could be abandoned with impunity. But in the all-important meantime, they would provide content to the nonabandonable commitment to Christ.

Although these attempts have been fundamentally unsuccessful, they are often interesting. There is at least one sense in which the Bible does, to use

[22]Niebuhr, *Christ and Culture*, pp. 11–12.
[23]Henrik Ibsen, *Peer Gynt*, act 5, scene 9.

Barth's phrase, "stand in judgment" on us all: it is a magnificent record of human experience at the highest level. Since contemporary culture is as prone as its predecessors to dally with superficialities, the material found in the Bible might deepen, and often correct, modern approaches to some recurring human problems.

Reinhold Niebuhr was one of the most stimulating of the contemporary plunderers of biblical wisdom. The words "stimulating" and "plunderer" are used advisedly. For Niebuhr is stimulating: his remarks on intellectual and political history, on contemporary politics, on psychology, are often brilliantly perceptive. And yet the use he makes of his insights does amount to a kind of piracy.

That reading the Bible should animate Niebuhr's thinking is hardly a matter for objection. Even the most methodologically minded psychologist does not depend on the accumulation of data to reach his discoveries or achieve his insights. He can use any method that helps him—from immersion in literature, to Bible reading, to swallowing amphetamine—to achieve insight. And there is, of course, no guarantee that any of these will work. Scientific method comes in *later,* when he subjects his visions to test in order to determine whether they correspond to fact or are just exciting ideas. Niebuhr was not always critical of his ideas, but he presented them in an unpretentious way.

Another good example of this Gestalt method can be found in Michael Foster's book *Mystery and Philosophy.* Foster thought that he had discovered in the Bible a theory of knowledge far superior to the Hellenist theories of knowledge which culminated in twentieth-century positivism. Arguing that the biblical theory provided a corrective on precisely those epistemological points where the Hellenist theories broke down, Foster pointed out that the Hellenist tradition had tended to maintain that "the riddle does not exist", that there is no ultimate mystery in the world, that there is a *method for attaining certainty* which at least some men can operate. Such positivist views, as Foster knew, had been undermined quite independently of any criticism from theologians.

In contrast to the Hellenist idea of the "unhiddenness" of Being, Foster argued, the biblical view maintains that God is hidden. The Israelites held no simple belief in the capacity of human reason to penetrate the mystery of ultimate reality, or in the "self-disclosure of Being" to the contemplating mind. According to the Israelites, man must *wait upon* God for a revelation; according to the Greeks, man can reach Him by himself, by mastering the technique.

One can agree with Foster in rejecting what he calls the Hellenist view; it is less certain that *his* biblical view of epistemology is indeed *the* biblical view. But the acceptable parts of the theory he expounds—and most parts of it are acceptable—are not uniquely biblical. They correspond very closely to the pre-Socratic *Greek* emphasis on mystery, the "hiddenness of truth", and the conjectural nature of knowledge.[24] Interesting as such attempts are, some questions must be raised about them. In the first place, thinkers like Niebuhr and Foster tend quite arbitrarily to identify a true view which is found in the Bible with *the* biblical view. In fact, there are a variety of competing biblical views on most subjects; and no theologian so far has provided any method for discriminating between the biblical views that are found in the Bible and the "nonbiblical" views that, embarrassingly enough, are also found in the le. Walter Kaufmann, in his brilliant *Critique of Religion and Philosophy,* has given many examples which illustrate this point.[25]

The method of contemporary theologians can often be reduced to three rather simple steps: (1) Run through the Bible picking out profound ideas about certain contemporary problems. (2) Run through contemporary secular literature picking out superficialities concerning these same problems. (3) Match the two in a book, thus providing an easy demonstration of the superiority of the Bible and the Christian tradition to contemporary secular culture. The basic unsoundness of the approach is aggravated by the ambiguity with which the results are often presented. If one interprets them one way, they seem undeniable commonplaces. If one interprets them another way, they seem ridiculous. Much of the appeal, as well as the apparent novelty and profundity, of theological commentary depends on its talent for bestriding two horses at once—sometimes even when they are galloping in opposite directions.

Another question concerns the significance of the undoubted presence of a great deal of wisdom in the Bible. Many contemporary theologians do little more than list and elaborate on the wisdom contained in the Bible as if thereby to establish the superiority of Christianity. Such a numerical approach, being a kind of stepdaughter of the old argument for design, need only be formulated to be rejected by almost any theologian. But, of course, the assumption is not usually formulated.

Although most neo-orthodox thinkers, like Niebuhr, were disturbed by the rift between reason and Christian commitment, the disturbance often did not go very deep philosophically. A theologian who was disturbed on a deeper philosophical level, and who also made an elaborate attempt to

---

[24]I discussed this point with Foster at Oxford in the summer of 1959, shortly before his death. He told me that the pre-Socratic Greek philosophers had not occurred to him when he called the view he opposed the "Hellenic" view. He was thinking of the tradition, and the "quest for certainty", which began with Plato and Aristotle. See Foster, *Mystery and Philosophy* (London: SCM Press, 1957), and *Mind,* 1934, pp. 446 ff.; 1935, pp. 439 ff.; and 1936, pp. 1 ff. Compare Foster's remarks with Tillich, *Protestant Era,* pp. 30–31; and Popper, "Back to the Pre-Socratics".

[25]Kaufmann, *Critique* (New York: Harper & Brothers, 1958), esp. chap. 6.

combine commitment to reason with commitment to Jesus the Christ, was Paul Tillich, to whose ideas I wish now to turn.

4. Paul Tillich and Objective Truth

R. G. Collingwood once wrote that it was impossible to reconstruct historically or intellectually anything that had failed: be it the strategy of the losing side in a battle or the thought of a philosopher who had been unable to solve his problems.[26] Collingwood was not only wrong here; his own archaeological researches in the history of Roman Britain refute his statement. Yet a study of Tillich's writings helps one appreciate how Collingwood could have come to such a conclusion. Tillich gives the impression that what he is trying to say is of vital importance. But it is difficult to determine just what he has said, let alone measure his success.

Behind this obscurity, however, some problems and ideas do lie. Like his spiritual colleagues, Tillich has seen that many traditional Christian concepts—such as that of original sin, echoing as it does in Freudian psychology—have not outworn their usefulness. His first task, then, is to restate and redefine such concepts, with the hope of eliminating their supernatural features and of bringing their valid aspects into focus. "You must first save concepts", he once wrote, "before you can save souls".[27] Specifically, his strategy is to point up certain contemporary human problems—classified under the five headings of rationality, finitude, sin, unity, destiny—and to show that certain biblical themes—which can be grouped under the five concepts of Revelation, God, Christ, Holy Spirit, and Kingdom of God—provide, when interpreted in a certain way, important insights into these problems.[28]

To give a simple example of how this approach can work: Niebuhr's doctrine of original sin could possibly be reinterpreted on Tillichian lines somewhat as follows.[29] The Genesis story of Adam's original sin—for which God is said to be punishing the subsequent generations of men—can be understood in part as a primitive explanation of the fact that there is evil already in the world when any of us arrive here: "structural evil", which is "there", beyond our control. Each child that is born this year will grow up

---

[26]Robin George Collingwood, *An Autobiography* (London: Oxford University Press, 1939), pp. 69–70.
[27]Tillich, "The Existentialist Challenge and the Religious Answer", speech delivered at Dartmouth College (Great Issues Course), May 11, 1953, p. 7 (mimeographed). See also Tillich's "Introductory Remarks" to his *Dynamics of Faith* (New York: Harper and Brothers, 1957).
[28]The five biblical concepts just named correspond to the five parts of Tillich's system.

in a world torn by war which he is in no way responsible for bringing about but which will condition his daily life and perhaps even lead him to personal destruction. Other children will inherit the diseases of their parents; still others, their parents' economic plight or broken marriages. Even where the original situation can be corrected externally, scars often remain in the form of neuroses. We are unable by ourselves to cure all the ills we are born with. If healing does occur, it is often more a matter of luck—the theologian might say "grace"—than of our own efforts.[30]

Tillich tries to preserve such acceptable implications in the old concepts and to disarm the supernatural and magical aspects that are no longer tenable, such as—on a very elementary level—the belief that God actually punished a fellow named Adam for eating an apple. The result is a "broken myth", symbolically true. Tillich's practice up to this point has won him many admirers, and thus far, his procedure is largely acceptable.

Right here, however, an important problem arises for all recent Christian apologetical theologians. Namely, other faiths—not to mention literature, such as Greek tragedy and Shakespeare, and ordinary folklore—also possess symbols and myths embodying important truths about the way men should confront life. What, then, is to preserve the claims of Christianity to religious superiority? What is to mark off the "true faith" of Christianity from competing faiths?

Many contemporary theologians do not even try to face this question; when it is raised, they appeal to their original commitment to Christ. Similarly, the presence of a treasure of wisdom in the Bible is not usually religiously significant except to the person who has already committed himself to Christ but whose faith is not firm enough to dispense with such buttressing.

To Tillich's credit, he does face the question. In answer, he maintains that the Christian tradition contains, in a unique way, a symbol that satisfies what he calls "the Protestant principle". The Protestant principle, a rather primitive attempt on Tillich's part to define an anti-idolatrous principle of criticism—indeed, the principle of criticism which he believes is the *criterion* of "objectively true faith"—is that no man or institution possesses the ultimate truth. To satisfy this principle, a symbol must "express the ultimate which is really ultimate" by implying its own "lack of ultimacy". Such symbols, then, are themselves not permanently valid or unrevisable; what is most important is something beyond themselves to which they are "pointing".

At its very center, Tillich claims, the Christian religion possesses just such a symbol. Jesus, by sacrificing himself on the cross, indicated his own lack of ultimacy as a historical figure. Hence, for Tillich, the religion whose central

---

[29]See Tillich, *The Protestant Era*, pp. xx, 165.
[30]Ibid., p. xxi.

symbol is Christ's cross is, when the Calvary event is properly interpreted, the "objectively true faith".

Three important questions arise here:
(1) How does Tillich know that the symbols of an objectively true faith will be those which imply their own lack of ultimacy?
(2) Suppose he is right. Does the Calvary event, as Tillich maintains, really provide such a symbol?
(3) Suppose it does. Is this the only such symbol? Do such symbols appear only in Christianity? Or do other religions also possess them? And if they do, how does Tillich's answer meet the original problem of distinguishing Protestant Christianity as the most meritorious religion?

These questions may be considered in turn.

(1) Tillich's answer to the first question leads to the topic of definitions. That an "objectively true faith" will "imply its own lack of ultimacy" simply follows from Tillich's definition of an objectively true faith. But, then, even if Christianity *were* the only religion possessing such a symbol, the matter would still rest on an arbitrary definition. The whole issue of Christianity's superiority would turn not on fact or on a point of view but on a stipulation. Moreover, even if it should be agreed that any objectively true faith will "imply its own lack of ultimacy" in some sense, it hardly follows that any faith which implies its own lack of ultimacy is an objectively true faith.

(2) But suppose that Tillich's definition were in some sense acceptable. Does the Calvary event, as Tillich argues, provide such an objectively true symbol? Unfortunately, it does not satisfy his definition in any clear way. Jesus did indeed sacrifice his person to the cause to which he was dedicated and to what he thought was God. In so doing, he can be said to have sacrificed himself for the "ultimate beyond himself". But the question arises whether Jesus, in order to act as the incarnation of a principle that is intended as a principle of criticism, would not have had to be willing *to sacrifice not only himself but also his conception of his message*. Was Jesus at all critical of the symbols through which he himself apprehended "the ultimate"? There seems to be nothing in the Gospels to indicate that he was; and independent New Testament scholarship does not seem to disagree, at least on this point. Rather, the Calvary story seems to be that of a man who sacrificed part of himself (his life) for the sake of a greater cause but who never sacrificed or seemed willing to sacrifice or seemed even slightly critical of that other part of himself—his message—for the sake of an ultimate truth beyond that message. To put it less sympathetically, Jesus sacrificed his life but not his delusion.[31]

Only if Jesus's conception of his message is identified in advance with the

---

[31]Tillich took a contrary view, but provided no clear supporting arguments. See *Systematic Theology*, vol. 1, p. 36.

ultimate truth does he satisfy Tillich's definition. Certain other features of Tillich's thought, however, would prevent him from equating Jesus's own conception of his message with the ultimate truth.

(3) But suppose we overlook such objections and assume that Jesus does fulfill Tillich's definition. Do other non-Christian sources contain no symbols that also satisfy the definition and thus qualify as symbols of the "objectively true faith"?

That there are many such symbols can be easily shown. I shall do so in a roundabout way—one that should incidentally bring out the dangers inherent in procedures like Tillich's—by comparing Tillich's program with that of the logical positivists, which I believe was equally misguided. My aim here, as it was in dealing with the second question, is to show that even if one were to accept Tillich's definition, his system would *still* break down.

As Tillich wished to demarcate true faith from its competitors, so the positivists wished to demarcate true science from its rivals—pseudo-science, metaphysics, and especially theology. Any statement, at least in earlier positivism, had to be either logical, scientific, or meaningless. One would determine to which of the latter two categories a nonlogical statement belonged by determining whether it could be verified. At first some positivists claimed that this criterion simply recorded a fact about the world. Later they, too, admitted that it was just a definition, or—as they preferred to say—a "stipulation".

The positivists were intellectually routed as early as 1931, when Sir Karl Popper, then a young Viennese schoolteacher, showed the positivists of the famous Vienna Circle that their criterion of meaning would not work.[32] He pointed out that according to their criterion *all scientific laws are meaningless*. Later he showed that "arch-metaphysical assertions" about an omnipotent and omniscient creature (such as a god) *are* meaningful *on the positivists' criterion*.[33] One *could* demarcate science from pseudo-science (such as astrology) and religion; but not through a criterion of meaningfulness. Theology (like astrology) might be untenable—and it was certainly unscientific—but it was not necessarily meaningless. Positivism, hence, not only was objectionable philosophically; it could not even account for science, let alone support it!

Tillich's program can be criticized in a parallel way. Not only is it philosophically objectionable; it doesn't even benefit Protestantism. Many non-Christian symbols fit Tillich's definition of objectively true faith. Perhaps the clearest example is one most rationalists have always held dear:

---

[32]Popper, *Logik der Forschung* (Vienna: Springer Verlag, 1934), translated as *The Logic of Scientific Discovery* (New York: Basic Books, 1959). See also Popper, *Unended Quest* (La Salle: Open Court, 1976, 1982).

[33]Popper, "The Demarcation between Science and Metaphysics", *Conjectures and Refutations*.

the death of Socrates. In Tillich's way of speaking, the argument might go something like this: Socrates, who sought throughout his spatiotemporal existence to achieve the Good in his own person, sacrificed his person as Socrates, the embodiment of the Good, to the Good which was beyond himself. For Socrates refused the opportunity to escape the death sentence imposed on him by the tribunals of democratic Athens, lest he deny the Good as it expresses itself in a respect for the rule of law in a democracy. Moreover, Socrates was critical of his own conjectures about the nature of the Good.

Now, I hardly want to deify Socrates. The only point is that, *on Tillich's own definition*, Socrates is as divine as Jesus.

It might be objected that the example just given is rather academic and artificial, and certainly too abstract. For the purpose of the argument let us accept this objection. C. G. Jung has provided, in his *Memories, Dreams, Reflections,* a most vivid and concrete symbol which such an objection could hardly touch.[34] Reflecting on a boyhood experience, probably in 1886, Jung begins his narrative as follows:

> One fine summer day I came out of school at noon and went to the cathedral square. The sky was gloriously blue, the day one of radiant sunshine. The roof of the cathedral glittered, the sun sparkling from the new, brightly glazed tiles. I was overwhelmed by the beauty of the sight, and thought: "The world is beautiful and the church is beautiful, and God made all this and sits above it far away in the blue sky on a golden throne and . . ." Here came a great hole in my thoughts, and a choking sensation. I felt numbed, and knew only: "Don't go on thinking now! Something terrible is coming, something I do not want to think, something I dare not even approach . . ."

Jung continues for several pages with this stream-of-consciousness reporting of his memories of this childhood episode; he tells how he attempted to resist the terrible thought, how he regarded it as the unforgivable sin, the sin against the Holy Ghost, which—if committed—would send him to hell, to the desolation of his parents. But resisting the thought was easier said than done: sleepless nights ensued—or else the troubled youth awoke, terrified, in the middle of the night. "I felt my resistance weakening", Jung continues.

> Sweating with fear, I sat up in bed to shake off sleep. "Now it is coming, now it's serious. *I must think.* It must be thought out beforehand. *Why* should I think something I do not know? I don't want to. . . . But *who* wants me to?

Jung concludes that it is God himself who demands that he think this thought; and this thought, he reports,

---

[34]Jung: *Memories, Dreams, Reflections* (New York: Pantheon, 1963), pp. 36–43.

liberated me instantly from my worst torment. . . . There was no question in my mind but that God Himself was arranging a decisive test for me, and that everything depended on my understanding Him correctly. I knew, beyond a doubt, that I would ultimately be compelled to break down, to give way, but I did not want it to happen without my understanding it, since the salvation of my eternal soul was at stake.

Jung resumes his internal dialogue:

God knows that I cannot resist much longer, and He does not help me, although I am on the point of having to commit the unforgivable sin. In His omnipotence He could easily lift this compulsion from me, but evidently He is not going to. Can it be that He wishes to test my obedience by imposing on me the unusual task of doing something against my own moral judgment and against the teachings of my religion, and even against His own command-ment, something I am resisting with all my strength because I fear eternal damnation? Is it possible that God wishes to see whether I am capable of obeying His will even though my faith and reason raise before me the specters of death and hell? . . .

I thought it over again and arrived at the same conclusion. . . . I gathered all my courage, as though I were about to leap forthwith into hellfire, and let the thought come. I saw before me the cathedral, the blue sky. God sits on His golden throne, high above the world—and from under the throne an enormous turd falls upon the sparkling new roof, shatters it, and breaks the walls of the cathedral asunder.

So that was it! I felt an enormous, an indescribable relief. Instead of the expected damnation, grace had come upon me, . . . It was as though I had experienced an illumination. A great many things I had not previously understood became clear to me. That was what my father had not under-stood, I thought; he had failed to experience the will of God, had opposed it for the best reasons and out of the deepest faith. And that was why he had never experienced the miracle of grace which heals all and makes all comprehensible. He had taken the Bible's commandments as his guide; he believed in God as the Bible prescribed and as his forefathers had taught him. But he did not know the immediate living God who stands, omnipotent and free, above His Bible and His Church, who calls upon man to partake of His freedom, and can force him to renounce his own views and convictions in order to fulfill without reserve the command of God. In his trial of human courage God refused to abide by traditions, no matter how sacred . . . At that time, too, there arose in me profound doubts about everything my father said. When I heard him preaching about grace, I always thought of my own experience. What he said sounded stale and hollow, like a tale told by someone who knows it only by hearsay and cannot quite believe it himself.

This powerful, vivid, and highly concrete symbol—God defecating on his own cathedral—fulfills Tillich's criteria for the "truth of faith" perfectly. It evokes a response in most people—and to that extent is, according to Tillich's criteria for "subjectively true faith", a symbol that is subjectively true. And it is intensely anti-idolatrous, and consequently "objectively true" according to Tillich's criterion for the objective truth of a symbol. Moreover, it might be argued that it is, as a symbol of criticism, far preferable to the crucifixion symbol. For here in Jung's vision we find a suggestion of intellectual criticism of tradition which is lacking in Tillich's account of the crucifixion symbol. And Tillich's account sounds stale and hollow by comparison with Jung's.

Tillich could doubtless evade such objections. He might avoid the counterexample of Socrates, for instance, by *redefining* "objectively true faith" so as to exclude Socrates. By continuously redefining, one can save any system. If in a game of chess one player is allowed to change the rules whenever he is in danger of checkmate, the second player is unlikely ever to win.

Tillich, of course, would not be the first to resort to such gamesmanship; nor would he be the last. After Einstein presented his theories of relativity, a number of leading physicists tried to save Newtonian mechanics in a similar way—by reinterpreting, redefining, and adjusting the old concepts, and by introducing auxiliary rules.

If Socrates were an obscure counterexample from a little-known tribal religion, one could excuse Tillich for overlooking him. As it is, one can only wonder at his statements that "Christianity expresses itself in such a symbol in contrast to all other religions" and "the fact that this criterion is identical with the Protestant principle and has become reality in the Cross of the Christ constitutes the superiority of Protestant Christianity".

The point is important enough to stress. If Tillich could once admit either that Christ did not provide an incarnation of the Protestant principle or else that his incarnation of it was not in any clear way special,[35] he would have to give up either his Protestant principle or his Christianity. In fact, this is a point about which Tillich did, at least once, express some tentative doubts. In an article published in 1958, he wrote of the encounter of Christianity with other religions:

> I do not think this encounter, which becomes more concrete and existential every day, has been taken seriously enough in Christian theology, including my own ststem. The statement that Jesus is the Christ and therefore the incarnation of the universal Logos of God is a matter of continuous testing, not only in view of secular culture but also in view of the other world religions.[36]

Tillich's liberality here is, however, tempered and complicated by certain remarks he made earlier—remarks which make it extremely difficult to interpret the statement just quoted. In *The Protestant Era,* for example, Tillich wrote:

[35]But see Tillich, *The Protestant Era,* pp. xi, xix.
[36]Tillich: "Beyond the Usual Alternatives", *Christian Century,* May 7, 1958.

In the power of the New Being that is manifest in Jesus as the Christ . . . the Protestant protest comes to an end. Here is the bedrock on which it stands and *which is not subjected to criticism.* Here is the sacramental foundation of Protestantism, of the Protestant principle and of the Protestant reality.[37]

If the objections to the claim that Jesus fulfills the Protestant principle in some special way are correct, Tillich's thought is due for drastic revision. But what happens when positivists or followers of Tillich meet objections like these? For a number of years after their program came under fire, the positivists attempted to make definitional adjustments in their criterion of meaning. Some remnants of this revisionist program are still very much alive, but positivism is for the most part being abandoned; those who were once under its influence today argue a more modest empiricism.[38] Unlike the positivists, however, Tillich and his followers continue spinning definitions and multiplying criteria.

This is not because theologians as individuals tend to be less objective or open-minded than positivists, or because positivists, any more than other people, like to see their pet theories smashed. Philosophers are just as human as theologians; if their sin is more original than that of the theologians, that may be more a matter of intellect than of virtue. Perhaps philosophers generally take a more flexible position than theologians because they are more exposed to internal criticism. A crucial part of the endeavor of philosophy is to expose one's theories and those of others to criticism. Philosophers are engaged in following the argument where it leads and in encouraging and listening to criticism; they are members of the critical community. There is criticism within the theological community, too. But it is usually *constructive* criticism—in the worst sense of the word. Its aim is to evade the criticisms of those who are outside the theological circle. Tillich, for example, has said that theologians should emphasize the areas in which they *agree,* not those in which they disagree. This may be good form within the club, but it is not notably helpful in avoiding error.

Reinhold Niebuhr in his later books has championed democracy as the best means developed by man to rid society of bad rulers. But the political

---

[37]*Protestant Era*, pp. xxii ff. (the italics are mine). On p. 234 Tillich states that the Protestant principle may not be subjected to criticism. See also Martin Luther, who, during his attack on Erasmus, wrote: "A Christian ought . . . to be certain of what he affirms, or else he is not a Christian." (*De servo arbitrio, Werke* [Weimar, 1908], vol. 18, p. 601) and H. A. Hodges's statement: "Not only the content, but also the manner of religious belief is different from that of our belief in the truth of a scientific hypothesis . . . it is the result of reflection on . . . evidence by experts in scientific research; and they put it forward and the layman accepts it from them, always as something provisional, open to revision in the light of fresh evidence which may at any time be found. There may be people in the world who accept the belief in the existence of God in this spirit, but they are probably few in number. Such is not genuine religious belief. Religious belief . . . is held not as a theory which further evidence might modify, but as a fundamental and immutable truth." ("What Is to Become of Philosophical Theology?", *Contemporary British Philosophy* [New York: Macmillan, 1956], p. 229.) For other views on these lines, see H. R. Niebuhr, *The Meaning of Revelation* (New York: Macmillan, 1941), p. 139; and Barth, *Church Dogmatics*, vol. 1, part 2, pp. 239–40.

[38]See Popper, "Who Killed Logical Positivism?", in *Unended Quest*. But see also my "A Popperian Harvest", in Paul Levinson, ed., *In Pursuit of Truth* (New York: Humanities Press, 1982), pp. 249–89.

aspect is only one side of a broader problem: how to get rid of error whenever and however it appears. The question is whether the structure and institutions of the theological community are such that erroneous ideas can be removed; or whether it is not rather easy for a false idea to entrench itself within theology.

5. Philosophical Queries

The new Protestant thought presents a number of more general difficulties. One of these revolves around the contemporary focus on symbols in theology and in other fields. Behind this concentration of attention is the hope that thereby (often through approaches influenced by Husserl's phenomenology) it will be possible to attain absolute presuppositions or categories of thought. The theologians have failed to see that symbols will not do the job; and this mistake is rather ironical. In their attack on empiricism, theologians eagerly point out—quite rightly—that sense experience is not "given" but is itself a matter of interpretation, since it is "theory-impregnated". But they have not applied this observation to the *apprehension of symbols*. This can be done as follows: (1) *Symbols* are not "given" either; they do not interpret themselves. (2) We need rules in terms of which to interpret symbols and evaluate and state the claims of any particular symbol. (3) Symbols, then, are *dependent* on interpretational rules. (4) *Therefore, symbols cannot be ultimate,* i.e., independent, any more than the "given" sense observations of the positivists can be ultimate and incorrigible.[39]

Another, perhaps equally important, difficulty arises from the acceptance, by almost all the theological writers concerned, of a conception of the nature of *science* which combines phenomenalism, positivism, and instrumentalism. Some of the central tenets of Barth's and Tillich's thought—such as their belief that it is impossible in principle for theological beliefs to conflict with scientific hypotheses—rest on this concept. This conception of science, however, has been refuted.

It has been shown, for example, that although untestable metaphysical assertions cannot conflict with *reports* of *scientific* observation, they *can* conflict with scientific hypotheses, or "laws of nature".[40] To be sure, such metaphysical assertions cannot be *disproved* by the fact that they are in

---

[39]For an application of similar ideas to symbolism in art, see E. H. Gombrich's brilliant book, *Art and Illusion* (New York: Pantheon Books, 1960).

[40]See J.W.N. Watkins's excellent series of articles on this subject: "Between Analytic and Empirical", *Philosophy*, April 1957, esp. p. 129; "Confirmable and Influential Metaphysics", *Mind*, July 1958, pp. 345 ff.; and "When Are Statements Empirical?", *British Journal for the Philosophy of Science*, February 1960. See also my appendix 2, sec. 10, below.

conflict with accepted scientific hypotheses—for scientific hypotheses cannot be conclusively verified in the way the positivists would wish. Scientific hypotheses remain forever conjectural (and highly *im*probable, to boot).

This is only one aspect of a broader point. Many twentieth-century religious thinkers, including the Roman Catholic Pierre Duhem and others, have been able to avoid the old clash between science and religion by accepting a view of science which so denatures it that it could not in principle conflict with metaphysics and religion. These thinkers strongly disagree with the positivists not over the *nature* of science but over the positivist claim that there is no meaningful or legitimate sphere of intellectual activity *beyond* "science" interpreted positivistically. This assumption about science is so integral a part of recent theological thought that much of it would topple were this view refuted—as it has been.[41] The claim that no conflict between science and religion is possible is only one of the ways in which men have tried to solve the conflict between science and religion.

Within Tillich's own system, in his central concept of "ultimate concern", the boundary line between science and religion is not clear. Tillich argues that all men have ultimate concerns, and that one's God is the object of one's ultimate concern. Several questions arise here: Is the statement that all men have ultimate concerns a psychological scientific statement subject to empirical refutation? If so, a major part of Tillich's theological system is in potential clash with science. If not, what is the status of the claim? Again, does a person with a "split personality" have an ultimate concern? Rather, does not a great deal of the personal neurosis that Tillich stresses result from the fact that men do *not* have some ultimate concern but are inconclusively torn between two or more concerns? David Riesman has observed: "We will find that the same pluralism which exists in the society exists in many of its individuals, and that we are talking to one part of a person and against another."[42]

6. *Lingering Liberalism*

Whatever their faults, Protestant thinkers such as Niebuhr and Tillich had grounded their theological reflections in historical scholarship. This ground-

---

[41]See the articles by Watkins cited in the previous footnote. See also Popper, "Three Views Concerning Human Knowledge", *Contemporary British Philosophy*, ed. H. D. Lewis (New York: Macmillan, 1956), and "A Note on Berkeley as Precursor of Mach", *British Journal for the Philosophy of Science*, May 1953; and Joseph Agassi, "Duhem versus Galileo", *British Journal for the Philosophy of Science*, November 1957.

[42]See his "Values in Context", *American Scholar*, 22, no. 1 (1952). For an illustration of how readily other theologians accept a positivist view of science, see Barth, *Church Dogmatics*, vol. 3, part 1, pp. ix–x, and p. 344; and vol. 1, part 1, pp. 7ff. In the latter Barth cites Scholz's incorrect discussion of the role of proof in science as embodying the "concept of science for our time".

ing lends their work realism and candor. The same is not true of all contemporary Protestant thought. For it should not be supposed that Protestant liberalism disappeared utterly in the wake of Schweitzer's historical investigations and the new orthodoxy of Barth, Niebuhr, and Tillich. Rather, Protestant liberalism has continued a half-life existence, particularly among certain British and American philosophers. A good example is the approach represented in *An Empiricist's View of the Nature of Religious Belief*, by R. B. Braithwaite, of Cambridge University.[43]

Whereas Protestant liberalism and the movements and ideas associated with it were lively and interesting phenomena, Braithwaite's approach is constructed on naïve and uninformed historical scholarship and philosophical analysis.

His chief concern is with the meaning of religious expressions, and his problem is set by the early logical-empiricist criterion of meaning according to which only those utterances have meaning which can be empirically verified or else are truths of logic. Braithwaite adopts a move common among postwar logical empiricists. Without going so far as to state bluntly that the empiricist criterion of meaning is incorrect, Braithwaite is bold enough to suggest that it is not sufficient, and suggests that when one approaches certain subjects, such as morality and religion, one may study meaning in terms of the way assertions are *used* in these areas, without worrying about whether they may be verified in the ways required by early logical empiricists. Claiming that the meaning of any statement will be given by the way it is used, Braithwaite sets out to explain how religious statements are used by those who express their religious convictions thereby.

Braithwaite reaches the conclusion that religious assertions are used primarily as moral assertions and may thus be "assimilated" to moral assertions. Like moral statements, religious statements are not scientifically verifiable; but they do nonetheless have a use: to wit, they express "conative intentions". A moral assertion expresses the intention of its asserter to act in a particular sort of way. The primary use of religious assertions is the same: religious assertions, within the context of the religious system within which they appear, are declarations of adherence to a policy of action or way of life or pattern of behavior.

There is, however, Braithwaite declares, an important but subordinate

---

[43]R. B. Braithwaite, "An Empiricist's View of the Nature of Religious Belief", in I. T. Ramsey, ed., *Christian Ethics and Contemporary Philosophy* (London: SCM Press, 1966), or in John Hick, ed., *The Existence of God* (New York: Macmillan, 1964). The study was first printed separately by the Cambridge University Press as the Eddington Memorial Lecture in 1955. For another example of ethics-oriented Christianity since Barth, see W. W. Bartley, III, "The Bonhoeffer Revival", in the *New York Review of Books*, August 26, 1965, pp. 14–17. See also my "Some Theological Interactions: Germany, England and America", in *Die Philosophie und die Wissenschaften: Simon Moser zum 65. Geburtstag* (Meisenheim am Glan: Verlag Anton Hain, 1967), pp. 228–34.

sense in which religious assertions may differ somewhat from some moral assertions. Namely, religious assertions, unlike moral assertions, will be accompanied by particular stories. These stories, drawn from the Christian tradition, help support an "agapeistic" policy of behavior.[44] The difference between agapeistic behavior patterns as recommended by Christians and exactly the same behavior patterns as recommended by proponents of other, non-Christian religions, such as Judaism and Buddhism, will be that in the case of Christians one set of stories will be borne in mind; in the case of Jews, another set of stories borne in mind; in the case of Buddhists, yet another set of stories borne in mind, and so on. It is not at all necessary, on Braithwaite's account, for the asserter of a religious assertion to believe that the story he tells is true; he "entertains" the story mentally in order to help him—psychologically, causally—to follow a pattern of behavior which he might otherwise resist. Braithwaite notes that he has chosen the word "story" as the most neutral word he could think of, and allows that other writers whom he admires, such as Matthew Arnold, have used words like "parable", "fairy tale", "allegory", "fable", "tale", "myth", and so on to express a comparable idea. All of which brings us to this definition of the professing Christian: "A man is not, I think, a professing Christian", Braithwaite writes, "unless he both proposes to live according to Christian moral principles and associates his intention with thinking of Christian stories; but he need not believe that the empirical propositions presented by the stories correspond to empirical fact".[45]

Braithwaite's account of religion has been taken seriously by several distinguished philosophical writers. In the issues of the *Cambridge Review* devoted to discussion of Braithwaite's essay, J. N. Schofield, to be sure, made no secret of his poor opinion of Braithwaite's lecture. But Professor D. M. MacKinnon and Ian Ramsey, bishop of Durham, treated it with respect, MacKinnon even describing it as a stimulating contribution to the philosophy of religion for which one should be grateful.[46] Among other writers, Professor John Macquarrie has written that Braithwaite gives "quite a plausible analysis of religious language",[47] although several pages later in the same book Macquarrie writes that Braithwaite has "surely exaggerated his thesis beyond what is plausible".[48] Macquarrie's position is, then, unclear. On the other hand, we find Renford Bambrough writing that his colleague Braithwaite's study "is the most philosophically sophisticated of numerous recent writings in the same vein".[49]

[44]The neologism is Braithwaite's idiosyncratic way of rendering the Greek ἀγαπή into English as an adjective.
[45]Braithwaite, in *Christian Ethics and Contemporary Philosophy*, p. 68.
[46]These discussions, together with Braithwaite's reply, are reprinted in *Christian Ethics and Contemporary Philosophy*.
[47]John Macquarrie, *Twentieth-Century Religious Thought* (London: SCM Press, 1963), p. 312.
[48]Ibid., p. 316.
[49]Renford Bambrough, *Reason, Truth and God* (London: Methuen & Co., 1969), p. 74.

Part of the explanation for the attention paid to Braithwaite's contribution to the philosophy of religion may have been the perhaps inevitable association of this essay with a Cambridge event: namely, the conversion of Braithwaite to Christianity. One writer, reporting the reminiscences of a Cambridge don, wrote of this:

> There has always been a touch of King's College religion about Cambridge—the very beautiful King's Chapel, with its very beautiful choir, where anyone, religious or not, would like to go to church—which means a touch of intellectualism and eccentricity. For instance, Richard Braithwaite, who is a professor of Moral Philosophy here, was persuaded—philosophically—to become a Christian in his adult life, but, apparently, only after an exchange of several letters between him and the church. He certainly behaved as though a private treaty had been made, with a table of exemptions for him, and everyone in Cambridge believed that this was so. When he was baptized, practically everybody who was anybody in Cambridge was there, except Wittgenstein.[50]

One difficulty facing readers of Braithwaite's treatise is to determine just what he means. His key words, such as "agapeistic", are so vague that it is difficult to know what might count as such behavior. Although Braithwaite has, in the course of replying to some of his critics, specified some of the things that he did not mean—such as a "general policy of benevolence"—what he did mean remains unclear.

So let us adopt as an experiment Braithwaite's own proposal: that the meaning of an expression is to be found in its *use*—in order to determine what Braithwaite himself, by his own definition, may have meant. How does Braithwaite treat his own rule—or philosophical behavior policy—that the meaning of an expression is to be found in its use? To be more specific, what does he mean when he indicates that the meaning of a Christian religious assertion is to be found in its use? Does he mean that its meaning is to be determined by the way in which Christians have traditionally used it? Or by the ways in which they use religious assertions today? No: neither of these is even considered. Rather, we find that the rule that Braithwaite is following is this: *The meaning of a Christian religious assertion is to be determined by the use that I (Braithwaite) make of it.* There is a rapid *unvoiced* transition from *the* use to *my* use, from the definite article to the personal pronoun.

Earlier Protestant liberalism, as we have seen, had been undermined when historical biblical exegesis uncovered the *falsity* of the liberal portrait of Jesus, a portrait deeply permeated by a wrong interpretation of the Sermon on the Mount. Thousands of Protestant liberals soberly abandoned their Christian affiliations because they could not accept what appeared really to have been the "Christian ethic" as objectively determined by biblical scholarship.

For Braithwaite such considerations as what the "Christian ethic", i.e.,

[50]Ved Mehta, *The New Theologian* (New York: Harper & Row, 1965), p. 70.

the morality preached by Jesus of Nazareth, really may be are beside the point. Not only is the truth of the stories which he uses to prop up his agapeistic policies unimportant to him; it is apparently of no importance to him whether whatever stories he *finds* in the Christian tradition, or imagines to be there, are really there at all. He writes:

> Since different people will take different views as to what these fundamental moral principles are, the typical meaning of religious assertions will be different for different people. I myself take the typical meaning of the body of Christian assertions as being given by their proclaiming intentions to follow an agapeistic way of life, and for a description of this way of life—a description in general and metaphorical terms, but an empirical description nevertheless—I should quote most of the Thirteenth Chapter of I Corinthians. Others may think that the Christian way of life should be described somewhat differently, and will therefore take the typical meaning of the assertions of Christianity to correspond to their different view of its fundamental moral teaching. (p. 63)

Again, Braithwaite writes of the stories which are to be used to prop up moral behavior: "The empirical story-statements will vary from Christian to Christian; the doctrines of Christianity are capable of different empirical interpretations, and Christians will differ in the interpretations they put upon the doctrines" (p. 66). And at the very close of his essay, Braithwaite concludes, with certainty, that "it is of the very essence of the Christian religion" that the questions "What shall I do?" and "What moral principles should I adopt?" *must be answered by each man for himself.*

In brief, for Braithwaite the very essence of the Christian religion is a subjective—arbitrary—choice of moral principles. Or one might say: *The very essence of Christianity is doing whatever you choose provided that you decorate whatever you chose to do with stories from the Christian tradition which you may interpret in any way you please.*

This is, however, preposterous as an interpretation of the Christian tradition *as it is used*; it is an eccentric legislative proposal on Braithwaite's part about how the Christian tradition might be used. If nothing more could be found in Christianity save a few moral homilies, Braithwaite might indeed be doing Christians a service by championing such a use, however little it had to do with the tradition. But this is clearly not so. His lip service to science to the contrary, Braithwaite ignores the objective findings of scientific historical biblical scholarship when he defines the essence of Christianity as agapeistic behavior.

Christianity is, of course, made up of a multitude of different and conflicting policies, stories, doctrines, and also of scientific and metaphysical assertions. There are, to be sure, parts of the tradition that stress what one might translate into something like what Braithwaite evidently means by agapeistic behavior—the thirteenth chapter of I Corinthians (which Braithwaite cites), the Sermon on the Mount (as interpreted by the liberals, prior to Schweitzer's work). But to concentrate on these is arbitrary. Anyone might of course say that one particular strand of the Christian tradition appeals to him more than another. But there is a logical leap from "I find such and such an aspect of Christianity appealing" to "I am a Christian". If one finds some aspect of Buddhism appealing is one then a Buddhist too? Nor does it help to say that seemingly conflicting parts of the tradition will support an agapeistic interpretation if put into context. One might as well argue that a different claim which some have advanced—namely, that Christianity is essentially a prudential ethic—would also be borne out if put into context. By picking and choosing, one can find biblical backing and context for dozens of different behavioral policies.

It can be instructive, if we really do want to put agapeistic accounts of Christianity such as Braithwaite's into context, to ask what Christians pray for. How many prayers in the Book of Common Prayer ask for support in agapeistic behavior? Very few. Quite the contrary, prayers tend to ask for protection against dangers and enemies. The second Collect, for peace, in the Church of England service for Morning Prayer, reads:

O God, who art the author of peace and lover of concord, in knowledge of whom standeth our eternal life, whose service is perfect freedom; Defend us thy humble servants in all assaults of our enemies; that we, surely trusting in thy defence, may not fear the power of any adversaries, through the might of Jesus Christ our Lord.

And for what does one pray at night? The second Collect at Evening Prayer reads:

O God, from whom all holy desires, all good counsels, and all just works do proceed; Give unto thy servants that peace which the world cannot give; that both our hearts may be set to obey thy commandments, and also that by thee we being defended from the fear of our enemies may pass our time in rest and quietness.

And one of the most famous of all prayers, the beautiful prayer of St. Chrysostom, reads:

Almighty God, who has given us grace at this time with one accord to make our common supplications unto thee; and dost promise, that when two or three are gathered together in thy Name thou wilt grant their requests: Fulfil now, O Lord, the desires and petitions of thy servants, as may be most expedient for them; granting us in this world knowledge of thy truth, and in the world to come life everlasting.

Or ought one to consider the Creed of St. Athanasius, also in the Book of Common Prayer, and although not much used in contemporary times, directed nonetheless to be recited in place of the Apostles' Creed on Christmas Day, the Epiphany, Easter Day, Ascension Day, Whitsunday, Trinity Sunday, and on the Feast Days of eight of the saints? It is very long, and wears the dress of an ancient and now obsolete philosophical terminology. I shall quote only from the beginning and the end:

> Whosoever will be saved: before all things it is necessary that he hold the Catholick Faith. Which Faith except everyone do keep *whole and undefiled*: without doubt he shall perish everlastingly. And the Catholick Faith is this: That we worship one God in Trinity, and Trinity in Unity; Neither confounding the Persons; nor dividing the Substance. . . .

And so on for four columns of very small print. *Not a single word is said of love*, not a single word in this great creed of the Church which ends in these words: "This is the Catholick Faith: which except a man believe faithfully, he cannot be saved." For that matter, there is not a word about love in the Apostles' Creed, the most widely used creed of the Christian churches. Why? Part of the answer seems to be that the creeds were intended in part to define heresies to be avoided, and to pronounce on matters over which there had been some disagreement in the early history of the Church. That Jesus preached some vague gospel of love has rarely been contested—it was *so* vague that there were few doctrinal disputes about it; and also, I fear, it was so *uninteresting* to the majority of Christians that it was not considered necessary to incorporate a reference to it in the creeds. What was wanted was protection against dangers; give us that, dear God, and we may even do some loving.

But if there were in the early centuries of the Church few doctrinal disputes about love, historical scholarship has had something to say about it. As we have seen, one result of nineteenth-century biblical criticism was that the Sermon on the Mount, which many took as the paradigm statement of Jesus's gospel of love, was not meant as a general policy of behavior even for Christians, but was rather what Schweitzer called an interim ethic, a prudential ethic to be followed by a small group of Christians isolated from general society expecting the imminent return of a God who would protect them from the dangers of that society and indeed set them up as lords over it.

Braithwaite's account of Christianity is, then, somewhat simple-minded. The same may be said of his view of literature in general: for Braithwaite, the chief function of Christian stories is, like that of myths, parables, and other kinds of literature, to give us fodder to bolster our moral intentions. The function of literature, and in particular the question whether it is morally uplifting or morally degrading, has been discussed by philosophers and critics from Plato to F. R. Leavis—with many rather different conclusions. It is perhaps worth remarking that one important thing that may happen when one confronts great literature is that one's perceptions may be heightened and changed by the artistic and imaginative presentation of human situations. Literature does not simply strengthen one's moral resolutions; and it would on any account be superficial to say that this is *the* function of literature. Literature has no single function and has in fact been used for many different purposes in the course of its history. Few who have read such writers as Marcel Proust, Robert Musil, Richard Hughes, Virginia Woolf, E. M. Forster have failed to be both affected and *changed* by the encounter. Sometimes, of course, material from this literature may be used to help support one's previous moral resolutions. But just as often its effect may be at once destructive and constructive—to alter radically one's moral resolutions.

Before concluding this discussion of contemporary Protestant thought, I should comment briefly on some of the ideas and expressions that have been used, such as "religious assertions" and "religious language". Some philosophers now refer to "religious language" as if that were a unique category of discourse, quite separate from such categories as "historical narrative", "scientific explanation", "poetry", "symbolic discourse", "allegory", "myth", and several other ways and modes of speaking. Such approaches to "religious language" tend to originate with the intention of marking it off as one of a number of *illegitimate* forms of discourse to be distinguished from legitimate forms of discourse such as formal logic and mathematics on one hand and scientific explanation on the other. Later, as this logical and scientific imperialism was abandoned, some philosophers—Braithwaite is a good example—persisted in speaking of "religious language", but dropped the earlier pejorative tone. Now "religious language" was to be construed as something with properties all its own, even with its own unique criteria in terms of which religious statements could be validated or rejected. Such thinkers would sometimes maintain that just as there could be developed a logic of scientific discourse, or a logic of scientific discovery, so could there be developed a logic of religious discourse—neither of which could be judged in terms of the criteria held valid by any of the others.

The results of contemporary investigations in philosophy, philology, linguistics, anthropology, comparative religion, and other fields provide little support for either of these approaches. Language is used importantly in religion, but there is no such thing as "religious language", any more than there is a single thing, "Religion", which has a kind of language appropriate and peculiar to it: there are many different religions, each with its own distinctive style of discourse; and even within a particular religion, such as Christianity, many different kinds of language are used. There is the rich poetic language, filled with metaphor and hyperbole, simile, allusion, of the Psalms or the Song of Solomon. There is the comparatively straightforward historical narrative of much of the Books of Samuel and Kings and Joshua, or again, of the Gospels and the Book of the Acts of the Apostles. There are at one extreme the letters of Paul, occasionally bordering on the ordinary, and at the other extreme the altogether extraordinary language of the Book of Revelations. Also to be mentioned are the various prayer books and liturgies, the hymns of the churches, and the oral traditions. So, we may speak of the languages of religions, or of the language of religions; but we begin to go astray if we think that there is something which might be called "religious language", or that there is a category of assertions that can easily be pigeonholed as "religious assertions". There is no "language of religion" which could be studied exhaustively like, say, the language of the Hopi Indians during a particular decade; nor is there a category of religious assertions which could be studied intensively like an axiom system of symbolic logic or mathematics. One great theologian, Karl Barth, did say that the *Word of God* (which is not to be identified with any human report of it) could not appropriately have the criteria of disciplines other than theology brought in judgment upon it. But even theological criteria remained hypothetical for Barth; and he would have scoffed at the idea of "religious language".

4

THE DILEMMA OF
ULTIMATE COMMITMENT
AND THE RATIONALIST
SEARCH FOR INTEGRITY

1. The Tu Quoque Argument

> Contemporary Christians should support
> those who relativize world and man.
> —Karl Heim[1]

Some of the dramatic argumentative themes discussed in the preceding chapter, which are characteristic features of the writings of such theologians as Tillich, Niebuhr, Brunner, and Bultmann—ideas of sin and symbol, broken myth, and biblical *Weltanschauung*—are so intriguing and familiar that many people have come to regard them as the most important features of contemporary Protestantism. This is a mistake: as perhaps only Barth has adequately appreciated, such arguments are quite unimportant.

They are unimportant not because, as Barth might say, they are irreverent, but because they are not taken seriously. Although they are billed as arguments in support of the Christian position, they are not treated as such: when some of these arguments are toppled, the theological edifice they are supposedly buttressing does not even lean. When a person sees no reason to abandon a position when an argument put forward to support it is refuted, that indicates that his position, far from *depending* on the argument, was held independently of it. He may use the argument as a tool to convert others or to exorcise his own doubts; such arguments are the neon lights, not the foundations, of the theological edifice.

Fortunately, this "heads I win, tails you lose"[2] technique for using arguments without taking them seriously can usually be detected. One need only determine whether the advocate of a particular position would abandon it if his argument was shown to be false. If he would not, then his position does not depend on that argument; in so far as a serious defense of the position is concerned, the argument is therefore superfluous.

---

[1]*Religion and Culture: Essays in Honor of Paul Tillich*, ed. Walter Leibrecht (New York: Harper and Brothers, 1959), p. 194.

[2]I owe this apt name to Joseph Agassi.

The only serious argument for Christian commitment today concerns the problem of the limits of rationality. This is the argument that both Kierkegaard and Barth relied upon.

The three principal problems of philosophy are the problem of knowledge, the problem of rationality, and the problem of reconciling knowledge and rationality.

The third problem, that of conflict between knowledge and rationality, typically arises when it is found that according to one's theory of rationality, knowledge is impossible; or that according to one's theory of knowledge, rationality is impossible. This conflict is usually occasioned by the existence of another conflict within the theory of rationality itself, a conflict that appears when it is discovered that according to one's theory of rationality, rationality is impossible. The problem of resolving the latter conflict I take to be central to the *problem of rationality, or of the limits of rationality.* It is also often called the dilemma of ultimate commitment and the problem of presuppositions.

This problem is crucial, not only because no one has seemed able to solve it but because the Christian commitment of many Protestants *depends upon the assumption that it cannot be solved.*[3] For the argument provides a *rational excuse* for irrational commitment. If due weight is given to the fact that the dilemma involved was believed to be inescapable when, at the breakdown of Protestant liberalism, many theologians decided to remain within the Protestant tradition, one can hardly fault them intellectually for doing so. But if the argument of this and the following chapter is correct—if I succeed in refuting what I call the *tu quoque* argument and in solving the problem of rationality in which it is rooted—then this excuse will be invalid for future irrational commitment, Protestant or otherwise.

Just what is the powerful *tu quoque* argument? It argues that (1) for certain logical reasons, rationality is so limited that *everyone* must make a dogmatic irrational commitment; (2) therefore, the Christian has a right to make whatever commitment he pleases; and (3) therefore, no one has a right to criticize him (or anyone else) for making such a commitment.

The correctness of the two closely related conclusions depends on the contention about the limits of rationality. This contention—which arises out of the need to stem an infinite regress and from the fact that arbitrary

---

[3]For examples, see David E. Roberts, "Tillich's Doctrine of Man", especially sec. 3, "The Limitations of Objectivity", in *The Theology of Paul Tillich,* ed. R. W. Bretall and C. W. Kegley (New York: Macmillan, 1956). Roberts writes (p. 110): "Everyone must take a stand somewhere. . . . no matter what center is chosen, it cannot be objectively demonstrated—partly because it is the expression of ultimate concern, and partly because all value-arguments presuppose its acknowledgement before they can have any point." For other examples, see Karl Heim, *Christian Faith and Natural Science;* Basil Mitchell, ed., *Faith and Logic* (London: George Allen and Unwin, 1957); Alasdair MacIntyre, "The Logical Status of Religious Belief", *Metaphysical Beliefs* (London: SCM Press, 1957); James William McClendon, Jr., and James M. Smith, *Understanding Religious Convictions* (Notre Dame: University of Notre Dame Press, 1975); and Basil Mitchell, *The Justification of Religious Belief* (Oxford: Oxford University Press, 1973).

dogmatic commitment seems the only way to do this—relies on an analysis of what is regarded as the rational way to defend or justify ideas. No matter what belief is advanced, someone can always challenge it with: "How do you know?", "Give me a reason", or "Prove it!" When such challenges are accepted by citing further reasons which entail those under challenge, these may be questioned in turn. And so on forever. If the burden of proof or rational justification is *perpetually* shifted to a higher-order premise or reason, the contention originally questioned is never effectively defended. One may as well never have begun the defense: an infinite regress is created.

To *justify* the original contention, one would eventually have to stop at something not open to question for which one does not and need not provide justificatory reasons. These would be the halting points for rational discussion. These "standards", "criteria", "ultimate presuppositions", "ends", or "goals" are simply accepted.

However, if all men do not cease their questioning at the same point—if ultimate standards are perceived not to be certain or if different people deem conflicting "ultimate" standards to be certain—then "ultimate relativism" results. Some way of arbitrating *rationally* among competing ultimate stopping points by appeal to a common standard is now excluded in principle. If these ultimate statements are matters of contention, then there will be no Archimedes' lever with which to decide among competing sets of ultimate standards. Indeed, even if everyone did subjectively happen to stop at the same place or accept the same standard, there still would be no way to prove rationally that this universal subjective standard led to objectively true statements about the world. Suppose someone says: "I've got Archimedes' lever right here; with it I can decide objectively between x and y. And y, my position, comes out on top." The opponent can reply: "How do you know that that is Archimedes' lever? Actually, you are quite mistaken. *I* have Archimedes' lever, and it differs from yours. Not only does it show that your position is wrong; it also shows that your so-called Archimedes' lever is wrong."

In fact, such situations are common: people do not accept the same standards, and individuals accept different standards at different times of their lives. Standards vary, often sharply, from brother to brother, man to man, village to village, nation to nation, historical period to historical period. Many persons, in fact, think they possess Archimedes' lever.

Obviously, one cannot, without arguing in a circle, justify the rationality of a standard of rationality by appealing to that standard. Yet, if certain beliefs—for example, the standard itself—are held to be immune from the demand for rational justification and from the question "How do you know?", they can be said to be held irrationally or dogmatically. And, so it is claimed, argument about the radically different beliefs held in this way is pointless. For rational argument consists in mutual criticism, with each person supporting all his beliefs with good reasons.

The limits of rational argument within any particular way of life seem, then, to be defined by reference to that object or belief in respect to which commitment is made or imposed, in respect to which argument is brought to a close. Thus reason is relativized to one's halting place or standards, and cannot arbitrate among different standards. Different halting places—i.e., standards, criteria, presuppositions, conventions, dogmas, articles of faith—are taken by different individuals and define irreconcilable communities. Whatever may explain how such differences arise, reason can never dissipate them.

If this account of rational argument and of its limits is accepted, the two consequences stated above seem to follow immediately. If one must, then . . . one *may*: one may choose without justification the set of standards, or the Archimedes' lever, one pleases. The "truth" of one's beliefs is then ultimately rooted not in their self-evidence or in their universality but in one's whim, or in the belief, say, that God has commanded one to accept these standards. A man's standards are *true for him* because of his subjective commitment to them. An irrationalist thus has an *excuse for subjective irrationalism,* and a secure refuge from any criticism of any subjective commitment: he has a *tu quoque* or boomerang argument. To any critic, the irrationalist can reply: *"tu quoque",* reminding him that people whose rationality is similarly limited should not berate others for admitting to and acting on the limitation. If everyone—as a matter of logic—must make an irrational commitment at some point, if no one can escape subjective commitment, then no one can be criticized simply because he has made such a commitment, no matter how idiosyncratic. "Error" in these important matters would be only a matter of submission to a *different* authority. This limitation is the more telling in being accompanied by the remark that in those things which matter most, reason is incompetent: that such things are beyond or above rational scrutiny; and that those things which reason *can* decide are of relatively minor importance.

Neither the Western sceptic nor the Indian yogi would dispute this argument. They agree from the outset that truth is not to be attained through rational argumentation. Since no position can be defended by reason, they might say, so much the more *reason* for suspending judgment. But it is the *fideist* who *glories* in the argument, and who challenges the sceptic and the yogi too. His claim is simple: since an eventual halt to rational justification is inevitable and *cannot* be made with objective and universal reason, it must be made with unreason, subjectively and particularly: one must choose or commit or attach oneself subjectively. Thus the fideist deliberately makes a final, unquestionable, subjective commitment to or choice of some way of life, or some presuppositions, or of some authority or tradition claiming to possess the competence or the right to make such decisions for him.

The reader may protest that people have argued this way during various romantic periods of the past, but that they no longer do so. Do people really argue this way *today?* Is the *tu quoque* argument still widely in use? It is well to remember Michael Polanyi's remark, with reference to this argument, that

> It was a mistake to regard the Nazi as an untaught savage. His bestiality was carefully groomed . . . His contempt for humanitarian ideals had a century of philosophic schooling behind it. The Nazi disbelieves in public morality in the way we disbelieve in witchcraft. It is not that he has never heard of it, but that he thinks he has valid grounds to assert that such a thing cannot exist.[4]

It may, however, be insisted that there are no Nazis any more. It is therefore pertinent to quote a more recent political proclamation by a young student at Harvard, just as a reminder that this is no academic discussion. I shall quote a few philosophers (including some of this mere boy's teachers) later:

> The only reason I wouldn't blow up the Center for International Affairs is that I might get caught. But the desire is there. As it is for the 7094 Computer, the Instrumentation Labs, and the Center for International Studies at M.I.T., draft boards, army bases, the Pentagon, the White House, the Capitol, New York City, Los Angeles, Las Vegas, and Harvard University. . . . What has happened to our generation is that we never got what we wanted. . . . We have an irreconcilable tension in our existence. . . . Blowing up a bad thing will relieve much of that tension. . . . I may have learned only two things in my four years at Harvard. *The first is that an equally intelligent, rational, and valid argument can be made on all sides of any question from any and all premises. The second is that those arguments have no relationship to anything but themselves.* . . . The point is that *arguments are based on reason and the valid laws of discourse can prove anything within their system.* It is the feeling I have in my stomach against the war that matters. Any argument in favor of it does not. . . . We are told continually that knowledge will make us free. *We are taught to ignore irrational consequences and to put our faith in reason.* . . . *We are fed reason in order to give an inferiority complex to the rest of our emotions and senses.* . . . We are trapped in a philosophical system of cause and effect. *Rationality binds the mind and restricts the soul.* It might even destroy brain cells. We need to be liberated.[5]

This young writer, if typical of his generation, may even think more highly of witchcraft than of "public morality" and rationality. Yet as long as the *tu quoque* argument goes undefeated, this sort of irrationalist, even

---

[4]Michael Polanyi, *The Logic of Liberty* (London: Routledge & Kegan Paul, 1951), p. 106.
[5]Published in *Harvard Crimson*, October 22, 1969; reprinted in Sidney Hook's fine essay, "The Ideology of Violence", *Encounter*, April 1970, p. 30. Italics mine.

terrorist position, is intellectually plausible—*indeed, the rationalist has no reply to it that is effective even from within his own point of view.*

To test whether the *tu quoque* is indeed unanswerable we might select several competing ways of life and probe them to determine whether in the last resort any choice between them is arbitrary. Before making such a test, we must decide which ways of life to compare. There appears, at least at first, to be little guidance for the selection; on the assumption that they are mutually exclusive, we might as well contrast Buddhism and Christianity; or asceticism and hedonism; or (as the Christian philosopher H. A. Hodges, for instance, has done)[6] Marxism, positivism, and "metaphysical Christianity".

However, comparisons of *such* ways of life miss the point of the difficulty. Hence, a further consideration of the original problem may provide a clue to guide our selection. First, the problem concerns the *limits of rationality* in the making of a decision about a way of life. Second, one of the most important contemporary ways of life is that of the *rationalist,* a position that might be described loosely for the time being as one whose supporters are eager to make *all* their decisions—moral, scientific, or otherwise—rationally, on rational grounds, or with good reasons. Therefore, we might turn the problem on itself as it were, strike a deeper level, and perhaps even solve it, *by asking what the limits of rationality are when it comes to making a decision between the rationalist way of life and some other way of life.* Must the rationalist also begin with an irrational commitment?[7]

Although almost any way of life would do as a contrast to rationalism, the fact that here we are primarily interested in the Protestant tradition may enable us to focus our task better. For Protestantism, by contrast to many other ways of life, such as Nazism or the beatnik life, has from its inception been intimately associated with reason.

To the theologians we have discussed, the answer to the question has seemed clear: the choice between rationalism and Protestantism has indeed appeared to be just as arbitrarily irrational as any other.[8] It was distinguished only, if at all, by the apparent blindness of would-be rationalists, who rarely would admit to being real irrationalists. When the conscious

---

[6]H. A. Hodges, *Languages, Standpoints and Attitudes* (London: Oxford University Press, 1953).

[7]It is not often enough noticed that the rationalist and scientific tradition contains more or less explicit moral codes adhered to or subscribed to voluntarily by a large proportion of its members. These codes are not usually *called* "moral codes"; their most important components may be labeled "heuristic rules" or "rules of scientific procedure". Yet they have a typically moral force. For example, sanctions may be applied to those who depart from them or appear to depart from them. Some of the most important components of these rationalistic codes can be reconstructed from the epistemological theories developed within this tradition. Epistemologies, as found in the writings of the great Western philosophers, are documents of moral codes.

[8]See H. R. Niebuhr, *Christ and Culture*, p. 252; and Reinhold Niebuhr, "Reply to Interpretation and Criticism", in *Reinhold Niebuhr: His Religious, Social and Political Thought* (New York: Macmillan, 1956), p. 450.

irrationalist talks of the "Leap of Faith", he sincerely believes he is referring to a universal human condition. Moreover, since we all value self-awareness, he contends that a man who makes such a choice in full awareness of its arbitrariness is not only no more irrational than anyone else; he is a superior being—superior to the mass of men who never even know they have standards, far superior to the blind "bourgeois" rationalist liberal who believes his own beliefs to be objective. More extreme irrationalists have gone so far as to suggest that almost *any* deliberate commitment is better than a rationalism which is, they say, typically unaware of its commitments. The soul-impoverished rationalist, not realizing that he cannot avoid making an irrational commitment, makes one blindly without knowing what he is doing. The irrationalist, on the other hand, is *free*. Recognizing that his commitments are *necessarily arbitrary,* he becomes free to *choose* them and to be true to himself in his choice. The rationalist, in trying—hopelessly—to ensure that all his beliefs are determined by objective standards, merely succeeds in ensuring that none of his beliefs is "truly his own".

To use the terminology of some existentialist proponents of the argument, it is in his self-conscious deliberate selection of the kind of world in which he is going to live, or of the way of life he is going to lead, that a man achieves *authentic* human existence.[9] The theologian makes an irrational commitment to Christ; he admits it—he glories in it. But the rationalist has made an equally irrational commitment to reason—despite his insolent claim to "hold no dogma sacrosanct".[10] The theologian, it appears, is intellectually more honest—indeed, even more rational—than the rationalist. If even the most radical rationalist must hold some of his beliefs immune from criticism, the theologian can write in good conscience, as Brunner did in his book *The Mediator*:

> Faith may indeed be combined with criticism of the biblical tradition about the life of Jesus, perhaps even with a very radical form of criticism, but it is not possible to combine faith with *every* kind of criticism; for instance, it cannot be combined with the kind of criticism which denies the existence of Jesus altogether. . . .

---

[9]However, existentialists are no more agreed about the importance of deliberate choice than they are about many other issues. In particular, Protestant existentialists often deny that this is a matter of picking and choosing, stressing that *we are chosen* in the sense that God decides who shall "choose" Christian presuppositions. But there is greater agreement on a more important point: the identification of the *worth* and the *validity* of a commitment with its *source*, whether that source be a "self-conscious decision" or "God".

[10]See Dancey, "In Defense of Liberalism".

2. How Shoes Can Be Danced into Holes

> Judge not, that ye be not judged. For with
> what judgment ye judge, ye shall be
> judged; and with what measure ye mete, it
> shall be measured unto you. And why
> beholdest thou the mote that is in thy
> brother's eye, but considerest not the
> beam that is in thy own eye? Or how wilt
> thou say to thy brother, Let me cast out
> the mote out of thine eye; and lo, the
> beam is in thine own eye? Thou hypocrite,
> cast out first the beam out of thine own
> eye . . .
>
> —MATTHEW 7:1-5

If correct, the argument about the limits of rationality can provide a
Protestant with a rational excuse for his irrational commitment to Christ
and a secure refuge from any criticism of this commitment. The theologian
can reply *"tu quoque"* to his critic, and remind him that people whose own
rationality is limited should not admonish others for admitting that the
limitation exists; that people who live in glass houses should not throw
stones.

Fair as the retort seems, and even if the argument is valid, its use involves
some serious disadvantages. One of these concerns the practical matter of
settling disputes in social life. A typical rationalist might say that there are
two principal means of settling disputes among people with basically
differing outlooks: (1) argument, and (2) force or appeal to irrational
authority. And a rationalist, he would add at once, is one like himself who
prefers the first course. Yet, typically, such a rationalist is unable to escape
the dilemma of ultimate commitment; and thus is unable to defeat the great
excuse of proponents of force and irrationalism (such as the student quoted
in the preceding section): since, for certain logical reasons, argument is
severely restricted, force—possibly violent—*must* be employed when a
decision is necessary. As the American pragmatist and Supreme Court
justice, Oliver Wendell Holmes, Jr., put it, "the ultimate ratio is force." That
is, if it is *futile* to try to *argue* a person with different commitments into
one's own position rationally, then one must—if a decision must be
reached—resort to irrational persuasion or force. If disputes that must be
settled cannot in principle be settled by argument, then they must in practice
be settled by force.

Another ironic consequence of using the *tu quoque* is rarely noticed. To the extent that anyone employing it strengthens his own position by insuring that it is parallel to his opponent's, to that extent he increases the invulnerability of the *opponent* to criticism.[11] For the opponent, if criticized, may also use the *tu quoque*. Those who gain a refuge of safety for themselves through appeal to the limits of rationality thereby provide a similar refuge for all others whose commitments differ from theirs. Thus, the many criticisms which the Protestant theologians have leveled at rationalism and liberalism become as pointless as those the liberals have directed at theology. Ultimately, the use of the *tu quoque* makes nonsense of the idea of the historical development and change of ideas in the face of criticism.

Among those who have employed the argument of the limits of rationality to defend their own commitments from criticism, there are two kinds of writers who, ignoring such disadvantages, have continued to criticize the commitments of others. The first kind consists of those who simply have not seen the point, who have not appreciated that this "defense" forces them to abandon the practice of criticism. The second kind consists of those who do seem to see the point but who go on criticizing all the same. I shall cite two examples of the latter type to illustrate some of the pitfalls involved.

The first is Professor Herbert Butterfield of Cambridge University. In his book *The Whig Interpretation of History* and in many essays,[12] Butterfield has stated that the task of the historian is simply to report the facts, not to criticize morally, not to praise or blame men of other times. Himself a nonconformist Protestant Christian, Butterfield urges the historian to embrace the precepts: "Judge not (that ye be not judged)" and "To know all is to forgive all". The task of the historian, he argues, is that of the detective, not of the judge or advocate. Ultimately, Butterfield suggests, the only moralizing one can allow oneself is moralizing about oneself.

Butterfield fits easily into our picture of the relativist: he allows that a man may make his own moral decisions and commitments but forbids criticism of others for differing moral stances. At the same time, there is in his approach a highly misleading air of "objectivity" which needs to be pointed out. Butterfield is not simply saying that the historian should avoid moralizing and misleading value-charged words and emphases in his descriptive narrative; nor is Butterfield simply enjoining the historian not to slant his narrative in favor of the faction he personally prefers. Among Western historians, there is little serious controversy about such matters.

Butterfield's claim is much stronger. He is saying that the historian should

---

[11]One of the few philosophers who seems fully to have appreciated this point, although he has applied it critically only to contemporary linguistic philosophy, is Ernest Gellner. See *Words and Things* (London: Victor Gollancz, 1959), chap. 8.

[12]See "Moral Judgments in History", in *History and Human Relations* (London: William Collins Sons & Co., 1931), pp. 101–30; and *Christianity and History* (London: Collins Fontana Books, 1958), p. 85.

not step into the picture to praise or condemn the men whom he is terms of discussing, even after he has presented the facts about them as objectively as he can.

Though he presents his position attractively, Butterfield fails to practice what he preaches. For he has also been one of the most enthusiastic champions of the idea that historians should study the history of historical writing. His *Whig Interpretation,* his *Man on His Past,* and many of his other writings provide examples of such investigations into the history of historical writing. Now, the historians like Lord Acton whom he studies are themselves men of the past acting in the past. *Yet Butterfield, the historian of historical writing, praises those historians who do not praise or blame, and blames those historians who do.* In Butterfield's hands, the thesis that one should make no moral judgments about men of the past is itself a moral judgment on men of the past.

Untenable as this thesis is, it nonetheless plays in much of Butterfield's work the role of a powerful summons to historical responsibility and to reverence for the context and particularity of past events and men. Butterfield's error is understandable and almost inevitable in a framework wherein the dilemma of ultimate commitment cannot be resolved. Moreover, he might try to avoid my objection by distinguishing intellectual from moral criticism. At any rate, I certainly do not blame him for blaming other historians. But in failing to blame him for blaming others, I am not embracing his position. I abstain from blaming him for blaming historians who blame, only because I believe that the historian, Christian or not, has a right, and at times a duty, to blame and criticize the subjects of his studies.

A second illustration of what may happen when the consequences of using the *tu quoque* argument go unheeded may be found in the writings of Paul Tillich.[13] Tillich might claim that all the criticisms made in the preceding chapter are not only wrong—as they certainly could be—but simply "meaningless". For he has said that "all speaking about divine matters which is not done in the state of ultimate concern [that is, in our terminology, "commitment"] is meaningless . . . that which is meant in the act of faith cannot be approached in any other way than through an act of faith".[14]

The argument cuts both ways—and cuts Tillich. For like Barth, Brunner, Niebuhr, and most of the others, he is a thinker with one "ultimate concern" or ultimate commitment who has done a lot of critical "speaking about" ultimate concerns he does not share. For example, he has sharply criticized ultimate commitments to the "bitch goddess" success, or to

---

[13]The criticism of Tillich presented here was stated, in preliminary form, in my review "Dynamics of Faith and Technology of Iconoclasm", *Harvard Crimson,* March 15, 1957. I owe the inspiration that Butterfield is involved in a similar difficulty to a brilliant lecture by Morton White at Harvard in the autumn of 1957.

[14]*Dynamics of Faith,* p. 10.

nationalism or totalitarianism, or to traditional and literal religion. Yet, in his position, one would be forced to conclude that his own remarks on these matters are, by *his* definition, "meaningless". Nor can this word be explained away as no more than a careless lapse on Tillich's part into a kind of behaviorism or "theological positivism". He has extensively elaborated and complicated his position:

> The assertion that something has sacred character is meaningful only for the asserting faith. As a theoretical judgment claiming general validity, it is a meaningless combination of words. . . . The outside observer can only state that there is a correlation of faith between the one who has faith and the sacramental object of his faith. But he cannot deny or affirm the validity of this correlation of faith. He can only state it as a fact. If a Protestant observes a Catholic praying before a picture of the Virgin, he remains observer, unable to state whether the faith of the observed is valid or not. If he is a Catholic he may join the observed in the same act of faith. There is no criterion by which faith can be judged from outside the correlation of faith.[15]

It is questionable whether the position Tillich espouses here could even be carried out internally. On just what basis, for instance, can one Catholic judge the validity of the faith of another *Catholic* whom he observes praying before the picture of the Virgin? On Tillich's own criteria he can do no more than note that both he and the observed person have a correlation of faith with a certain sacramental object; he cannot tell whether they both have the *same* correlation. And lacking this information, how can he judge validity? Tillich's problem is parallel to many in subjectivist, relativist ethics. For example, what is the line of demarcation between the inner group and the outside observers? Tillich is here in an even more difficult position than the average subjectivist. Not only can his outsider not evaluate or judge the validity of another faith; he cannot even approach it meaningfully. Again, how would Tillich reconcile his statement that "it is meaningless to question the ultimacy of an ultimate concern" with his own practice of setting up criteria for ultimacy?[16]

In making the claims he does, Tillich, like Butterfield, has clearly labeled as impossible the very activity in which he himself has been engaged throughout his writings: the criticism and judgment of other commitments. So in talking about "ultimate concerns" other than his own, Tillich also fails to practice what he preaches. For he rarely stops at stating that certain "correlations of faith" exist. He goes on to evaluate them, to label many of them idolatrous, to deny many of them validity in his sense of that word: as expressive of the "ultimate which is really ultimate". Apparently Tillich believes that all men are equally faithful, but some are more faithful than others. According to the brothers Grimm, there was, once upon a time, "a King who had twelve daughters, *each more beautiful than the others*". The

[15]Ibid., pp. 58 ff.
[16]Ibid, p. 46.

name of the Grimms' fairy tale is "The Shoes That Were Danced into Holes".

Significantly, a recalcitrant Tillichian might reply to this criticism with another, different *tu quoque*: he might point out that certain rationalists, like the early Wittgenstein in his *Tractatus Logico-Philosophicus,* also made judgments that were, by their own definitions, meaningless. However, any Protestant theologian who indulges in this *tu quoque* at once sacrifices the accrued integrity that the first *tu quoque* afforded him. He had *differed* from the rationalist in not claiming for himself more than he could do: he, unlike the would-be rationalist, admitted his limitations. But as soon as Protestant theologians who embrace a position that makes criticism of other commitments impossible begin to criticize other commitments, a loss of integrity occurs in Protestant thought, too.

In sum, the belief that rationality is ultimately limited, by providing an excuse for irrational commitment, enables a Protestant, or any other irrationalist, to make an irrational commitment without losing intellectual integrity. But, at the same time, anyone who makes use of this excuse pays a high price for it. For any one who uses it may no longer, in integrity, *criticize* the holder of a different commitment. One gains the right to be irrational at the expense of losing the right to criticize. One gains immunity from criticism for one's own commitment by making any criticism of commitments impossible.

And it is just here that the story of the stone-throwing tenant of the glass house becomes most relevant. There is a particularly modern irony in the idea of a glass house inhabited by a subjective relativist. Only one kind of glass is suitable for such a building: that ingenious modern one-way window-mirror glass which one sometimes finds fitted in zoo cages, especially in monkey houses. The world can look in at the subjectivist and watch his antics; but when the subjectivist looks outward, he sees only his own face in the mirrors that imprison him. This is an odd sort of "palace of crystal".[17] And perhaps it does afford the subjectivist a Pickwickian kind of freedom. He is at any rate free to make any face he pleases in his mirror. Since his world is his mirror image, he is free to create his world. Moreover, if everyone *has* to be a subjectivist, there is a sort of consolation: nobody can look in from the outside. Everyone is alone, inside his own mirror cage, staring at his own face. No wonder the existentialists are bored. No wonder they complain of isolation, loneliness, "a little death".

---

[17]See Dostoevsky, *Notes from the Underground,* part 10.

3. Is a Rationalist Possible?

> The symptom that a particular branch of
> science or art is ripe for a change is a
> feeling of frustration and malaise, not
> necessarily caused by any acute crisis in
> that specific branch—which might be
> doing quite well in its traditional terms of
> reference—but by a feeling that the whole
> tradition is somehow out of step.
> —ARTHUR KOESTLER[18]

The fact remains that anyone who is bored of being bored must answer the
tu quoque. Is it really inescapable? A would-be rationalist who is convinced
that it cannot be so gets little consolation from the dominant rationalist
philosophies of the mid-twentieth century. Although contemporary philosophers have had their share of successes "in traditional terms of reference",
the feeling of frustration and malaise to which Koestler refers is their
familiar, almost companionable, bedfellow. In particular, those who have
dealt with problems connected with rationality have often suspected, in
their bewilderment, that something must be wrong with the problems of
philosophy.[19] And they have gone on to wonder aloud whether relativism of
the kind discussed in these pages might seem unavoidable only because
something is deeply out of order in our entire philosophical tradition. But it
is easier to feel uneasy than to detect the error. The "discovery" of the
"error" and with it the "revolution" in philosophy have in fact themselves
become regular features of modern philosophy.

Generally speaking, the various revolutions in philosophy can be characterized by reference to the solution they offer to what I believe is the
fundamental problem of modern philosophy. This is the problem of
defeating the *tu quoque* by showing that it is possible to choose in a
nonarbitrary way among competing, mutually exclusive theories, and—
more broadly speaking—among competing "ways of life". This is, I believe,
more fundamental than what has been called the "central problem of the

---

[18]*The Sleepwalkers*, p. 520.

[19]For two out of hundreds of examples, see H. A. Prichard, "Does Moral Philosophy Rest on a
Mistake?", in A. I. Melden, *Ethical Theories*; and S. E. Toulmin, *The Place of Reason in Ethics* (Cambridge:
Cambridge University Press, 1953), pp. 202-21. See also Richard Rorty, *Philosophy and the Mirror of
Nature*, which argues the end of epistemology; Ian Hacking, "Is the End in Sight for Epistemology?", *Journal
of Philosophy*, vol. 77 (October 1980), pp. 579–88; and Jaegwon Kim, "Rorty on the Possibility of
Philosophy", *Journal of Philosophy*, vol. 77 (October 1980), pp. 588–97.

theory of knowledge": namely, the demarcation of science from non-science.[20]

The broader problem became important in modern intellectual history during the Renaissance, when for the first time since antiquity men were faced with a great number of radically competing views and the need to decide among them. During the Reformation, the Counter Reformation, and the attendant scientific revolution, it explicitly became one of the main preoccupations of philosophers. And the interest in it is far older than the Renaissance. Indeed, one of the main stimulants to discussion of the problem during the immediate post-Reformation period was the translation and popularization of the writings of the ancient Pyrrhonian sceptic, Sextus Empiricus.

Behind the early modern attempts to solve this problem lay a very practical aim: namely, to show that philosophical disputes could be settled in an orderly and rational way, to show that the traditional political, intellectual, and religious authorities—which had in many cases come to seem arbitrary and irrational—could be *displaced* without intellectual chaos, *since* they would be *replaced* by the authority of reason. The various schools of philosophy arose in an attempt to adjudicate among competing views by providing *rational* authorities to substitute for unwanted forms of traditional and hereditary authority.

Practically every revolution in philosophy since then has disclosed that the previous candidate for intellectual authority was unsatisfactory and has proposed a new, supposedly more satisfactory, rational authority. The church should be replaced by intellectual intuition, intellectual intuition by sense experience, sense experience by a particular language system. And so on. These revolutions have had a depressingly similar pattern. And since, as we shall see, the pattern itself dooms the revolutions to failure, future philosophical revolutions that remain within this pattern cannot succeed. However, I propose to break the pattern by calling attention to it and showing that it is not necessary.

But just why have previous revolutions failed? And what is the structural defect, the pattern, that dooms them to failure?

First, these revolutions may be understood as stages in the search for *rationalist identity*. And practically the same criticism has defeated them all—the criticism that the rationalist identity proposed by each revolution claimed to do more than it could, that it overcommitted its adherents to an ideal that was impossible in principle to attain, and thus threatened them with a perpetual crisis of integrity.

---

[20]Popper, *The Logic of Scientific Discovery*, p. 34. These two problems, as well as the different problems of demarcating rational beliefs from irrational beliefs and of demarcating true beliefs from false beliefs, have often been identified, thus causing considerable confusion, including the positivist identification of non-science and non-sense. See my "Theories of Demarcation between Science and Metaphysics", in I. Lakatos and A. E. Musgrave, eds., *Problems in the Philosophy of Science* (Amsterdam: North-Holland Publishing Company, 1968), pp. 40–119, and my book *Come demarcare la scienza dalla metafisica* (Rome: Edizioni Borla, 1983). See also appendix 2 below.

I contend, then, that the perpetual crisis of integrity into which rationalists are continually falling or being forced is due to a neglected crisis of identity in the rationalist tradition; neglected partly because of a general failure on the part of philosophers to make deliberate efforts to develop a theory of rationality as well as a theory of knowledge. Because of these crises, the valuable handy man in the house of irrationalism—the *tu quoque*—is the skeleton in the cupboard of rationalism. Rationalists are overcommitted to a notion of rationality, or rationalist identity, that is impossible to attain; and the inevitable frustration of the effort to satisfy this overcommitment prevents them from achieving integrity. At the same time, the failure of the rationalist tradition to resolve its crisis of integrity enables many irrationalists, whatever their affiliations, to preserve their own identities without loss of integrity.

My attitude toward this situation is suggested by an anecdote about Gottlob Frege that Karl Popper used to enjoy telling in his lectures. When Frege heard about Russell's discovery of paradoxes in his own and Frege's theories, the latter cried out: *"Die Arithmetik ist in's Schwanken geraten!"* (Roughly, "Arithmetic has been set spinning!"). In fact, it was not arithmetic, but Frege's theory of arithmetic, that was set spinning. Such mistakes Popper has dubbed examples of "Frege's mistake". A similar mistake is made about rationality and the possibility of being a rationalist. The blame for continued failure by rationalists to answer sceptical and fideistic arguments about the limits of rationality should, in fact, be placed on the inadequacy and primitive character of our *theories of rationality*, or on our conception of rationalist identity, rather than on our rationality or reasoning capacity itself, where Pascal, Kant, and many others have put it. It is not simply the miserable state of the human creature that sponsors irrationalist fideism and scepticism, but the miserable state of the philosophical theory of rationality that that human creature has accepted.

Let us consider this search for identity and integrity in rationalism, and in so doing examine three possible conceptions of rationalist identity:[21]

> *panrationalism* (or *comprehensive rationalism*)
> *critical rationalism*
> *pancritical rationalism* (or *comprehensively critical rationalism*).

The story of modern philosophy can be told to a large extent in terms of the history of panrationalism or comprehensive rationalism. It is, for the most part, the story of the failure of panrationalism to defeat sceptical and fideistic contentions about the limits of rationality. Traditionally dominant, panrationalism remains, despite its failures, a very commonly held conception of rationality. In a review of contemporary literature, W. P. Alston and

---

[21]The three categories are not intended as exhaustive. Obviously, a number of historical positions would not easily fit any of them.

R. B. Brandt call it the "Establishment" view.[22] Yet most contemporary philosophies are forms of critical rationalism. Both panrationalism and critical rationalism share the structural defect I have mentioned. To go from critical rationalism to pancritical rationalism involves a change in the *structure* of philosophical revolution. This third account, which fuses the comprehensive aims of panrationalism with the critical spirit of critical rationalism, is my own attempt to salvage the good intentions of the other two accounts while avoiding the attendant difficulties. That is, I shall try to reach a new conception of rationalist identity which will satisfactorily solve the problem in response to which theories of rationalist identity originally arose—while also avoiding those aspects of previous theories that engendered the crisis of integrity in rationalism.

Before beginning the story of panrationalism, it is important to distinguish between the essence of being a rationalist, or rationalist identity, and the essence of rational belief. Just as in the Christian tradition the essence of being a Christian, or of Christian identity, had been traditionally subordinated to the essence of the Christian message, so in the rationalist tradition rationalist identity has often been subordinated to the essence of rational belief. Criteria for distinguishing a rational from an irrational belief (or more often, a "true" belief from a "false" belief) were set up, and the rationalist was characterized as one who made his evaluations on the basis of these rational criteria or authorities, and the irrationalist as one who did not. This emphasis on the criteria for rational *belief* is suitable only for the history of panrationalism and critical rationalism. The important structural shift to pancritical rationalism involves a change of emphasis to the problem of how to tell a genuine from a nongenuine rationalist.

This procedure will bring into proper focus the *tu quoque* argument, which claims to afford a rational excuse for irrationalism, and in accordance with which—even from a rationalist point of view—the deliberate irrationalist should be judged to be more rational than the rationalist who denies that he is himself fundamentally an irrationalist.

Our question, in brief, is this: Is a rationalist possible?[23] That is, is it possible, with intellectual integrity, to claim to be a rationalist?

---

[22]W. P. Alston and Richard B. Brandt, *The Problems of Philosophy*, 3d ed., 1978, p. 605. In the *Fontana/Harper Dictionary of Modern Thought*, rationalism as contrasted with irrationalism is defined as denying "the acceptability of beliefs founded on anything but experience and reasoning, deductive or inductive".

[23]In view of the title of the present section, and of passages like these, it is curious that a critic of this book, Roger Trigg, states that "Bartley ignores the most basic question of all, namely whether rationality is possible in the first place". See his *Rationality and Commitment* (Cambridge: Cambridge University Press, 1973), p. 150.

4. The Quandaries of Panrationalism

> Now in so far as this is a complete philo-
> sophical diagram of every ethical system,
> it must show the sort of authority on
> which every ethical proposition—every
> imperative—must rest.
>
> —James Balfour[24]

The traditionally dominant, and perhaps still most common, conception of rationalist identity—panrationalism—can be traced back at least to Epictetus, who wrote in his *Discourses* (chapter 2): "To be a reasonable creature, that alone is insupportable which is unreasonable; but everything reasonable may be supported." Such conceptions combine two main requirements for rationalist identity: (1) A rationalist accepts any position that can be justified or established by appeal to the rational criteria or authorities; and (2) he accepts *only* those positions that can be so justified. The second requirement forces the rationalist to be able to justify rationally everything he holds—including these two requirements. As W. K. Clifford put it in "The Ethics of Belief": "It is wrong everywhere and for anyone, to believe anything upon insufficient evidence." Rationalists have explicitly— but not necessarily rationally—embraced such requirements on many occasions. T. H. Huxley, for instance, comically yet humorlessly claimed that his own form of rationalism demanded "absolute faith" in the validity of the second requirement.[25]

In the stereotyped way in which it is usually told, the history of modern philosophy focuses attention on a number of basically subordinate questions that arise only if panrationalism is assumed to be correct. Among these, the most important has probably been: What is the nature of the rational authority or criterion to which a rationalist appeals to justify all his opinions? The various theories of knowledge are functions of the answers philosophers have given to this question. These answers fall into two main categories:

(1) *Intellectualism* (or Rationalism—with a capital "R"), according to which the rational authority lies in the intellect (or Reason). A rationalist justifies his beliefs by appealing to intellectual intuition or the faculty of Reason.

(2) *Empiricism,* according to which the rational authority lies in sense

---

[24]James Balfour, "On the Idea of a Philosophy of Ethics", *Readings in Ethical Theory*, ed. Wilfrid Sellars and John Hospers (New York: Appleton-Century-Crofts, 1952), p. 649.
[25]T. H. Huxley, "Agnosticism and Christianity", *Selections from the Essays of Thomas Henry Huxley* (New York: F. S. Crofts, 1948), p. 92.

experience. An empiricist justifies his beliefs by appealing to sense observation.

The history of these answers is one of failure. In order to make clear why, I shall sketch here a few of the most important steps in the development of pan- or comprehensive rationalism.

The great French mathematician, physicist, and philosopher René Descartes is usually regarded as the father of intellectualism. Faced by a plethora of competing theories on all subjects, many of which he believed to be incorrect; horrified that many intellectual leaders of his time had adopted a sceptical relativism in order to help combat the rationalist claims of the Protestant Reformation; and struck by the need for some rational means of assessing competing theories, Descartes set out to find something which by its very nature would be impossible to doubt and by means of which the worth of other opinions might be assessed. Had Descartes been successful in his search, he would, so he thought, have provided the means to cut off the infinite regress that produces the argument about the limits of rationality —without resorting to dogmatic commitment.[26] If it were impossible in principle to ask for a justification of an adequate standard of rationality— that is, if the standard were indubitable and thus self-justifying—the relativist sceptic could be stopped.

Descartes argued that a rationalist should base all his opinions on "clear and distinct" ideas presented to the intellect; of these, the famous indubitable *cogito ergo sum* was the paradigm of such a clear and distinct idea. Such ideas would not themselves need justification because to doubt them would be absurd—to doubt, indeed, the veracity of God. Like the Protestant Martin Luther, the Roman Catholic Descartes invoked God to objectify his subjective certainty. Complementing this theory of knowledge was a theory of error. Error is produced by the will, which leads men to claim to know something before they have reduced it to clear and distinct ideas.

This conception of rationalist identity began to be eroded almost at once in the seventeenth century, not only by sceptics like Gassendi and Sorbière and Aristotelians like Voetius, but even by philosophers like Leibniz who held views similar to Descartes's. In the eighteenth century, Locke and Hume advanced further strong arguments against the approach; and finally Kant radically and conclusively undermined it. There were hundreds of difficulties in intellectualism—not the least of which was that, far from being indubitable, our intellectual intuitions are notoriously unreliable and variable. But the basic objection to all intellectualistic varieties of comprehensive rationalism was (and is) that even if they are assumed to be indubitable themselves, *they still let in too much*; they are "too wide". As

---

[26]Descartes was expressly trying to do this. See his remarks about scepticism in *Discours de la méthode*, in *Oeuvres*, ed. Adam and Tannery (Paris: Léopold Cerf, 1897–1913), vol. 6, p. 32; and *Objectiones septimae*, in *Oeuvres*, vol. 7, p. 550. On Descartes, see my "Approaches to Science and Scepticism", *Philosophical Forum*, 1 (Spring 1969), pp. 318–31.

Kant showed with his "antinomies",[27] clear and distinct ideas could lead to two contradictory theories. It would be impossible, therefore, on the basis of clear and distinct ideas alone, to decide rationally between such theories. The fact that one's beliefs had been deduced from clear and distinct ideas was a distinctly insufficient guarantee of their rationality.

The other main answer to the question of the nature of the rational authority was the empiricist notion of sense experience. Modern versions of this view, stemming primarily from the work of Bacon, Locke, and Hume, culminate in such twentieth-century movements as logical positivism. According to most empiricist views, a rationalist derives all his knowledge from sense observation, stopping the infinite regress of demands for justification not with indubitable, clear, and distinct ideas of the intellect but with sense observations (sense data) which, it is suggested, are manifestly true, "incorrigible", unable to be challenged. Here it is usually nature, rather than God, which does not deceive. Whereas for Descartes an irrationalist was one who held beliefs that could not be derived from clear and distinct ideas, for the empiricist the irrationalist is one who entertains notions and theories which cannot be derived from sense observations or who holds theories with greater conviction than the sense observations warrant.

Convincing arguments against empiricism have existed since antiquity. But the attack that has had the greatest impact on modern philosophy is that of David Hume, who in his *Treatise* and *Enquiry* gave empiricism an empiricist routing. Developing and strengthening the arguments of the ancient Pyrrhonian sceptics as recorded by Sextus Empiricus (*c.* A.D. 200)[28] and revived in the sixteenth and seventeenth centuries, Hume reluctantly came to the conclusion that inductive (or, as he thought, scientific) reasoning was an irrational procedure.

Empiricists like Hume had hoped for a rational criterion, sense experience, on whose authority it would be possible to exclude various ideas like God, demons, angels, and the like, which obviously could not be derived from sense experience and whose existence could not be proved by appealing to the intellect either. Hume's arguments, however, showed that—quite apart from the question whether sense experience, far from being indubitable, was not really rather unreliable—the empiricist criterion was inadequate; it excluded not only belief in God and the angels but also belief in scientific laws, memory, and other people. None of these could be reduced to sense experience; empiricism in effect reduced to *solipsism*—that

---

[27]Anticipated in part, incidentally, by several other philosophers, including the American colonial theologian Jonathan Edwards. See "The Insufficiency of Reason as a Substitute for Revelation", chap. 7 of his *Miscellaneous Observations on Important Theological Subjects*; this chapter is reprinted in *The Development of American Philosophy*, ed. Muelder and Sears (Cambridge, Mass.: Houghton Mifflin Company, 1940), pp. 29–36.

[28]See esp. *Outlines of Pyrrhonism*, book 2, chap. 4. For a historical account of the sceptical argument, see R. H. Popkin, *The History of Scepticism from Erasmus to Spinoza* and *The High Road to Pyrrhonism*.

is, to one variety of the radical subjectivism of what I have called life in the mirror cage. Since it is unconvincing to say that it is irrational to believe that other people exist and have minds, empiricism also had evidently failed to provide an adequate characterization of the rationalist. Whereas the main fault of intellectualism had been to include too much, to ascribe rationality to untenable views, the main fault of empiricism was to exclude too much, to exclude obviously tenable views as irrational. It was, therefore, too narrow for the purpose at hand.[29]

Whereas empiricism had gained much of its influence and support because of its claim to provide an unimpeachable rational authority to counter tyrannical irrational authority such as that of the Roman Catholic church, submission to this so-called rational authority, sense experience, became for the post-Humean empiricists an irrational procedure too. And if scientific activity thus rested on illogical psychological habit, who could offer a convincing argument against a man with different habits? As Bertrand Russell put it, more strongly, if there were no answer to Hume's argument, there would be "no intellectual difference between sanity and insanity".[30]

In the years immediately following Hume's attack, and indeed throughout the nineteenth century, irrationalists taunted the empiricists about their dilemmas. However, these blows were cushioned by the influence of Kant, who in 1781 began to publish his bold critiques of pure and practical reason in an attempt to synthesize intellectualism and empiricism and to provide a place for religion, too. This attempt—a sophisticated and complicated variety of panrationalism—largely dominated philosophy, and the relations between philosophy and theology, during the nineteenth century. However, the philosophies of Kant and his followers, such as Russell himself, whose own final attempt in *Human Knowledge: Its Scope and Limits* was Kantian, have now also broken down.

Worse, the various kinds of panrationalism today seem to be in far greater difficulties than most eighteenth-century philosophers anticipated. One of these difficulties is connected with a number of principles—such as the "law of causality" and "determinism", as well as "the principle of induction"— which for several hundred years have been regarded as part of the intellectual equipment of any rationalist, whether or not they have been interpreted as essential to his rationality. However, it appears that these principles not only cannot be justified rationally through sense experience; more serious still, they lead to internal difficulties and inconsistencies, and

---

[29]It was also, but less importantly, too wide, just as intellectualism was also, less importantly, too narrow. The terms "too narrow" and "too wide" are used in this sense by Popper in his "Demarcation between Science and Metaphysics", and also by Bertrand Russell in *The Problems of Philosophy* (London, 1912), p. 132.

[30]*A History of Western Philosophy* (New York: Simon and Schuster, 1945), p. 673. See also Russell's "The Limits of Empiricism", *Proceedings of the Aristotelian Society*, vol. 36 (1936), pp. 131–50, where Russell states that the principle of induction cannot itself be based on induction and that therefore its adoption marks the limits of empiricism.

in some cases patently fail even to provide solutions for the problems they were intended to solve.

Despite these formidable difficulties, panrationalism has been able to stay alive—particularly in its empiricist forms—by a number of repair measures. One important secondary reason for this tenacity is that the practical effects of the crisis of identity in rationalism have been far less serious than those of its crisis of integrity. However difficult it may be today to identify a Christian by the way he argues, it is relatively easy to spot a serious rationalist. He is typified by his fervent opposition to "woolly formulation" and pretentious pontification in philosophical matters, and his devotion to science and "the scientific attitude".

One of the medicines modern panrationalists have tried in order to immunize themselves from the complaints that brought about the death of earlier intellectualism and empiricism is particularly ingenious. To deal with the fact that many seemingly rational beliefs—like scientific laws, the principle of induction, and the belief in the existence of other minds—could not be justified by appealing to intellect or sense experience, some rationalists argued that the trouble lay in the fact that the problem of justification was stated in terms of broad concepts like "belief". Actually, they insisted, our beliefs are of many different logical types. Some of them—those which do actually say something about the world—need to be justified by appeal to, say, sense experience. But other beliefs do not *describe* but perform some other job. In pragmatist or instrumentalist varieties of panrationalism, scientific laws, memory, and other minds, along with such troublesome principles as that of determinism, become "useful instrumental beliefs". Such statements say nothing descriptive about reality, but help us get around in it. From this it follows, so it is claimed, that such things need not be justified on factual grounds (i.e., derived from sense experience), but only on such grounds as their predictive or classificatory usefulness. They are in fact tools we have invented to help simplify and organize our basic sense experiences, to derive from one set of experiences the prediction of another, perhaps to engineer our activities better. Scientific activity is a sort of "glorified plumbing", but never glorified enough to "plumb the depths". Moreover, if such notions are just tools, their internal troubles hardly matter; we can use them when they are useful and discard them for other tools when they break down.[31]

This instrumentalist view has been very influential and seems, on the face of it, to work. But when it is probed a bit, most of the old troubles of panrationalism reappear. Like the *tu quoque* argument, instrumentalism is an ultimate weapon: once the other side learns how to use it, there is no such thing as winning or losing any more.

[31]Yet another device to deal with the fact that scientific theories could not be derived from observational experiences was "inductive logic", an attempt to support scientific theories with "probability". These attempts have also foundered: Popper has shown that a scientific law has *zero* probability (*Logic of Scientific Discovery*, passim; and *Realism and the Aim of Science*, part 2).

To begin with, irrationalists were delighted to find empiricists being forced (by the inadequacies of their view) to justify instrumentally beliefs that were empirically unjustifiable—not only grand principles like causality, but even scientific theories which, in making assertions about the hidden structure of the universe as a whole, cannot be strictly justified or verified by experience. Irrationalists could take to instrumentalism as a duck takes to water since instrumentalism removed the possibility of a clash between science and any irrational commitment. The idea of intellectual instruments or *tools*, with its overtones of carpentry and plumbing, grew into the more dignified and aesthetically appealing notion of *symbols*. God, freedom, immortality, and even angels reappeared as instruments, "heuristic fictions", and then as symbols. They, too, could not be proved or justified empirically; they, too, were full of internal conflict. But who could deny that it might be *useful* to believe in God? Who could deny that such beliefs might help simplify and organize our experience, particularly if we added "moral experience" to the sense data of the empiricists?

The dangerous opening to irrationalism which instrumentalism allowed can be seen in some of the classic statements of the pragmatist-instrumentalist position which appear in William James's famous essays, "The Sentiment of Rationality" (1879) and "The Will to Believe" (1896); and in his book, *The Varieties of Religious Experience* (1902). The first essay contains a penetrating and largely sound polemic on some views W. K. Clifford developed in his *Ethics of Belief,* a famous nineteenth-century statement of panrationalism which is still influential today.[32] Himself a scientist and a kind of empiricist, James demanded that philosophers honestly admit that men cannot help going beyond the evidence; that they require beliefs for which they can provide no justification in sense experience. He went on to state that men have a right to choose as they wish—that is, on "non-intellectual grounds"—whenever they have a genuine option, i.e., when it is impossible to avoid making a choice, and when the opinion they prefer is not ruled out either by logical grounds or sense observations.

From the pragmatist philosopher William James to neo-orthodox theologians like Tillich and Niebuhr, such arguments have not changed much basically. In some respects they have grown more refined; and terminology and details have altered. In particular, the idea of "symbol"—especially when linked with either Adlerian or Jungian psychologies—has taken on a somewhat more substantial form.[33]

---

[32]For example, J. Bronowski uses and endorses Clifford's views in the last section of his *Science and Human Values* (New York: Julian Messner, 1956), pp. 84 ff.

[33]Adler appropriated the instrumentalist idea of the "heuristic fiction" from Hans Vaihinger's *The Philosophy of 'As If'* (London: Routledge & Kegan Paul, 1924). Tillich and Niebuhr have both been deeply influenced by Jung as well as by Freud. The tendency of the argument here should not be misunderstood. Undeniably, standards, criteria, categories, and so on do have a history of their own which is affected by factors that are not purely cognitive. What I wish to combat is the leap from the fact of such revision and change to the advocacy of relativism. Noncognitively motivated revision does not in itself imply relativism.

Another unintended consequence of pragmatism and instrumentalism is the opening they allow for the contention that many of the opinions men hold can not only be correlated with but can be reduced to arbitrary irrational factors like environment, social class, religion, financial position, geographical location, nationality, historical period. For example, the Marxist position, according to which an ideology is the instrument or tool of an economic class, a function of the material conditions of life, links beautifully with the instrumentalist stance. Who could deny rationally that some of these commitments might not be due to the intervening action of Barth's God?

So the retreat into instrumentalism, far from resolving the crisis of integrity in rationalism, seems to have backfired, to have furthered the *irrationalist* cause. And the *tu quoque,* incidentally, crops up all over again: the decision to use one set of instruments rather than another is said to be arbitrary—either historically determined or subjective; so the defensive stratagems are not successful in preventing the problem from rearising.

Faced by such objections, a recalcitrant panrationalist might shrug his shoulders and admit that perhaps he had not yet put forward an adequate characterization of rationalism or a standard by which all rational beliefs could be justified and all irrational beliefs excluded. But this, he might aver, indicates no more than a temporary lack of success; eventually, panrationalism would triumph.

Any such optimism about the future of panrationalism is quite misguided. For it can be shown that panrationalism is unattainable *in principle.* Let us for a moment return to the two requirements for a panrationalist cited above. These are: (1) that any position which can be justified or established by rational argument is to be accepted; and (2) that *only* positions which can be justified or established by rational argument are to be accepted. The panrationalist accepts anything that can be rationally justified, and also is ready to justify rationally anything that he accepts.

Arguments undermining panrationalism logically existed long before Descartes or the empiricists composed their theories. But it took the practical breakdown of intellectualist and empiricist forms of panrationalism to bring home to most philosophers the fact that arguments showing that their position was theoretically impossible were not simply intellectual cheats.

There are many ways to demonstrate that panrationalism is not attainable. I shall begin by showing that the two requirements cannot be held simultaneously: if we take the second requirement seriously, then we must try to justify the first requirement. But this cannot be done. First, the requirement is not in fact justifiable by sense experience, by intellectual intuition of clear and distinct ideas, or by any other rational authority ever proposed. Second, any such justification of the practice of accepting the results of argument, even if it could *per impossibile* be carried out, would be pointless unless it were already accepted that a justification should be accepted at least here—which is just what is in part at issue. The argument would be generally convincing only to those persons who had *already adopted* the belief that arguments should count. To put the point in a stronger form: it is pointless to try to prove something to a person who does not accept that proofs should be accepted.[34] So it is in fact impossible to quell doubts about the principle by justifying it through argument. It seems that an argument in favor of this requirement, in order to be effective, would presuppose a commitment to argument. Tillich's statement, quoted above, seems to be relevant: "That which is meant in the act of faith cannot be approached in any other way than through an act of faith."

But if the rationality of the first requirement cannot be justified either theoretically or practically through argument, then one cannot after all maintain *both* the first and second requirements. For the second requirement forbids the holding of any unjustifiable principles. On the assumption that we must then choose between the two requirements, the question becomes which to reject.

Now there are several good reasons for rejecting the second requirement rather than the first. Since we are searching for an adequate rationalist identity, we shall hardly want to abandon the demand that the rationalist

---

[34]The common philosophical arguments to the effect that you cannot persuade a person to be moral unless he is moral, or persuade someone to be logical with logical arguments unless he accepts logic, etc., are clumsy applications of the more general and approximately correct point that you cannot argue an individual into a position, including the position of listening to argument, unless he or she has accepted that argument counts. If both morality and immorality are arguable positions, then you can argue someone into either *if* he accepts that argument counts. For examples of this sort of reasoning, see Plato's question (*Meno* and *Protagoras*) whether virtue can be taught; also Aristotle's *Nichomachean Ethics*, book 1, sec. 4, and book 2, sec. 9; F. H. Bradley, "Why Should I Be Moral?", in *Ethical Studies*, Essay 2, 2d ed. (Oxford: Oxford University Press, 1927); H. A. Prichard, "Does Moral Philosophy Rest on a Mistake?" in *Mind*, N.S. 21 (1912), and *Moral Obligation* (Oxford: Oxford University Press, 1949); A. I. Melden, "On the Nature and Problems of Ethics", in Melden, *Ethical Theories*, and Karl Popper, *The Open Society*, chap. 24. See also footnote 60 below.

Even the statement that one cannot argue a man into a position unless he has accepted that argument counts, however, is unsatisfactory. It is a bit verbal; and it is more concerned with the question of the *source* of the decision to adopt a particular position or way of life than with the more important question whether that decision and position are open to criticism. (And such questions of source blend all too readily into justificationist arguments.) Thus when one is concerned with the question whether a decision is criticizable, it hardly matters whether that decision was originally made as a result of argument, whether the individual concerned just stumbled into it, or whether he or she decided by tossing yarrow stalks or by some other arbitrary method. Most important, even if the rationalist position had originally been adopted as a result of an irrational arbitrary decision, it is possible that the person who made the choice would, by living in accordance with rationalist traditions and precepts, gradually become very rational, open to criticism *as an unintended consequence* of his original choice. (See in this connection my "Ein schwieriger Mensch: Eine Porträtskizze von Sir Karl Popper", in Eckhard Nordhofen, ed. *Philosophen des 20. Jahrhunderts in Portraits* (Königstein: Athenäum Verlag, 1980), esp. p. 59. See also the "Introduction to the Second English Edition, 1984" in the present book, sec. 1, above. Important choices, such as those of philosophical positions and ways of life—are often not the result of argument, any more than scientific theories are the result of sense observation. Theories are put forward; choices are made. The question of the sources of the theories and choices is not so important. The question, rather, is whether such theories and choices are open to criticism. If they are, then they are *held* rationally, even if they were not originally *made* rationally as, for instance, the result or conclusion of an argument.

accept any position that can be rationally justified. Moreover, the second requirement can be shown by argument to be self-contradictory. (To be sure, had we rejected the first requirement instead, this contradiction need not have bothered us: for if we are not obliged to accept the conclusions of argument, we are not obliged to accept that the second requirement is self-contradictory or that it should therefore be rejected.) The second requirement is self-contradictory because it, too, cannot itself be justified by requirement is self-contradictory because it, too, cannot itself be justified by appeal to the rational criteria or authorities. *Therefore, if it is true, it must, by its own directions, be rejected. It asserts its own untenability.*

Hence, if these arguments are sound, the second requirement is logically impossible and rationally impermissible. And since it is responsible for the comprehensive character of this theory of rationalist identity, it appears that a panrationalist not only does not *happen* to exist, but is a logical impossibility.[35]

Such a collapse of panrationalism obviously seems to strengthen the position of the subjective dogmatists, and to make the position of the rationalists who seek to escape irrational dogmatism appear even more futile. In the seventeenth century, when Protestants claimed rational support for their views, Catholic counter reformers taunted them with similar arguments about the limits of rationality. Now that Protestantism has broken with rationalism, it has taken up these once-resented weapons and turned them on its former ally. If the so-called rationalist not only cannot justify his own presuppositions rationally, if his position is basically self-contradictory, why should a Protestant worry if *his* beliefs seem irrational and unable to be justified? He is actually better off than the rationalist, since he did not claim to be able to justify them; and thereby he at least preserves his integrity. Some men believe in reason, some in inspiration, dictators, intuition, prophets, medicine men, fortunetellers, gypsies, or the Word of God. World and man are "relativized",[36] subjectivity is complete; relativist existentialism is the order of the day. Make a free decision; commit yourself to the oracle you like or obey the oracle that has chosen you. There are, it has seemed, many "true" ways to see the world; you needn't even "pay your money to take your choice".

While the crisis of rationalism engendered by the collapse of pan-

---

[35]Some of the components of my argument here are taken from Popper, *Open Society*, chap. 24, p. 416, and passim. Popper's formulation, which shows that the position, by asserting its own falsity, is self-contradictory in a way analogous to the original (strictly speaking, nonparadoxical) statement of the "liar paradox", seems to be an important improvement on previous attempts to refute panrationalism. Panrationalism of the sort that I have discussed here was identified by Popper in *The Open Society*, where it is referred to as "uncritical or comprehensive rationalism", and further criticisms of it are to be found there. See also Hayek's discussion of "naive" or "constructivist" rationalism in his "Kinds of Rationalism", chap. 5 of *Studies in Philosophy, Politics, and Economics* (Chicago: University of Chicago Press, 1967), pp. 82–95.

[36]See the passage from Karl Heim in Leibrecht, p. 194, which I used as an epigraph for this chapter. See also Heim's book *Christian Faith and Natural Science* (New York: Harper & Brothers, 1953).

rationalism remains unresolved, all would-be rationalists who are aware of their tradition will be pitched into a perpetual crisis of integrity, a perpetual *crise pyrrhonienne*.[37] For whenever a rationalist accuses another of irrationalism, the irrationalist can reply that what is impossible cannot be morally demanded, and that the sort of panrationalism which the rationalist demands is, *rationally speaking*, impossible.

As Santayana put it, in such a situation the "moment is rather ill chosen for prophesying the extinction of a deep-rooted system of religion because your own studies make it seem to you incredible; especially if you hold a theory of knowledge that regards all opinions as arbitrary postulates, which it may become convenient to abandon at any moment".[38] The panrationalists deified Reason, "and all she gave . . . in return was doubt, insecurity, self-contempt, insoluble contradictions".[39]

5. Critical Rationalism—Its Advantages and Defects

Although these difficulties have battered rationalists severely, they have driven comparatively few of them into outright irrationalism. Rather, rationalists have sought some way to minimize the importance of their critics' arguments while acknowledging their cogency; to make their critics' *victory* "bloodless" or even "fictitious", as A. J. Ayer puts it. After admitting that their own position contained the germs of irrationalism, they have taken businesslike steps to immunize themselves from further contagion and to prevent the disease from spreading.

A few have pushed the minimizing to extremes and dismissed the *tu quoque* argument, along with the internal difficulties of panrationalism, as sophistical cheats rooted in unserious "pseudo-problems". Others have blamed the troubles on overly abstract theory that was of little if any relevance to the more important problem of the practical limitations of rationality. Occasionally, such attitudes may be appropriate. Where the limits of rationality are at issue, however, they sponsor ostrich policies; for in this debate theory is much more important than practice. If a thoroughly open mind were just *practically* impossible—and few would deny that—one might still legitimately urge people to try to keep their minds as open as possible. But if a *closed* mind is *theoretically necesssary,* such exhortations lose their point. Not to mention their persuasive force.

Here I shall be concerned not with those who dismiss the difficulties but

---

[37]And to be sure, many would-be comprehensive rationalists, such as Alfred North Whitehead, capitulated to irrationalism after the disillusionment of realizing that panrationalism was impossible. See Popper, *Open Society,* chap. 24.

[38]Santayana, *Winds of Doctrine,* p. 40.

[39]Isaiah Berlin, in his Hermon Ould Memorial Lecture, "Tolstoy and Enlightenment", as reported in the *Times Literary Supplement,* November 25, 1960, p. 759.

rather with some philosophers who have been sufficiently concerned about them to attempt new theories of rationality to replace panrationalism. One of the most interesting and important of these responses to the rationalist crisis might be called *critical rationalism*. Since adherents of this view differ widely among themselves on fundamental philosophical issues, I shall use the name—which I take from Karl Popper, who uses it to describe his own position—merely to refer to several points on which they generally agree: (1) They concede that rationality *is* limited in the sense that some matters, such as the principles and standards of rationality, cannot be justified. The point of calling this a *critical* rationalism is indeed that its adherents begin with this acknowledgment. Critical rationalism is thus in the tradition of what Henry David Aiken calls "a tradition to end all traditions, which is committed, at bottom, only to the principle of reasonableness itself, the principle, that is, that a reason may be properly requested for any proposition whatever".[40] As Morton White, a philosopher who has taken this problem very seriously, concludes: "There is no rock which can serve as a fulcrum on which . . . claims . . . can be weighed in some absolutely decisive way. The notion that there is such a rock is one of the great chimeras of western thought."[41] (2) They claim that this concession is unimportant, or at least not important enough to give any consolation to irrationalism. (3) If challenged, they tend to ground or justify their rationalist position in personal or social commitment to standards which are beyond challenge.

Whatever its faults, this position does possess one obvious advantage: its honesty about justification. By dropping the comprehensive claim that all legitimate positions must be rationally justifiable and by candidly admitting his supposed limitations, the critical rationalist saves himself, at least provisionally, from a crisis of integrity—from either claiming to be able to do more than he honestly can or demanding impossible performances from others. Therein, indeed, lies his claim to be critical.

Sir Alfred Ayer is one of the best-known proponents of such a viewpoint. Ayer began his career with a panrationalist positivism of sense experience, as published in his *Language, Truth and Logic* (1936). But by the mid-fifties he began to develop a variety of critical rationalism, as may be found in his book *The Problem of Knowledge* (1956).[42] Along with Morton White's *Toward Reunion in Philosophy*,[43] published in the same year, Ayer's argument provides a perceptive development of the general approach—and one which is lucid enough to make the implications of the position clear. Ayer's account has the added merit of being explicitly devoted to consider

[40]Henry David Aiken, *Age of Ideology* (New York: Mentor Books, 1956), p. 272.

[41]White, *Religion, Politics and the Higher Learning* (Cambridge, Mass.: Harvard University Press, 1959), p. 48.

[42]Ayer, *Language, Truth and Logic* (New York: Dover Publications, 1946), and *The Problem of Knowledge* (Baltimore: Penguin Books, 1956).

[43]Morton White, *Toward Reunion in Philosophy* (Cambridge, Mass.: Harvard University Press, 1956).

ing and answering the sceptic's claims. Like White, Ayer states flatly that it is impossible to provide a rational justification for basic philosophical standards, principles, procedures. It is impossible to give a proof "that what we regard as rational procedure really is so; that our conception of what constitutes good evidence is right". His strategy is to minimize the importance of the sceptical arguments against panrationalism while granting their cogency, to make the sceptic's *victory* "bloodless".

By his concession, Ayer seems at first to avoid claiming the ability to do more than he logically can. Yet simply to *discard* the demand that the standards of rationality be justified hardly suffices. Ayer must proceed to show how his approach, *as a theory of rationality,* can *afford* to dispense with the requirement that standards be justified. Initially, he seems alert to the scope of his task. He writes of the importance of showing "in a way that satisfactorily disposes of the sceptic's disproof", that the procedures "which sustain our claim to knowledge . . . do not *require* a proof of their legitimacy" (p. 74).

Yet Ayer fails to show anything of the sort. Why, on his account, do our standards of rationality not need rational justification? Simply because any such standard "could be irrational only if there were a standard of rationality which it failed to meet; whereas *in fact* it goes to set the standard: arguments are judged to be rational or irrational by reference to it" (p. 75). "When it is understood", he explains, "that there logically could be no court of superior jurisdiction, it hardly seems troubling that inductive reasoning should be left, as it were, to act as judge in its own cause. The sceptic's merit is that he forces us to see that this must be so" (p. 75). "Since there can be no proof that what we take to be good evidence really is so", then "it is not sensible to demand one" (p. 81).

Such a position, even if assumed to be coherent, fails as a theory of rationality. The nub of the attack on panrationalism was not simply that panrationalism is impossible, but that *since* it is impossible, the choice among competing ultimate positions is arbitrary. A theory of rationality that begins by admitting the unjustifiability of standards of rationality must go on to show that aribtrary irrationalism can be escaped *without* panrationalism. Thus Ayer's discussion begs the question and is itself a variety of fideism—and hence no answer to it.

Consider his argument more closely. He contends that our standards of rationality (in his case including scientific "induction") enjoy an immunity from the demand for justification since it would be impossible to judge them to be irrational. *For they set the standards on which any such judgment of their own irrationality would have to be based.* Now, an argument such as this could not be relevant, let alone valid, unless some particular standards and procedures of rationality, such as Ayer's own, *are assumed to be correct*

If some particular standards of rationality *are* correct, then there can exist no other rational standards which are also correct but which can nevertheless invalidate the former as irrational. This "if" marks a crucial assumption: *this is precisely what is at issue.*[44] Criticisms of putative standards of rationality have always questioned *whether* they were correct. Alternative conceptions of scientific method, such as Popper's, which deny the *existence* of inductive procedure, let alone its legitimacy, do claim that there are standards of rationality which positions such as Ayer's fail to meet.

Not surprisingly, a position that begs the question in this way turns out to be fideistic itself. Indeed, the "ultimate irrational commitment" of the fideist might alernatively be described as a self-conscious, deliberate begging of the question. The main doubt about whether Ayer's position is fideistic would be whether in this case the question begging is conscious and deliberate.[45]

Ayer's position is fideistic in other respects. Apart from suggesting that any critic's demands would not be sensible, Ayer says rather little about how an unjustifiable rationalist position might be defended against a critic— whether a fellow philosopher-critic or the most hyperbolical irrationalist— who simply does not "understand" why logically there can be no court of superior jurisdiction to arbitrate among standards like the principle of induction whose rationality he does not in fact accept.

On this point Morton White has been more explicit. White has made it clear that he shares Ayer's general position. In the course of a review of *The Problem of Knowledge,* White warmly endorsed Ayer's book and discussed some of its similarities to various philosophical movements in America, particularly pragmatism and its successors. When we want to defend something like "the general practice of basing our knowledge claims on experience", White suggests, "we can do no more than appeal to the

---

[44]Such question-begging approaches may be infectious. See Ed Helbig, "A Model of Rationality", in *Philosophic Research and Analysis*, vol. 7, no. 4 (1978), pp. 18–19. Helbig hopes to "alter the course of epistemology by proposing that *rationality* be understood as a device for judging the justification-status of statements". He contends: "it would be useless to require that a model of rationality be justified, except to the extent that it must meet its own requirements. To justify a statement is to submit it to a model of rationality and to have that model pronounce it justified. *To ask that the model itself be justified is to ask either that the model pronounce itself justified (which is legitimate)* or that the model be submitted to another model—and this presumably to another—*ad infinitum*, and that is useless." My italics.

[45]The sort of argument Ayer constructs here is rather extraordinary, and it is interesting to notice how widespread and persistent this tangled kind of thinking is. The *typical* response of critics who have considered my argument against Ayer has been to agree that Ayer is begging the question, and then to go on immediately to make *exactly the same mistake*, to beg exactly the same question themselves. Anthony O'Hear does this in his *Karl Popper* (London: Routledge and Kegan Paul, 1980), pp. 147–53, as Roger Trigg does in *Reason and Commitment* (Cambridge: Cambridge University Press, 1973), pp. 146. Trigg agrees that Ayer begs the question, and then argues that it is wrong, odd, and incoherent to think—as he appears to believe I think—that a commitment made outside the scope of rationality is irrational, for "It could not be at variance with what is rational, when rationality does not extend that far" (p. 150). Trigg also maintains, contrary to what I say repeatedly in this book, that I take it for granted "that one must be able to justify a position, but this could clearly only be so if it is logically possible that a justification be forthcoming. If it is not, there can be no shame in not being able to give one" (p. 150). Even Trigg's words echo Ayer's: "Since there can be no proof that what we take to be good evidence really is so", then "it is not sensible to demand one" (*The Problem of Knowledge*, p. 81).

accepted code for the transmissibility of the right to be sure . . . to the accepted way of speaking".[46] To test the adequacy of his analyses, the philosopher can do no more than check them "against the moral convictions which he and others share".[47] Consequently, the rationalist position, unable to be rationally based or justified, is finally based on irrational moral commitment. And the choice of this commitment is throughout dominated by *conservative* attitudes toward the best-entrenched standards already accepted by one's own philosophical community—indeed, just as conservative as those of the sixteenth- or seventeenth-century fideists who argue on similar grounds for adherence to the Church of Rome. How apt then, and how ironic, that in a different connection, in *Toward Reunion in Philosophy*, White should express his general preference for Erasmus rather than Luther. He writes:

> Sometimes . . . the sanitation [i.e., removal of intellectual "refuse"] can be carried on with crusading enthusiasm, with a sense of deep antipathy to a philosophy which one opposes on every major issue, and which one would like to see extirpated. But at other times criticism can be conducted in the spirit of Erasmus rather than Luther, by one who admires a philosophical framework so much that he wishes to cleanse it of its short-comings rather than demolish it. Much of the negative part of this book is intended in the second spirit, since I believe that the analytic, the empiricist, and the pragmatic movements . . . have been the most important and enlightening tendencies in twentieth-century philosophy.[48]

How, it might be asked, can one tell when to adopt the spirit of Erasmus and when that of Luther? If the final appeal is to the code and convictions of one's colleagues, and if the view under consideration is one shared with them—indeed, admired by them—then are the cards not stacked in favor of Erasmus? If White had lived during the Reformation and had practiced then

---

[46]Morton White, *Religion, Politics and the Higher Learning*, p. 47.

[47]Ibid., p. 8. This elitism with regard to one's own views and those of other expert professionals is complemented by an authoritarian attitude with regard to the remainder of the populace. The authoritarian, elitist tenor of the dominant community of contemporary philosophers is reflected everywhere in its publications. As one example, there is "Justification and the Psychology of Human Reasoning", published in *Philosophy of Science*, the organ of the Philosophy of Science Association. Its authors counsel that there is a higher court of appeal than an individual's own "reflective equilibrium". Namely, it is that of his "cognitive betters". "There are", these authors write,

> people in our subject's society who are recognized as *authorities* on one or another sort of inference. . . . He need only seek out the experts and ask them. The role of experts and authorities in our cognitive lives has been all but ignored by modern epistemologists. Yet it is a hallmark of an educated and reflective person that he recognizes, consults and defers to authority on a wide range of topics. . . . one of the principal effects of education is to socialize people to defer to cognitive authorities. . . . Deference to authority is not merely the habitual practice of educated people, it is, generally, the right thing to do, from a normative point of view".

See Stephen P. Stich and Richard E. Nisbett, "Justification and Psychology of Human Reasoning", *Philosophy of Science*, vol. 47 (1980), pp. 188–202. Harold I. Brown's *Perception, Theory and Commitment: The New Philosophy of Science* (Chicago: Precedent, 1977) conforms to this authoritarian, expert-oriented, deferential mood. Thus Brown argues for a relativistic conception of scientific truth according to which the truth of a scientific theory reflects or is a projection of the consensus of the scientific community, and a theory is false when it is rejected by that community; and if the scientific community has made no commitment, then the theory is neither true nor false.

[48]Morton White, *Toward Reunion in Philosophy*.

the method he advocates in the twentieth century, would he not, like Erasmus, have remained within the fold of the Roman Catholic church, fully critical of its shortcomings, but admiring its framework too much to want to see it extirpated? One further remark brings out even more clearly the fideistic character of positions like Ayer's and White's. However radically their substantive positions may differ, from a structural standpoint the positions of arch rationalists and anti-theologians like Ayer and White are closely parallel not only, as might be expected, to fideistic positions like contemporary Oxford theology, but also to that of the arch theologian and belligerently fideistic irrationalist, Karl Barth. To appreciate this parallel, note that, as an alternative to *justifying* rational standards, Ayer sees the task of the philosopher as that of *describing* them. (This would be an important task if critical judgments are to be made by reference to *accepted* procedures of rationality. Accurate descriptions of accepted procedures would then be needed.) For Ayer, the business of the philosopher becomes to analyze, and state as principles, the patterns of accepted ways of thinking and speaking. White agreed with Ayer that the business of the philosophically minded person is to analyze and to express in principles the patterns of the accepted way of speaking or reasoning.[49]

Following the same *pattern* of argumentation, Barth had maintained that although the content of the "Word of God" might be expounded or described, it is unnecessary for the theologian to apologize for it, to justify it before sceptical criticism. To do so is not only logically impossible, but unnecessary and irreverent for anyone who is committed. There can be no assessment of the Word of God or of the Christian's ultimate commitment to it *since* the Word of God is the standard or criterion which any such assessment would have to use.[50]

Ayer did not put the point much differently: "Inductive reasoning should be left, as it were, to act as judge in its own cause" (p. 75). In Ayer's case, as in Barth's, when we confront that to which commitment has been made, "it is we who are being judged".

The shift made by Ayer from panrationalism to critical rationalism can even be described in traditional theological terminology. Both Ayer and the Christian fideists abandon *apologetics* (in theology the procedure which gives rational justification for commitment) and replace it with *kerygmatics* (which is devoted to the exposition and description of the fundamental message). Unable to justify his basic position, the logical empiricist, just like

---

[49]For an illustration of some of the difficulties involved in describing these so-called principles, see Nelson Goodman, *Fact, Fiction, and Forecast* (Cambridge, Mass.: Harvard University Press, 1955). See also Ayer's comments on such difficulties in *Problem of Knowledge*, p. 31. See my "Goodman's Paradox: A Simple-Minded Solution", in *Philosophical Studies*, December 1968, pp. 85–88.

[50]Barth, *Evangelical Theology* (New York: Holt, Rinehart and Winston, 1963), p. 131. The italics are Barth's. See my discussions of Barth in "Karl Barth: 'The Last of the Protestants' ", *Encounter*, March 1970; and my *Morality and Religion* (London: Macmillan, 1971), chap. 3.

the neo-orthodox theologian, begins to describe the position, to preach it
without regard to the critical situation within which it is being considered.
without regard to the critical situation within which it is being considered.
As these basic similarities in their positions indicate, Ayer and like-minded
rationalist philosophers beg the main question as flagrantly as do Barth and
those who may share his commitments. While Barth begs the question of
the existence and righteousness of God and his Word, Ayer begs the question of the existence and legitimacy of induction. Ayer's position bars in
advance criticism of his fundamental standards by laying down a "persuasive definition" of "rational" in terms of which his own standards *are*
so.[51]

Presented with such a defensive definition, a critic may refuse to be
persuaded by its title and ask whether, if what is being suggested is "being
rational", it is right to be rational. He might also ask whether someone with
a genuine concern to criticize and test his standards should not—instead of
comparing them with the "accepted code" and the convictions of the group
of which he is a member—seriously explore the views of those who are
convinced the code is wrong but who may, for all that, be able to defend
their ideas, and perhaps even be right.

Thus Ayer's position, his critical rationalism, like thousands of similar
stands taken by contemporary philosophers, is hardly a satisfactory theory
of rationality. To be satisfactory, a theory of rationality which, like Ayer's,
began with the admission that the standards of rationality were unjustifiable, would have to go on to show—without begging the question—that the
arbitrary irrationalism of scepticism and fideism could be escaped without comprehensive justification. This task Ayer's theory fails even to attempt.

A position similar to that of Ayer and White has been stated by Hilary
Putnam. After objecting (as White had also done) to the sharp demarcation
of scientific, political, and ethical ideas, Putnam addresses the problem of
ultimate justification, writing: "Circular justifications need not be totally
self-protecting nor need they be totally uninformative . . . The fact that a
justification is circular *only means that that justification has no power to
serve as a reason, unless the person to whom it is given as a reason already
has some propensity to accept the conclusion.* We do have a propensity—an
a priori propensity, if you like—to reason 'inductively', and the past success

---

[51]This last point was made (but of course not in reference to Ayer) by Herbert Feigl in a paper published over four years before Ayer's book appeared. See "Validation and Vindication: An Analysis of
the Nature and the Limits of Ethical Arguments", in *Readings in Ethical Theory*, p. 676. Feigl's article
gives a clear exposition of the problem as well as a criticism of various proposed solutions. Later, however,
he lapsed into the sort of mistake that Ayer is making. Thus, in "On the Vindication of Induction",
Philosophy of Science, April 1961, p. 212, he writes: "It is true that one important component of
the meaning of such words as 'reasonable' or 'rational' is indeed the employment of inductive procedures."

of 'induction' increases that propensity. . . . Practice is primary."[52]

To cater to a propensity—inclination or predisposition—to accept something which would, *apart from* such a predisposition, be unacceptable is, however, precisely what is meant by "to be prejudiced" or "to act as judge in one's own cause". Practice is not "primary"; *it is simply practice.* It is unclear from Putnam's discussion whether this "a priori" prejudice is also supposed to be innate. In any case, the point of rationality is to review prejudices, attachments, propensities (a priori and otherwise) and to examine and criticize them. A good reason, as opposed to a rationalization, is one that works independently of prejudice. If the problem of rationality cannot be solved, there are no good reasons; there are only rationalizations.

The approach to rationality, and the kind of critical rationalism that appears in the work of Ayer, White, and Putnam, also is to be found in Wittgenstein, and that is some token of its influence. To by-pass here the familiar problems of Wittgensteinian exegesis, I refer the reader to my discussion of that issue elsewhere.[53]

But the most important kind of critical rationalism today—one that differs importantly from those just discussed—appears in some of the early writings of Sir Karl Popper. Popper has different standards of rationality from those of Ayer, White, and Putnam. In particular, he denies the very existence, let alone the legitimacy, of "scientific induction". So there is some

---

[52]Hilary Putnam, "The 'Corroboration' of Theories", in *The Philosophy of Karl Popper*, ed. P. A. Schilpp (La Salle: Open Court, 1974), p. 239. Italics mine. Compare Putnam's "The Analytic and the Synthetic", in *Minnesota Studies for the Philosophy of Science*, ed. Herbert Feigl and Grover Maxwell (Minneapolis: University of Minnesota Press, 1962), pp. 358–97, where Putnam manages to combine circularity with an argument from authority: "Does the fact that everyone accepts a statement make it rational to go on believing it? The answer is that it *does*, if it can be *shown* that it would be reasonable to render the statement immune from revision by stipulation, *if* we were to formalize our language."

[53]See my *Wittgenstein* (New York: J. B. Lippincott Co., 1973), and the extensively revised and augmented German translation published by Matthes & Seitz, Munich, 1983). Wittgenstein's position emerges in the *Philosophical Investigations*, his "Bermerkungen über Frazers *The Golden Bough*," *Synthese*, 1967, pp. 233–45, and other writings, and is stated perhaps most clearly in *On Certainty* (Oxford: Blackwell, 1969). Wittgenstein's position is straightforwardly reported by his student Norman Malcolm in "The Groundlessness of Belief", in Stuart C. Brown, ed., *Reason and Religion* (Ithaca: Cornell University Press, 1977), pp. 143–57. Wittgenstein writes in *On Certainty*, p. 192: "Of course there is justification; but justification comes to an end." Malcolm explains that he means that hypotheses are put forth and challenged *within* a system; justification occurs within a system. We should not, however, expect that there might be some sort of rational justification of the framework itself. "The framework propositions of the system are not put to the test". It is, Malcolm explains, a conceptual requirement that inquiries stay within boundaries. By contrast to Popper, however, Malcolm explains that, on the Wittgensteinian view, one does not *decide* to accept framework propositions. Rather, "we are taught, or we absorb, the systems within which we raise doubts . . . We grow into a framework. We don't question it. We accept it trustingly. But this acceptance is not a consequence of reflection". Scientific and religious frameworks are on a par here, Malcolm stresses. As he states: ". . . the attitude toward induction is belief in the sense of 'religious' belief—that is to say, an acceptance which is not conjecture or surmise and for which there is no reason—it is a groundless acceptance. . . . Religion is a form of life . . . Science is another. Neither stands in need of justification, the one no more than the other." Malcolm says nothing of the critical examination of frameworks, and clearly believes it to be impossible—reflecting the relativity of criticism to frameworks. See my "Non-Justificationism: Popper *versus* Wittgenstein", *Proceedings of the 7th International Wittgenstein Symposium*, pp. 255-61; "A Popperian Harvest", in Paul Levinson, ed., *In Pursuit of Truth*, esp. sec. 4; and "On the Differences between Popperian and Wittgensteinian Approaches", *Proceedings of the 10th International Conference on the Unity of the Sciences*.

irony in taking Popper as an example of a critical rationalist—even though this is his own term for his position, and even though his position, like mine, arises in the course of a radical critique of panrationalism (which Popper dubs "comprehensive rationalism" and "uncritical rationalism"). Although the problem of the limits of rationality can, I think, eventually be solved only within the context of a Popperian-style fallibilism, Popper's own explicit first attempt to solve the problem is inadequate, is as fideistic as Ayer's and Putnam's, and seems to operate within a justificationist context foreign to the dominant themes of his own thought.

Popper's fideism is prominently displayed in his proposal, in *The Open Society and Its Enemies,* to adopt a "minimum concession to irrationalism".[54] He writes:

> whoever adopts the rationalist attitude does so because he has adopted, without reasoning, some proposal or decision, or belief, or habit, or behavior, which therefore in its turn must be called irrational. Whatever it may be, we can describe it as an irrational *faith in reason.* . . . the fundamental rationalist attitude is based upon an irrational decision, or upon faith in reason. Accordingly, our choice is open. We are free to choose some form of irrationalism, even some radical or comprehensive form. But we are also free to choose a critical form of rationalism, one which frankly admits its limitations, and its basis in an irrational decision (and so far, a certain priority of irrationalism).

This choice in which, as Popper says, we "bind" ourselves to reason, is for him not one between knowledge and faith, "but only between two kinds of faith. The new problem is: which is the right faith and which is the wrong faith?"[55] Now, if any adequate theory of rationality aims to escape fideism, Popper's discussion of rationality is inadequate. For it is itself obviously fideistic.

The position Popper takes in *The Open Society* is anchored in his earlier work. In his first book, *Die beiden Grundprobleme der Erkenntnistheorie* (The Two Basic Problems of the Theory of Knowledge), for instance, Popper had expressed himself similarly. Writing that "there can be very different purposes or objectives. I hold a rational decision among them to be impossible" (p. 394), Popper went on to state:

> We share with conventionalism the view that the final basis of all knowledge is to be sought in an act of free postulation, that is, in a fixing of an objective

[54]See *The Open Society and Its Enemies,* 1st, 2d, and 3d English editions, or the Princeton edition (1950), pp. 416-17. The point is repeated in "Utopia and Violence" (1948), reprinted in *Conjectures and Refutations,* p. 357. One finds a similar attitude in Sidney Hook, who writes: "To be reasonable is to be absolute about nothing except being reasonable." See his *The Paradoxes of Freedom* (Berkeley: University of California Press, 1962), p. 15.

[55]*Open Society,* 1950 Princeton edition, p. 431.

which itself cannot further be justified rationally. It is in another form Kant's idea of the primacy of practical reason.[56]

Popper happened to be admirably open and forthright about his fideism, whereas the fideistic character of Ayer's and Putnam's positions is not displayed and may not even be recognized by them. This openness does not, however, solve the problem.[57]

Such remarks as those quoted have seemed to me to be out of step with Popper's own approach. Thus in 1960 I discussed these matters with him, and suggested how the problem could be dealt with within the general framework of his own approach, in terms of my distinction between justification and criticism, to be introduced presently. In response, Popper altered the terminology of chapter 24 of *The Open Society and Its Enemies* (fourth and subsequent English editions) to mute its fideism, and introduced a polemical addendum on relativism. In *Conjectures and Refutations*, chapter 10, and in his *Realism and the Aim of Science*, part 1, section 2, he introduces my distinction between justification and criticism, and this distinction is now routinely presented as a feature of Popperian thought.[58] Despite these alterations, Popper's earlier fideistic approach has been corrected only in a patchwork manner, dropping some of the old notions, but retaining the old terminology—"critical rationalism" for instance—and the old slogans.[59] This results in a confused situation. In the next chapter, I attempt to show how the problem can after all be solved through a generalization of Popper's approach which is thoroughly in the spirit of his work but dispenses with the justificationist and fideistic remnants in his early thinking.

Whatever the problems that arise in the accounts of Ayer, Putnam, White,

[56]*Die beiden Grundprobleme der Erkenntnistheorie* (Tübingen: J.C.B. Mohr Verlag, 1979). When Popper turns deliberately to deal with the irrationalist, as in chap. 24 of *The Open Society*, he does not engage those persons who possess an argument, a "rational excuse for irrationalism". Rather, he engages those who despise reason altogether, who are willing to *shoot* those who attempt to argue with them. Whereas, the sort of irrationalist with whom I am chiefly concerned here is one who attempts to reply to arguments against irrationalism with *arguments* to show that the rationalist position is defective on its own terms and that rationalism suffers from those very defects which it ascribes to irrationalism. The second type of irrationalist is stronger and more worth debating: since a rationalist claims to be moved intellectually only by arguments, even if he is compelled by force to act physically contrary to his views, a putative argument against his rationalism is far more of a threat than is force against it.

[57]Whatever the shortcomings of Popper's account of rationality, they are not those wrongly attributed to him by Harold I. Brown, who suggests that Popper's rejection of induction and his theory of falsifiability show that he is unwilling to allow "the inferences on which rationality is based to share . . . uncertainty". In trying to show that a logical relationship sometimes obtains between fact and theory, Popper does not maintain *at all* that inferences must always be certain; quite the contrary, he emphasizes their hypothetical and criticizable character. Nor does he do anything like seeking "an algorithm which will allow us to compute when a claim has been disproven". See Brown, "On Being Rational", *American Philosophical Quarterly*, 15, no. 4 (October 1978), p. 244; and also Brown's book, *Perception, Theory and Commitment: The New Philosophy of Science*, wherein the structural innovations in Popper's thought are ignored, wherein he is characterized as a transitional figure on the way to . . . the *new* philosophy of science . . . relativism!

[58]*Realism and the Aim of Science*, vol. 1 of the *Postscript to the Logic of Scientific Discovery*.

[59]See "On Reason and the Open Society", *Encounter*, May 1972, p. 18.

Popper, and others, it might be asked whether critical rationalism might not be formulated in a different, broader way wherein these objections do not arise. For instance, the rationalist position might be characterized not by its commitment to some particular activity or set of standards, but—more broadly—in the simple commitment, itself impossible to justify by argument, that the results of argument are to be accepted no matter where the argument leads.[60] If radical argument about various rational standards were permitted within such a commitment, the objections raised against Ayer would not arise.

This conception of critical rationalism, although still unsatisfactory, is stronger than the former. Its strength stems from the fact that the *tu quoque* argument breaks down at at least one minor point when applied against it. That is, an unjustifiable commitment to accept the results of argument is not strictly parallel to the unjustifiable commitments that existentialists, Protestant theologians, or Marxists speak about.

An argument on behalf of any position—in order to be relevant and intellectually effective—presupposes in the hearer a rational attitude in respect to itself. Thus, an argument on behalf of rationalism (the practice of accepting the results of argument) presupposes in the hearer the agreement that the result of at least this argument should count. The same is true also of an argument on behalf of any *other* position, such as Marxism or one or another of the forms of Christianity. The significance of this fact is this: whereas an argument on behalf of Marxism presupposes in the listener a rationalist attitude in respect to itself, an argument on behalf of rationalism does *not* presuppose in the listener a Marxist attitude in respect to itself. What is true of Marxism holds also for other popular ultimate commitments, such as those to Christ—and, indeed, for any other commitments I know about. And to the extent that his position is not precisely parallel to these, the critical rationalist might be thought to enjoy an advantage.

The explanation of this rather trivial asymmetry is probably that the rationalist position, characterized in a broad sense as obedience to the results of argument, is logically more basic than the various other positions and ideologies. Thus, even if a commitment to argument is like the other commitments in *some* respects (in being unjustifiable, for instance), it differs from them here. Nonetheless, there remains even here the idea that the rationalist position must be justified irrationally in the subjective decision or commitment to accept argument. And this is enough to let the *tu quoque*

---

[60]Popper writes that attempts to justify the rationalist attitude presuppose the rationalist attitude. His formulation is a bit loose and might be improved as follows. First, what presupposes a rationalist attitude is not the attempt to justify it, but the attempt effectively to convince someone of it *by argument*. Second, Popper's formulation is too general. What is presupposed is a willingness on the part of the irrationalist to listen at least to *that particular argument* (on behalf of rationalism). All that is presupposed is his openness to *this* argument, not to argument in general. Of course, if this argument succeeds, then he may become open to all argument, at least in principle. See footnote 34 above for further qualifications.

back in. For it might be argued that the critical rationalist must subjectively decide to commit himself to a position that is logically more basic. To be sure, a minimum remnant of subjectivism seems hardly implausible here. The idea that a rationalist is committed to rational argument appears, on the face of it, as convincing and inescapable (whatever the differences) as the idea that a Christian is committed to Christ. Yet plausible or not, this concession to irrationalism allows the dilemma of ultimate commitment to linger on unresolved, threatening rationalist identity.

5
PANCRITICAL RATIONALISM

1. The Pattern of Failure

The failure of critical rationalism, like that of panrationalism, was foreordained by the structure of the questions it emphasized and the criticism it permitted.[1] Any theory of rationality that is to succeed where these have failed in resolving the dilemma of ultimate commitment must bring this hidden structure to light, break it, and put forward an alternative. I shall attempt to do this in this chapter. My argument revolves around two historical observations, the first of which is the following.

The Western philosophical tradition is authoritarian in structure, even in its most liberal forms. This structure has been concealed by oversimplified traditional presentations of the rise of modern philosophy as part of a *rebellion against authority.* In fact, modern philosophy is the story of the rebellion of one authority against another authority, and the clash between competing authorities. Far from repudiating the appeal to authority as such, modern philosophy has entertained only one alternative to the practice of basing opinions on traditional and perhaps *irrational* authority: namely, that of basing them on a rational *authority.*

This no doubt at first served an urgent need. Those challenging ecclesiastical and political authorities needed to be able to show that disputes could nevertheless be settled in an orderly way: that traditional political, religious, and intellectual authorities could be displaced without producing social anarchy and intellectual chaos since they would be replaced by the authority of reason. Thus arose the various schools of modern philosophy whose careers we have sketched in reviewing panrationalism. These hoped to adjudicate among competing positions by providing rational authorities to substitute for unwanted forms of traditional authority. The structure embodied in these schools has been meticulously maintained. Each successive philosophical revolution, each being a phase in the search for an adequate theory of rationality, disclosed that the previous candidate for rational authority was unsatisfactory and proposed a new, supposedly more satisfactory, rational authority. The church was to be replaced by intellectual intuition; intellectual intuition by sense experience; sense experience by a certain language system, and so on. The story is always the same: past

[1]Both panrationalism and critical rationalism arise within the polluted metacontext of justificationist philosophy of true belief. (See appendix 1.)

109

philosophical error is to be given a positive explanation by attributing it to the acceptance of a false rational authority.

This may be seen by examining the main questions asked in all these philosophies. Questions like: How do you know? How do you justify your beliefs? With what do you guarantee your opinions? *all beg authoritarian answers*—whether those answers be: the Bible, the leader, the social class, the nation, the fortuneteller, the Word of God, the intellect, or sense experience. One of the main tasks within Western philosophies has long been to extricate these supposedly infallible epistemological authorities from difficulties. For not only did they all prove fallible and questionable in themselves; even if they were assumed, *per impossible*, to be indubitable, they still turned out to be inadequate justifications or guarantees for all the positions that the rationalist wished to hold—including the rationalist position itself.

This historical observation about the structure of Western philosophy I owe to an address by Karl Popper before the British Academy in 1960.[2] His simple observation—the sort of simple observation it requires genius to make—has an almost revelatory character that throws a very different light on the history and problems of philosophy. I shall try to build on this observation, first by putting it in some philosophical context, then by explaining it, and finally by suggesting the principal outlines of my own account of rationality—pancritical rationalism—which can be erected within the new, roomier, structure which the observation makes possible.

Since the entire argument which follows—which calls for a fundamental change in traditional ways of thinking about these matters—depends on this observation, I wish to make as clear as possible what is meant by it. Perhaps what is involved can be illustrated initially in terms of the related but far more concrete case of political philosophy.

Among the most important questions of traditional political philosophy are: Who should rule? What is the supreme political authority? Both questions beg authoritarian answers, such as: the people, the proletariat, the king, or the dictator. This authoritarian character of traditional political philosophy—although also generally unrecognized—is one of the most important causes today of the so-called theoretical breakdown of traditional political theory. The liberal democratic attempt to locate political authority in the people was largely motivated by the desire to replace the irrational, arbitrary, and often absentee rule of traditional monarchs by a rational authority. Political authority, it was argued, should, rationally speaking, stem from the people because, among other reasons, they would know their

[2]"On the Sources of Knowledge and of Ignorance", *Proceedings of the British Academy*, 1960; published separately in 1961 by Oxford University Press (Henriette Hertz Trust monographs); also published as the introduction to *Conjectures and Refutations* (London: Routledge and Kegan Paul, 1963). A preliminary statement of the view appeared in his "On the Sources of Our Knowledge", *Indian Journal of Philosophy*, August 1959.

own needs best. However, as Walter Lippmann and others have argued, illustrating their cases with historical examples, a populace can also become an arbitrary and irrational political authority. And political affairs might in certain situations become so complex that the average man would not in fact be able to judge his own best interests. A ballot-box majority in such a situation might be as irrational an authority as the most arbitrary king. So democratic liberalism, by tying itself to *traditional* forms of democracy, is in danger of embracing *irrationalism* despite its intentions.

The practical problems involved in such situations are far from easy to solve. Nevertheless, the *theoretical* difficulties that have troubled Lippmann and others so much may be escaped with remarkable ease by recognizing the authoritarian character of the traditional questions and simply *changing the political question* from: Who should rule? to: How can we best arrange our political institutions so as to get rid of bad rulers when they appear, or at least restrict the amount of harm they can do?[3]

This seemingly minor change in the political question is enough to topple the authoritarian structure of political philosophy. The recognition that there is *no best kind of supreme political authority for all situations,* but that *any* authority—people, king, or dictator—may turn into a bad ruler, is implicit in the question. The change is important not only because absolute power corrupts absolutely. The ruler may simply become tired and old and lose touch with the realities that should govern the discharge of his responsibilities. Or he may, with the best of motives, become attached to an idea or ideology that thwarts his own intentions while also defeating the best interests of those he is charged with governing.

Even with this change in the traditional political question, practical political answers will not be easy to achieve. Imagination and dedication are required if men are to devise governmental institutions containing built-in mechanisms of self-criticism which will work efficiently in concrete geopolitical and economic contexts. But formulating the problem in this way reopens the door to a *rational* approach and enables one to be a political rationalist and a kind of democrat without committing one to the belief that any majority is right. And it helps explain why apparently undemocratic institutions might perhaps be unavoidable, at least at first, in some situations. If the ballot box itself is not an effective mechanism for eliminating bad leadership, even the ballox box may have to be subjected to institutional checks—which are themselves, in turn, open to check.

In his memoirs, Charles de Gaulle has described the traditional concept of sovereignty or authority as well as anyone: "a last resort designated in advance." It is hardly necessary to add that he was referring to himself. What is challenged by the proposed change of question is the whole idea that political institutions of the last resort need to be designated in advance.

[3]Popper, *The Open Society,* chap. 7.

For conditions may change, and a good last resort in one situation may be disastrous in another. The ballot box, the national assembly, or the general who lives in the country, each may prove a good locus for political authority, and each may conceivably become tyrannical or ineffectual. The problem, then, should not be how to designate in advance an infallible source of political authority, but how to take out *insurance* against the wreck of whatever flagship happens at a particular time to be handling the navigation for the fleet of state. A country that happens to possess a brilliant and humane, if rusticated, general, who is willing and able to assume leadership when needed, has a potentially valuable piece of insurance as well as a potentially dangerous explosive. But a state whose institutions are so broken down that she must rely on such chance occurrence is poorly insured indeed. Perhaps both considerations apply to the Fourth Republic; it was "the fortune of France", as de Gaulle might put it, that the one *happened,* at one point in her history, to balance the other.

What holds true for political philosophy applies perhaps even more significantly to philosophy in general. All proposed intellectual authorities have turned out to be both intrinsically fallible and epistemologically insufficient. Infallible sources of knowledge and intellectual authority appear to be as unavailable as infallible political authorities. Yet those who readily admit the unreliability of political leaders often retain their hope for and trust in manifestly unworkable intellectual authorities. Perhaps the two are connected, so that political instability encourages uncritical escapist faith in intellectual systems within which chaos can more easily be concealed.

2. A Nonjustificational Approach

The authoritarian structuring of philosophy's fundamental epistemological questions can be remedied by making a shift comparable to the one suggested for political philosophy. We may not only reject (as did the critical rationalists) the demand for rational proofs of our rational standards. We may go further, and *also* abandon the demand that everything else *except* the standards be proved or justified by appealing to the authority of the standards, or by some other means. *Nothing gets justified.* Instead of following the critical rationalists in replacing philosophical *justification* by philosophical *description,* we may urge the philosophical *criticism* of standards as the main task of the philosopher. *Nothing gets justified; everything gets criticized.* Instead of positing infallible intellectual authorities to justify and guarantee positions, one may build a philosophical program for counteracting intellectual error. One may create an ecological niche for rationality.

The philosophical questions that would have to be asked within such a program would show a striking structural change. The traditional demand for justification—the "How do you know?" question—would not legitimately arise. And if it arose in fact, the philosopher would have to reply: "I do not know; I have no guarantees."

If he wanted to be a little clearer, he might elaborate: "Some of the beliefs I hold may in fact be true; but since there are no guarantees or criteria of truth, no ways of definitely deciding, I can never know for sure whether what I believe to be true is in fact so." For such a philosopher, a different question would become important: *How can our intellectual life and institutions be arranged so as to expose our beliefs, conjectures, policies, positions, sources of ideas, traditions, and the like—whether or not they are justifiable—to maximum criticism, in order to counteract and eliminate as much intellectual error as possible?* In effect, we shall attempt to learn from our mistakes, to adapt to the unforeseen and unanticipated. Even though we may never reach definitive, authoritative, justified answers any more than we achieve total adaptation, we may learn to pose more and more probing questions. This concern could hardly clash more sharply with that of the traditional rationalist for whom the main intellectual offense was to hold an unjustifiable belief.

The shift from authoritative justification to criticism is a genuine innovation in philosophy whose importance cannot be overemphasized. Nonetheless, it might be objected immediately that there is no real shift or clash here; that the idea of criticizing competing views rationally, far from being novel, has been the main theme of modern philosophy from its outset—as I myself have stressed in the previous chapter. In this case, my so-called shift from justification to criticism would seem to be just another refrain of the song, "You must be critical", which has been in the philosophical litany from the pre-Socratics to Socrates himself, through Descartes and Kant, to Nietzsche, to the latest enthusiastic student of philosophy. Almost everybody is in favor of the critical attitude these days; it has become a rather old story. And one grows bored of paeans to criticism, however eloquent and right-minded, which never grapple with a belief that is so widespread it is taken quite uncritically for granted: that there is a fundamental theoretical limit to the role of criticism and, *ipso facto,* of rationality—as illustrated by the dilemma of ultimate commitment.[4]

So, until the dilemma of ultimate commitment is resolved, this hypotheti-

---

[4]In writing this paragraph I was thinking in part of Walter Kaufmann's *Critique of Religion and Philosophy* (New York: Harper, 1958). A brilliant and exciting book, it neglects to deal significantly with the *tu quoque* argument, and to that extent fails to treat the main defense of much contemporary religious and philosophical thought.

cal objection might continue, stress on the importance of criticism does no good; for this dilemma makes it futile for one philosopher to accuse another of being uncritical. The defendant usually can, and often does, reply that his is the point at which the limit to criticism should be drawn and that his accuser is himself uncritical in forgetting that he, too, limits its role.[5]

Although this objection is invalid, it should be taken very seriously. For in terms of the new theory of criticism to be outlined here, the notion of criticism, far from being trite, becomes one of the most unexplored, puzzling, and rewarding areas of philosophy. To show why such reactions are mistaken, I wish to bring out as clearly as possible the crucial difference between the new idea of criticism which is being advocated here and the old familiar themes of traditional critical philosophy.

This can be done in a straightforward way by asking for an explanation of our historical observation: Why has an authoritarian structure been retained—and even gone unnoticed—in modern philosophies that have been intentionally anti-authoritarian and critical in spirit? Has it perhaps been retained because it is inescapable?

These questions can be answered by a further historical observation. Namely, the task of solving the problems of rational critical arbitration among competing positions has been frustrated from the start by the fact that *in almost all traditional and modern philosophies—those that called themselves critical as well as those that did not—the idea of criticism has been fused with the idea of justification.* Since demands for justification are satisfied by the appeal to authority, the dilemma of ultimate commitment arises *in regard to criticism* within such philosophies; and authoritarianism remains inescapable. (The fusion of justification and criticism in Ayer's thought, for instance, explains why he turned to *description* when justification broke down. For criticism only appears as an *alternative* to justification after the two notions are separated.) As a group, the philosophies in which this fusion of justification and criticism occurs may be called *justificational philosophies of criticism.*

The purpose of the view proposed here is to escape this dilemma—and perhaps help make future hymns to the critical attitude worthwhile—by explicitly eliminating the notion of justification from the notion of criticism,

---

[5]Such an objection is entirely understandable. Western justificationist philosophy of true belief (see appendix 1) *does* contain many *theories* of criticism; it pays lip service to progress; it avows the critical attitude. Yet within the polluted metacontext of justificationism, criticism can function only within the limitations set down by commitments and attachments. Western justificationist philosophy does not ecologize: it does not provide a metacontext in which avowals of criticism can be effectively pursued. An embryonic fallibilist critical metacontext may, for instance, be interpreted by—and contained and stunted within—a more developed justificationist metacontext. Hitherto, fallibilism has been largely confined to the level of well-intentioned World 2 (in Popper's terminology) resolves, and has been contextualized within a justificationist World 3 institutional framework. Thus its limited success. The progress of criticism, and even the success of Western science, have hitherto occurred *in spite of* the context in which they have been couched. (For an account of Worlds 1, 2, and 3, see Popper's *Objective Knowledge* [Oxford: Oxford University Press, 1972].)

and by aiming not simply to encourage criticism and objection but to do so within the framework of a *nonjustificational philosophy of criticism.* In this lies the difference between the view advocated here and many other critical philosophies.[6] But what does it mean to talk of the fusion of justification and criticism? They have been fused in a number of different ways. One way, which is historically probably the most important, is dominant in most kinds of panrationalism. On this view, the way to criticize a view is to see whether it can be logically derived from—i.e., "justified by"—the rational criterion or authority. On an empiricist view, such as Hume's, for instance, the strongest criticism of any particular theory was that it could not be justified or established properly—in his case by an appeal to sense experience. If one examines Hume's philosophical writings, one finds him making fairly consistent use of the following basic strategy of criticism: He takes one idea after another—the idea of God, of the soul, of memory, of other minds— and asks whether it can be justified by being derived from sense experience, which he regards as man's only source of knowledge, or rational authority. If it can be justified as required, he accepts it; and if it cannot, he either rejects it or implies that at least from a rational point of view it *should* be rejected. As he writes: "When we entertain . . . any suspicion that a philosophical term is employed without any meaning or idea (as is all too frequent), we need but enquire, *from what impression is that supposed idea derived?* And if it be impossible to assign any, this will serve to confirm our suspicion."[7] Descartes's method "for conducting the reason well and for searching for truth in the sciences", however different in other respects, is closely parallel to Hume's in this. Descartes's program of reductive analysis is a form of justificational criticism, and his program of synthesis is a particular form of justification. Ideas that cannot be reduced to clear and distinct ideas, and thus rationally justified, Descartes thinks should be rejected—just as everything that is to be accepted must be so justified. For both philosophers, the rational way to criticize an idea is to see whether or not it can be rationally justified.

Another strategy of criticism which is quite popular, although both weaker in its demands and more difficult to apply than the first, also fuses justification and criticism. It is weaker than the first strategy because it employs a kind of "elastic clause" similar to that in the United States

---

[6]See, for example, Henry David Aiken, *The Age of Ideology.* Aiken's failure to distinguish explicitly the problems of justification and criticism puts much of his discussion out of focus and results in the following expression which, however well-intentioned, is less than coherent. He writes (pp. 241–42): ". . . a tradition to end all traditions, which is committed, at bottom, only to the principle of reasonableness itself, the principle, that is, that a reason may be properly requested for any proposition whatever, and that no principle is ever exempted from critique, so long, at any rate, as the latter is conducted honestly and in good faith."

[7]*Enquiry Concerning Human Understanding,* sec. 2.

Constitution. What matters is not whether a belief can be derived from the rational authority but whether it *conflicts* with it. In other words, it is not irrational to hold a belief that cannot be derived from—i.e., justified by—the rational authority unless its denial *can* be derived from the rational authority.

This strategy has been adopted not only in various intellectualist, empiricist, and pragmatist epistemologies, but also in many religious theories of authority. For instance, few theories that grant the Bible preeminence as an authoritative source of truth require that the faithful repudiate any belief that lacks biblical sanction. Beliefs not specifically endorsed or implied by the Bible—such as Newtonian theory—may be held for other reasons provided they do not conflict with views that do enjoy biblical justification. The Roman Catholic church has adopted one variant of this strategy: the authoritative preeminence of the pope applies only to matters of faith and morals.

This second strategy can be varied in many subtle ways. Indeed, a typology of theories of authority, developed in terms of the different possible moves consistent with the general strategy, would illuminate some of the particular twists taken now and then in historical controversies. Yet, all varieties I know continue to fuse justification and criticism in one way or another: to criticize a position, one must show either that it cannot be derived from, or else that it conflicts with, the rational authority, which is itself not open to criticism.

(A semantic account of justification completely in line with the position just outlined, and fusing justification and criticism, has now been reported in *The Journal of Symbolic Logic* as capturing the "intuitive concept of justification"! Thus a sentence is justified on this account if it follows deductively from justified sentences. A sentence not justified at one time may become justified later, but once justified it remains justified. The author notices how justification values assigned at present constrain future assignments. Of those sentences which are not justified at one time, some are consistent with the justified sentences and are thus weakly unjustified, whereas other sentences are inconsistent with the justified sentences and are thus strongly unjustifiable.)[8]

When combined, the two historical observations introduced in this chapter—Popper's observation that traditional philosophy is authoritarian or justificational in structure, and my observation that these philosophies have fused the ideas of justification and of criticism—suggest the conditions under which the dilemma of ultimate commitment might be resolved. In fact, three precise questions may now be posed which, if pursued in turn, lead directly to a resolution of the dilemma:

---

[8]John T. Kearns, "A Semantics Based on Justification rather than Truth" (Abstract), *Journal of Symbolic Logic*, vol. 43, no. 3 (September 1978), p. 614.

(1) Is it possible, *within* a justificational or authoritarian theory of knowledge, to resolve the dilemma of ultimate commitment? If not, the justificational character of traditional philosophies might explain why all traditional attempts to resolve it have failed.

(2) Is an alternative nonjustificational, or nonauthoritarian, approach to philosophy possible?

(3) Within a nonjustificational approach, is it possible to resolve the dilemma of ultimate commitment? If so, how might this be done?

Definite answers to these questions, even negative ones, would be of considerable value. For example, negative answers to the first two questions would show rationalists that the dilemma could not be escaped at all, and would excuse them for lapsing without further effort or complaint into some candid, if limited, form of rationalism like that of Ayer. On the other hand, positive answers to questions 2 and 3 could lead to a resolution of what I believe is the main intellectual dilemma both of theoretical philosophy and of practical moral reflection.

Previous efforts to resolve the dilemma—many of them made by men like Bertrand Russell who passionately wanted to escape intellectual and moral relativism—have not taken into account the justificational framework in which philosophy is caught. Consequently, the possibility of an alternative has not been raised and the attempts have failed.

The answer to the first question must be negative. The dilemma of ultimate commitment cannot be escaped within an authoritarian theory of knowledge. This should be abundantly clear already from the difficulties encountered by panrationalism and critical rationalism. Indeed, the only fundamental way in which the present question differs from those encountered above is in its limitation in scope to justificational philosophies—an irrelevant limitation if previous philosophies have really all been justificational. Whether that limitation can ever become relevant, or can be escaped, is the problem involved in the second question.

The answer to the second question is affirmative. An alternative nonjustificational philosophy is in fact possible.

I shall try to bring out the character of such an approach in the next two sections.

3. Pancritical Rationalism—the Tu Quoque Reconsidered

Implicit in such a nonjustificational approach are a new philosophical program and a new conception of rationalist identity. The new framework permits a rationalist to be characterized as one who is willing to entertain any position and holds *all* his positions, including his most fundamental standards, goals, and decisions, and his basic philosophical position itself, open to criticism; one who protects nothing from criticism by justifying it irrationally; one who never cuts off an argument by resorting to faith or irrational commitment to justify some belief that has been under severe critical fire; one who is committed, attached, addicted, to no position. I shall call this conception *pancritical rationalism*.

The new conception of rationalist identity shares its comprehensive aims, but not its justificationism, with the first type of rationalism. It also follows from, or is implied by, the traditional requirement. That is, a panrationalist who succeeds in justifying *all* his positions rationally clearly need not justify any of them irrationally. Nonetheless, the two requirements are not equivalent; if they were, the traditional requirement would also be implied by the new one—and that would mean that any refutation of the traditional requirement would destroy the new conception too. But in fact the new requirement does not imply the traditional one. It does not follow that a man who justifies none of his beliefs irrationally will justify them all rationally.

The last point indicates how much the new conception differs from both its predecessors. It differs from comprehensive or panrationalism in having altogether abandoned the ideal of comprehensive *rational* justification. And it also differs from critical rationalism, wherein a rationalist accepted that his position was rationally unjustifiable but went on to justify it irrationally by his personal and social moral commitment to standards and practices that were not themselves open to assessment or criticism since—as in Ayer's theory—criticism and rational justification are fused. Within a justificational approach, such a move might seem unavoidable. We cannot go on justifying our beliefs forever since the question of the correctness of the conclusion shifts back to the question of the correctness of the premises; and if the premises are never established or justified, neither is the conclusion. Since we want to justify and cannot do so *rationally*, irrational justification or commitment seems the only resort. So, if rationality lies in justification, it is severely limited by the necessity for commitment. But if rationality lies in criticism, and if we can subject everything to criticism and continued test, including the rationalist way of life itself,[9] without leading to infinite regress,

---

[9]Also including (see appendix 1) *the fallibilist metacontext.*

circularity, the need to justify, or other such difficulty, then rationality is in this sense unlimited. The pancritical rationalist does not justify at all. If all justification—rational as well as irrational—is really abandoned, there is indeed no need to justify irrationally a position that is rationally unjustifiable. The position may be held rationally without needing justification at all—*provided that it can be and is held open to criticism and survives severe examination.* The question of how well a position is justified differs utterly from the question of how criticizable it is, and how well it is criticized.

The proviso just italicized masks a potential objection. So the hypothetical critic with whose arguments we grappled in the previous section might be revived long enough to make one further sally. "Suppose", he might grant, "that you are probably right in thinking that it is *generally* possible to separate the notions of justification and criticism. But can this separation be extended to the examination of the rationalist position itself? The logical impossibility of the program of comprehensive justification could be shown quite independently of the question whether any particular 'rational standards' were justifiable. Why should the story be different for comprehensive criticism? Would it not meet some of the same difficulties as the former? Indeed, is it really possible to eliminate justification entirely from criticism?"

These questions can perhaps be pinned down in the following formulation: Under traditional conceptions of rationalism the rationalist position itself was not rational. The rationalist identity excluded rationalist integrity. Under the new conception, can a comparable crisis be avoided? Is the new rationalist position itself rational? Does it satisfy its own requirements? Can the program of following an argument where it leads and of holding everything open to severe criticism itself be held open to criticism and survive it? Does not a paradoxical situation arise in regard to the criticism of the practice of argument just as it did in regard to the justification of that practice?

Surprising as it might seem, the practice of critical argument can be criticized without contradiction or any other logical difficulty. The general separation of justification and criticism can be extended to the examination of the rationalist position itself. Under previous conceptions of rationalism, the rationalist position, being unjustifiable, was itself not rational. But pancritical rationalism satisfies its own requirements: without any contradiction or other difficulty the very practice of critical argument can be criticized.[10] Just as it is possible for a democracy, through democratic processes, to commit suicide (e.g., through a maiority vote to abolish

---

[10]Anyone who continues to insist that rationalists just *cannot* hold their basic positions open to criticism and rejection, *or cannot* be willing to contemplate adopting some sort of irrationalism, ought to explain how this view can be reconciled with my own attempt to criticize my position as severely as possible. Again, how would he explain how it happened historically that many other similarly "prejudiced" rationalists nevertheless came to be driven by rational arguments like the *tu quoque* into irrationalism? He also has a more serious task: he must produce detailed argument to show that pancritical rationalists really must be irrationally committed. Then he might find out how sincere they are.

democracy in favor of dictatorship), so a pancritical rationalist who was not *committed* to the belief that his position was the correct one could be argued, or argue himself, out of his rationalism. Continued subjection to criticism of his allegiance to rationality is explicitly *part* of his rationalism. For example, someone could devastatingly refute this kind of rationalism if he were to produce an argument showing that at least some of the unjustified and unjustifiable critical standards necessarily used by a pancritical rationalist were uncriticizable to boot, that here, too, *something* had to be accepted as uncriticizable in order to avoid circular argument and infinite regress.

Although I doubt it, such an argument may be possible. But the onus is on the critic to produce it. I have, in the meantime, done what I can. After arguing that the old difficulties in rationalist identity were due to the demand for justification, and that criticism might be had without justification, I have just now gone so far as to specify what sort of argument I would accept as a refutation of my position. Thereby, I may have helped my opponents to think of ways to attack it. I try to help them even more, in my remarks on the revisability of logic in the next section, by constructing an argument against my position that is as strong as I can make it. Although I am able to refute this particular argument, I may not be able to do the same with a similar argument in the future.[11]

Until such an argument is produced, pancritical rationalism—the position or way of life which holds everything, justifiable or not, open to criticism— can be held as an approach that is *itself* open to criticism. And if rationality is located in criticizability rather than in justifiability, this position can be held rationally. This conclusion has an important, if by now obvious, consequence:

The answer to the third question is affirmative. Within the nonjustificational, pancritical or comprehensively critical rationalism just outlined, the dilemma of ultimate commitment can be resolved and the *tu quoque* avoided. The case for arbitrary ultimate commitment rested entirely on the claim that rationality was so limited logically that such commitment was inescapable. As we have seen, there are no such logical limitations for rationality in the proposed nonjustificational critical approach.

Consequently, the *tu quoque* argument cannot be used at all against pancritical rationalism. Theologians have argued that not only to abandon allegiance to Christ, but even to subject that allegiance to criticism, is to forsake Christianity. But for a pancritical rationalist, continued subjection to criticism of his allegiance to rationality is explicitly *part* of his rationalism.

---

[11]To refute pancritical rationalism, it would not be necessary to show that it is uncriticizable. If it could be shown that justification and criticism are generally, or even largely, inseparable in principle, that would be sufficient at least to damage pancritical rationalism badly. See appendix 4.

Because of these differences, the core of arbitrary relativism and of the defense of contemporary Protestant theology as well as of other forms of thought such as existentialism—the so-called rational excuse for irrational commitment—is defeated. If a pancritical rationalist accuses his opponent of protecting some belief from criticism through irrational commitment to it, he is not open to the charge that he is similarly committed. Criticism of commitments no longer boomerangs.

To avoid serious misunderstanding of this claim, and of the position proposed, several warnings should be sounded here. *First,* the claim that a rationalist need not commit himself even to argument is no claim that he will not or should not have strong convictions on which he is prepared to act. We can assume or be *convinced* of the truth of something without being *committed* to its truth.[12] As conceived here, a rationalist can, while eschewing intellectual commitments, retain both the courage of his convictions and the courage to go on attacking his convictions—the courage to think and to go on thinking. The word "courage" is appropriate here. The submission of one's peripheral and unimportant beliefs to criticism requires no courage, but the willingness to subject to the risks of criticism the beliefs and attitudes one values most does require it.

Second, a pancritical rationalist, like other people, holds countless unexamined presuppositions and assumptions, many of which may be false. His rationality consists in his willingness to submit these to critical consideration when he discovers them or when they are pointed out to him. Charles Darwin's example is a good one here. "I had", he wrote, "during many years followed a golden rule, namely, that whenever a published fact, a new observation or thought came across me, which was opposed to my general results, to make a memorandum of it without fail and at once; for I had found by experience that such facts and thoughts were far more apt to escape from the memory than

---

[12]Since *The Retreat to Commitment* was first published, some writers on religion, accepting its argument, have maintained that Christian faith can be expressed in terms of *conviction,* as described here, rather than requiring *commitment.* See David R. Griffin, *A Process Christology* (Philadelphia: Westminster Press, 1973), pp. 154–55. For an attempt to bring Roman Catholic theology into a pancritical framework, see Reinhold Oswald Messner, "Über Möglichkeit und Wünschbarkeit eines Pankritischen Katholischen Dogmenglaubens", in *Die Philosophie und die Wissenschaften: Simon Moser zum 65. Geburtstag* (Meisenheim: Verlag Anton Hain, 1967), pp. 206–27. See also the sketch of "falsifiable theism" in John King-Farlow and William Niels Christensen, *Faith and the Life of Reason* (Boston: D. Reidel, 1972), pp. 3 ff.

On the other hand, other writers have not noticed such possibilities. Thus William H. Austin, in "Religious Commitment and the Logical Status of Doctrines", *Religious Studies,* vol. 9, pp. 39–48, states that the price of being a rationalist in my sense is too high since the rationalist "can preserve his rationalist integrity only by refraining from embarking upon any disciplined scientific inquiry. For every discipline has its assumptions, which give shape and direction to its inquiries, and to abandon them is simply to resign from the discipline". This objection is beside the point, for I do not suggest that all assumptions be *abandoned,* only that they be held open to criticism! And I allow within this (see text above) that one might be convinced of such an assumption without being committed to it.

Nietzsche says: "A very popular error: having the courage of one's convictions; rather it is a matter of having the courage for an attack on one's convictions!" Quoted in translation from Nietzsche's *Musarionausgabe* by Walter Kaufmann, *Critique of Religion and Philosophy,* p. vii.

favourable ones. Owing to this habit, very few objections were raised against my views which I had not at least noticed and attempted to answer".[13]

When one belief is subjected to criticism, many others, of course, have to be taken for granted—including those with which the criticism is being carried out. The latter are used as the basis of criticism not because they are themselves justified or beyond criticism, but because they are *unproblematical at present.*[14] These are, *in that sense alone and during that time alone,* beyond criticism.

We stop criticizing—temporarily—not when we reach uncriticizable authorities, but when we reach positions against which we can find no criticisms. If criticisms of these are raised later, the critical process then continues. This is another way of saying that there is no theoretical limit to criticizability—and to rationality. One belief that is nearly always taken for granted when one or another belief is being criticized is the belief in criticism itself. But the fact that most of a man's beliefs are beyond criticism at any one time does not mean that any of them has to be beyond criticism all the time: this is not so logically, and probably not even practically. Nor does it mean that the belief in criticism itself may not come up for critical review from time to time. Such a willingness unattachedly to hold open to revision even those positions supposed most surely to be true is part of the spirit of pancritical rationalism.

Pancritical rationalism is therefore compatible with one kind of relativism. The survival of a position is relative to its success in weathering serious criticism. And a position that survives at one time may be refuted later. This kind of relativism—which is due to the fact that we are not gods, are ignorant, lack imagination, and are pervasively fallible—is quite harmless. It is an example of how learning proceeds by trial and error—by making conjectures and trying to criticize them. The making and destroying of theories is part of, and parallel to, the evolutionary process.

One will not begin to question statements that seem to be true simply in the face of arguments that it is, say, *logically* possible that they are not! In that sense, one calls a halt to criticism. One will, however, begin to question this "halting place" when a *particular* argument is produced to challenge it—when an argument is produced that renders it *problematical.* In regard to standard sceptical arguments, all positions are *equally* problematical— equally indefensible—and equally defective because equally unjustifiable. In order to compare positions intelligently we need a theory of criticism in

[13]Charles Darwin, *Autobiography*, p. 123. See my "What Was Wrong with Darwin?", *New York Review of Books*, September 15, 1977.

[14]Our objective structure of belief will be relative to the basic critical statements we accept ("basic statements" in scientific criticism). If we were to make these basic critical statements at which we stop absolute, *then* we would get subjectivity or relativism of the vicious kind. But this we have not done. See my discussion of this problem in regard to Fries's "trilemma" in appendix 3 to this book.

terms of which positions differ in problematicality. This becomes possible once the aim of justification, which is responsible for equality of problematicality, is abandoned.

Third, it should be remembered that our problem is a logical one, and that the point being made here is logical, too. The classical problem of rationality lay in the fact that, for logical reasons, the attempt to justify everything (or to criticize everything through justification) led to infinite regress or dogmatism. But nothing in logic prevents us from holding everything open to nonjustificational criticism. To do so does not, for instance, lead to infinite regress.

There may, of course, be other nonlogical considerations which lead one to grant that it would be pointless to hold some particular view as being open to criticism. It would, for instance, be a bit silly for me to maintain that I held some statements that I might make—e.g., "I am over two years old"—open to criticism and revision.

Yet the fact that some statements are in some sense like this "beyond criticism" is irrelevant to our problems of relativism, fideism, and scepticism. I may in fact hold some such views as beyond criticism; but I do not have to do so logically: I do not have to be dogmatic about any of these matters. In holding everything open to criticism I, of course, do not deny that there are true statements and valid arguments; nor do I maintain that for every proposition there must exist some sound argument against it! Holding such statements as beyond criticism in a practical sense has nothing to do with stemming an infinite regress. What is needed for the effort to state a consistent theory of rationality is to show that it is logically possible (without leading to infinite regress, vicious circle, or other logical difficulty) to hold such statements open to criticism. When this is done, no tu quoque can be mounted.[15]

Many issues of course remain. Of these, perhaps the most important are the technological problems of what means of criticism to adopt and how to organize these means, our critical intellectual institutions, so as to achieve maximum criticism. Before turning to these matters in the next section, one further possible objection needs to be noted. It has to do not with the substance of the viewpoint I have presented but with my general method of approaching the problem. The question is whether my theory of rationalist identity is not simply a redefinition of the word "rationalist"—of the suspect sort I have criticized in theology—designed to fit my desires and prejudices while avoiding philosophical difficulties.[16]

It is not: any attempt to resolve the dilemma of ultimate commitment this

---

[15]See A. A. Derksen, "The Failure of Comprehensively Critical Rationalism", Philosophy of the Social Sciences, 1980, and my reply, "On the Criticisability of Logic", in the same issue.

[16]Wolf-Dieter Just makes this accusation—without argument or explanation—in "Kritischer Rationalismus und Theologie", Zeitschrift für Evangelische Ethik, vol. 15 (January 1971), pp. 1–19.

way could succeed only at the expense of cheapening the whole quest for an answer and of turning a serious problem into a trivial verbal question. But just how does my view differ from such cheap solutions?

When a problem like the dilemma of ultimate commitment arises and a theory is proposed to solve it, that theory may use terms taken from language and tradition which have many different connotations, some held unconsciously. And some of those connotations may prevent the theory from adequately solving the problem. In such a case, one may sometimes be lucky enough eventually to *eliminate* a troublesome connotation in such a way that the resulting theory, while perhaps still using the same word, *does* solve the *original* problem—not a weakened version of it. What has taken place, however, is not *simply* a redefinition of a word—let alone a surreptitious redefinition. The theory *itself* has been fundamentally changed by the elimination of an assumption that had been smuggled "inside" one of the terms it uses.

Similarly, in presenting pancritical rationalism, I proposed a theory of rationality that I think can satisfactorily solve the original problem in response to which self-conscious theories of rationalist identity arose within the rationalist tradition. To do this, I explicitly separated, I believe for the first time within a theory of rationality, the notions of justification and of criticism; and I rejected the false assumption, usually held unconsciously, that these two notions *must* be bound together.

It is not difficult to see how such a program differs from some diagnostic programs in philosophy which are primarily concerned with definition of words: the "linguistic analysis" of ordinary language, for example. My aim is to unburden the idea of rationality of excess and troublesome meanings; *not* to *explicate* its meaning and use as they occur in ordinary language but to *eliminate* from it an ordinary assumption about rationality which prevented the solution of the problem that accounts of rationality were intended to solve.

Two of the professors of philosophy at Cambridge University during the present century—G. E. Moore and Ludwig Wittgenstein (the latter particularly in his later period)—exerted an enormous influence on contemporary philosophy with their contentions that our intractable philosophical problems often arise because special, extraordinary, *philosophical* interpretations are superimposed misleadingly on ordinary language. We then become confused about how to describe certain situations and as a result ask rather odd questions—whether, for example, we really *know* that other people have minds. Concepts are used out of their proper context and "language goes on holiday", to use Wittgenstein's apt phrase. We may eliminate such perplexity, it is claimed, by going back over the problem and tracing by example after example how certain puzzling terms such as "knowledge" are used. We have then done all we can: we have shown how the usage of the term arose; how, in detail, it is used in varying circumstances; and in what respects the particular puzzling case before us differs from others. Thereby, we gradually "break the hold" words have on us and begin to stop stretching them. This method doubtless has a place in philosophy. Philosophical dust-throwing caused by the misuse of language does occur—perhaps even among linguistic analysts. However, in so far as the idea of rationality is concerned, the story is very different. Here the notions of justification and criticism are simply mixed. This is traditional and sanctioned by ordinary language, which is a great repository of tradition. Only by proposing something new, an *extraordinary* demarcation between these two notions, can the problem be solved. Ordinary, intuitive, traditional, and—so far as I can ascertain—*original* usage led philosophers into the dilemma of ultimate commitment. Thus, I have not defined a term or engaged in linguistic analysis of meaning. If the activity I advocate must have a name, it might be "diacritical analysis".[17]

My approach also differs from Tillich's "word healing". It is true that we both emphasize the importance of the process of elimination in conceptual analysis. That some men are no longer "at home" in the world but are estranged in it and from it, Tillich ascribes in part to their "looking at the world in the wrong way"—a state that might be cured by eliminating certain attitudes, assumptions, prejudices, and commitments which prevent their attaining to the ecstatic communion with reality whose possibility is revealed in the "New Being" of Jesus.

But whereas in Tillich's system the elimination is akin to Restoration, mine is closer to Revolution. His conviction that Revelation happened in the biblical events forces him to "heal" words like "faith" by amputating only the accretion of philosophical and psychological views that have become attached to them over the years but are no longer acceptable. Such surgery is sadly insufficient: the conceptual operations demanded for the solution of philosophical problems sometimes must be directed to *vital* parts of the *original* view. That is, not all conceptual disease in philosophy is acquired; some is congenital; and in both cases some diseases are incurable. This means that philosophical theories are sometimes beyond restoration and must die.

And even if a cure is possible, new ideas and new medicine may be required in addition to surgery. There is not only disease and rebirth in philosophy; there is also conception, creation, and new birth.

---

[17]I owe this term to a conversation with Popper, who suggests that a number of philosophical achievements of the twentieth century which prima facie resemble definitions, and which perhaps have helped encourage the fad for analysis of meaning, are in fact "diacritical analyses" in the sense described here. Examples are Russell's theory of descriptions and Tarski's theory of truth.

Later Popper used the word "dialysis" to refer to such analyses. See his *Unended Quest*, sec. 7, and also his *Realism and the Aim of Science*, vol. 1 of the *Postscript to the Logic of Scientific Discovery*, part 1, Addendum, pp. 261–78.

4. Technological Considerations: What Counts as Criticism?

Under the approach to philosophy suggested here, many technical and technological questions become central to the theory of knowledge. But I do not intend to explore these in detail now—any more than I have tried to solve in this essay the institutional problems I believe should replace much of traditional political philosophy.

The question of what critical means to use to reduce error in philosophy is, however, related to a number of current disputes. So I shall make some brief programmatic remarks that may help indicate where further attention might profitably be directed. Popper has already focused attention on one of the means—the check of empirical experience—in *The Logic of Scientific Discovery* and elsewhere. The problem of how to criticize, how to reduce error in those of our theories, such as the metaphysical ones, which are *not* subject to empirical check, has been discussed within a similar framework by Popper himself and by J.W.N. Watkins (political philosophy, ethics, and metaphysics), J.O. Wisdom (metaphysics and psychoanalysis), Joseph Agassi (nonempirical principles of interpretation in physics), and Imre Lakatos (mathematical conjecture).[18]

Since there is considerable disagreement about what sort of criticisms should apply against various theories, it might appear that we are on the verge of stepping right back into the dilemma of ultimate commitment. This does not happen, however; for when the abandonment of the old aim of *establishing* our views is taken seriously, it must be held that we cannot decisively refute theories either. For any theory will be refuted only relative to our acceptance of critical arguments that are incompatible with it. This means that we must be willing to reopen to examination and further criticism and possible rejection all the critical arguments and critical institutions we have accepted. *But within our new approach, this presents no difficulty.* Such a willingness to hold open to revision in principle even those notions that we believe most surely to be true is part of the spirit of pancritical rationalism.

All this is important with reference to theologians who claim to be in irreconcilable opposition to the presuppositions of modern rationalism. *Although theologians and rationalists appear to be in very sharp disagree-*

---

[18]See the articles by Watkins cited above. See also Popper, *Conjectures and Refutations*, esp. chap. 15; his *Realism and the Aim of Science*, esp. part 1, chaps. 1–3; and his *Quantum Theory and the Schism in Physics*, esp. chap. 4. See also Joseph Agassi, "Sensationalism," *Mind*, 1964; and "The Nature of Scientific Problems and Their Roots in Metaphysics", in Mario Bunge, ed., *The Critical Approach*; Imre Lakatos, "Infinite Regress and Foundations of Mathematics", *Proceedings of the Aristotelian Society*, Supplementary Volume, 1962, and *Proofs and Refutations*; J. O. Wisdom, "The Refutability of 'Irrefutable' Laws", *British Journal for the Philosophy of Science*, February 1963.

ment about their high-level metaphysical theories, they are in considerably closer agreement with respect to the kinds of considerations they in principle, if not always in practice, accept as proper critical institutions.

Moreover, although logic is the critical institution about which theologians differ most sharply from rationalists, I shall try to show that most theologians presuppose logic in practice *even where they deny it in principle.*

We have at least four means of eliminating error by criticizing our conjectures and speculations. These checks are listed in descending order according to their importance and the rigor with which they may be applied.

(1) The check of *logic*: Is the theory in question consistent?

(2) The check of *sense observation*: Is the theory *empirically* refutable by some sense observation? And if it is, do we know of any refutation of it?

(3) The check of *scientific theory*: Is the theory, whether or not it is in conflict with sense observation, in conflict with any scientific hypotheses?

(4) The check of the *problem*: What problem is the theory intended to solve? Does it do so successfully?

Almost all prominent Protestant theologians today accept the second consideration: they have by now abandoned those traditional theological theories that are actually contradicted by sense observation.

A smaller, yet still large, majority of theologians accept the third consideration: they are willing to abandon any theories that conflict with well-tested scientific hypotheses. The ambivalent attitude that occasionally appears here stems from the widespread acceptance of an instrumentalist view of science, and the possibility it opens for a theologian to hold a belief that contradicts a scientific *theory* without at the same time contradicting any statements about empirical observation. Moreover, since no scientific theory can ever be fully verified by experience—the best we can do is to *test* scientific hypotheses—a genuine possibility remains *forever* open, even on a realist view of scientific theories, that any particular hypothesis may be refuted by experience. Thus, when a theological statement conflicts with a scientific theory, the theological statement *could* in principle be correct.

About the fourth critical consideration—what I have called the check of the problem—there is considerable controversy among Protestant theologians, although I expect that at least a bare majority accept it, too. Those who side with Barth, however, while not denying that their Revelation helps solve human problems, claim that the Word of God, being a Revelation of God, *need not* do so: it is *thrown* at man, like a stone, not fitted on him like a suit of clothes. Those influenced more by Niebuhr and Tillich take a contrary view, arguing that the Revelation is revelatory in respect to certain permanent human problems.

I agree with the followers of Tillich in believing that ideas must be evaluated in terms of their capacity to solve problems. This is true not only of theological ideas but even of scientific theories: these, too, can be judged only by reference to a definite problem situation. Whether or not a theory is scientific, and whether or not it can be justified in some particular way, we have to ask questions of it, such as: Does it solve the problems it was intended to solve? Or does it merely shift the problem? Does it solve the problem better than competing views? Or does it create still worse difficulties? Does it contradict other philosophical theories needed for solving other problems? Is it fruitful in suggesting new problems?

At the same time I think that the followers of Barth are perfectly right in claiming that *if* one takes the original absolute *commitment* seriously, then it is at least theoretically irrelevant whether the Revelation to which one is committed solves any human problems. It is precisely because I cannot make Barth's or any other ultimate commitment that I think the problem-solving consideration important—partly as a means of bringing erroneous commitments under critical fire.

The idea of the "check of the problem" is of perhaps even greater importance for philosophy generally. Although Max Weber, Collingwood, Popper, and some other philosophers have emphasized the importance of criticizing philosophical theories by comparing them historically against the problems they were intended to solve, the idea of the critical effectiveness of this check is sometimes dismissed as a vague popular notion. Now, the idea of the problem is indeed a bit vague and popular. But it is popular to call it vague; and the unadorned charge that something is vague is, by itself, a vague criticism. I hope to have illustrated in my own argument above the usefulness of the critical comparison of philosophical theories against problems, and thereby to have made the notion clearer. For I argued that panrationalism, in failing to solve its problem, led to a crisis of integrity; that critical rationalism attained integrity at the expense of ignoring the problem; and that pancritical rationalism can solve the original problem with integrity.

One reason why the notion of the problem has seemed so vague is that most contemporary philosophies tend to devalue the importance of the history of philosophy. To tell which philosophical view best solves important philosophical problems it is necessary to go to the historical texts and examine concretely what those problems were and how they have developed and changed. Consequently, the historical study of philosophical problems is of crucial importance for even the most theoretical and analytical of philosophers.

By far the most controversial critical consideration, however, is the first: logic.[19] Although most theologians will compliment logic "in its proper

---

[19]My discussion of logic here has been much misunderstood. For a more elaborate presentation and defense of my views, see the appendices to this book, esp. appendix 5.

place", many of them seem willing, in a jam, to reject it. Usually they are far more ready to reject logic than to deny empirical experience or even a scientific hypothesis.[20] Reinhold Niebuhr, for example, has indicated his willingness to defy logic over substantially the same issue that led William James to pragmatism and a kind of irrationalism: the problem of free will and moral responsibility. Niebuhr writes:

> The doctrine of original sin remains absurd from the standpoint of a pure rationalism, for it expresses a relation between fate and freedom which cannot be fully rationalized . . . unless the paradox be accepted as a rational understanding of the limits of rationality and as an expression of faith that a rationally irresolvable contradiction may point to a truth which logic cannot contain. . . .[21]

Niebuhr assumes that "from the standpoint of a pure rationalism" determinism is an inescapable theory and believes that it conflicts with the idea of free will and human responsibility.[22] But he is committed by his religious views to the idea that human beings are responsible and free. Since he feels he can abandon neither free will nor determinism (although he believes the two are logically inconsistent), he relinquishes logic. His alternative course is to embrace a kind of Hegelian logic, probably the most discredited logical theory in the history of the subject.

Similar views about the dispensability of logic—indeed, that the main difficulty in many of our most important intellectual and spiritual conflicts probably lies in our submission to its oppressive authority—rebound today throughout our literature of cultural diagnosis. "If a true prophet should appear", Norman Podhoretz has predicted, "his revelation would be acceptable to reason because it would illuminate life so powerfully as to compel rational assent; it would, in other words, provide a new way of understanding the world, new categories, even a new logic".[23] J. D. Salinger echoed this mood in his striking short story *Teddy*. Teddy, a precocious ten-year-old and a kind of prophet, is talking, on board ship in the mid-Atlantic, with Nicholson, an Ivy League intellectual who teaches education:

---

[20]See Barth, *Dogmatics in Outline* (London: SCM Press, 1949), p. 15, and *Church Dogmatics*, vol. 1, part 1, p. 8: "The very minimum postulate of freedom from contradiction is acceptable by theology only upon the very limited interpretation, by the scientific theorist upon the scarcely tolerable one, that theology will not assert an irremovability in principle of the 'contradictions' which it is bound to make good." Other theologians who seem to prefer to retain logic nonetheless treat such things as the law of noncontradiction as *categories* that are in principle revisable. See Hodgson, *For Faith and Freedom*, vol. 1, p. 50.

[21]Niebuhr, *The Nature and Destiny of Man* (New York: Charles Scribner's Sons, 1941), vol. 1, p. 278.

[22]It is no longer at all clear that there need be any contradiction here. Popper's arguments have convinced me that determinism is a scientifically untenable view. See his *The Open Universe* (London: Hutchinson, 1982), being vol. 2 of *Postscript to the Logic of Scientific Discovery*; his "Indeterminism in Quantum Physics and in Classical Physics, Parts I and II", *British Journal for the Philosophy of Science*, 1950; and "On the Status of Science and Metaphysics". For an excellent explanation of why Hegelian dialectic seems so attractive to many intellectuals, see his "What Is Dialectic?" in *Conjectures and Refutations*, chap. 15.

[23]*Commentary*, March 1960, p. 276.

"You're just being logical," Teddy said to him impassively.
"I'm just being what?" Nicholson asked, with a little excess of politeness.
"Logical. You're just giving me a regular, intelligent answer," Teddy said.
"I was trying to help you. You asked me how I get out of the finite
dimensions when I feel like it. I certainly don't use logic when I do it. Logic's
the first thing you have to get rid of."
Nicholson removed a flake of tobacco from his tongue with his fingers.
"You know Adam?" Teddy asked him. . . . "You know that apple Adam
ate in the Garden of Eden, referred to in the Bible?" he asked. "You know
what was in that apple? Logic. Logic and intellectual stuff. That was all that
was in it. So—this is my point—what you have to do is vomit it up if you
want to see things as they really are. I mean if you vomit it up, then you
won't have any more trouble with blocks of wood and stuff. You won't see
everything stopping *off* all the time. And you'll know what your arm really is,
if you're interested. Do you know what I mean? Do you follow me?"
"I follow you," Nicholson said, rather shortly.
"The trouble is," Teddy said, "most people don't want to see things the
way they are" . . . He reflected. "I never saw such a bunch of apple-eaters".[24]

Prevalent as such ideas are, the attempt to reject logic at once raises a host
of problems of which many theologians, apple-eating and otherwise, seem
quite unaware. One serious difficulty is that "from a contradiction everything follows". If a contradiction is admitted into a set of views, it will
follow from that set of views, for instance, that John F. Kennedy is identical
with Nikita Khrushchev *and* that John F. Kennedy is not identical with
Nikita Khrushchev. And any other statement, as well as *its* contrary, also
follows. This sort of result inclines one to regard the logic repudiator as
someone who really does not know what he is doing.

However, simply to dismiss this point of view is rash. For even the fact
that "from a contradiction everything follows" is perhaps not so telling as it
might seem. The logic repudiator might retort that everything follows from
a contradiction only within our very inadequate logic, and that this will not
happen in the "higher logic" of God or of the future "prophet". In any case,
Niebuhr's claim that logic might be rejected in the face of certain considerations, in the course of rational argument, and during our search to learn
more about the world and how to act in it, has to be taken seriously—if only
because some contemporary logicians of the highest rank have said things
that appear to support it. I have in mind the epistemological holism W. V.
Quine espoused in his well-known article, "Two Dogmas of Empiricism".
This position is influential throughout American neo-pragmatist thinking,
and has antecedents in some remarks John Dewey and C. I. Lewis had at
different times made about logic. Morton White endorsed a position similar
to Quine's in *Toward Reunion in Philosophy*.[25]

[24]J. D. Salinger, *Nine Stories, 1953*; or *For Esmé with Love and Squalor* (London: Hamish Hamilton,
1953), pp. 207–8. See also Barth, *Church Dogmatics*, vol. 1, part 1, p. 8.
[25]W. V. Quine, "Two Dogmas of Empiricism", *From a Logical Point of View* (Cambridge, Mass.:
Harvard University Press, 1953), chap. 2; and Morton White, *Toward Reunion in Philosophy*.

Writing in a vein reminiscent of Aristotle's description of logic as a tool of the educated man, Quine asked that formal logic be pictured "as one phase of the activity of a hypothetical individual who is also physicist, mathematician, *et al*".[26] According to Quine, when a critical individual brings the body of his beliefs to the test of criticism, *any* part of that body may be revised and rejected in the light of unfavorable criticism. There is *no* segment of it—such as the set of "analytically true" statements, including logic—which is so insulated from such continuous criticism and revision that we could say in advance that "the mistake could not be here". Quine has vividly described his approach:

> The totality of our so-called knowledge or beliefs, from the most casual matters of geography and history to the profoundest laws of atomic physics or even of pure mathematics and logic, is a man-made fabric which impinges on experience only along the edges. Or, to change the figure, total science is like a field of force whose boundary conditions are experience. A conflict with experience at the periphery occasions readjustments in the interior of the field. Truth values have to be redistributed over some of our statements. Reëvaluation of some statements entails reëvaluation of others, because of their logical interconnections—the logical laws being in turn simply certain further statements of the system, certain further elements of the field. . . . But the total field is so underdetermined by its boundary conditions, experience, that there is much latitude of choice as to what statements to reëvaluate in the light of any single contrary experience. . . . If this view is right . . . it becomes folly to seek a boundary between synthetic statements, which hold contingently on experience, and analytic statements, *which hold come what may.* *Any statement can be held true come what may,* if we make drastic enough adjustments elsewhere in the system. Even a statement very close to the periphery can be held true in the face of recalcitrant experience by pleading hallucination or by amending certain statements of the kind called logical laws. *Conversely, by the same token no statement is immume to revision.* Revision even of the logical law of the excluded middle has been proposed as a means of simplifying quantum mechanics; and what difference is there in principle between such a shift and the shift whereby Kepler superseded Ptolemy, or Einstein Newton, or Darwin Aristotle?[27]

Accepting Quine's framework, White adds that not only empirical experience but also "moral experiences" can occasion us to revise the totality of our beliefs—including logic. Moreover, he thinks that those beliefs which are revisable in the light of moral feelings cannot be demarcated from those beliefs which are not revisable in the light of moral

---

[26]See Quine's article in *Mind*, October 1953. Compare with the passage quoted, and with other parts of his article, Aristotle's *Nichomachean Ethics* (1094b23), *De partibus animalium* (639a5), (639b7), and *Metaphysics* (1005b1). These passages from Aristotle are particularly relevant since Quine's article was critically directed toward "ordinary language" critics of logic like Gilbert Ryle, P. F. Strawson, and S. E. Toulmin. Acknowledging that logical language has its roots in ordinary language, Quine, like Aristotle, argues that its categories and terms are not meant to impose a false model on ordinary discourse. For another discussion of some of the issues arising here, see Popper's comments on some of Ryle's views in "Why are the Calculuses of Logic and Arithmetic Applicable to Reality?", in *Conjectures and Refutations*.

[27]"Two Dogmas". Italics are mine.

feelings. Thus the distinction between fact and value is rejected along with the distinction between analytic and synthetic.

Several things may be said about this extreme holism. In the first place, although it looks like the pancritical rationalism I have just championed, we shall see in a moment that there are important differences.

In the second place, there are a number of senses in which logic is no doubt open to revision and in which there are "alternative logics". To take only two examples: the traditional Aristotelian logic of categorical propositions has been abandoned or, at best, retained for a very limited use. It is too clumsy and restricted to enable us to formulate many of the rules of inference which are valid in our ordinary discourse, not to mention the inferences of physics and mathematics. In addition, various artificialities may have to be introduced into our logical systems in order to avoid the famous logical paradoxes of Russell, Grelling, and others.

In the third place, in order that the position Quine and White take not be seriously misunderstood, it is important to remember that both are rationalists who do not *personally* reject logic. Indeed, both seem to doubt that circumstances could ever require us to deny the logical laws. White, for example, in an explicit discussion of Niebuhr's views, has emphasized his own loyalty to logic.[28]

Still, their approach seems to open the door, even if only nonlogicians will pass through, to a Niebuhrian sentiment about logic. Because of this, the next point is quite important. Our logical theories may, to be sure, be repaired and revised far more than we at present expect, and it is impossible to predict when such repairs will be necessary. Whether empirical observations or moral feelings could ever occasion such legitimate revision is quite another question, and I shall not tangle with it here. *Nonetheless,* however much the various alternative systems of logical rules of inference may differ among themselves, they have one important feature in common: whenever we observe these rules and, *starting with true premises,* argue in accordance with them, *we arrive at true conclusions.* The question arises whether we can revise logic in the sense of denying that true premises need always lead, in any valid inference, to true conclusions.

As Niebuhr's conception of "dialectic" shows, he apparently does regard logic as revisable in this way. And, although Quine and White seem nowhere explicitly to have faced this question when making their remarks about the revisability of logic, certain of their comments suggest that they also regard this revision as *in principle* possible. In the following paragraphs, where I speak of the revision of logic, I shall have *this* kind of revision in mind; I have no objection to the others.

The view that logic, in *this* sense, is part of our system of beliefs, which we bring to the test during critical argument and which is revisable in the light of the results of such critical argument, is untenable. For there is an *absolute difference in principle* between the replacement of logic with another "logic" and the replacement of other views, such as (to refer back to the passage quoted from Quine's "Two Dogmas") Ptolemy's with Kepler's, or Newton's with Einstein's.

The reasons for these contentions are complicated, but the basic structure of my argument is this: the "argument situation" in terms of which Quine and White (and, I think, Niebuhr, too) envisage the revisability of logic *presupposes logic.* To put this another way: we cannot regard logic as part of the set of beliefs that are put to the test in critical discussion, for the notion of testing and revising in accordance with the results of the test presupposes logic. And this is so regardless of what other critical checks one does or does not allow.

This rather abstract point can be explained as follows. The idea of *testing* and *revising* in the light of tests, or—more simply—the idea of critical argument, presupposes the notion of *deducibility,* i.e., the idea of the *retransmission of falsity* from conclusions to premises and, *ipso facto,* of the *transmission of truth* from premises to conclusion. That is, when the conclusion of a valid argument is discovered to be false, that falsity is retransmitted to the premises whence it must have come: at least one of these premises must be reevaluated. If our totality of beliefs implies "x", and if, upon testing, we get the result "not x", then there is a mistake in our set of beliefs which *needs to be corrected.* However, this idea of deducibility is practically equivalent to the second minimum sense of logic previously discussed.[29]

Hence, the idea that a set of beliefs might be brought "in closer correspondence with reality" by abandoning logic is mistaken, since the tool of logic is needed in order to argue and learn about reality—in order to bring the rest of our theories into closer correspondence with reality. Logic, then, cannot be part of the totality that is brought under test. In this consists the absolute difference in principle between the revision and correction of our nonlogical (as distinguished from illogical) beliefs, and what must amount to the rejection of logic.

An observant reader—particularly if he or she was struck by the apparent similarity between Quine's idea that everything is open to revision and my

---

[29]Moreover, it has been argued that from the notion of deducibility alone, the validity of most of logic, including propositional logic and the lower functional logic, may be established, without presupposition of axioms or primitive rules of inference. See Popper, "New Foundations for Logic", *Mind*, 1947; "Logic Without Assumptions", *Proceedings of the Aristotelian Society*, 1947; "Functional Logic Without Axioms or Primitive Rules of Inference", *Proceedings Koninklijke Nederlandsche Akademie van Wetenschappen*, vol. 50, no. 9 (1947), p. 1214; "On the Theory of Deduction", parts 1 and 2, ibid., vol. 51, no. 2 (1947), pp. 173 ff.; vol. 51, no. 3 (1947), pp. 322 ff.; "The Trivialization of Mathematical Logic", *Proceedings 10th International Congress of Philosophy*, 1948; and "Why Are the Calculuses of Logic and Arithmetic Applicable to Reality?" For a further discussion of the revisability of logic, see also appendix 5 below.

theory of pancritical rationalism—may, or perhaps *should,* have started to wonder whether in the last few paragraphs I have not tacitly been backing out of pancritical rationalism. It might seem as if I were now insisting that we are *committed* to logic.

But this is not so.

The point is that the practice of critical argument and logic are bound together. We can reject logic, but to do so is to reject the practice of argument. What we cannot do is to go on arguing critically after we have rejected the idea that true premises must, in a valid argument, lead to true conclusions. If we want to learn about, or even to describe, the world, we need to be able to derive true conclusions from true premises.

To be sure, to abandon logic is to abandon rationality as surely as to abandon Christ is to abandon Christianity. The two positions differ, however, in that the rationalist can, from his own rationalist point of view, consider and be moved by criticisms of logic and of rationalism, whereas the Christian cannot, from his own Christian point of view, consider and be moved by criticisms of his Christian commitment.[30]

I have not shown, as Descartes tried to do, that universal doubt is absurd; nor have I shown that the rationalist must hold something (namely, logic) immune to criticism. I have argued: (1) that *everything,* including the practice of arguing and revising (and using logic), is open to criticism and rejection. But (2) *as long as* we do continue to revise and criticize—as long as we have not rejected this practice—we presuppose logic, for it is entailed by the idea of revision. If we reject the practice of argument and revision we may reject logic, but we cannot reject logic so long as we continue in this practice.

Thus I have stated an absolute presupposition of argument to which we are committed not *as human beings,* because of our biology, psychology, or sociology, but *as arguers about the world.* No human being need argue unrestrictedly about the world: therefore he need not, as a human being, be committed to logic; only as arguer about the world. In so far as the practice of critical argument is the core of the process of learning about the world, this presupposition is important. The point also has philosophical and theological implications. Most importantly in the philosophical realm, the absolute difference just stated makes it possible to demarcate between those beliefs that are revisable *within* the argument situation and those that are not. Thereby it draws a sharp line which, although not corresponding to the traditional "analytic-synthetic" dichotomy, does mark off one portion of the class of truths traditionally known as "analytic truths" and thus refutes claims made by Quine, White, and others, that *no* boundary between

---

[30]See Barth, *Dogmatics in Outline,* chap. 2. "And faith is concerned with a decision *once for all.* . . . Everyone who has to contend with unbelief should be advised that he ought not to take his own unbelief too seriously. Only faith is to be taken seriously".

analytic and synthetic truths may be drawn. This makes it possible to introduce what might be called a "revisability criterion"; namely, that whatever is presupposed by the argument-revisability situation is not itself revisable *within that situation*.

Now, if we accept (1) Popper's "falsifiability criterion" as marking off scientific from nonscientific beliefs, and (2) my "revisability criterion", as just proposed, to demarcate those beliefs that are revisable within the argument situation from those that are not, then the spectrum of our claims can be sharply divided into at least three parts. To speak metaphorically, in a small area on the left would be logic and in a small area on the right would be empirical science.[31] In between, in a much larger section, would be some claims which have traditionally been called analytic and others which have traditionally been called synthetic, but which we can say are *neither* empirically refutable (and hence scientific) nor presupposed by the activity of argument (that is, logic). This middle area would contain, at least, all of metaphysics, some of mathematics, and part of that curious class of statement such as "all brothers are male siblings" around which much of the analytic-synthetic controversy has revolved.

The theological ramifications of these remarks can be put more simply. Most contemporary theologians, following Barth, speak in terms of continuing conjecture about the Word of God and of revision of conjecture in the face of various kinds of experience. Hence, in their own basic activity they presuppose logic, even when in respect to certain specific theories they claim to abandon it. Moreover, many theologians like Tillich and Niebuhr (or Butterfield) who advance apologetic arguments against their opponents presuppose in so doing that their opponents presuppose logic, *unless* they regard these arguments as merely persuasive gimmicks. Thus, when the theologians claim to abandon logic, they are usually defying the presuppositions of their own programs, thwarting their own intentions.

These remarks about logic are pertinent to the more general argument. If theologians would add logic to those critical intellectual institutions such as empirical observational experience whose value they already accept; and if they also took seriously their own claims to be self-critical, they would soon find that most of their theories are indeed untenable—that is, they will not stand up under criticism—that they raise far more difficulties than they deal with, and that most of them even ignore the most pressing problems; and that for these reasons (not because they cannot be *justified*) they are held irrationally when they are held at all. Theologians have in the past drawn their own and others' attention away from decisive criticisms of their theories by insisting—quite rightly—that their opponents could not justify their views either. But, as we have seen, the notion of justification can be

---

[31]See diagram in appendix 5 below.

eliminated from the notion of criticism.

Whereas many philosophers have argued that we can decide as we please, freely and irrationally, between two unjustifiable theories, I suggest that we can decide freely and irrationally, as a matter of taste, only between two theories against which there exist no criticisms one is unable to defeat. This reduces the area of whim considerably: there are no important positions that can be justified in the required way, but there are few important traditional philosophical positions against which no decisive criticisms exist. Moreover, once the retreat to commitment involved in the justificational framework is no longer necessary, then it is also no longer possible to avoid facing these criticisms by citing the *tu quoque*.

6
THE
BREAKDOWN
OF COMMUNICATION

"Where do you come from?" said the
Red Queen.
Alice explained that she had lost her
way.
"I don't know what you mean by *your*
way", said the Queen, "all the ways about
here belong to me—but why did you come
out here at all?" she added in a kinder
tone. "Curtsy while you're thinking what
to say. It saves time."
—LEWIS CARROLL

So far, our discussion has focused on the historical and philosophical
ramifications of the new Protestant thought; we have not inquired into its
practical implications. If Protestant theology were, as is sometimes suggested, a subject mainly for seminaries and theologians, the matter could
perhaps rest here—the story of an interesting and understandable, if
unfortunate, intellectual development. However, the new Protestant
thought and its strategy of defense have occasioned some important
practical results, a few of which I shall try to indicate in this and the
following chapter. As soon as we turn to the practical aspects, the issue of
integrity within Protestantism becomes more complicated than it was on the
strictly theoretical level. The very fact that Protestant leaders were able to
preserve a considerable degree of philosophical integrity seems to have
afforded many of them rather easy consciences about a number of practical
matters. I shall turn first to some of these results within Protestantism, then
to some of the broader social repercussions.

1. Agreement and Disagreement

An observer of contemporary Protestant life who is familiar with its history
must often be struck by a kind of paradox. Whereas Protestants agree and
cooperate more than ever before, they also disagree more radically than

ever—and about far more fundamental issues than those which caused their predecessors to splinter into hundreds of sects.

The agreement, which is more tangible, has been given more publicity. While the old denominationalism is breaking down, the growing strength of the ecumenical movement, symbolized by the Manhattan skyscraper headquarters of the National Council of the Churches of Christ in the U.S.A., has surpassed in promise the hopes of its founders and early supporters. The splits, schisms, divisions, and "heresies" of the eighteenth and nineteenth centuries which produced the more than two hundred and fifty registered American Protestant groups have dwindled to practical unimportance, although they have not disappeared, especially among the more fundamentalist groups. Ministers now move rather easily from one denomination to another; even where rigid formal barriers remain, clerical leapfrog is common. Several denominations also cooperate in their educational programs by planning and publishing jointly the materials needed in Sunday-school classrooms.

More important, new mergers are flourishing. Various Baptist, Methodist, and Presbyterian groups, which had been split not only by doctrinal schism but by the more geographical animosities of the Civil War, have been reuniting. Two groups which differ considerably in polity and tradition, the Episcopalians and the Presbyterians, have for years been carying on serious, although as yet unsuccessful, merger negotiations. Most remarkable, the independent covenantal Congregational Christian Churches (themselves the products of several mergers) and the Evangelical and Reformed Church (also the result of several mergers) have merged to form the United Church of Christ. Not only have two such diverse groups united politically; they have been able to produce a broad credo, or statement of faith. Significantly, the negotiations and discussions that preceded the statement of this credo were often described as part of a search for a "formula".

But the new *disagreement*, if less often discussed, is no less striking. Never before, not even at the time of the Reformation, have Christians differed over such fundamental issues. Past disputes have focused on matters like evolution, the nature and number of the sacraments, the form of baptism, the organization of the clergy. Atheism was largely left to those outside the church. Today, there is disagreement within the churches over such matters as whether the traditional God exists and whether there is an afterlife.

For example, Nels F.S. Ferré has reported about the "extensive agnosticism" that characterizes young Protestants. Writing that "even in our theological seminaries we can no longer take for granted that students believe Christianity to be true, even at the heart of its message concerning the living God", he has observed: "Acceptance of Christianity as a way of life, of integrity and love . . . with rejection of the 'old doctrines', is a common occurrence not only among students but among laymen and a number of ministers when they dare to be honest with themselves."[1] Ferré taught at a moderately liberal New England seminary. W. Norman Pittenger, who was a professor at New York City's General Theological Seminary, an Episcopalian school with strong high-church tendencies, seems to have encountered a very different situation among his own students. "Anyone who knows the situation in our leading seminaries", he writes, "can testify that authoritarianism is gaining ground and that students want to be told".[2] The apparent contrast between the situations could hardly be more marked. Yet it is typical of the religious situation today that as soon as one begins to probe beneath the surface, one loses confidence that things are quite so different. For example, if one were to accept that the desire "to be told" may often indicate a lack of inner conviction, Pittenger's observation might be interpreted as indirectly corroborating Ferré's.

However this may be, another characteristic report deplores a situation wherein the "religiously indifferent" remain theists or "slide back into a socially acceptable belief in 'God', while the student with the deepest concern for finding out the nature of religious reality concludes that he cannot honestly make the ambiguous affirmation, God exists. . . . Those who hold these views believe that they can show that there are not good reasons for believing in the existence of God. And some of them believe that they can show that religion and the church nonetheless have an important place in the examined life".[3]

Clearly, differences that would have splintered denominations in the nineteenth century are commonplace *within the churches* today. How is this possible? If interpreted in the light of the earlier chapters, the development is not surprising. These seemingly antagonistic tendencies can flourish side by side, and even stimulate one another, because of the choice made by the leading Protestant thinkers when Protestant liberalism collapsed. The most brilliant Protestant theologians, led by Karl Barth, chose a form of irrationalism that was as rational as seemed possible and also rationally excusable in terms of the problem of ultimate commitment and the limits of rationality. On the one hand, by declaring that any statement about the essence of the Christian message was to be in principle revisable, they showed a dramatic flexibility that ruled out any future fundamentalism or fixed interpretations of the Christian message. On the other hand, they sharply located the limits of this flexibility in a basic inflexibility: whatever his message might turn out to be, "assent to Jesus" was presupposed and required by all who were properly to call themselves Christians. Since what is meant by "assent to Jesus" is itself open to extremely different interpreta-

---

[1]Ferré, "Letter" to the *Christian Century*, July 1, 1959.
[2]Pittenger, "Wanted: A New Christian Modernism", *Christian Century*, April 6, 1955.
[3]Louis B. Potter, of Swarthmore College, in a letter to the *Christian Century*, July 1, 1959.

tions, the resulting flexibility is wide indeed. At any rate, it was wide enough—cast as a vague formula—to be written into the constitutions of the new ecumenical organizations as the key to admission to membership in them.

With such an ingenious framework at its disposal, one might have expected Protestantism to have rejuvenated itself as common heir to the unity of a shared commitment and the healthy stimulation of good-natured diversity. The framework would seem to provide just what many people have been clamoring for: a unified ideology plus free speech. To a certain extent, the enthusiastic cooperation among denominations does satisfy this sort of expectation. Moreover, the new Protestant thought has lent strength to institutional Protestantism in other ways. For example, it provides a powerful *explanation of failure*, past, present, and future. Such explanations are useful in accounting for the apparent failure of the old Protestantism: the search for the essence of Christianity, and the constant modification and revision of a system of belief that purported to contain certain truth. But of course similar themes can also easily account for the *present* failure of Protestantism: for example, the waning of its intellectual influence in modern society.

Such an explanation is needed because the society Protestantism serves has become embarrassingly secular: not in the sense that its practice no longer matches Protestant Christian ideas—this it had never done—but in the sense that its most articulate and sensitive thinking and feeling are not Protestant. An explicitly Protestant Christian poet or man of letters, like W. H. Auden or T.S. Eliot, has become an object of special interest and attention, not only for the merits of his work but also for his religious identification.

It is true that such interest in the contemporary Christian is rarely hostile: the Christian thinker is now a phenomenon to be studied. Yet many Protestants would prefer open hostility. For although some dignity perhaps still attaches to being hated, being scrutinized can be embarrassingly debasing. The proud descendant of the Founding Fathers becomes the "native", to be photographed and questionnaired by the intellectual colonist-gone-tourist who has captured the land. As if the secular tourist were not enough, the Roman Catholic colonists, growing in numbers and influence daily, seem to threaten to take Protestantism's social prestige and place even as a religion.

The themes and defenses of the new Protestantism provide immediate explanations and justifications for this development. For example, the contention that genuine communication between two or more groups with different ultimate commitments is quite impossible is a handy notion for a group under pressure. It "explains" why one's opponents seem so lacking in "understanding", without admitting the unpleasant possibility that they might be right. The resulting argument, which may be found in almost any handbook of American Protestantism, goes something like this: These tourists do not understand us, do not adopt our way of life, our truth, because of the different ultimate presuppositions to which they are committed. It is necessary to share presuppositions in order to communicate; otherwise, our minds will never meet and we shall talk past each other forever. That so many of our contemporaries have abandoned worshipful commitments to our presuppositions in order to take up touring explains why our culture is in such a mess. Not only is one social group unable to communicate with another; even the greatest intellectuals have so specialized and narrow a view of things that they cannot understand one another. Parochialism is the inevitable result of tourism. So if our contemporaries would only come back to *our* parochialism, the old reliable highway, we would be able to understand one another again; we would be united; we would trade our confusion for strength.

In this way, the difficulties of Protestantism can be externalized and linked with the popular cry for a return to the old Protestant America.

2. The Breakdown of Communication

There is then no doubt that the new Protestant thinking has been valuable in increasing cooperation among Protestants and providing an excuse for failure. However, when one turns from such immediate political and practical achievements, its success becomes less certain. For the main aims of Protestantism, as a community claiming a kind of custodianship of a religious message, are neither the political strong arm nor the convincing excuse. As a religious tradition, Protestantism hopes to provide rich saving help to individual human beings who are confused about themselves and their world, to provide an identification that, unlike other "false ultimates", does not "refute itself in experience".[4] Here, facing their most important task, Protestant theologians have—despite quite contrary intentions—sown the seeds of their own failure: their intentions have been drastically frustrated by the results of their policies. Although vast religious confusion and loss of meaning do exist in contemporary life, theology is as much responsible for the situation as is antitheology or theological indifference; God-saving breeds as much confusion as does the death of a God. I wish to support this contention in the remainder of this chapter, partly impressionistically, partly by explicit argument.

---

[4]Robert Bretall, Introduction to *A Kierkegaard Anthology* (Princeton: Princeton University Press, 1951), p. xxi.

In Protestant Christendom today, communication has broken down. The beliefs and religious expectations of those learned in theology are very often not only different from and more complex than those of the average man in the pew; they *contradict* them. Agreement is no longer over beliefs but over *passwords,* which one may take literally, symbolically, or in some other way, depending on one's theological sophistication.

Since many clergymen are not at all eager to communicate their beliefs to the "believers", the ordinary gulf between pulpit and pew and between one parishioner and another is widened by the new circumlocutions which make the break with traditional Christianity seem less serious than it is: we get different kinds of "truth", different kinds of "belief", different kinds of "knowledge".

The resulting church services are weird pantomimes. Kneeling before the same altar in the same service, saying the same creeds and singing the same hymns, one man worships the God who acts literally, another worships the God who acts metaphorically, a third worships the God who acts symbolically, and yet another worships the God who doesn't act at all.[5]

"Well, yes", the theologian nods when pressed. "I don't believe that there is an afterlife, but the notion of an afterlife is *symbolically true,* you know."

"Yes, Virginia, there is a God."[6]

At the source of this internal breakdown of communication is the widespread tendency among Protestant thinkers today to make traditional doctrines fit new situations by redefining the words in which the doctrines are phrased. The traditional doctrines now become counters in an elaborate game. "To be a Christian" begins to resemble "to go dancing". All that is required of a couple who wish to dance is that they both know and follow the rules. They need agree about no substantial issue: neither morals, nor politics, nor art, nor science. A married couple who quarrel bitterly may *enjoy* dancing together; here is one activity in which they *can* cooperate smoothly, while leaving their disagreements unspoken.[7]

But do two such people communicate when they dance? Similarly, in the case of two Christians who agree about nothing substantial but who both know when to say the proper phrases and when and how to carry out the appropriate actions together—are they communicating? *Can* they communicate? They are doubtless *cooperating;* and they may enjoy each other's

---

[5]Compare Ernest Gellner, *Words and Things,* p. 221. Citing a statement by A. M. Quinton in *The Twentieth Century,* June 1955, that "I don't decide whether a man is my co-religionist by seeing how he argues, but by whether I find him kneeling beside me at Church", Gellner comments: *"Manners makyth faith,* it appears, *and not convictions.* . . . It does not appear to have occurred to Quinton that the inability to tell a man's nominal faith from the way he *argues* is only possible in an age when nominal faith has indeed become nominal."

[6]Above I have used some sentences from my article, "I Call Myself a Protestant", *Harper's,* May 1959; reprinted in *Essays of Our Time,* ed. L. Hamalian and E. L. Volpe (New York: McGraw Hill, 1960).

[7]I am indebted to J. W. N. Watkins for the suggestion that I illustrate this point with this example.

company. Protestants now, like Alice, curtsy while they're thinking what to say.

Satisfactory communication with a person must involve appreciation of what *he* means when he says: "I believe in God" or "Jesus Christ is Lord". Only a theologian who accepts something like a positivist or behaviorist stipulation that meaning lies in usage can maintain that two people, because they use certain phrases in certain ways and play the game together, are really communicating. No one, of course, has direct access to another's mind. How, then, can anyone tell whether he understands what another person means? There is probably only one practical way: he can make a guess as to the proper interpretation of the other person's behavior and conversation, ask him whether that conjecture is correct, and continue to test the conjecture against the other person's future behavior. There is no more, and probably far less, certainty here than in other matters.

Such a procedure of guessing and correcting guesses may break down in many obvious situations; for example, if the other person deliberately chooses to be evasive and indulges in answers that are intended to throw the questioner off the track. This may, of course, be legitimate behavior, particularly when the questioner is simply invading the other's privacy.

Another such situation arises when the language in which the guessing must be done has become so debased and ambiguous that it is impossible to know when one is *disagreeing* with the person with whom one is talking. Communication demands that both parties be able to find out in what respects they disagree: *two people cannot understand each other if they have no way of determining when they are disagreeing.*[8] But the practice of "word healing" and the "ceremonial use of language", so important in contemporary theology, have made it exceptionally difficult for contemporary Protestants to ascertain when they are disagreeing on religious questions. To the extent to which articulation of disagreement ceases to occur, to the extent to which what I call the "indiscernability of disagreement" prevails, any kind of communication, including that religious communication which is supposed to possess saving power, falters.

It is worthwhile to place these polemical remarks about religious language in the broader context of the theory of language, with special attention to Karl Bühler's famous book *Sprachtheorie*.[9] Bühler analyzed the communicative function of a language into three components: (1) *the expressive function,* where the communication serves to express the emo-

---

[8]Some linguisitic philosophers have attempted to make a point at least vaguely resembling the one just italicized, and have done so in terms of a misapplication of the notion of unfalsifiability. I believe that it is what I may call the "indeterminability of disagreement", rather than unfalsifiability, which is the crux of the matter here. See *New Essays in Philosophical Theology,* ed. A. G. N. Flew and A. MacIntyre (New York: Macmillan, 1955).

[9]Karl Bühler, *Sprachtheorie: Die Darstellungsfunktion der Sprache* (Stuttgart: Gustav Fischer Verlag, 1965). On Bühler see Robert E. Innis, *Karl Bühler: Semiotic Foundations of Language Theory* (New York: Plenum Press, 1982).

tions or thoughts of the speaker; (2) the *signaling* or *stimulative* or *release* function, in which the communication serves to stimulate or to release certain reactions in the hearer; (3) *the descriptive function,* which is present to the extent that the communication describes some state of affairs. These three functions are separable in so far as each is accompanied by its preceding one but need not be accompanied by its succeeding one. That is, one may express without signaling; one may express and signal without describing. But one cannot signal without expressing, or describe without both expressing and signaling. Yet another function has been added to Bühler's set: namely, the *argumentative function,* to which the same hierarchical ordering applies: one cannot argue without describing, signaling, expressing.[10] The first two functions apply, of course, to animal languages. Animals surely do express and signal. But the second two functions, describing and arguing about those descriptions, may possibly be characteristically human—although those who research into the life and languages of animals may well hope for discoveries which will refute at least some of our views about the limitations of animal communication. There is, for instance, some sense in which bees describe.

As an aid in the understanding of his ideas, Bühler developed the diagram facing.[11]

The triangle in the middle denotes the linguistic *sign.* This sign may be used by the sender or speaker to express himself; it may be received by the receiver or listener as a signal or appeal which may or may not have been intended by the speaker. And the same sign again may be used—by sender, receiver, or both—to symbolize some objective state of affairs independent of the receiver and sender. An application of the scheme to contemporary art, music, and poetry can be very instructive. Extend the sign beyond conventional language to such things as works of art. A work of art may express certain subjective states of mind or intentions on the part of the artist; those who receive or respond to the work of art may or may not decode it as it was intended by its original sender. And the work of art may

[10]This was added by Popper. See his *Conjectures and Refutations,* pp. 134 and 295. See also, on the relations between Popper and Bühler, my "Sprach- und Wissenschaftstheorie als Werkzeuge einer Schulreform: Wittgenstein und Popper als österreichische Schullehrer", in *Conceptus,* April 1969; my "Theory of Language and Philosophy of Science as Instruments of Educational Reform: Wittgenstein and Popper as Austrian Schoolteachers", in Robert S. Cohen and Marx W. Wartofsky; *Methodological and Historical Essays in the Natural and Social Sciences* (Dordrecht: D. Reidel, 1974); and my "Die österreichische Schulreform als die Wiege der modernen Philosophie", in *Club Voltaire: Jahrbuch für Kritische Aufklärung,* vol. 4 (Hamburg: Rowohlt, 1970). See also Arne Friemuth Petersen, "On the Role of Problems and Problem Solving in Popper's Early Work on Psychology", in the Popper Festschrift issue of *etc.,* ed. Paul Levinson, 1984; Arne Friemuth Petersen, Pierre Garrigues, and Guilhem de Roquefeuil, "Jeu et activité autorégulatrice: Le jeu en tant que résolution de problème chez l'animal et l'enfant", in Josyane Guillemaut and R. Soulayrol, eds., *Le jeu chez l'enfant,* (Paris, 1984). See also Jürgen August Alt, *Die Frühschriften Poppers—Der Weg Poppers von der Pädagogik und der Psychologie zur Spätphilosophie* (Frankfurt: Peter Lang Verlag; 1982); and *Vom Ende der Utopie in der Erkenntnistheorie* (Königstein/Ts.: Forum Academicum; 1980).

[11]*Sprachtheorie,* p. 28.

or may not be representational. To coordinate various contemporary theories and modes of artistic expression with Bühler's schema is an exercise both instructive and amusing.

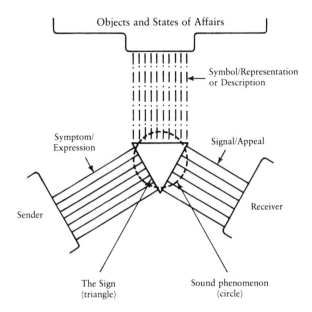

The Sign
(triangle)

Sound phenomenon
(circle)

If we look fairly at the history of religion, rather than at art, to determine how these comments about language apply, we find the following. Despite the attacks of logical empiricists who would permit religious expressions at best an emotive meaning, and the views of such as Braithwaite (see chapter 3, section 6) who would assimilate religious assertions to signaling and appeal policies for moral behavior—things to be analyzed roughly in terms of Bühler's first two functions—it can hardly be doubted that religious discourse was in its origins often intended to be descriptive and explanatory as well as expressive and stimulative, and that this remains true today. Moreover, the history of religion is full of quite genuine and often rigorous arguments about the truth of these explanations and descriptions.

This heritage is in danger of being lost today; religious discourse is in danger of being reduced—as if this were a favor to religion—to the first two functions. Ironically, perhaps the most serious danger of this happening comes from the attempts of theologians to defend religion.

I have mentioned how the very coin of religious discourse may be debased by excessive ambiguity of meanings. It is worth mentioning another self-defeating strategy to which the Bühler schema is particularly relevant.

Some theologians such as Reinhold Niebuhr, as we have seen, suggest that human logic is responsible for having led us into difficulties in trying to comprehend and defend religious doctrine, and have recommended that instead of trying to reconcile seemingly contradictory doctrines we instead abandon logic, together with its laws of noncontradiction and *tertium non datur*. Now, logic has a way of avenging herself on those who treat her lightly. *If we abandon logic, we lose the power of argument*: for argument consists, in essence, in showing that two claims are incompatible. *And if we abandon logic we also diminish enormously our powers of description*: for to say what something is, to describe it, is at the same time to say a great deal about what it is not. And if we allow contradictions to be introduced, we permit all descriptions at once. Thus one defensive move—the scuttling of logic—forces us step by step down the hierarchy of linguistic functions. We lose the power to argue, we lose the power to describe; we are left with the powers to express and to signal. Such *may* be sufficient in poetry. It *may* be sufficient in, say, music. There can be no doubt that the expressive and stimulative functions of our various languages are by themselves alone astonishingly rich and deep. But are they rich and deep enough, do they suffice, for religion? Or do they debase and emasculate it? Some persons, like myself, who sympathize with the rich heritage of traditional Christianity even though we are critical of it, would wish that more theologians would keep these elementary linguistic considerations in mind when defending religion. For their cures may indeed be far worse than the disease. Moreover, these cures are infectious and may spread to areas other than religion. For example, historical writing and political argument may be debased by tactics similar to those used unintentionally to debase religious discourse.

The ambiguities of language are great gifts—and great dangers.

A good example of cooperation without communication is found in the history of the membership policy of the National Council of Churches. Its founders wrote the commitment to Christ into the constitution of the group with their decision that any religious body which wished to join must accept the doctrine of the divinity of Christ, the idea which is loosely expressed today in the statement that "Jesus Christ is Lord". This provides a formula for cooperation, yet—because it is itself open to endless interpretation— allows all the flexibility that is needed for hypocrisy. One of the favorites of the National Council is Tillich, an acknowledged atheist in most traditional senses of that term. Less favored are Unitarians, who are often more conservative theologically than Tillich and who in many cases could agree to Tillich's interpretation of Christ's divinity; the Unitarians are excluded as a group from council membership. What is the difference? Tillich has provided in his systematic theology a formula and a concept of truth which enable him to say that it is true that Christ is divine. Unitarians are not producers of formulae. So, lacking the password, they lack membership too.

It is hardly surprising that ecumenical Protestant thinkers draw such odd lines around denominations, for they no longer can easily ascertain the views of their denominational fellows. When a prospective clergyman has been trained in the new theology almost anything can happen during the creedal examination many denominations require of candidates. The bishop may ask his postulant: "Do you believe in God?" (meaning "Do you believe that it is a true statement that the God of traditional theology exists?"). The candidate, who may be an atheist, or perhaps—even more fashionable in the seminaries these days—a pantheist, is often able quite legitimately to substitute a special Tillichian reinterpretation of "belief in" and reply: "Yes, I *believe in* God."

There has been verbal agreement, and the candidate is usually passed. But one wonders not only whether the candidate has been candid but also what was the point of holding the interview under such conditions in the first place.[12] Such practices are probably less the product of willful deceit than of the difficult situation in which many contemporary clergymen find themselves. Clear communication and statement of one's theological idiosyncrasies may involve one in awkward situations with conservative fellow clergymen and unsophisticated members of one's flock. So why bother to communicate if cooperation can be achieved without it? To the personal tension and anxiety that the educated clergyman must share with most contemporary men, he must now add the burden of playing a double role.

Professor Wesley Shrader has attributed the high incidence of nervous breakdowns among clergy not so much to initial psychological weaknesses as to the multiple roles the clergy are now expected to play. His remarks about role playing are supported by many recent reports. A former Methodist minister, J. B. Moore, has depicted the dilemma of clergymen who cannot, "in good conscience, play the role of good, sound, orthodox, conventional, safe" Protestants; who "no longer believe in the Gospel *as they are expected to preach it,* and no longer believe in the denomination they are expected to support".[13] A former Congregational, now Unitarian, minister, Thomas S. Vernon, has sorrowfully described the churchly game of "Let's pretend." The church members confide to each other that they no longer believe the doctrines of their church but "would not dare to let their minister know they felt that way". And the minister tells *his* confidants (when he dares to have any) that he doesn't believe the doctrines either, but "would not dare to say so from the pulpit".[14]

---

[12]Above I have used in paraphrase several lines from my review of Kaufmann's *Critique of Religion and Philosophy*, in *Commentary*, November 1958.

[13]James B. Moore, "Why Young Ministers Are Leaving the Church", *Harper's*, 1957.

[14]See also Vernon's talk in *Monthly Newsletter*, November 1958, published by the First Congregational Church of Bay City, Mich.; and Von Ogden Vogt, *The Primacy of Worship* (Boston: Starr King Press, 1958), p. 85.

7
THE
"REPUDIATION OF OTHERNESS"

> If the older liberalism sometimes seemed to make "what Jones will accept" the criterion for Christian truth, the newer tendency is to employ *any* device through which Jones can be persuaded to accept, for religious purposes, whatever is thought to be said in the particular heritage of the popular apologist. . . . One cannot accuse them of actual dishonesty. But one must wonder if that kind of integrity and utter honesty which should mark those who serve God with their minds is not sometimes neglected.
>
> —W. NORMAN PITTENGER[1]

1. Some Intended Consequences

For the most part, the internal breakdown of communication in institutional Protestantism has been an accidental, unintended consequence of the new Protestant theology. Public dissension over Protestant doctrine has deliberately been discouraged in order to prevent any weakening of the various programs for cooperation. An editorial that appeared in the *Christian Century* in 1959 illustrates this attitude. After decrying the "party spirit" and "factionalism" into which "we Protestants have fallen", the editor found that public disagreement was "playing into the hands of Protestantism's enemies". His solution, which indicated no awareness of the importance, for communication, of articulating disagreement, was for Protestants to listen more closely to "the talk around the tables at ecumenical gatherings".[2]

Once a breakdown of communication has occurred, however, the way is open for authoritarian and even totalitarian attitudes such as flourish today

---

[1]"Wanted: A New Christian Modernism".

[2]"A Protestant Believes in God", *Christian Century*, May 20, 1959. Later (July 1, 1959, p. 782), in the Letters to the Editor, an eminent theologian challenged the editor on the grounds that a "unity of concealment" would be "insipid and false", and stated that an ecumenical organization would lose its right to support by Christians on the day it began to conceal honest differences among its participants. Several other equally distinguished Protestants, however, wrote to congratulate the editor for his stand.

in Protestantism, expressed both in policies implemented within the churches and in the policies that guide the relationship of the churches and the community. Unlike the breakdown of communication that originally bred the attitudes which made such policies possible, the policies themselves are often quite coldly calculated; for they are conscious responses to felt needs. Some sort of unity seems necessary in a religious group; yet, when the members of the group have lost the means of communicating with one another, the spiritual unity offered by the open and critical exchange of beliefs disappears.[3] If there is to be any unity, it must be achieved in some other way; and the only other available ways appear to be authoritarian, at least in temper.

The transition to authoritarian attitudes is greatly facilitated if the leaders of the group feel no responsibility to rationality. Believing that the cultural turn away from Protestantism is due to wrongful abandonment of Protestant presuppositions, thinking that those presuppositions are true, that rational argument about presuppositions or ultimate commitments is impossible, that society is hence divided into a host of rationally irreconcilable groups, and that social unity under the banner of a dominant ideology is necessary, Protestant theologians have decided to advocate nonrational means and illiberal measures to propagate their presuppositions.

And when those leaders individually are ridden by bad conscience, an authoritarian attitude can quickly take hold. A man who is secure in his own faith can be more tolerant toward one who differs from him than can a man who is uneasy in his faith. The uncertain man must, like Kierkegaard, prove his faithfulness to himself by the violence of his rejection of any competing faith. Thus he represses at least partially and temporarily his dread of losing what he has—no matter how tenuously he is tied to it—lest he sink into still greater confusion.

In the first chapter, I suggested that much of the alienation and confusion of identity in our society may be due to the fact that our leading intellectual and spiritual traditions are so involved in crises of identity and integrity that those who affiliate with them can hardly do so without bad conscience and confusion. My suggestion, if correct, will help explain the phenomena of intolerant authoritarian "repudiation of otherness" which now abound in Protestantism and which are not altogether absent from various forms of traditional rationalism, such as pragmatism.

By examining some of these phenomena, we may get a clearer notion of how the various elements of the picture—the intellectual uneasiness of the Protestant leaders who know what difficulties Protestantism is in, the gap that exists between the leaders and the ordinary laity, the abnormal difficulties of communication, the repression of articulate disagreement, and

---

[3]Watkins, "Epistemology and Politics", *Proceedings of the Aristotelian Society*, 1957–58, pp. 79–102.

the plasticity of religious language—complement one another in a web of deception, partly intended and partly unintended.

Moreover, the presence of such authoritarianism in Protestantism needs to be discussed, if only because it is often masked by a popular image of the Protestant religion as a prototype of democratic activity. This image, reinforced during the nineteenth-century flowering of Protestant liberalism and the proliferation of sects whose members were still able to determine when they differed in opinion, is no longer so applicable today. Even the most vehement Protestant attacks on Catholicism for its authoritarianism and its antidemocratic tendencies are very often the result not of any basic difference about the role of religion in national life but of a sharp difference about whose religion is to play that role.

To indicate the extent of this calculated Protestant authoritarianism, it will be sufficient to consider the role it plays in: (1) the relations between clergy and laity within the churches; and (2) the policies for public education advocated by many leading Protestants.

2. Limping before the Lame

Crane Brinton once speculated that "the moral anguish of our age is rather the mark of the intellectual classes in our West than of the many".[4] If the intellectual classes are confused, the nonintellectual classes are *kept* in the dark. In the foreword to the 1946 edition of *Brave New World,* Aldous Huxley wrote:

> The greatest triumphs of propaganda have been accomplished, not by doing something, but by refraining from doing. . . . By simply not mentioning certain subjects, by lowering . . . an "iron curtain" between the masses and such facts or arguments as the local political bosses regard as undesirable, totalitarian propagandists have influenced opinion much more effectively than they could have by the most eloquent denunciations, the most compelling of logical rebuttals.

Contemporary Protestant theologians have lowered a curtain of formulae between the mass of Protestants and the problems of Protestantism. And this policy has during the past few years led to a practice that—although in itself an old policy—is rather new in American Protestantism.

Perhaps Dostoevsky has portrayed the policy, and the questions it raises, most vividly. In 1881 the Russian novelist placed on the lips of Ivan Karamazov, an atheist, the famous legend of the Grand Inquisitor, cardinal

[4]Crane Brinton, *A History of Western Morals* (London: Weidenfeld and Nicolson, 1959), p. 391 f.

of Seville, who deceived his flock for their own sakes. According to Ivan's tale, Christ had reappeared in Seville and had been promptly imprisoned by the Inquisition. Late at night the cardinal—whom Ivan describes as also an atheist—visits Christ in the dungeon in an attempt to defend before Him his suppression of intellectual and religious freedom in Spain. Describing the believers whom he and those who shared his priestcraft had deceived, the cardinal insists:

> We shall show them that they are weak, that they are only pitiful children, but that childlike happiness is the sweetest of all. . . . And all will be happy, all the millions of creatures, except the hundred thousand sufferers who have taken upon themselves the curse of the knowledge of good and evil. Peacefully they will die, peacefully they will expire in Thy name, and beyond the grave they will find nothing but death. But we shall keep the secret, and for their happiness we shall allure them with the reward of heaven and eternity. . . . Judge us if Thou canst and darest. . . . I too prized the freedom with which Thou hast blessed men. . . . But I awakened and would not serve madness. I turned back and joined the ranks of those who have corrected Thy work.

Four hundred years after the Grand Inquisitor, and three quarters of a century after Dostoevsky, Tillich has endorsed a similar kind of priestcraft. Like the Grand Inquisitor, Tillich does not believe in the popular "God of theism", the God who answers prayer and offers men a life beyond the grave. Frequently he has emphasized the contrast between his own theology and faiths that hold to a more literal interpretation of the biblical teachings. For instance, Tillich writes:

> The primitive period of individuals and groups consists in the inability to separate the creations of symbolic imagination from the facts which can be verified through observation and experiment. *This stage has a full right of its own and should not be disturbed, either in individuals or in groups, up to the moment when man's questioning mind breaks the natural acceptance of the mythological visions as literal.*[5]

Tillich contrasts this stage with

> the second stage of literalism, the conscious one, which is aware of the questions but represses them, half consciously, half unconsciously. The tool of repression is usually an acknowledged authority with sacred qualities like the Church or the Bible, to which one owes unconditional surrender. *This stage is still justifiable, if the questioning power is very weak and can easily be answered.* It is unjustifiable if a mature mind is broken in its personal center by political or psychological methods, split in his unity, and hurt in his integrity.[6]

Tillich and the Grand Inquisitor seem agreed on a number of points. Both

---

[5] *Dynamics of Faith*, p. 52. Italics are mine.
[6] Ibid., p. 53.

believe that it is better to let *innocent* ignorance prevail. When doubts arise in an individual, they leave it to his minister to decide whether his doubts are weak enough to be refuted, or whether he must be made one of the "hundred thousand sufferers" who inhabit the inner circle of the broken myth. Tillich and the Inquisitor most clearly *disagree* over a positive program of enforced ignorance: Tillich would sponsor no inquisition.

I have not brought these two passages together either to condemn Tillich or to suggest that his motives are similar to the Inquisitor's. Much as Dostoevsky hated the cardinal's policy, he could not help portraying him sympathetically as one who "all his life loved humanity". At least as much must be said for Tillich. Indeed, it is ironical that the suggestion of such a comparison could even arise; for in his intellectual autobiography Tillich specifically mentions his personal *fight* against the figure of the Grand Inquisitor as "a decisive element of my theological thought".[7]

Although it is easy enough to deplore such ideas, certain questions arise: Aren't such practices inevitable? Isn't Tillich's approach in fact the only *realistic* one? Must we not simply accept the fact that people are different in their capabilities, that most men are simply beyond the reaches of theological interpretation? On this level at least, isn't a breakdown of communication unavoidable?

These questions sound reasonable, and some of them may be answered affirmatively. Certainly Tillich is not alone in his opinions about them: other philosophers, such as C. E. M. Joad, have raised similar points. "Is it wise", he asked, "to continue to erode the foundations in history and metaphysics upon which the Christian faith is based? If we can't accept them ourselves, may it not, nevertheless, be well that we should at least pretend, remembering in our emergency Plato's hint about the social beneficence of the useful lie?"[8]

Huston Smith has specifically defended Tillich's position with similar arguments. Every great historical religion, Smith argued, has a "layered character". "Indian thought", he points out, "has never hesitated to commend to persons at different levels of understanding different concepts of God, ranging from graven images to the absolutely formless Nirguna Brahman". Smith contends that although Western theology has allowed "less latitude", it, too, has accepted the principle. He gives as an example an old story about St. Thomas Aquinas: "When an old woman asked St. Thomas whether the names of all the blessed were written on a scroll exhibited in Heaven, he wrote back with untiring calm: 'So far as I can see

---

[7]"Autobiographical Reflections", in *The Theology of Paul Tillich*, ed. Kegley and Bretall (New York: Macmillan, 1956), p. 8.

[8]As quoted by Brand Blanshard in "The Morality of Self Respect", *New Republic*, February 28, 1955.

this is not the case; but there is no harm in saying so'." There is, Smith blandly concludes, no duplicity in this activity; it is simply founded on a basic fact about human nature.[9] Christ's wisdom, once unattainable to the wise and prudent and best available to the simple and to babes, has undergone a curious reversal.

Such "benevolent sowing of ignorance", like many other theological practices today, has a philosophical root in the new Protestantism. Smith's idea of a "layered truth" is in many respects an *internal* application of the notion of "truth for the committed group" which has helped the theologians defend their general commitment *vis-à-vis* the wider external culture.

Yet, as Joad's remark suggests, Smith might have gone far back in the Western tradition, to one of its most respected sources, to find further defense for his position. He could have resorted to Plato's famous policy of "the royal lie", described in the *Republic* and the *Laws,* which allows the rulers, for the good of the state, to introduce certain myths designed to arrest social change and mobility. All that is really needed, Plato suggests, is "just one royal lie".[10] However, the great philosopher who immortalized Socrates's quest for truth explains *his* royal fib with some embarrassment— considerably more than Tillich, Smith, or even, apparently, St. Thomas, in his "untiring calm", seemed to show. "Well then", Plato says, "I will speak, although I really know not how to look you in the face, or in what words to utter the audacious fiction, which I propose to communicate gradually".

Hidden persuasion, then, is an old art. Yet Tillich's program cannot be explained by anything so simple as a "desire to deceive", or to arrest social change. Quite the contrary. The trouble with Tillich, as contrasted with Plato, is that Tillich's policy is not founded on a very realistic interpretation of human nature: his policy is surprisingly naïve. For one becomes neither profound nor realistic by making the rather obvious observation that most men are not very bright. To judge the role of religion, one must heed the logic of the situations in which the traditional religious stories are told today.

Such caution is particularly important for anyone who, like Tillich, plays the part of a "physician of society", a cultural psychiatrist who is concerned to "break the hold" of misleading "models" that are causing societal neurosis. Although one of the chief concerns of psychiatry is *preventative* medicine, Tillich and similar thinkers often attack neurosis—if they treat it at all—only *after* it has arisen. The question arises whether Tillich—by urging that the Christian myths be taught to unsophisticated people as "the truth", by encouraging children to acquire a literal understanding of them, and by arguing that this kind of religion is "justifiable" as long as no one is being *forced* to think this way—is not really spreading the seeds of conflict.

---

[9]Smith made these remarks in a letter to *Harper's* which appeared in the section "Protestant Voices", July 1959.
[10]Plato, *Republic*, 3.414.

Consider the possible biography of a believer. Having been taught Bible stories as the truth in his nondoubting period, he grows up a devout believer. Then he reads a book or goes away to college and learns about the difficulties in religious belief. The resulting conflict may jeopardize not only his belief but his mental balance as well. His whole scheme of values may totter and fall. Before this point, ideally, the Tillichian minister comes along, asks a few astute questions to determine just how strong the doubt is, learns that the fellow's doubts cannot be quashed, and so reveals to him that the Christian stories are *really* symbolically true. "They are symbols, no less", the preacher says. "Didn't you know *that?* Why, that's what I meant all the time". The wise and realistic farmer need not destroy his own harvest.

The problem, of course, is a general one:

> A diseased state of an organism, a society or culture, is characterizied by a weakening of the integrative controls, and the tendency of its parts to behave in an independent and self-assertive manner, ignoring the superior interest of the whole, or trying to impose their own laws on it.[11]

Part of Tillich's mistake here was to let his love and often deep understanding of the Christian stories and traditions blind him to the daily tragedy of not-so-simple men who are shattered by the discovery that the creeds in which they put their trust are false and by the obvious inference they tend to make that *everything,* their whole world, is breaking down. Perhaps theologians will some day ponder how much of the mental disorder and meaninglessness that they say is prevalent among young people today is due to their discovery in late adolescence that the "true" biblical stories they learned in their youth are literally false, and to their being accustomed from early childhood and from many traditions of Western culture to a peculiar *standard* of "ultimate satisfaction" and "ultimate meaning" that is both psychologically unrealistic and philosophically untenable.

But suppose it *were* realistic to think that ignorance could be sown benevolently and successfully by the representatives of Protestantism or of some other ideologically oriented group, in some "brave new America" of the future. Every would-be Protestant theologian must still answer for himself the question whether he intends to participate in such deception, however benevolent it might be.

Even if Tillich's main fault here was in fact lack of realism—perhaps a kind of social blindness linked with the dismal failure of the "religious socialism" he tried to lead to political power in Germany during the 1920s—he still cannot entirely be excused from the charge of having yielded to an old temptation that seems especially seductive to intellectuals: the urge to take it upon oneself to decide what is best for other people; the willingness to keep other people unconscious in order to prevent them from

---

[11]Koestler, *The Sleepwalkers,* p. 517.

making errors. Perhaps this is an especially grave mistake for a Protestant theologian. For it involves a social policy that seems quite at variance with at least one of the traditional conceptions of Protestantism—the idea of the priesthood of all believers. According to a common interpretation of this idea, each man can and should seek out God for himself; no man is *dependent* on the intermediary activity of a church or priest, although he may, if he wishes, make use of such intermediaries. When joined, as it often has been, with the more obviously rationalized idea of the Quest, this principle has been one of the most important and fruitful concepts in the development of Western spiritual traditions. Together, the two ideas have nourished the belief in the importance of the individual human being. Here, the *quest* for God becomes most important for the individual, and it really does not matter greatly if someone on his own comes to a "wrong" conception of God. It may be immaterial that an old lady thinks the names of the blessed are exhibited on a scroll in heaven; or that someone else devotes his life to discovering whether angels are able to read and write. But it can be very serious if someone who believes that the names of the blessed are not so exhibited, or that there are no angels anyway, leads other gullible people, for his own purposes, to believe that there is such a heavenly exhibition—or that angels are literate. Protestantism, then, seems lost in the business of selling a product, whereas the quest for truth is something that can be neither sold nor bought.

To search after truth is to start to scale a mountain of infinite height. It is no more possible that some climber will reach the top than it is that some mathematician will count all the numbers. Yet, at least from the foothills below, the most distant reaches seem infinitely attractive. The visible snowcaps seem bathed in sunlight; and who knows what wonders are beyond the clouds? Most men go climbing at least for a while—with or without equipment and preparation, with or without natural strength.

Some of the most talented climbers have always been disappointed, soul-chillingly disappointed, on reaching the first snowcaps. It looked so much better from down below; and the climb itself was far more satisfying than the plateau. The mountain winds are real and cold, and the warmth of the sunlight is only an illusion. Self-pity often sets in—the self-pity that flees from itself to pity others. "The poor people down below!" the story goes. "They are really better off where they are, while they still have such great expectations." And so the people on the plateau set up a cloud factory to slow up the others for their own sake.

> You are good when you walk to your goal
> firmly and with bold steps.
> Yet you are not evil when you go thither
> limping.

Even those who limp go not backward.
But you who are strong and swift, see
that you do not limp before the
lame, deeming it kindness.[12]

3. The Educational Unifiers

It is difficult to become very excited about the personal ideological and spiritual tyranny, deplorable as it is, which goes on within the church. Religious affiliation is voluntary; and throughout much of the Western world an individual is able to criticize the church before any audience whose attention he can gain. Besides, there are worse terrors in the world than a tyranny of holy words to which one owes obeisance whether or not they are rationally interpretable. This situation begins to grow dangerous in the uncritical attitude toward authority which it can encourage. If it is in the "unswept corners of our intellectual universe that the germs of epidemics are often bred",[13] an attempt to sweep some of the usually skirted corners may be worthwhile.

There are many such germs in *education* today, often sown by men who, frustrated and battered by the present, would like to try to control the future by conditioning the young people who will comprise it. One example of the call to national ideological unity through the educational system apeared in 1956, in a paper by the Christian philosopher John Wild.[14] Wild attributed many of the troubles of the West to its lack of a unified educational structure and insisted that just such a structure "is the most desperate need of our time". Claiming that the great contemporary world cultures—his examples are Buddhism, Hinduism, Mohammedanism, and the Marxism-Leninism of the U.S.S.R.—"are guided by overarching patterns of religious and philosophic thought which are cultivated in their schools, and which elicit voluntary devotion", Wild called attention to the roots of Russian culture in the philosophy of Marx's teacher Hegel:

> This semi-religious philosophy has been corrected and refined by several generations of thinkers, including Marx and Lenin. At the present time it includes fundamental ontology based on evidence accessible to all which can give an intelligible account of the results of the different sciences, a philosophy of man and human history which takes account of many facts, an

[12]Kahlil Gibran, *The Prophet* (New York: Alfred A. Knopf, 1948), p. 73 f.

[13]E. H. Gombrich, *Art and Scholarship,* Inaugural Lecture delivered at University College, London (London: H. K. Lewis & Co., 1957), p. 14.

[14]"Philosophy of Education in the West: A Desperate Present Need", *Harvard Educational Review,* 1956. See Wild's letter to the *New Republic,* May 5, 1958, p. 12, and my reply, *New Republic,* May 19, 1958.

ethics which claims to be grounded in the dialectic laws of nature, and a penetrating analysis of class conflict which has already offered unequivocal guidance for social action, and which has a profound appeal to many scientific minds, and to millions of oppressed people all over the world. Hence it is no accident that this integrating culture is far more formidable than any other now confronting us. The view of the world which binds it together is taught as a compulsory subject in every Russian high school as well as in every technical school and university. What do we have in the West corresponding to this great overarching structure of ideas? What integrating view of the world now guides our Western life and policy? . . . There is none!

One might prod Professor Wild's statement in many places, beginning with a few questions about this "compulsory subject" which elicits such "voluntary devotion". Such criticism is unnecessary here. Wild's address was only an especially excited version of a point of view one often encounters in Protestant as well as Catholic discussions about the place of religion in higher education: in Sir Walter Moberly's *Crisis in the University*; in Henry P. Van Dusen's *God in Education*; in George A. Buttrick's *Faith and Education*; in Howard Lowry's *The Mind's Adventure*; in T. S. Eliot's *The Idea of a Christian Society*; in the Kent School Symposium on *The Christian Idea of Education*.

Broadly stated, the view diagnoses that in order to destroy the Western tower of Babel, its self-doubt, hesitation, anxiety, lack of effective communication, and disagreement, the West needs to adopt a comprehensive cultural ideology—usually some form of Christianity. Very few advocates of such views suggest communist-type enforcement of their "overarching faith". Certainly Wild does not. Most, like Wild, give no directions at all, indulging in a latter-day "belling of the cat". A few, to be sure, have been somewhat more explicit. In his book *Christ and Man's Dilemma*,[15] George A. Buttrick, the former chaplain to Harvard, argued that "an agreed-upon syllabus of religious studies" should be instituted in the American public-school system. But if it were impossible to achieve such a syllabus, Buttrick proceeded, very seriously, to argue:

> it would be better—however unfortunate and schismatic—for each faith to build its own schools rather than continue with a merely secular education. . . . I hold the conviction regarding Protestant denominations that, however worthy and heroic their respective origins, the crisis of our time now requires their unity. So deep is this conviction that I suspect the phrase "unity, not uniformity," for I wonder how there can be unity without *some* clear form, since unity cannot be a disembodied spirit. The tragic dismemberment of Protestantism is more tragic because it cripples Protestantism in its task of real education. A united Protestantism could help offset the blight of secularism in education; a dismembered Protestantism is a tragedy, and may now be a crime. But, if secular education is to remain merely secular, any substitute in truer basic faith, even though I would deplore a dismembered

---

[15]George A. Buttrick, *Christ and Man's Dilemma* (Nashville: Abingdon Press), chap. 6.

substitute, would be a gain. . . . By whatever worthy means, at the price of whatever temporary chaos, secular education must become religious, or the religious community must establish its own schools.[16]

Similar ideas about how American education might combat secularism in a more unified way—"at the price of whatever temporary chaos"—appeared in some remarks made by a Catholic, Father John Courtney Murray, at the predominantly Protestant Kent School Symposium:

> We have the older students in the college and the university. Shouldn't it be possible to make an impact upon their imaginations with the humanities and with Christian doctrine in such wise that we would, as it were, immunize them from the impact of the scientific experience?

Students would also be immunized, apparently, from the disintegrating effects of intelligent reflection and searching examination. Moberly, for instance, has written:

> In Europe amoralism is widely prevalent; and our own abler young men will accept nothing from tradition without searching examination. We academic people are too little awake to this disintegration. . . .

In this flip way, searching examination of oneself and one's tradition, activities that have, at least since the time of Socrates, stamped man as civilized, are pronounced marks of disintegration.

Many questions reaching far beyond the bounds of educational theory arise out of the various proposals for unification. Two of the most important are: Does the West need a common faith in its battle with communism? And if so, is this faith Christianity? It is practically impossible to answer the second question affirmatively. There are too many different Christianities for Christianity to act as a system that Western men might agree on today, whatever its unifying power half a millennium ago. Moreover, it is difficult to see how any Protestant theologian who maintains that any future intellectual synthesis, when and if it does come, must be a Christian synthesis can escape being justly accused of precisely the sort of intellectual pride that Protestant theologians so automatically deplore when it appears among non-Christians.

An approach toward an answer to the first question is available in James Bryant Conant's book *The Citadel of Learning*. There Conant gives a critique of Soviet education which serves almost as a point-by-point rebuttal of the kind of theory many of the contemporary Christian unifiers espouse.

---

[16]For an illustration of such worthy means and temporary chaos in action, see the literature relating to the religious controversy at Harvard University, March and April 1958, beginning with my article "Religion at Harvard", *Harvard Crimson*, March 28, 1958 (reprinted in the *New Republic*, April 21, 1958). Several paragraphs in the text above are paraphrased from this article. See also the almost daily correspondence about this matter printed in the *Crimson* during April 1958, and the reports of the controversy and its results which appeared in the *St. Louis Post-Dispatch*, May 11, 1958; *Harvard Crimson*, April 23, 1958; and *Time*, April 14, 1958. See Greg Lawless, ed., *The Harvard Crimson Anthology: 100 Years at Harvard* (New York: Houghton Mifflin, 1980), pp. 76–79.

Writing of some of his experiences as American ambassador to the Federal Republic of Germany, Conant noted that no one "uses the word 'unity' more frequently than those who are attempting to force the Soviet ideology on the people of the Russian zone". Their educational syllogism, he states, goes like this: Education is concerned with truth, truth is everywhere the same, therefore education should be everywhere the same. Pointing out the pernicious effects of such a doctrine in practice, as in the Lysenko case, for example, Conant argues that a scientist or a scholar, to the degree that he is dedicated to the advancement of learning as such, must aim to contribute to a long-range human enterprise, not to an immediate undertaking or battle. "If anyone in the free world believes that a unifying philosophy is a goal to be desired at whatever price", Conant suggests, "then he should drive from the free sectors of Berlin eastward through the Brandenburg Gate".

The words "at whatever price"—recalling Buttrick's phrase "at the price of whatever temporary chaos"—should be underscored. For some Protestant philosophers of education apparently are willing to unify the curriculum at whatever price. So distinguished and genuinely liberal a Christian educator as Henry P. Van Dusen, president of Union Theological Seminary, a charter member of the board of trustees of Princeton University, has written:

> Instructors might protest that, if they were adequately to teach their several subjects in conformity to the basic premise of the Unity of Truth, they would be compelled to recast the underlying structure of their minds. To which it might be replied, perhaps that is just what is required, if they are to fulfill their central loyalty to Truth.

One wonders how the recasting of the "underlying structure" of one's mind differs from brainwashing. Since it is structural, perhaps it is meant to be more thorough than mere washing. And, of course, the "compelling" would doubtless be voluntary.

These calls for ideological unity often reflect a desire that society have the symmetry and internal order of a painting, a formula, a building. When juxtaposed with some other themes of contemporary Protestantism, however, such aestheticism evokes a special irony. For one of the soundest distinctions made popular by this theology is that between the "I", the "thou", and the "it"—a distinction which the theologians have used in deploring the "scientific" practice of treating man as an *object* instead of as a *subject*. Yet what objectifies man more than the attempt to paint him fast and predictably into the order of a social canvas?[17]

---

[17]Compare T. S. Eliot, *The Idea of a Christian Society* (New York: Harcourt, Brace and Company, 1940), p. 26; and Aldous Huxley, *Brave New World* (London: Penguin Books, 1955), Chap. 17.

EPILOGUE

The leading Protestant theologians of the twentieth century have, then, embraced as fact the philosophical contention that rationality is logically limited, that every man—willy-nilly—makes some ultimately irrational commitment; and they have used this contention to excuse rationally their own irrational commitment to Christ. Thereby, they have been able in principle, although not in practice, to avoid loss of intellectual integrity.

I have tried to refute the philosophical theory about the limits of rationality by turning the tables, by showing how we can shift the emphasis in rational discussion from justification to a nonjustificational criticism of our beliefs and commitments. I hope, in this way, to have helped clarify the issues of identity and integrity in both Protestantism and rationalism, and to have made the choice at least clearer to individuals who are torn between them. If my argument is sound, there can no longer be a general rational excuse for ultimate irrational commitments. Those who continue to make them will *really* be irrationalists, in the sense that they will not be able to retain their Protestant or other irrationalist identity with the intellectual integrity which the argument about the limits of rationality afforded them, so long as it went unrefuted.

Still, my argument does not force anyone to be a rationalist; it only shows that there is no rational or logical excuse for being an irrationalist. Anyone who wishes, or who is personally able to do so, may remain an irrationalist. And it may be difficult indeed to argue with any such person, for he will have abandoned argument. No one, for instance, can expect to convince a psychotic that he is ill if he cannot or will not accept the diagnosis. The person who fervently believes that one is equal to zero need never admit that two and two equals four. I cannot convince Hitler that murder is wrong. And I hardly know where to begin arguing with the Anglican canon who has announced that mental patients are not ill but are *really* possessed by evil spirits.

How should a man who is trying to be a rationalist act toward such people? If the rationalist were in fact *committed* to rationalism, he would be entitled to treat such people as they treat him: he could regard them as members of a different *ecclesia,* or ultimately committed religious community, whom—since real argument was impossible—he could best hope to convert through nonrational persuasion.

But since the rationalist, as I have tried to show, need be committed neither to his rationalism nor to any other of his beliefs, he need not repudiate people with whom he fundamentally disagrees. In principle, he can act toward them in a remarkable way.

In the old story, the Pennsylvania Dutchman says to his wife: "Everybody is crazy but me and thee, Hanna, and sometimes I wonder even about thee." Anybody, from the neurotic to Reinhold Niebuhr, can play Pennsylvania Dutchman and ask us to "take the leap of faith"—whether it is a "great leap forward", a great leap backward, or a somersault on the status quo—to his own irrational commitment. That commitment may carry consolations; there are, as Ibsen knew, such things as "saving lies". But if we look before we leap—and when the chasm is very wide, he who hesitates is not necessarily lost—many of us will be unable to crucify our intellects without impaling our integrity.

As long as the *tu quoque* argument about the limits of rationality stood unchallenged, it was possible for a man to crucify his intellect, to make an irrational commitment, without impaling his integrity. For those who claimed to be rationalists had clearly impaled *their* integrity. However, having discovered why that argument is invalid, I no longer need to make that leap; and I think no one else has to do so either. People can, like Lessing, be engaged without being committed.[1]

Yet anyone who has grappled with the arguments about ultimate commitment and the limits of rationality, and who has appreciated what a strong case the irrationalists have been able to put up, should have acquired at least one virtue: a measure of intellectual humility. For rationalists can and very often do make mistakes, too. I used to think a good approach in almost any disagreement (provided none of the disputants had the power to impose his opinions) was Hamlet's reply to the queen:

> *My pulse, as yours, doth temperately keep time,*
> *And makes as healthful music. It is not madness*
> *That I have uttered. . . .*
>   *. . . Mother, for love of grace,*
> *Lay not that flattering unction to your soul,*
> *That not your trespass, but my madness speaks!*

Although I still think Hamlet's advice is sound, I have altered my attitude toward it. The would-be panrationalist, as I once was, usually presumes that his opponent is a fool. For the self-conscious panrationalist knows in his heart that his own position is riddled with inconsistencies, and "whoever is hard put to feel identical with one set of people and ideas must that much

[1]See E. H. Gombrich's fascinating account in his "Lessing, Lecture on a Master Mind", *Proceedings of the British Academy*, 1957 (Oxford: Oxford University Press, 1958).

more violently repudiate another set".[2] Hence, I used to picture myself self-righteously repeating Hamlet's words to those who practiced the "queen of the sciences". Today, wiser in a *pancritical* rationalism which makes no claims that it cannot carry through, which recognizes that although rationality is indeed unlimited we are all nonetheless prone to error, that "while differing widely in the various little bits we know, in our infinite ignorance we are all equal",[3] I try to imagine my opponents reciting Hamlet's passage back to me; and I try to listen to it as good advice for me, *as well as for them.*

Such an attitude, which helps us to treat our opponents as sane men, or perhaps simply as *men,* and which is rooted in the admission that "I may be wrong and you, even you, a poor irrationalist, may be right", makes argument, and learning—scientific, moral, metaphysical, and religious— possible. For each of us plays Pennsylvania Dutchman at some time of his life. And sometimes the Pennsylvania Dutchman is right.

Perhaps surprisingly, the practice of asking one's opponents for criticisms of one's own position, and of taking these criticisms seriously, resembles in certain ways a Christian position. It recalls the Sermon-on-the Mount idea of turning the other cheek, and this resemblance, however faint, leads to some interesting reflections.

When Jesus, in his Sermon, admonished his listeners to turn the other cheek and go the second mile, he probably had in mind practical human relationships. The exegetical problem of whether his suggestions were intended to apply only to a short period preceding the imminent coming of the Kingdom of God, or to a longer period, does not arise here. What is important is that few people today would put much faith in such utopian policies. They have learned too much from the times and from recent moralists, both Protestant and secular, to treat the Sermon on the Mount as a rule book for practical politics.

The situation is different if one applies the Sermon's injunctions not to politics but to the business of argument and discussion. Where argument about the world and discussion of problems are concerned, some of the advice contained in the Sermon on the Mount is highly realistic. Perhaps this is not so surprising as it might sound in isolation—or even in the present context. For if we treat our opponents in discussion *not as they treat us, but as we would have them treat us,* it is we who profit. When our object is to learn rather than to win a debate, we must take our opponents' arguments seriously and not reject them unless we can refute them. As far as our aim, learning about the world and ourselves, is concerned, it does not matter whether our opponent reciprocates, or whether he treats our own arguments as no more than emotive signals. We may learn from the criticisms of our opponents even when their own practice prevents them from learning from us. Whatever his real motive or intention may be, the rationalist acts in his own interest (provided his interest is learning) when he takes his opponents' thoughts seriously, when he treats his opponent as a person rather than as a tiresome talking machine he would like to switch off.

I have mentioned this parallel not in order to come back to Christianity through the attic window, but to point out yet another irony in the new theology. When it comes to critical discussion, those who divide the world into "us" and "they", appeal to the so-called limits of rationality and the necessity of commitment, and then preach to their opponents rather than argue with them, at once forget their own advice and also fail to use one of the most appealing features of Christianity—the Sermon on the Mount—in one of the very few practical contexts in which it may occasionally be appropriate.

The last, but far from imaginary, opponent whose arrows I shall face before closing is no cupid, though he speaks in the name of love.

My position, he will say, is far removed from any religion of love. The pancritical rationalism I have championed, he will add, is a ruthless policy that replaces loving commitment with cold scrutiny. For the relationship of commitment is like the relationship of love. We do not argue ourselves into love, and once in love we do not try to argue ourselves out again. No one who loves truly will deliberately subject his loved ones to danger. But criticism may be dangerous; to subject our love commitments to criticism is therefore to endanger them. By advocating pancritical rationalism, I advocate a harsh, cruel attitude unworthy of sensitive and civilized men. Love *should* be blind.

In an unloving world, the ability to love is precious, and not just because it is rare. If certain people have nothing better to love than some idea—or perhaps a fancy about a prophet who lived and died long ago, leaving traces so scanty and conflicting that some of his most dedicated modern biographers say that we can know little of what he was like or what he did—who can condemn such people? Let them love when and what they can.

But what a sorry kind of love. Love is not for ideas but for individual people, real and alive, and—already in a different sense—for our live and vivid memories of people we once loved directly.

And what a dangerous kind of love. For when the love of ideas and fancies becomes a substitute for the love of living people, the lover, the committed man, often subordinates the requirements of human beings to the claims of his idea—the "demand of the object". Thus, that most inhuman of transformations occurs: human beings become objects, to be bent, broken, molded, even "educated," for the love of an idea.

There is yet another and still more important objection to the would-be spokesman for love. Although I have suggested that a sound ethic for argument could be read into Jesus's words in the Sermon on the Mount, I did not intend that ethic as an endorsement of Christianity or as a divine sanction for pancritical rationalism or, most important, as part of a religion of love. Too many people who do not love anyone in particular like to talk grandly about their love for humanity. If anything, there is too much rather than too little of this love of humanity in the world today. Such talk of love, which can cover almost any sentiment or policy, suggests the danger and difficulty, if not the impossibility, of attempting to spread love too widely, of trying to make it into a universal religion. Love should not be treated like a commodity: offered to a few people with lavished care, it can flourish and return itself beyond expectation; but anyone who pretends to offer it to all comers at once misrepresents himself and turns his would-be gift into a mass product.

The ethic of argument that I endorse invokes a different sort of sentiment, which can be spread far more widely: *respect* for people. Whether one owes love to few people or many, one owes respect to all—at least until they very definitely show themselves unworthy of it. One of the most important ways of indicating prima facie respect for a person is to attempt to take his views seriously. This would be impossible if rationality were so limited that critical argument was impossible. I have tried in this essay to promote this sort of respect by showing that the critical argument it calls for is possible and by illustrating some of the unfortunate consequences of the retreat to commitment.

APPENDICES, 1984

APPENDIX 1. A METACONTEXT
FOR RATIONALITY

1. Three Problems of Rationality

There are three separate problems of rationality with which this book is concerned directly or indirectly. They are:

(1) the problem of the (logical) limits of rationality;
(2) the *demarcational* problem of rationality;
(3) the problem of *the ecology of rationality*.

The first problem, that of the limits of rationality, is the chief problem treated in the body of the book, and is elaborated particularly in appendices 3, 4, 5, and 6. The second—the demarcational problem of rationality—is treated in appendix 2.

The third—that of the ecology of rationality—is the main subject of this first appendix; and is also treated in appendix 2, section 11. The solution to the first two problems contributes to, and indeed licenses, the broader problem-program of the ecology of rationality.

2. No Boat Goes to the Other Shore Which Is Safe and without Danger

> I have taught a doctrine similar to a raft—it is for crossing over, and not for carrying.
> —THE BUDDHA
> *MAJJIHIMA-NIKAYA I*

Several years ago, well after first publishing *The Retreat to Commitment,* there came to me a line of thinking which seems to be important, and which I would like to share with my readers. It is a line of thinking which preserves and enhances the argument of this book, and yet takes it to a new dimension.[1]

[1]See my book *Werner Erhard: The Transformation of a Man* (New York: Clarkson N. Potter, 1978), chap. 10.

169

My line of thought has to do with what I call *"metacontext"*, and with my realization that rationality—although treated implicitly in this book as if it were a matter of *context* ("the rationalist identity"), should be treated metacontextually.

The terms I have just introduced will be foreign to most readers, and thus what I have said will have made no sense. Let me explain what I mean.

I can begin to do this best, I think, by speaking in terms of *ecology*, for the problem that will emerge is that of *the ecology of rationality*.

Ecology is, of course, the theory of the interrelationship between an organism and its environment, and has to do with survival. The pertinent part of the human environment, of course, contains people, plants, animals, and various things (objects, chemicals, and so on). It also contains certain ideas and patterns of thought which are every bit as real as the organisms, objects, and physical conditions of the environment. These ideas and patterns of thought are not all of a piece, but are of different sorts. They can be partially classified as follows:

(a) *positions*—these include (1) a variety of descriptions, representations, or portrayals of the environment; and (2) a variety of recommended ways of behaving within the environment so represented;

(b) a variety of *contexts* for these positions;

(c) *criticisms* of and objections to various positions and contexts —these criticisms may themselves be positional or contextual;

(d) various *contexts of contexts* or *metacontexts*.

The human econiche is one in which people hold conflicting positions *in* conflicting contexts and *in terms of* conflicting metacontexts.

An example of a *position* could be a simple statement purporting to be true or right: e.g., "The human soul is immortal", or "abortion is wrong".

Similar-appearing positions may be embedded in quite different *contexts*. Christianity, Buddhism, Hinduism, and humanism, for instance, provide different contexts for the position-statement, "The human soul is immortal". Examples of contexts are belief systems, ideologies, traditions, institutions.[2] Such a context is not simply the sum of the positions it contains, but is also the framework and even the sensibility in which these positions are couched; and it weights positions with regard to importance and significance.

To illustrate how a sensibility casts a context over a statement, one might notice the way in which I, in the comfort of my study, reach out to the overflowing bowl of strawberries on my table, take and eat one as I read,

---

[2]Most Kuhnian paradigms are contexts in my sense; most Kuhnian paradigm shifts are contextual shifts in my sense. See Thomas S. Kuhn, *The Structure of Scientific Revolutions*, 2nd ed. (Chicago: University of Chicago Press, 1970).

and comment in a self-satisfied way to myself, "This strawberry is so sweet". And one might contrast this with the Zen sensibility of the doomed Samurai, trapped on a collapsing bridge over a deep ravine, who, savoring the moment, reaches out to pluck the strawberry growing wild on the steep bank and says, "This strawberry is so sweet".

Many persons find personal identification or "identity" in the sense of this book—and in the sense of the psychologist and sociologist Erik H. Erikson—in contexts. They employ contexts to define themselves and their relations to others and to the world. Their allegiance is to the context; allegiance to particular positions sponsored within that context generally flows from allegiance to the context rather than vice versa. Thus, as an example, opposition to abortion (a position) is likely to flow from one's Roman Catholicism (a context) rather than Roman Catholicism's flowing from one's opposition to abortion.

In the complicated world of ordinary practice, however, it is not always easy to tell a position from a context. Thus what one might have thought to be a position may act contextually, and vice versa. Some politician—or the notorious Vicar of Bray—may shift his party or his church for the sake of some position that has taken on a contextual character. If, for example, his political ambition sets the context for his life, the selection of a party may be a matter of position within that context. Within the justificationist meta-context (to be explained in a moment) such action almost always smacks of disloyalty.

Rationality—as embedding the search for knowledge and the critical attitude—can hardly be a matter of positions or contexts. There is nothing intrinsically rational about any particular position or context—including that particular context known as "rationalism" or "the rationalist identity" or "the rationalist tradition". Positions and contexts may further or hinder the search for knowledge and the critical attitude. Rather, rationality would have to be a matter of the *context of contexts,* or the *metacontext.*

A metacontext differs from a context as understood here. *A metacontext has to do with how and why contexts are held,* subjectively and objectively. While there are endless positions and thousands of contexts, there are comparatively few metacontexts. (I believe, in fact, that there are exactly three: see below.)

Theory of rationality and ecology of rationality are thus metacontextual: they are theory about how and why to hold contexts and positions; and they depend in part on goals: e.g., is it one's goal to justify or defend a particular position? or to attain a more adequate representation of the way in which things are?

People have, throughout history, differed fundamentally about how and why to hold contexts and positions; these differences, as we shall see, have a religious dimension. Yet what I call metacontext has hardly been noticed and is rarely discussed—although without such a discussion one cannot characterize the nature of the most fundamental differences among men: *one cannot define the way in which they differ about the ways in which they differ.*

A few writers, however, have occasionally reached the metacontextual level. Robert Michels used to write that the humanist tradition possessed a myth of mission but lacked—and needed—a myth of origin. Such a myth of origin for the rationalist tradition, and also an idea of what metacontext represents, may be found by contrasting the development of ideas in the pre-Socratic schools of the Pythagoreans and the Ionians.[3] Among the Pythagoreans a *second-order tradition* was developed of defending, preserving, and passing on to others the doctrines of the founders of the school. This metacontextual second-order tradition had the effect of restricting development in the ideology; and of limiting changes to those that could be handled surreptitiously—as, say, a restatement of the master's real intentions, or as a correction of previous misinterpretations. For the master's teachings were assumed to be correct. Whereas among the Ionians, by contrast, one has the first recorded instance of widely different viewpoints being explicitly handed on, without dissent or schism, by the same school in successive generations. There a metacontextual second-order tradition was developed of criticizing and of trying to improve upon the doctrines of the master for the purpose of getting *closer* to the truth. Within this second school, the origins of the critical tradition may be located. Here a true history of ideas begins to develop, in which, along with the ideas of the leaders of the school, criticisms and changes are also taught, respected, and recorded.

Thus far, only three metacontexts have been developed. These are:

(1) The metacontext of true belief—or justification philosophy. This metacontext, in the Pythagorean tradition, aims to justify or defend positions and contexts: in Jacob Bronowski's words, "to honour and promote those who are right".[4]

(2) The oriental metacontext of nonattachment. This aims to detach from positions and contexts.

(3) The metacontext of fallibilism, or of pancritical rationalism. This aims to create and to improve positions and contexts.

As I have argued in this book, most Western philosophies—philosophies

---

[3]See James Luther Adams's comments on some of Michels's ideas in "Tillich's Concept of the Protestant Era", in *The Protestant Era* (Chicago: University of Chicago Press, 1948), p. 279. See K. R. Popper, "Back to the Pre-Socratics", Presidential Address, *Proceedings of the Aristotelian Society*, 1958–59; and "Towards a Rational Theory of Tradition", and "The Nature of Philosophical Problems and Their Roots in Science", reprinted in *Conjectures and Refutations*. See also n. 38 to chap. 10 of *The Open Society and Its Enemies*. See also W. I. Matson, "Conford on the Birth of Metaphysics", *Review of Metaphysics*, 8, no. 3 (March 1955), pp. 443–54.

[4]J. Bronowski, *A Sense of the Future*, p. 4.

of science and epistemologies as much as philosophies of religion—are justificationist. That is, *they sponsor justificationist metacontexts of true belief.* This was true among the Pythagoreans, and it is just as true today. Such philosophies are concerned with how to justify, verify, confirm, make firmer, strengthen, validate, vindicate, make certain, show to be certain, make acceptable, probabilify, cause to survive, *defend* particular contexts and positions. Most such philosophies—again, philosophies of science as much as philosophies of religion—end up in commitment and in identification.

There is, I believe, a simple historical explanation for the entanglement of Western philosophy of science in this metacontext: Western science *might,* for instance, have developed in the Ionian tradition and have avoided justificationism. But it did not do this. Rather, *Western science grew up in debate with a justified-true-belief religion, Christianity.* Responding to a true-belief religion, Western science became, in its philosophy, a justified-true-belief science.

At the other extreme, there is the oriental metacontext of nonattachment. In most varieties—in Hinduism, Buddhism, and in the yogic tradition underlying both[5]—oriental philosophy opposes *attachment*: attachment to anything whatever: one's body, habits, wishes, lusts, cravings, aspirations, ideas, beliefs, ideologies, relationships, affiliations. Most Western accounts of oriental thought neglect ideas and beliefs, and concentrate on themes of nonattachment with regard to lust and ambition. But such emphasis stems from our Western distortion. From the oriental perspective, it is as important not to be attached to particular *beliefs* as it is not to be attached to particular *lusts and cravings.* As the Buddha says: "Even this view, which is so pure and so clear, if you cling to it, if you fondle it, if you treasure it, if you are attached to it, then you do not understand that the teaching is similar to a raft, which is for crossing over, and not for getting hold of."[6] Nonattachment is demanded with regard to "high spiritual attainments as well as pure views and ideas".[7]

In calling this metacontext "oriental", I do not wish to subscribe to the view that all orientals are alike, and that they differ completely from westerners—who are in turn all alike.[8] In taking care not to commit such a solecism, however, I also do not want to avoid marking this real, important, and deeply pervasive difference between those systems of thought that are associated with the West, and those that are associated with the East.

From this oriental perspective, the westerner erects positions and contexts

[5]See Georg Feuerstein, *The Essence of Yoga* (New York: The Grove Press, 1974), p. 25; and E. Conze, *Buddhist Thought in India* (London, 1962); and H. Beckh, *Buddha und seine Lehre* (Stuttgart, 1956), p. 138.

[6]*Majjhima-nikaya* (PTS edition), vol. 1, p. 260.

[7]Walpola Rahula, *What the Buddha Taught* (New York: Grove Press, 1974), chap. 1.

[8]See Edward W. Said, *Orientalism* (New York: Random House, 1979).

—belief systems—for particularly ignoble ends, related to a kind of craving: the westerner commits himself to, identifies himself with, such systems in order to justify himself and invalidate others, to dominate and to avoid domination, to survive and make others fail to survive. By identifying with his positions, the westerner automatically becomes *positional*: he is oriented toward the perpetuation of his positions rather than toward the truth. He causes those positions and contexts with which he has identified to persist as part of his own combat for survival. This is seen as the source of that vaunted "hunger and thirst after righteousness" of which Western moralities speak fondly and which orientals (and a few others, such as Nietzsche) see as a kind of vampirism, sapping the strength of Western culture.

It is interesting and—so far as I can tell—hitherto unremarked that the oriental concept of *attachment* and the Western idea of *commitment* are closely similar. Both, in turn, resemble the idea of *addiction*. The dictionary defines an addict as one who has "given himself over" to a practice, a habit, a pursuit. Thus it is not surprising that Supreme Court Justice Oliver Wendell Holmes, Jr., in explaining the force of his philosophical commitments or presuppositions, chooses the language of the addict: he calls these *Can't Helps!*[9] The chasm between the dominant trends of Eastern and Western thought is nowhere so evident as here: the metacontext of oriental philosophy sponsors nonattachment; the chief metacontext of Western philosophy sponsors attachment, commitment, addiction.

It is alien to an Eastern metacontext to see *any* position or context as a source of identification and commitment *in the Western sense*. Yet oriental writers—and some westerners[10]—sometimes speak of another, different sense of identity: "true identity" or True Self. True Self in this sense is *the context of all contexts* (including metacontexts). Beyond any individual, identification, form, process, context, position, or econiche, True Self is the matrix that gives rise to them. Not a position, True Self is the space in which all positionality in life occurs.

Within this Eastern metacontext, commitments, belief systems, ideologies, traditions, identifications, and so-called ultimate values provide contexts—often valuable contexts—for individual existence; but these do not determine who or what one is; nor does it make any sense to be attached to, identified with, or committed to such things. True Self, being the context of all contexts, is the context in which things such as commitments, identifications, ideologies, metacontexts, and so on emerge, flourish for a time, and then decline. Thus one is the matrix in which content is crystallized and process occurs, and is not any particular content or process,

[9]Oliver Wendell Holmes, Jr., "Natural Law", in *Collected Legal Papers* (New York: Harcourt, Brace, 1920), pp. 310–11. See the discussion of Holmes in Morton White, *Religion, Politics, and the Higher Learning* (Cambridge, Mass.: Harvard University Press, 1959), pp. 130–31.

[10]See my *Werner Erhard*, and Gregory Bateson, *Steps to an Ecology of Mind* (New York: Ballantine, 1972).

not any individual form. Here there is a profound sense of the limitation inherent in form, and of the opportunity latent in lack of attachment to form: the capacity to take on any form—and to create form anew. Here identity as fixed identification is seen as a liability: the more fixed one's identity, the less experience of which one is capable, the less one *is*. The point is not *to lack* a position or context, but not to be positional: not to be attached or committed to whatever position and context one does have at any particular moment. To adapt Sartre's terminology: one may *have* a position or *do* a position, but may not *be* a position.[11]

Two Western writers, Hermann Hesse and Hermann Keyserling, found in such Eastern thought a "protean sensibility", writing of the "supple individual" of infinitely polymorphous plasticity who, "in order to experience enough must expose himself a great deal", and who "gains profundity from every metamorphosis".[12] As Keyserling's protean figure—in the course of trying out different forms and experiences, different positions and contexts—discovers how limited each is, and how one is linked to another, he passes beyond the danger of placing an exaggerated value on any single form, phenomenon, position, or context. Personality and character, being forms, also imply limitation. "No developed individual", Keyserling writes, "can reverence 'personality' as an ideal; he is beyond prejudices, principles and dogmas". Such a supple individual, though perceived to be without character, may be as securely and firmly positive as any rigid individual.

This is not the confused and disordered state of one in the throes of "identity diffusion". The Yogi says "neti, neti: I am not that" to all nature, until he becomes one with Parabrahma. After that, as Keyserling says, "no manifestation limits him any more, because now each one is an obedient means of expression to him . . . A God lives thus from the beginning, by virtue of his nature. Man slowly approaches the same condition by passing through the whole range of experience".

On the other hand, such a godlike being may seem capricious—like Proteus, the Greek sea god, the "old man of the sea", who not only had the power to assume any form he wished, but was also "as capricious as the sea itself". One finds such capriciousness also in some Hindu accounts: the capriciousness, say, of credulity, which accepts all things, however contradictory, as vessels of the truth; which, regarding everything as holy, yet takes nothing seriously. *Within limits.* For to consider and discard another metaphor, the oriental approach does *not* commend the *chameleon*, that remarkable lizard with a greatly developed power to change the color of his skin. Lightning-change artistry is a superficial sort of suppleness, skin-deep, for which the chameleon's characteristic slow power of locomotion is itself a metaphor.

---

[11]Jean-Paul Sartre, *Being and Nothingness* (New York: Washington Square Press, 1975), part 4.
[12]Hermann Keyserling, *Travel Diary of a Philosopher*; and Hermann Hesse, *My Belief.*

All this may remind one somewhat of ordinary Western scepticism, but it is hardly the same. Western scepticism, to be sure, also arches its brows at all attempts at knowing, all formulations, definitions, identifications—including any definition of its own position. But it is posed more as a position or context, not as a metacontext; and it is born out of the defeat of, and permeated by the spirit of, justificationism. It rejects attachments not out of a positive quest for nonattachment but out of reaction to the internal contradictions of the Western justificationist metacontext. Usually, Western scepticism is regretfully or resignedly nonattached, permeated by epistemological disappointment. None of the majesty of nonattachment appears in, say, Sextus Empiricus or Hume, as it does in the Eastern writers. Scepticism is a *defense* against uncertainty.

This Eastern way of thinking, and of approaching thinking, is, then, far removed from the metacontext of belief, identification, and commitment that one finds in most Western philosophies. It is less distant, but still *very* different, from the fallibilism of Xenophanes or of Popper, or of the pancritical rationalism presented in this book.

Such fallibilism—which provides a third metacontext—also allows for the fallibility, the distortion, of all forms, of all existing crystallizations in language, and yet maintains (unlike the oriental) that one may, through form, through language, come *closer* to the truth, measuring one's *progress* through . . . fallible criteria. Although the oriental is right to stress how language can mesmerize us and solidify and rigidify our positions, it is also language that *permits* one to dissociate from, to detach from, one's own positions and hypotheses: to make them into *objects,* not subjective states, not identified with ourselves: objects that then may be examined.

While rejecting the identification, commitment, and positionality into which Western justificationist philosophies are forced, fallibilists yet champion the *growth* of knowledge and of science and the "rational way of life" as leading in this direction. In the interaction between ourselves and our intellectual products, so the fallibilist maintains, we are most likely to transcend ourselves. Here there can be progress without commitment.

Unlike most oriental philosophies, which tend to be noncompetitive, and which are rarely interested in the growth of knowledge, fallibilism demands, and encourages competition for, a more adequate model or representation of the world. *Like* the oriental, the fallibilist gives no importance to "right belief", and searches for a pervasive condition of nonattachment to models and representations generally. For one must detach from, must *objectify* one's theories in order to improve them. The very asking of the fallibilist question—"Under what conditions would this theory be false?"—invites a psychological exercise in detachment and objectification, leading one to step outside the point of view shaped by that theory. While fallibilists, however, emphasize progress in knowledge and rationality, for the oriental the apparentness of progress is illusory and the pursuit of it is a manifestation of addiction. The oriental and the fallibilist also seek detachment for different reasons: the oriental, to attain distance from all models of the world, and thereby to win freedom from illusion, and peace; the fallibilist, in order to further the growth of knowledge, to attain a more adequate model of the universe. The products which they seek differ.[13]

3. The Gnostic Texts

> Jesus said, "If you bring forth what is within you, what you bring forth will save you. If you do not bring forth what is within you, what you do not bring forth will destroy you".
> —THE GOSPEL OF THOMAS[14]

> "For whoever has not known himself has known nothing, but whoever has known himself has simultaneously achieved knowledge about the depth of all things".
> —JESUS TO THOMAS.[15]

> . . . who we were, and what we have become; where we were . . . whither we are hastening; from what we are being released; what birth is, and what is rebirth.
> —THEODOTUS[16]

It is possible that all three metacontexts—the Western metacontext of justified true belief, the oriental metacontext of nonattachment, and the fallibilist metacontext—met, tangled, and parted ways forever in one

---

[13]Jagdish Hattiangadi objects to my discussion of metacontext, arguing that contexts and metacontexts should not be distinguished, and that only one natural context stands over and above the others: namely, evolution. We disagree here. Evolution is, from my point of view, not a context but part of the background circumstances or conditions in terms of which we operate, whether we know it or not, and no matter what our metacontext. It is no more a context than gravity—which is another condition or circumstance. A knowledge of circumstances, or a theory of circumstances—such as the theory of gravity or the theory of evolution—may, once it is acquired, contextualize. So far, however, the theory of evolution has not fully been assimilated into any of the three metacontexts. It stands in opposition to the first two: it contradicts them. And while it is fully compatible with fallibilism, only a start has so far been made on integrating them. Hattiangadi also objects that my account makes metacontexts provide cultural casts for the preformation of its ideas. But the metacontext does not preform ideas, only the ways in which ideas are held. Thus it may affect to some extent the ways in which they change and develop; but it will not determine positive content. It functions in some respects similarly to what Hayek calls a "context of constraint".

[14]The Gospel of Thomas, in J. M. Robinson, ed., The Nag Hammadi Library (New York: Harper & Row, 1977), p. 126.

[15]The Book of Thomas the Contender, in The Nag Hammadi Library, p. 189.

[16]Theodotus, cited in Clemens Alexandrinus, Excerpta ex Theodoto, 78.2.

paramount encounter that would have had to be discussed in the body of this book had it been written some years later than it was.

I have in mind the new debate about the nature of early Christianity that has arisen from the discovery of the Nag Hammadi papyri: the discovery, that is, of the so-called Gnostic gospels.[17] These early Christian documents, although discovered in 1945, did not become generally available to scholars until long after the first edition of this book. The story of this delay— described as a "persistent curse of political roadblocks, litigations, and, most of all, scholarly jealousies and 'firstmanship'" which has "grown by now into a veritable *chronique scandaleuse* of contemporary academia"[18]—has been told elsewhere and is not our concern here.

The Nag Hammadi papyri, discovered in an earthenware jar in Upper Egypt in 1945, consist of some thirteen leather-bound papyrus books containing some fifty-two texts dating from the early centuries of the Christian era—some of them no later than A.D. 120–150, and *possibly* much older: possibly at least as early as, if not earlier than, the New Testament gospels. These Coptic translations of Greek originals contain a collection of Christian gospels previously unknown, as well as various texts attributed to followers of Jesus, and also poems, cosmological descriptions of the origins of the universe, magical works, and works of instruction in mystical practices.

These texts challenge fundamentally the picture of the historical Jesus and the conception of God that was presented by Schweitzer and championed by Barth and the neo-orthodox movement. As we have seen above (chapters 2 and 3), God is regarded by Barth and his followers as *wholly other* than man, and opposed to the conceptions, philosophies, and cultural creations of man. Man cannot, on this view, by seeking find out God; rather, he requires revelation and authority.

The Gnostic Christian texts, by contrast, go far beyond anything known in Protestant liberalism—in their individualism, and in their focus on self-knowledge as the starting point of the religious quest. As the Gnostic teacher Monoimus states: "Abandon the search for God and the creation and other matters of a similar sort. *Look for him by taking yourself as the starting point.* Learn who it is within you who makes everything his own . . . Learn the sources of sorrow, joy, love, hate . . ."[19]

More surprising, these Gnostic texts have a strong flavor of Buddhism and Hindu religion about them. In fact, there is some possibility that the Gnostic writers were influenced by Indian sources. The Gospel of Thomas,

---

[17]On this discovery and its interpretation, see Elaine Pagels, *The Gnostic Gospels* (New York: Random House, 1979).

[18]See Hans Jonas, *The Gnostic Religion*, 2nd ed. rev. (Boston: Beacon Press, 1963), p. 290; and Pagels, p. xxv.

[19]See Hippolytus, *Refutationis omnium haeresium* 8.15.1–2.

one of the chief Gnostic writings, is named after that disciple who, according to tradition, travelled to India. And at the time when these Gnostic texts were written, Buddhist missionaries were active in Alexandria. However the question of influence turns out, many of the Gnostic texts begin, as the Buddha did, in the recognition of the suffering of ordinary human existence: ordinary existence is one of oblivion or unconsciousness, of illusion. It is a nightmare. But there is a route out of, a release from, this suffering: through discipline, meditative and ascetic practices, and interior, spiritual search, one may come to *enlightenment*, an experience or state in which one recognizes who one really is, a state in which one enjoys self-knowledge. This self-understanding is the key also to the knowledge of existence, of God, and of the universe in which we live.

Although the Gnostic texts are quite distinctively Christian, they firmly reject the creeds, professions of faith, rituals, hierarchy, authority, and other marks of the orthodox churches. They deny the literal understanding of the virgin birth of Jesus, the real physical suffering of Jesus on the cross, and the bodily resurrection, as well as the coming of the Kingdom of God on earth. All this they see as naïve misunderstanding, as magical thinking, as "the faith of fools". Those beliefs that they deny are precisely those that are most incredible, those that have required blind belief, irrational commitment, and conformity to authority to support them within orthodox Christianity. The Gnostics see these things, rather, in more symbolic and metaphorical terms. One attains resurrection, for instance, through the experience of enlightenment; and the Kingdom of God is already here on earth: it is a state of transformed consciousness. Jesus himself does not, as Schweitzer put it, "stand over against" man; rather, he is seen as a teacher or guide who leads men to greater self-understanding, in the course of which they themselves attain to a spiritual state comparable to his. As the Gospel of Philip puts it: "You saw the spirit, you became spirit. You saw Christ, you became Christ."[20]

Although Elaine Pagels and other scholars have suggested that, provided the names were changed, the Buddha could have said what the Gospel of Thomas and other Gnostic writings attribute to Jesus,[21] there is nonetheless an important difference between Buddhism and these Gnostic texts—quite apart from names, dates, and historical references. This difference is especially important with regard to the oriental metacontext of which I wrote in the previous section. The Gnostic texts do not really participate in that metacontext. In particular, they do not advocate relativism or scepticism or indifference to all human formulations of the truth. On the contrary, there often seems to be in them a fallibilistic advocacy of progress toward the truth through the use of reason! While rejecting particular

[20]*Nag Hammadi Library*, p. 137.
[21]Pagels, p. xx.

claims, especially those of the orthodox church, the Gnostics nonetheless encouraged speculation and disputation and the "storming of the citadel of truth". One can, they taught, go beyond, improve upon, even the teachings of the apostles, even the most hallowed tradition. Here, they contrast markedly with their orthodox, and deeply justificationist critics, such as Tertullian, who—referring to such Gnostic teachings—wrote: "We want no curious disputation after possessing Christ Jesus, no inquiring after enjoying the gospel! With our faith, we desire no further belief." [22]

The Gnostic writers inhabit an utterly different sensibility, an utterly different approach to religion. It is not simply a matter of difference in belief. Thus the Gnostic writer Silvanus, in his *Teachings,* sounds almost Socratic when he writes: ". . . a foolish man . . . goes the ways of the desire of every passion. He swims in the desires of life and has foundered . . . he is like a ship which the wind tosses to and fro, and like a loose horse which has no rider. *For this [one] needed the rider, which is reason. . . .* before everything else . . . know yourself. . . . The mind is the guide, but reason is the teacher. . . . Enlighten your mind . . . Light the lamp within you." [23]

The Gnostic texts are complicated and difficult; scholars have only in the past decade begun the vast task of interpreting and comparing them; the themes on which I have just commented are not the only ones present in them. Thus I do not want to give the impression that there is one clear Gnostic teaching, or that scholars have settled what it is. Nor do I have the slightest wish to endorse that teaching, whatever it may be. Nonetheless, it is already evident that, had these texts been available when Schweitzer or Barth were writing, the story told in chapters 2 and 3 of this book would have been very different. The problem situation confronting Protestant liberals would have differed radically. These texts would inevitably have strengthened the position of Protestant liberalism against the attacks of the neo-orthodox. They might even have saved Protestant liberalism.

But the texts were *not* available then, and I do not mention them now in order to revive Protestant liberalism. I remind the reader only that there was once a moment when Christianity might have gone in a quite different direction, and that we can, through these texts, now for the first time savor that moment. "We find ourselves now in possession of a massive literature of 'lost causes' from those crucial five or so centuries, from the first century B.C. onward, in which the spiritual destiny of the Western world took shape: the voice of creeds and flights of thought which, part of that creative process, nourished by it and stimulating it, were to become obliterated in

[22]Tertullian, *De praescriptione haereticorum* 7.
[23]*Teachings of Silvanus*, in *Nag Hammadi Library*, pp. 347–56.

the consolidation of official creeds that followed upon the turmoil of novelty and boundless vision."[24]

When the orthodox church crushed Gnosticism, that opportunity for a different and undogmatic Christianity was lost forever. What was left, what is today generally considered as Christianity, represents in fact only a small selection of the available sources—those compatible and agreeable sources which could survive the book burning and the persecution of the heretics. Those who made that selection, the triumphant orthodox forces, wiped out the Gnostics, and attempted with quite amazing success—a success frustrated after 1600 years only by the accidental discovery of an earthenware jar in a mound of soft soil, next to a massive boulder—to wipe out all traces of their teachings. In doing so, a true-belief religion was entrenched in the West, with fateful consequences for our history.

The knowledge of this possibility—of this historical "might-have-been"—we owe to that unknown scholar, perhaps a monk from the nearby monastery of St. Pachomius, who buried those papyrus books in that earthenware jar at Nag Hammadi just as the orthodox authorities swept through the ancient world, destroying and burning such books, and making their possession a criminal offense.

4. An Econiche for Rationality

The controversy just mentioned—that in which the Gnostics were defeated by the forces of orthodoxy—is one of thousands of possible illustrations of a simple truth: that it is much harder to institutionalize and to create a viable econiche for a program of unrelenting growth, development, and criticism than it is to create institutions and viable conditions for a self-perpetuating system of beliefs.

The main problem for the growth of rationality—and for the theory of rationality—as I see it, is therefore an ecological problem.

In a fallibilist metacontext, the ecological problem is to create the most lethal environment for positions, contexts, and metacontexts, in which the production of positions, contexts, and metacontexts yet thrives. Popper approached this understanding of the problem in *The Logic of Scientific Discovery*, where he wrote: "What characterizes the empirical method is its manner of exposing to falsification, in every conceivable way, the system to be tested. Its aim is not to save the lives of untenable systems but, on the contrary, to select the one which is by comparison the fittest, by exposing

[24]Hans Jonas, p. 290.

them all to the fiercest struggle for survival" (p. 42) and "a supreme rule is laid down which serves as a kind of norm for deciding upon the remaining rules . . . It is the rule which says that the other rules of scientific procedure must be designed in such a way that they do not protect any statement in science against falsification" (p. 54).

Popper extended his approach to apply not only to empirical science, but also to political institutions, in *The Open Society and Its Enemies,* chapter 7, and in 1960, in "On the Sources of Knowledge and of Ignorance" *(Conjectures and Refutations,* p. 25), he advocated replacing traditional questions about the source of knowledge with the question: *"How can we hope to detect and eliminate error?"* In this book, I have stated the problem more generally: *How can our intellectual life and institutions be arranged so as to expose our beliefs, conjectures, policies, positions, source of ideas, traditions, and the like—whether or not they are justifiable—to maximum criticism, in order to counteract and eliminate as much intellectual error as possible?*

This formulation, while incomplete, captures something very good. What is good about it is that it sees the production of heightened rationality not individualistically, not as something that one does by oneself; it places the problem, ecologically, in a framework that contains not only the individual but also the institutions, policies, traditions, culture, and society in which he lives. For let us suppose that we have an individual who has achieved in himself that state of flexibility combined with keenness for the truth that we have referred to as "rationality" in this book. Such an individual will inevitably be frustrated if he tries to express himself in institutions which are formed under and function within the justificationist metacontext. Such institutions, and the traditions in terms of which they operate, will act to perpetuate themselves at whatever cost—and certainly at the expense of rationality: at the expense of those conditions for a rational environment which include truthfulness, criticism, full communication, acknowledgment and correction of error, and acknowledgment of contributions.[25]

This is presumably why so many of the saints in India are said to live in caves, separate from the institutions of mankind. If rationality is to be brought out of the cave, or out of the study, it must be embedded in institutions and traditions that work against positionality and self-justification, instead of just in individuals who have transcended position-ality. If a rational individual is one who can tell the truth, a rational environment will be one in which the truth can be told.

The formulation italicized above is nonetheless incomplete in that it is stated too negatively in terms of the reduction of error. For an essential

---

[25]See my "A Place to Tell the Truth", *Graduate Review,* San Francisco, May 1978; and my *Werner Erhard,* pp. 214–21. See also my "Knowledge Is a Product Not Fully Known to Its Producer", in *The Political Economy of Freedom,* ed. Kurt Leube and A. Zlabinger (Munich, Philosophia Verlag, 1984).

requirement is the *fertility* of the econiche: the econiche must be one in which the creation of positions and contexts, and the development of rationality, are truly inspired. Clumsily applied eradication of error may also eradicate fertility. Criticism must be optimum rather than maximum, and must be deftly applied. Also, my initial formulation overemphasizes matters intellectual—such as beliefs, conjectures, ideas, and such like. Explicitly included for review should be not only aims, beliefs, conjectures, decisions, ideas, ideologies, policies, programs, and traditions, but even etiquette, manners and customs, and unconscious presuppositions and behavior patterns that may pollute the econiche and thereby diminish creativity, criticism, or both. The ecological problem of rationality is *how* this is to be done.

In the past, pursuit of this problem has been hindered by the claim that what it calls for *cannot* be done. This claim challenges the very possibility of any fallibilist metacontext in which it is assumed that one can make progress toward a more adequate and objective representation of the world. Instead, it asserts that, from a rational point of view, there can be no progress; that the choice between competing positions and contexts, whether scientific, mathematical, moral, religious, metaphysical, political, or other, is not reasoned but is arbitrary. If the argument of this book is sound, this claim has at last been refuted. We might now take some steps toward dealing with the question of *how,* assuming that the question of *whether* has now been resolved.

APPENDIX 2. LOGICAL STRENGTH AND DEMARCATION

1. The Problem of Demarcation Reconsidered

With the first publication of this book, I proposed a generalization of Karl Popper's theory of falsification.[1] This generalization, having to do with a separation between justification and criticism that transcends the separation between verification and falsification, has been useful, and nowadays Popperian thought is most often presented and interpreted in terms of it.

Almost as soon as I had achieved this generalization, however, I began to feel uncomfortable about parts of Popper's early work. This is hardly surprising: indeed, one of Popper's themes is that any broader theory will both explain and correct earlier theories. The part of Popper's thinking that I felt most uncomfortable about was his theory of demarcation.[2]

Demarcation is an important issue in philosophy of religion, and in the examination and critique of ideology. The story of the philosophy of religion in this century, and to some extent in earlier centuries, is indeed the story of the response to a series of criteria of demarcation brought forth in judgment on religious utterances: criteria of meaningfulness, empirical character, verifiability, and so on.

In this appendix, I consider anew the problem of demarcation. Although the discussion involves some correction to Popper's account of demarcation, it presupposes the approximate validity of Popper's own results, and could not have been carried out without them.

2. Demarcation and Justification

The fundamental problem to be considered is that of distinguishing between a good idea and a bad idea, a good practice and a bad practice. This may be called a *problem of demarcation*.

[1] For a recent statement, see my "Critical Study: The Philosophy of Karl Popper. Part III: Rationality, Criticism, and Logic", *Philosophia*, Israel, February 1982, pp. 121–221.

[2] W.W. Bartley, III, "Theories of Demarcation between Science and Metaphysics", in I. Lakatos and A. E. Musgrave, eds., *Problems in the Philosophy of Science* (Amsterdam: North-Holland Publishing Co., 1968), pp. 40–119.

The reader who is familiar with such problems as they are treated in contemporary philosophical literature is asked to pause here and note that I am *not* at the moment speaking of a demarcation *between science and metaphysics,* or a demarcation *between meaningful and meaningless utterances,* or of any demarcation other than the one specified: between a good idea and a bad idea, between a good practice and a bad practice.

In a simpler world, one might solve such problems without any explicit recourse to philosophy. For example: if faced with a choice between one idea and another, or one course of action and another, I might simply ask my friend Harry which to choose. Or I might flip a coin. This procedure could, of course, be said implicitly to involve a primitive theory of criticism, and to that extent a primitive philosophy. The theory—whether expressed or consciously entertained or not—is that any idea that Harry approves is good; and any that he disapproves, bad. Or similarly for heads and tails.

We do not live in so simple a world. Yet our own, complicated, answers to the problem of demarcation are no better: rather, our approaches are arranged so as to preclude the possibility of satisfactorily answering the problem. We live in a world contaminated by a particular philosophical idea about how *any* such demarcation would have to be obtained. I call this "justificationism". In brief, it is the view that the way to criticize an idea is to see whether and how it can be justified. Justificationism deeply permeates all Western culture, and virtually controls all traditional, modern, *and* contemporary philosophy. This idea shapes the thinking of Plato and Aristotle, of Descartes, Spinoza, and Leibniz, of Locke, Berkeley, and Hume, of Kant and Hegel, of Whitehead and Russell—and also of Wittgenstein, Carnap, Ayer, Ryle, Austin, Quine, Husserl, Heidegger, Barth, Bultmann, Tillich, or almost any other philosopher one might want to name. It shapes phenomenology as much as it does the so-called analytical philosophy that is more characteristic of the English-speaking countries. All these periods, men, and movements participate in what I call the "justificationist metacontext".[3]

The word "justify" is not essential here. A variety of other words and phrases have been used for the same purpose, including: verify, probabilify, confirm, make firm, validate, vindicate, prove, make certain, show to be certain, make acceptable, authorize, defend.

Such justification—or whatever it may happen to be called—involves the following:

(1) an authority (or authorities), or authoritatively good trait, in terms of which final evaluation (i.e., demarcation of the good from the bad) is to be made;
(2) the idea that the goodness or badness of any idea or policy is to be

---

[3]See appendix 1 and "Rationality, Criticism, and Logic".

determined by reducing it to (i.e., deriving it from or combining it out of) the authority (or authorities), or to statements possessing the authoritatively good trait.[4] That which can so be reduced is justified; that which cannot is to be rejected.[5]

The first step is already found in the decisions made by asking Harry or tossing a coin. The second step moves beyond this.

Note that these requirements do not speak of *rational* justification, in the sense of a justification that might be approved by rationalists or scientifically minded individuals. Justification is sought by rationalist and irrationalist alike. Rationalism and irrationalism have justificationism in common. Justificationism has the same structure, and the same requirements, whether the authority in question be the local wizard, the Ouija board, sense-observation reports, or the light of pure reason.

3. The Justificationist Pattern of Demarcation

Many superficially very different theories of demarcation conform to this underlying justificationist pattern. Consider this check list, which consists of demarcations proposed primarily within the Western rationalist traditions:

good traits	bad traits
true	false
probable	improbable
clear and distinct	unclear and indistinct
demonstrable by reason	undemonstrable by reason
empirical	unempirical
verifiable	unverifiable
meaningful	meaningless
scientific	unscientific

Which indicators of goodness and badness are taken most seriously depends on in which part, and in which period, of the justificationist metacontext one finds oneself. Thus, for Descartes, good ideas are demarcated from bad ones by finding which can be reduced to clear and distinct

---

[4]Compare Bertrand Russell, *The Problems of Philosophy* (London, 1912), p. 58: "knowledge concerning what is known by description is ultimately reducible to knowledge concerning what is known by acquaintance", and p. 109: "Our *derivative* knowledge of truths consists of everything that we can deduce from self-evident truths by the use of self-evident principles of deduction." Or as Rudolf Carnap writes: "This requirement for justification and conclusive foundation of each thesis will eliminate all speculative and poetic work from philosophy. . . . It must be possible to give a rational foundation for each scientific thesis. . . . the physicist does not cite irrational factors, but gives a purely empirical-rational justification. We demand the same from ourselves in our philosophical work". *The Logical Structure of the World* (Berkeley and Los Angeles: University of California Press, 1967), Preface to the First Edition, p. xvii.

[5]Cf. Russell, *Problems*, p. 111: "It is felt by many that a belief for which no reason can be given is an unreasonable belief. In the main, this view is just."

ideas; for Hume, good ideas are demarcated from bad ideas by finding which are empirical, i.e., which can be reduced to reports of sense observation. And so on. As to bad ideas, on some demarcations they are simply undesirable in some respect: being confused, unclear, or poorly related to evidence, and so on. On other demarcations, they are much worse: e.g., straying beyond the bounds of human understanding or of human language.

The items on the list have a staying power. Thus, even though clarity and distinctness are now commonly regarded as insufficient, they are, in and of themselves, still prized. As to *truth,* although no modern philosophy claims a criterion of truth, all still agree that truth is a good trait, when it can be had. Yet truth is certainly not sufficient: a falsehood of high content may be preferable to a trivial or tautologous truth.[6] The focus of attention in modern and contemporary philosophies has, however, been on probability and on the last four items on the list. Most forms of positivism and empiricism, for instance, agree that good theories will be of high probability, and will also be empirical, verifiable, meaningful, and scientific. Demarcations focusing on *science* have been of prime importance since Kant.

The examples given are those most important within Western philosophy and the rationalist tradition. Such justificationist resolutions of demarcational problems are, however, by no means restricted to philosophy and science: they invade every aspect of our culture.

Theologians would cite among good demarcational traits: endorsement by the Bible, or by the Pope, or by some other religious authority. Others, both in and out of religion, would appeal to "conscience" and "the inner light". Still others, arguing from political ideologies, might find such traits as authorization by class interests (however that might be figured) as hallmarks of good theory and practice. Rationalists and irrationalists alike are justificationists.

4. Problems of Logical Strength

Any theory of demarcation, any theory of criticism, that is set up in this way can, potentially, produce a problem of logical strength.

What is meant by a problem of logical strength?

The problem of logical strength arises when the statement or policy under evaluation, although not in conflict with the authorities, has a logical strength greater than that of any authority or combination of authorities, which hence cannot be reduced to or derived from the authorities, and

[6]See Popper, *Conjectures and Refutations,* pp. 229–30.

which must therefore be rejected as not sanctioned by the authorities.[7]

This is, of course, only a *problem* when proceeding in this way causes one *to reject something that should obviously be retained.*

It is, however, not anticipated that any such problem will arise. Justificational accounts of demarcation are set up with the expectation, with the presumption, that the authorities will be sufficient to sanction all good theories and policies, and that statements or policies that are *not* reducible to the authorities are simply to be rejected.

In fact, however, such problems arise all the time. Much of the history of philosophy, and almost all of the history of epistemology, is the history of problems of logical content.

This thesis could be illustrated with virtually every demarcational approach tried hitherto in the history of philosophy. And the whole history of philosophy could be rewritten in terms of this insight. For reasons of length, I shall restrict my discussion in this appendix to showing this for *empiricist* approaches to demarcation, which have usually taken sense-observation reports as authoritative.[8]

5. Logical Strength: An Elementary Lesson

Before explaining how these matters work, we need to consider the notion of logical strength.

What is meant by logical stength?

The idea is so elementary that some readers may protest any explanation. Yet the idea is also so important, and plays so crucial a role in this discussion, that I ask readers to forgive a brief review.

Statements differ in their logical strength or content; that is, some statements say more than others. For instance, the statement: "John is tall" says less than the statement: "John is tall and thin".

Or to take a more interesting example, the statement: "This normal die will turn up 3 on the next throw" is stronger than the statement: "This normal die will turn up either 3 or 5 on the next throw." And this latter statement, in turn, says more than: "This normal die will turn up either 1 or 2 or 3 or 4 or 5 or 6 on the next throw." This last statement, in fact, makes

---

[7]Another way of putting this is to say that such statements "possess a surplus meaning over against their evidential basis; they are not equivalent with or reducible to . . . any set of actual or possible confirming statements". See Herbert Feigl, "Existential Hypothesis", in *Philosophy of Science*, vol. 17 (1950), p. 45.

[8]It will not be necessary in this connection to challenge the authorities themselves. In a discussion of the problem of logical strength, the authorities under consideration (whether they be sense observation or intuition or whatever) need not themselves be questioned—not even when, as is always the case, they *are* highly questionable. For the problem of logical strength is independent of the question of the virtue of the authorities, and arises even when the authorities are granted as unimpeachable, unquestionable.

no assertion whatever; although it is certainly true, its content is nil.

Considerations of logical strength play an important role in valid argument and derivation (and thus in justification). It is an elementary point of logic that a valid derivation is one in which, when the premises are true, the conclusion must also be true. If any given conclusion can be validly derived from (or reduced to) a particular premise, then it is equal to or else logically weaker than the premise. By the same token, in such an argument the premises are equal to or logically stronger than the conclusion. In no circumstances may a stronger statement be validly derived from a weaker one.

Since I have mentioned that statements *equal* in strength may be derived one from the other, it may be useful to take as our first example of a valid argument such a case. Thus:

> Premise: My cat is Siamese
> _____
> Conclusion: My cat is Siamese

is a valid derivation. Here the premise and conclusion, being identical, are equal in strength. And it is obviously impossible for this derivation to be invalid. Here is a clear case in which it would be impossible for the premise to be true without the conclusion's being true as well.

Consider another example of a valid argument:

> Premise: My cat is Siamese
>   (and)
>   My cat is male
> _____
> Conclusion: My cat is Siamese.

Here is an example of a valid argument in which the premise is not equal to but stronger than the conclusion, richer in content than the conclusion. And here again, the argument is valid precisely because when the premise is true then the conclusion *must* be true.

To produce an example of an invalid argument, we may easily juggle our example. Thus the argument:

> Premise: My cat is Siamese
> _____
> Conclusion: My cat is Siamese and male

is invalid. The conclusion is stronger than is the premise. Although both premise and conclusion here *may* be true, that is a contingent matter having nothing to do with the validity of the argument: the conclusion here *need not* be true when the premise is true. The possibility that my cat is both Siamese and female is not excluded by this argument.

6. The Traditional Problems of Epistemology as Problems of Logical Strength

We are now in a position to return to the program announced in section 4 above: to illustrate, with particular attention to empiricism, the claim that many traditional problems of philosophy are problems of logical strength: that these central problems of philosophy are little more than illustrations of different sorts of situations in which a desired and desirable conclusion is too strong to be derived from the available authorities.

To illustrate the range of applicability of my claim, I select for detailed consideration two problems from different parts of philosophy: the first, *the problem of induction,* is a problem of the philosophy of science; the second, the is/ought problem, is a problem of ethics. The well-known "mistake" of deriving evaluative (ought) conclusions from descriptive (is) premises has in common with inductive reasoning at least this much: both arise from attempts to derive stronger conclusions from weaker premises.

In both inductive reasoning and in the so-called is/ought mistake, we have statements the merits of which must be decided—in the first instance these statements being scientific projections about the future (or "universal statements") and in the second instance the statements being of an evaluative character. The problem in both cases is to "justify" such statements, taken as the conclusions of arguments of justification, when it can be shown that the available justifiers, or statements which might be used as premises in such a justifying argument, are not sufficiently strong to entail the statements in question.

Take a straightforward example of inductive argument:

Premise: Mars is a planet and moves in an ellipse
             Jupiter is a planet and moves in an ellipse
             Earth is a planet and moves in an ellipse

Conclusion: All planetoid objects move in ellipses.

This simple textbook illustration of inductive reasoning is of course invalid. There may well be some planetoid object in our very large and possibly infinite universe which does not move in an ellipse. It is possible for our premises to be true, and our conclusion to be false. More broadly than our particular example, the problem of induction is that universal laws of science, applying as they do to an infinite number of cases, cannot be derived from a finite number, however large, of observation statements.

Now consider the kind of argument that one might and indeed can find treated in books on ethics:

Premise: I like x
                _____

Conclusion: x is good.

The argument happens to be invalid. Those who discuss such arguments sometimes suggest that they are invalid *because* a conclusion about goodness or value has been derived from statements about matters of fact or past experience: that the mistake or even fallacy has been committed of deriving an "ought" statement from an "is" statement. But this is not why this particular argument is invalid. This argument is invalid simply because, as it stands, there is no relation between the premise and the conclusion. The argument can be formalized in various ways: e.g.,

$$p \rightarrow q$$

or alternatively,

$$A \text{ is } B \rightarrow A \text{ is } C.$$

In either case, *any argument of this logical form* would be invalid, *independently of* any question about the evaluative or factual character of the premises and conclusion.

The premise and conclusion can, of course, be related through augmenting the premise thus:

Premise: I like x
                Whatever I like is good
                _____

Conclusion: x is good.

The argument is now valid. But it is no longer an example of attempting to derive an evaluative conclusion from premises which are purely factual. For the second premise is itself an evaluative statement.

Moreover, a problem completely parallel to the problem of induction—namely, a problem of logical strength—arises with regard to the second premise. For how would one justify it? Try this:

Premise: I like x and x is good
                I like y and y is good
                I like z and z is good
                _____

Conclusion: Whatever I like is good.

This argument, too, is invalid. But once again, the reason why it is invalid has nothing to do with the presence of factual statements in the premise and an evaluative statement in the conclusion. In fact, the premise statements are not purely factual. But even if they were themselves purely factual, the argument would remain invalid just because it is inductive; and an inductive argument is invalid because its conclusion is stronger than the collective strength of its premises. Here in one argument we find an evaluative conclusion and a straightforward example of inductive reasoning. In our examples, it has been impossible to derive an ought statement from an observational premise without adding, as an additional premise, another statement which itself is too strong to be derived from empirical observation reports.

Many other traditional problems of epistemology exactly parallel the problems of induction and the is/ought problem. These other problems include, among others, the problems of justifying:

(1) the existence of bodies and objects in the world, or even of the external world itself, independent of our sense observations thereof;

(2) the continued real existence of the personal self;

(3) the existence of other minds independent of our sense observations thereof;

(4) the uniformity of nature: i.e., the expectation that the future will follow the same laws as did the past;

(5) the existence of the past;

(6) the existence of matter;

(7) the existence of physical space independently of our sense perception thereof;

(8) the existence of time independently of our perceptions and measurements thereof;

(9) the principles of science, however these may be understood—as principles of induction, verification, causality, logic, whatever.

This is no arbitrary listing of epistemological problems. These are the problems treated by Bertrand Russell in his classic work, *The Problems of Philosophy* (1912) and by Sir A.J. Ayer in his *The Problem of Knowledge* (1956) and *The Central Questions of Philosophy* (1973). They are Hume's epistemological problems.

These apparently different problems are in fact one and the same problem, applied to different subject matters. Hence there are two crucial difficulties in traditional justificationist epistemology: (1) The authorities offered are too weak to justify some of the most obvious and important ideas of science and everyday life. In this consists the problem of logical strength. (2) The authorities are hence evidently unable to demarcate good ideas from bad. In this lies the failure of traditional epistemologies to solve the problem of demarcation.

All attempts to resolve this situation have neglected to deal with the underlying structure which generates it and have, instead, tried one of the following alternatives:

(1) They have attempted *to strengthen* the authorities by supplementing them with *a priori* or other principles—as in Bertrand

Russell's *a priori* principle of induction—so as to permit a deduction or reduction in terms of this principle; or

(2) they have attempted *to weaken* the requirement that the justified statements be logically reducible to the authorities. For example, the justified statements might only be "inductively" related to the justifiers—thus once again making use of some principle of induction. Or—to mention a currently fashionable approach—the justifiers and justified statements may be linked informally through the alleged rules of the alleged "language game" which is in play.[9]

7. *Turning the Tables: Nonjustificational Criticism*

It is the justificationist structure in which the problem of demarcation is embedded which generates all the difficulties we have considered. These other problems are wholly created by, arise *automatically* from, and are rendered insoluble by the presuppositions of justificationism. The problem of induction, for instance, *arises* only when the problem of demarcation is approached justificationally. And the same is true of the other problems. It is unconscious and uncritical justificationism which is the chief reason why the problems of philosophy are so often said to be "perennial"—which is a polite way of saying that they never show any progress, let alone are solved.

In fact, a nonjustificational approach—one dispensing with both of the two requirements mentioned in section 2—is not only possible, but is the usual practice in science. To have effective criticism, it is not at all necessary (a) that one have unchallengeable, uncriticizable authorities; or (b) that good ideas be reducible to, derivable from or justifiable by such authorities.

To show this, let us try out two proposals:

First, let us propose that all the individual steps of our arguments—our logically valid arguments—be considered not as authoritative or justified in any way, but as *unjustified conjectures or hypotheses.*

Second, let us momentarily stand the argument structure on its head, as it were. Let us put the hypothesis which is under consideration among the premises of the argument, and put the observational reports which are to be brought in criticism of it in the conclusion.

The second suggestion may seem arbitrary, since any argument can—through the simple manipulation of certain logical rules for denial, contraposition, and such like—be reversed. To make the contrast for which I am aiming, therefore, I need a steady point of reference. For this purpose, I use

---

[9] This would be the approach of Renford Bambrough in his "Unanswerable Questions", *Proceedings of the Aristotelian Society, Supplementary Volume,* 1966, pp. 151–72, esp. pp. 165–66.

the argument that was employed in section 6 above to illustrate inductive reasoning:

Observational Premises:	Mars is a planet and moves in an ellipse
	Jupiter is a planet and moves in an ellipse
	Earth is a planet and moves in an ellipse
Conclusion:	All planetoid objects move in ellipses.

This argument is invalid. As shown above, its premises, even if true, do not ensure the truth of the conclusion, which is of a logical strength greater than the combined strength of the premises.

So take this valid argument instead:

Premises:	All planetoid objects move in ellipses
	Mars is a planetoid object
Conclusion:	Mars moves in an ellipse.

Now, suppose that the conclusion is found to be false—that Mars is observed (a total of six sightings will do) *not* to move in an ellipse. The falsity of the conclusion is retransmitted to at least one of the premises (one of which is the universal law) by means of the logical rule of the retransmission of falsity from conclusion to premises.[10]

We can sum up the difference between the first—inductive and invalid—argument, and the second—valid and deductive—argument, by asserting that it amounts to an *asymmetry between verification* (a form of justification) *and falsification* (a form of criticism). Although it is impossible validly to verify (or justify) a scientific law in terms of observational statements, it is possible validly to falsify a scientific law in terms of observational statements. Another way of saying this is that a valid falsifying relationship, but not a valid verifying relationship, is possible in the "inductive direction", i.e., in an argument from singular observation statements to universal statements of scientific law.

The proposal just stated is, in essence, Popper's solution of the problem of induction.[11]

---

[10]Now that the point has been made, matters can of course be put differently, with the observational information among the premises, thus:

Observational Premises:	It is not the case that Mars moves in an ellipse
	Mars is a planetoid object
Conclusion:	It is not the case that all planetoid objects move in ellipses.

[11]This is, of course, only a brief summary of the solution and should be interpreted in terms of the elaborate presentation, restrictions, and qualifications in *The Logic of Scientific Discovery*. I believe not only that there is an asymmetry between verification and falsification, but that they are conducted in different metacontexts. See appendix 1.

Note the following features:

(a) There is no longer any problem of logical strength: a falsifying relationship is deductively possible between a weaker and a stronger statement.

(b) This is an account of criticism, of how a scientific law may be contested in terms of experiential or experimental evidence.

(c) There is no authority; and thus the first requirement is not needed. The agent of criticism, the observational report, is *also* conjectural, nonauthoritative (see appendix 3 below). This might be contested on the grounds that the test is made *in terms of* the observational statement. This is so, but does not imply that it is authoritative. To test a particular theory, one determines what sorts of events would be incompatible with it, and then sets up experimental arrangements to attempt to produce such events. Suppose that the test goes against the theory—as it did in our hypothetical example. What has happened? The theory definitely has been criticized in terms of the test: the theory is now *problematic* in that it is false *relative to* the test reports; whereas the test reports may *at the moment* be unproblematic. In that case, the theory may be provisionally and conjecturally rejected because it conflicts with something that is unproblematic or less problematic. Does this prove or establish or justify the rejection of the theory? Not at all. Test reports here are hypothetical, criticizable, revisable—forever—just like everything else. They may *become* problematic: they are themselves open to criticism by the testing of their own consequences.

(d) Hence the criticism in this case is nonjustificational. There is no question of proving or justifying the scientific law, or of somehow combining it out of observation statements. Nor is there any question of rejecting it on the grounds that it is not justified. The scientific law is, rather, presumed from the outset to be unjustifiable. Thus the second requirement is not needed.

(e) The problem of induction has disappeared. There is no problem of induction because there is no induction. Instead, there is conjecture and attempted refutation.

8. How Other Problems Are Resolved: Realism

The other problems mentioned earlier disappear along with the problem of induction. That statements about other minds, morality, the external world, and the like, are unverifiable, unjustifiable conjectures is no longer relevant. Everything is unjustifiable, and lack of justification is no longer grounds for objection. The question, rather, is how—within a nonjustificational framework—such statements may be criticized.

The resolution of these other problems proceeds in a way parallel to that of the problem of induction. But there are also some differences. Scientific laws had potential observational falsifiers: i.e., singular statements of existential form asserting that an observable event is occurring in a certain region of space and time. Popper calls these observational statements that conflict with scientific laws "basic statements". Many of the other controversial claims of traditional epistemology, unlike scientific laws, do not have potential observational falsifiers; they do not conflict with basic statements. Thus realism, the theory that there is an external world independent of human perception, is not testable in Popper's sense. The statement, "There exists an external world independent of human perception" is a *purely existential statement.*[12] Such statements are compatible with any observation whatever. The observation of a world independent of observation is precluded from the start.

This does not mean, however, that scientific information and evidence are irrelevant to the examination of realism. For it turns out that the denial of realism—i.e., *idealism,* the theory that there is no external world independent of human perception, that all reality is created by and composed of human perceptions—although also compatible with all basic statements, is *incompatible with some universal laws of science.* Among the laws in question are those of biology and evolutionary theory.

Related to this is a powerful argument against idealism (and thus for realism) that is curiously neglected in the philosophical literature. This argument arises particularly from studying and comparing the cognitive apparatuses of various life forms. According to evolutionary theory, we and other life forms have evolved in our diverse ways while coping with a common environment. The various cognitive structures employed by humans, animals, and insects make no sense individually or collectively in their mutual integration, in the way in which they complement one another, check and partly compensate for the inadequacies of one another, in their hierarchical arrangement and controls, except by reference to a common external world in which they function, which they attempt in various ways to represent, and in interaction with which they have evolved. Each cognitive structure—such as kinesthetic sense, vision, language, scientific representation, and others—can be explained in terms of natural-selection

---

[12]For discussions of purely existential statements, see Popper, *Logic of Scientific Discovery* (London: Hutchinson, 1959), sec. 15; J. O. Wisdom, "The Refutability of 'Irrefutable Laws' ", *British Journal for the Philosophy of Science,* 1963, pp. 303–6; J.O. Wisdom: "Refutation by Observation and Refutation by Theory", in I. Lakatos and A. Musgrave, eds., *Problems in the Philosophy of Science* (Amsterdam: North-Holland Publishing Company, 1968), pp. 65–67; J.W.N. Watkins: "Confirmable and Influential Metaphysics", *Mind* (1958), pp. 345–47; "Between Analytic and Empirical", *Philosophy,* 1957; and "When Are Statements Empirical?", *British Journal for the Philosophy of Science,* February 1960.

survival value only by reference to the others and to an external world. From the height of our own complex cognitive structures we can even see how the spatial and other cognitive equipment of various other life forms approximate, in however imperfect a way, to devices more elaborately and complexly developed in ourselves.

A hypothetical external world that exists independently of our senses clearly plays a crucial role here. Evolutionary theory claims the existence of a world millions of years prior to the appearance of human life or human perception as we know it. We need such an external world, and a history of interaction with it, in order to explain why our cognitive and perceptual structures are the way they now are; hence the contention that there is no reality apart from that created by human perception is, from the point of view of evolutionary theory, simply absurd. If one, however fastidiously and "justifiably", omits the external world, one is left with an inexplicable miracle, a piece of "preestablished harmony". Thus it can hardly be said here, as the philosopher Herbert Dingle wrote in defending idealism in physics: "the external world plays no part at all in the business, and could be left out without loss of anything . . . It is thus a useless encumbrance. . . . a will o' the wisp, leading us astray and finally landing us in a bog of nescience." [13]

Of course some idealist might dispute this argument, saying—let us suppose—that we had created out of our perceptions animals with cognitive apparatuses which *appeared* to be adjusted to the exigencies of an external world even though there is no such world. This megalomaniacal argument reminds one of those religious believers who, in the nineteenth century, defended seven-day creationism against geological discoveries on the grounds that God created a "pre-aged" world, one that contained structures that appeared to be fossil remains—just to try our faith. To be sure, one cannot conclusively disprove idealism: i.e., one cannot justify the contention that idealism is false. Thus one may not be able to convince a particular idealist. But one cannot conclusively disprove scientific laws—or anything else—either. Ad hoc and other defensive strategies may be invoked in defense of any and all theory and speculation.

[13]Herbert Dingle, *The Sources of Eddington's Philosophy* (Cambridge: Cambridge University Press, 1954), p. 25. For the biological and evolutionary accounts referred to, see Donald T. Campbell, "Evolutionary Epistemology", in P. A. Schilpp, ed., *The Philosophy of Karl Popper* (La Salle: Open Court, 1974), p. 414; K. R. Popper, *Objective Knowledge* (London: Oxford University Press, 1972); Konrad Lorenz, "Kant's Doctrine of the A Priori in the Light of Contemporary Biology", in L. von Bertalanffy and A. Rapoport, eds., *General Systems, Yearbook of the Society for General Systems Research*, 1962, pp. 112–14; Konrad Lorenz, *Behind the Mirror* (New York: Harcourt, Brace, Jovanovich, 1973); and W. W. Bartley, III, "Critical Study: The Philosophy of Karl Popper: Part I: Biology and Evolutionary Epistemology", *Philosophia*, September-December 1976, pp. 463–94; and W. W. Bartley, III, "Philosophy of Science", in Asa Kasher and Shalom Lappin, eds. *New Trends in Philosophy* (Tel Aviv: Yachdav, 1982; and New York: Humanities Press, 1984). See also my "Philosophy of Biology *versus* Philosophy of Physics", in *Fundamenta Scientiae* vol. 3, no. 1 (1982), pp. 55–78; and my "The Challenge of Evolutionary Epistemology", in *Proceedings of the 11th International Conference on the Unity of the Sciences* (New York: ICF Press, 1983), pp. 835–80. See also my "Knowledge Is a Product Not Fully Known to Its Producer".

In sum, the relationship between realism and observational evidence seems to be the following, indirect one: realism itself is untestable. However, the denial of realism, i.e., idealism, is contradicted by certain well-tested laws of science; and these are in turn testable by basic statements. Thus current scientific results leave hypothetical realism in possession of the field.

9. Factual Information and Moral Claims

The previous two sections have argued, with two examples, that traditional epistemological problems that were insoluble within a justificational approach can be resolved on a nonjustificational critical approach. Since we are concerned with illustrating the difference between the way in which sense observation is treated by traditional empiricism and the way in which it can be treated on a nonjustificational approach, we have concentrated on the ways in which observational evidence relates nonjustificationally to scientific laws and to the doctrine of realism.

In the present section I want to note how observational and other factual information relate to the evaluation of moral statements. And I do so just because many philosophers have been led, by the impossibility of justifying moral statements by factual statements, to deny that there is ever any connection between fact and value, and indeed even sharply to discourage any exploration of the possible logical connections between factual and evaluative statements. Rather, they accept G. E. Moore's verdict that "No truth about what is real can have any logical bearing upon the answer to the question of what is good in itself". Or they go so far as Hume, and declare that logic and reason play no part in moral argument.[14]

Yet this is clearly false. Truths about facts do bear logically on matters of value. A moral statement can sometimes be *rebutted* by factual statements. Here again, the crucial logical rule is *modus tollens,* retransmission of falsity.

In giving an example, I shall assume as correct the doctrine that "ought" statements imply "can" statements in respect to persons.[15] Thus, in saying

[14]G. E. Moore, *Principia Ethica* (Cambridge: Cambridge University Press, 1903), p. 118; David Hume, *Treatise of Human Nature,* Selby-Bigge edition (Oxford: Oxford University Press, 1888), book 3, part 2, sec. 1.

[15]See the discussion in my *Morality and Religion* (London: Macmillan, 1971). It might be objected that "counsels of perfection" conflict with what I am saying here. Thus Hermann Hesse, in *The Journey to the East,* writes: "One paradox, however, must be accepted and this is that it is necessary to continually attempt the seemingly impossible." Or, to take the perfect example: "Be ye therefore perfect, even as your Father which is in heaven is perfect." But such injunctions do not really enjoin the impossible, as is seen in the implicit expectations that such action is unattainable. Rather, as in Hesse, what is enjoined is an *attempt* in a particular rigorous direction. See also George I. Mavrodes, "Is and Ought", in *Analysis,* December 1964, pp. 42–44; and Alan Gewirth, "On Deriving a Morally Significant 'Ought'", *Philosophy,* vol. 54, no. 208 (April 1979), pp. 231–32.

that a person ought to do something, it is assumed that it is possible for him to do that thing, that he can do it. Morality posts guides to possible action. On this assumption, the following argument is valid:

Premise: Jones ought to be a genius

Conclusion: Jones can be a genius.

Suppose we have evidence indicating that the conclusion is false. We might learn, say, that Jones is suffering from extensive organic brain damage, or that he has an I.Q. far below normal. While one might reasonably question the results of an I.Q. test, and their import for genius, one would probably accept sound evidence of massive brain damage to show that Jones cannot be a genius. Here we have used a factual consideration in evaluation and criticism of a moral claim.

Take a more topical example, the punishment of criminals, an issue both of morality and of public policy. Suppose that it is argued that one ought not to punish criminals but to treat them all psychologically in order to cure them of criminal tendencies. To this proposal it may be retorted that "ought" implies "can", and that there exist some criminals—for example, those with certain genetic defects—whom it is impossible to cure by psychological treatment. The example is not fanciful: the XYY chromosomal abnormality has been widely associated by researchers with criminal behavior and/or low intelligence in adult males; and recent studies suggest that one male in 300 may be born with just this abnormality.[16] This factual information, which bears logically on the original proposal for a different public policy, will if taken seriously lead to a modification of the proposal. Thus Dr. Park S. Gerald of the Harvard Medical School has urged that a large-scale study of XYY incidence should be done, because "a great deal of social planning could be related to this. These people [with XYY syndrome] might still get into trouble despite present welfare programs".[17]

Such arguments in which factual claims rebut prescriptive remarks are by no means unusual. On the contrary, they are rather common. Bishop Robinson provided an interesting illustration when he reported the response to his proposal, in a sermon, that capital punishment be abolished in favor of attempts to reform even the most hardened criminals. The response is reported by the *Observer* as follows:

> Then came the letters; a week after the sermon they were piled on chairs and the floor in his study, a tide of sour disagreement. . . . "Well, you bloody

---

[16]JAMA, 205, no. 9 (August 26, 1968), p. 28.

[17]Since such arguments can easily be misused perhaps it is necessary to add here that a demonstration that one proposed alternative to punishment runs into difficulties in certain cases is in itself no argument on behalf of punishment. Whatever the facts concerning the XYY chromosomal abnormality may be, the problem of punishment remains to be dealt with.

fool", one began. A woman from Hampstead wrote briefly to say that "There *are* evil men who are unredeemable". "This is all rot," claimed an anonymous writer. "Just HANG 'em. I say dam the church and such talk".

Here again, an alleged fact, relating to possibility—"There are evil men who are unredeemable"—is used in rebuttal of a prescriptive policy.

In the *Observer* article from which these excerpts are taken, no mention of the XYY chromosomal abnormality is made. Outside an informed medical context, the claim that there just *are* "unredeemable men" might be dismissed as an admittedly factual but nonetheless untestable statement. The studies in genetics mentioned, however, indicate that such expressions may be given a quite hard and testable scientific interpretation, one harder to dismiss.

Moral claims are not, however, empirically testable. As we saw in the discussion of realism above, the notion of testability refers to refutability *by reports of sense observation*. And specific statements of impossibility—such as "Jones cannot be a genius"—although statements of fact, are not statements of observation. One cannot *observe* Jones's not being able to be a genius, although one may indeed so *infer* from certain observations one makes about him, in conjunction with laws of nature. Such statements are nonobservational inferences or conclusions of arguments which, themselves having nothing to do with morality, contend that certain kinds of facts and behavior are prohibited by natural law, given certain information (e.g., brain damage) relating to the party in question (e.g., Jones).

Nor is it claimed here that *all* moral statements may be rebutted in this way by factual information relating to possibility. Nonetheless, such factual criticism of moral injunctions plays a deeply pervasive role in the examination of morality. Almost all morality imposes some sort of obligation. Yet impossibility of performance generally releases one from obligation, or at the very least diminishes one's obligation. This is true in the law as well as in ordinary moral discussion. And it is also a matter of common reflection, as Undershaft indicates when, in *Major Barbara*, he says: "Well, you have made for yourself something that you call a morality or a religion or what not. It doesn't fit the facts. Well, scrap it. Scrap it and get one that does fit. That is what is wrong with the world at present." Information relating to impossibility also relates importantly to moral issues in connection with questions of freedom of action. Thus, if it can be shown that an action was forced, if it was impossible for one to resist it, then one may not be thought to have been obliged morally to have done otherwise, or to be morally culpable for having performed it. In this case, the argument that is constructed may be indirect: it may be argued that the impossibility to do otherwise renders the action unfree; and that the lack of freedom, in turn, defeats the obligation to do otherwise.

The connection between obligation and possibility is of course well known. A philosopher who has written of it most interestingly is H.L.A. Hart, who shows that a contract in the law is rendered "defeasible" by impossibility of performance.[18] The bulk of Hart's discussion is non-justificational (although not self-consciously so). Yet many writers in ethics who are aware of Hart's discussion nonetheless repeat the old refrain about the lack of logical connection—indeed the impossibility of any such connection—between factual and moral statements.

10. Two Problems of Demarcation

What results from this discussion? Several examples have been presented of the treatment of classical problems through nonjustificational evaluation. These examples should illustrate whatever power this approach has to deal with problems hitherto regarded as insoluble. In these examples, the role of observation and other factual information is not to justify but to winnow. Facts about the world are the grim reapers of our speculations. They play this role most strongly in the sciences, but also in other areas, including morality.

Other sorts of considerations may also be brought to bear in the nonjustificational evaluation of ideas. Among these the most important— and the most neglected—is the question of what problem the idea under consideration is intended to solve, and whether it does so successfully. I have discussed this question elsewhere,[19] and mention it here only to emphasize that the present discussion hardly exhausts the problem of nonjustificational criticism. Quite the contrary, it does no more than suggest some of the very first moves in opening up the issues of nonjustificational criticism. Pursuing this question further amounts to developing a new kind of epistemology. For it is difficult to find any real examples in science, morality, or other areas where justification is *of any importance whatever*. The supposition that it is important is due entirely to philosophical tradition, not to actual need and practice. Consequently, all traditional and most contemporary epistemology and meta-ethics are obsolete to the extent to which they are accounts of, and theories of, justification.

The discussion in this appendix has depended on the asymmetry between verification and falsification. This idea, which is of far-reaching importance,

[18]H.L.A. Hart, "The Ascription of Responsibility and Rights", in A.G.N. Flew, ed. *Logic and Language*, 1st series (Oxford: Basil Blackwell, 1952), pp. 145–66.

[19]See chap. 5, sec 4, above. See also my "Goodman's Paradox: A Simple-Minded Solution", in *Philosophical Studies*, vol. 19, no. 6 (December 1968), pp. 85–88; my "Eine Lösung des Goodman-Paradoxons", in Gerard Radnitzky and Gunnar Andersson, eds., *Voraussetzungen und Grenzen der Wissenschaften* (Tübingen: J.C.B. Mohr Verlag, 1981), pp. 347–58; and my "Rationality, Criticism and Logic", sec. 16.

is, however, often misinterpreted. Identifying and eliminating some of these misinterpretations may bring our discussion to a close, and will return us to the problem of demarcation with which this appendix opened.

(1) There is a very important problem—*What is the relationship between evidence and what is evidenced?*—which must interest every empiricist and every scientifically oriented individual. Popper has answered—I believe correctly—a very specific version of this question: namely, *What is the relationship between observational evidence reports and theoretical statements about the world?* His answer, as we have seen, is that it is a falsifying relationship, not one of verification.

Ironically, Popper's own clarification of this relationship somewhat diminishes the *philosophical* significance of that relationship. The relationship between theory and observation has been most important historically because of the assumption that observation is the source and justification of all knowledge. Where this assumption is dropped, the problem's significance changes accordingly, and becomes part of what I have elsewhere (appendix 1) called the larger ecological problem of rationality.

I do not, however, wish these words to suggest that the role of observation is practically unimportant in science and critical discussion. Quite the contrary, in creating a critical environment, the control of observation is crucial. It is always important to chart how any particular theory relates to potential observational refutation; and if it does not so relate, it is important to know that, so that examination of the theory can be enhanced in some other way. Fields and domains that lack any such connection with observation and experimentation at the very least "lack an important social system feature supporting honesty", as the psychologist and evolutionary epistemologist Donald T. Campbell puts it.[20] Under a nonjustificational approach, observation remains the most important winnower of theory, and—as Campbell reports—the experience of laboratory researchers is that "experimentation is predominantly frustrating and disappointing". That is, experimental observation is an effective winnower.

(2) Popper himself happened to identify his answer to the question of the relationship between theory and observation with his answer to another question: namely, *What is the demarcation between science and nonscience?* Thus, on his account, a scientific theory would be one that is testable by an observational report (in the exact sense characterized by his theory of basic statements). And nonscientific theories—of which there are various kinds, including metaphysics and pseudo-science—would be observationally untestable.

This identification has, however, the effect of placing outside science some

[20]Donald T. Campbell, "A Tribal Model of the Social System Vehicle Carrying Scientific Knowledge", in *Knowledge: Creation, Diffusion, Utilization*, vol. 1, no. 2 (December 1979), pp. 181–201, esp. pp. 195 and 197–98.

theories and principles that have played a very important role within science both historically and at the present time. We have already mentioned, in our discussion of realism, some such principles which are compatible with all sense observation, and which nonetheless do conflict with testable (and well-tested) scientific *theories,* and thus are criticizable in terms of them. J.O. Wisdom has called such theories "theory-refutable" (as opposed to "observation-refutable" or testable).[21] Thus "Every substance has a solvent" is irrefutable in principle in the sense that no *empirical* refutation is possible. It is compatible, for instance, with "Gold has never been observed to dissolve". But it is incompatible with—and thus refutable by—the theory "Gold is insoluble". As another example, there is Schrödinger's discovery of the wave equation, involving as it does discontinuities as consequences, which conflicts with (and thus "theory-refutes") the (observation-irrefutable, or untestable) principle that energy occurs in all possible quantities: i.e., is continuous. Some additional examples of these important principles are: "For every event there is a cause", "To every observable physical change there exists a corresponding change in arrangement of invisible atoms", "There exists a perpetual motion machine", "All apparent regularities are in fact regulated by a system of natural laws", "Matter can only be moved by contiguous matter", "All mental changes are due to physiological causes", "All bodily changes are due to physical causes".[22]

Where such theories are brought into clash with scientific theories, and thus are criticizable in terms of these scientific theories, one must not assume too readily, however, that the observation-irrefutable but theory-refutable statement is wrong and the observation-refutable scientific hypothesis is right. Since no scientific theory can ever be fully verified by experience, it remains possible that any particular such hypothesis may be falsified by experience at some later date. Thus, in the case of a conflict between a scientific theory and an irrefutable statement, the latter could in principle be correct.

Such possible conflict between untestable and testable theories thus has a twofold effect. Not only does it enable the testable theory to exert a critical force against the untestable theory; by contrast, the untestable principle may take the lead, and exert a significant regulative effect, leading one to

<hr/>

[21]See the references in note 12 above. See also my "Reply to J. O. Wisdom", in *Problems in the Philosophy of Science,* pp. 108–9. I disagree with Wisdom's contention that "this kind of refutation is hypothetical in a way that refutation by observation is not, for the refuting theory, though tested and confirmed, may later be falsified; then the programme it had refuted becomes 'derefuted'". This is a misunderstanding of the situation that obtains with observation-refutation. Observation-refutations are *and remain* quite hypothetical; and theories refuted by observations may *also* be "derefuted" if the observation is revised in further testing.

[22]Watkins has written brilliantly about such statements. See the references in note 12 above. Watkins modifies his position in "Metaphysics and the Advancement of Science", *British Journal for the Philosophy of Science,* June 1975, pp. 91–121, and in "Minimal Presuppositions and Maximal Metaphysics", *Mind* (April 1978), pp. 195–209.

discount testable theories that conflict with it, and to encourage testable theories compatible with it.[23]

For such reasons, I prefer to treat the question of the relationship between theory and observation neutrally, without linking it necessarily to the question of demarcating science and nonscience. In any case, it is far more important to obtain a correct general characterization of the relationship between theory and observation than it is to define "science".

(3) In his early, but not later, writings, Popper goes a step further. He implicitly tends to identify the demarcation between science and nonscience with the demarcation between good and bad—the demarcation problem with which we opened this appendix. His most extreme statement, which appears both in *Die beiden Grundprobleme der Erkenntnistheorie* and in *The Logic of Scientific Discovery,* denies that untestable or unfalsifiable theories even speak about reality. Thus he writes (his italics): "*In so far as a scientific statement speaks about reality, it must be falsifiable: and in so far as it is not falsifiable, it does not speak about reality.*"[24] Elsewhere he writes that theories that are untestable "are of no interest to empirical scientists", that "Irrefutability is not a virtue but a vice", and that the closer study of metaphysical statements is "not . . . the concern of empirical science".[25]

Whatever one may think of the identification between observationally testable and scientific theory, this further implicit identification between testable and good theory will not do, as Popper himself has long since recognized. As he reported in *Objective Knowledge* (1972) concerning his earlier work, and his change of mind: "In those days I identified wrongly the limits of science with those of arguability. I later changed my mind and argued that non-testable (i.e., irrefutable) metaphysical theories may be rationally arguable."[26] His own later work is, accordingly, a rich fusion of untestable interpretation and testable theory. This is so in his work in philosophical biology, in his defense of indeterminism against determinism in physics and in the social sciences, in his work with Sir John Eccles on the mind-body problem.

[23]See my "Commentary: Max Jammer on the Interaction between Science and Metaphysics", in *Proceedings of the 7th International Conference on the Unity of the Sciences,* New York, 1979.

[24]*The Logic of Scientific Discovery,* p. 314; *Die beiden Grundprobleme der Erkenntnistheorie* (Tübingen: J.C.B. Mohr Verlag, 1979), p. 10. See also *The Open Society,* vol. 2, p. 13.

[25]See *Conjectures and Refutations,* p. 257, and *Logic of Scientific Discovery,* p. 37. For discussion of the development of Popper's theory of demarcation, see the item listed in footnote 2 above.

[26]*Objective Knowledge,* p. 40n. See, for examples, K. R. Popper and J. C. Eccles, *The Self and Its Brain* (New York: Springer Verlag, 1977), and *The Open Universe.*

11. Evolution, Ecology, and Demarcation

What, then, *is* the criterion of demarcation between a good idea and a bad one?

There is none. There are, of course, certain qualities that are highly desirable in theories, and whose absence signals danger. These include testability and high empirical content. But these are not *criteria*: their presence is not required, and a theory lacking in them may turn out to be excellent. There are some objectionable characteristics in theories, and these include inconsistency and incoherency.[27] But their contraries are not criteria of goodness: consistency and coherency are desired, but they do not, in and of themselves, make a theory a good one.

How, then, does one get better ideas? How does one winnow out the bad from the good? The answer to this question is part of what the evolutionary epistemologist Donald T. Campbell calls "the general theory of fit".[28] The question is an evolutionary and ecological one; and its answer is related to the answer to the question of how animals and other organisms become better adapted to their environments. As it turns out, a nonjustificational theory of criticism is parallel to the neo-Darwinian account of evolution and adaptation, whereas a justificational theory of criticism is parallel to the discredited Lamarckian theory of evolution.[29] Which is not surprising, since the evolutionary adaptation of plants and animals is also a knowledge process.[30]

Darwinian evolution proceeds in three great steps or rhythms: (a) blind or unjustified variation; (b) systematic selection and elimination; and (c) retention and duplication.

Good and bad ideas demarcate from one another gradually, *in the setting of a critical, competitive, and creative environment, in accordance with these three steps.*

But what makes for such an environment? The epistemologist and methodologist who have set aside justificationism are freed of those powerful arguments on behalf of attachment and commitment which, so long as they were unanswered, served the interests of those who identify with, cling on to, and defend their positions and contexts, and thus

---

[27]See K. R. Popper, *Conjectures and Refutations,* chap. 10, and K. R. Popper, *The Open Society and Its Enemies,* 4th and subsequent editions, "Addendum: Facts, Standards and Truth: A Further Criticism of Relativism".

[28]See Donald T. Campbell, "Evolutionary Epistemology", William James Lectures, Harvard University, 1977. Preliminary mimeographed draft, October 1978.

[29]See Donald T. Campbell, "Unjustified Variation and Selective Retention in Scientific Discovery", in F. J. Ayala and T. Dobzhansky, eds., *Studies in the Philosophy of Biology* (London: Macmillan, 1974), pp. 144–46.

[30]See Donald T. Campbell, "Evolutionary Epistemology".

contribute to the maintenance of an uncritical environment hostile to the development of ideas.

What are the cultural ramifications of a change of metacontext in which justification is set aside? What must happen—intellectually, psychologically, socially, politically—for such a metacontext to be instituted? (For the idea of metacontext see appendix 1.) What would a culture lethal to positionality and attachment really be like? And would that be desirable?

The epistemologist who deals with such questions has as his goal the personal and institutional implementation of a transformed metacontext—one that involves the transformation of Western man away from the positionality and attachment that have marked his career. To reach such a goal, the epistemologist is faced with a charter for investigation whose ramifications extend far beyond traditional epistemology: how to create for our ideas the most lethal possible environment (systematic selection and elimination) in which the production of creative new ideas (variation) nonetheless thrives, and in which our intellectual heritage is preserved and transmitted (retention and duplication).

Put differently and more broadly, this question is: How can our intellectual life and institutions, our traditions, and even our etiquette, sensibility, manners and customs, and behavior patterns, be arranged so as to expose our beliefs, conjectures, ideologies, policies, positions, programs, sources of ideas, traditions, and the like, to optimum criticism, so as at once to counteract and eliminate as much intellectual error as possible, and also so as to contribute to and insure the fertility of the intellectual econiche: to create an environment in which not only negative criticism but also the positive creation of ideas, and the development of rationality, are truly inspired.

It is not easy to answer such questions, for existing traditions and even most institutions have evolved gradually; they are "complex phenomena": they enjoy a "spontaneously ordered" character and a usefulness that transcend anything that could have been produced by deliberate invention; they are the product of human action but not of human design.[31] Yet such spontaneous orders may also be fragile and difficult to maintain. Tampering with such traditions and institutions is hence fraught with the danger of unintended consequences, with the danger of making things far worse.

A first step in approaching such questions of reform and reconstruction of the intellectual econiche is to notice, to begin to identify, what existing traditions and institutions already contribute to goals of eliminating error and enhancing the advance of knowledge, and which ones work against those same goals. Some apparently trivial existing institutions—linguistic

---

[31]See Hayek, *Studies in Philosophy, Politics and Economics,* esp. chaps. 2, 4, and 6.

institutions, for instance—which of course were never developed for such purposes, in fact serve them rather subtly, economically, and effectively. There is, for instance, what I call *"marked knowledge"*, which is a kind of evolutionary precursor to falsified knowledge. We often use standard qualifiers, such as the phrase "so-called", to *mark* concepts or theories or practices about which there is already some doubt or question, or which are, at the very least, out of fashion. There are many such markers: others are the use of the phrase "First Draft" to mark a manuscript that is being circulated for critical comments, or the phrase "trial balloon", which one may use self-deprecatingly to offer a fresh but as yet unexamined idea. This sort of device should probably be used much more often: it could only do good if every published manuscript were prominently marked "Damaged Goods". The use of these markers proclaims to others that we are savvy, critical, and aware of, or anticipate, the defects in question—or at least aware that there is some question about such ideas. We use such devices to get optimum use out of such ideas: for our purpose is not to delete them too fast, not to eliminate what might be called *defective knowledge* before we have got as much as we can from it, but *just to mark it as defective*. Such knowledge can be transmitted *so marked*; whereas in natural selection in nature, there is only deletion (extinction).

To begin to become aware of, and to face, such ecological questions is to begin artificially to construct and to probe possible environments for the advancement of science and learning. Paramount in such construction will be the ecological question of *balance*—for evolution puts its three steps or rhythms permanently at odds with one another in a matrix of essential tensions. Thus variations and retention are always opposed. Methodologists —even nonjustificational methodologists—nonetheless frequently give unbalanced advice. Thus Paul K. Feyerabend overemphasizes variation; justificationists generally overemphasize retention; and Popper overemphasizes elimination—an overemphasis that could readily be corrected through judicious marking of defective knowledge.

In using the language of evolutionary theory to confront and treat problems relating to the advancement of knowledge, one should not forget that the mechanisms of organic evolution and those of cultural and intellectual evolution are not identical, despite their close parallels. We have already mentioned that marked knowledge has no real organic counterpart. There is also no meta-aim governing the evolutionary development of organisms in accordance with which variation or lethal elimination need artificially to be encouraged. The evolutionary development of ideas, however, may be governed by just such a meta-aim, a culturally instituted "plastic control", namely: the deliberate production of variation and the deliberate elimination of falsity and poor fit.

Such questions force the epistemologist out of the ivory tower into which the dilemmas of justificationism have seduced him, and make of him a psychologist, a sociologist, a political theorist—even a social reformer. Since the advancement of science and learning is not the only desirable goal of social life, the epistemologist, like all social reformers, will meet with opposition and conflict, as well as with opportunities.

APPENDIX 3. FRIES'S TRILEMMA AND THE EMPIRICAL "BASIS"

Although many ideas presented in this book are indebted to, and an extension of, the theories of Karl Popper, a few of Popper's ideas are directly opposed to my own. In Popper's work, and especially in his earlier writings, there is a tendency to demand conventional or irrational decision whenever some point is reached which cannot be justified. Thus we found an "irrational faith in reason" in Popper's first formulation of "critical rationalism" (see chapter 4, section 5 above) in *The Open Society and Its Enemies*. A similar move is also encountered in Popper's first book, *Die beiden Grundprobleme der Erkenntnistheorie*, where—appealing to Kant and the primacy of practical reason—Popper states that the final basis of all knowing is to be sought in an act of free postulation that cannot be justified rationally. These matters have been examined, and an alternative approach stated, in the text above (chapter 5).

There is, unfortunately, an additional such justificationist manifestation right at the heart of Popper's theory of knowledge, in his account of the "empirical basis" of science. I shall in this appendix argue that it is in no way essential to his approach, and can easily be rooted out while retaining the spirit of his critical philosophy. If the account presented in this appendix succeeds, then no conflict remains between Popper's approach and my own.

Since Popper's account of the empirical basis of science is stated in terms of the well-known Friesian trilemma, my argument develops in two stages: first, I present and reinterpret Fries's trilemma; then I show how the justificationist elements can be removed from Popper's account of the empirical basis of science.

1. Fries's "Trilemma"

It has become a matter of custom among many philosophers to present their views concerning the relation between theory and sense observation in terms of J. F. Fries's famous "trilemma", as presented in *Neue oder anthropologische Kritik der Vernunft* (1828–31).[1] This custom seems to me a bad one. First, Fries's problem is structured justificationally, and thus distorted from the outset; second, it is no true trilemma. It is, rather, a *dilemma-engendering dilemma.*

Fries had argued that, to avoid *dogmatism,* one must be able to *justify* the statements of science. But statements, he noticed, can be justified, logically, only by statements. This leads to *infinite regress.* To this the only alternative seemed to be what Popper calls *psychologism,* the doctrine that statements can be justified by the "immediate knowledge" of perceptual experience as well as by other statements. Presented with this trilemma—dogmatism vs. infinite regress vs. psychologism—Fries had opted for psychologism.

That this is no real trilemma, but a dilemma-engendering dilemma, can be readily seen from the following reconstruction:

If you are proving one proposition by another, either you go on forever—or you stop.

If you go on forever, there is no proof, only infinite regress. Therefore you cannot go on forever.

So suppose you stop. But can you stop? And if so, how?

There are a number of possibilities. It is a large number: I would guess that it is infinite. E.g.,

(1) You can just stop arbitrarily wherever you choose or decide to do so. (You can designate your stopping points as being those principles in terms of which you choose to lead your life.) In this case, you can either stick to your choice, come what may, or be prepared to give it up.

If you stick to your choice come what may, *then* you have a *dogma.*

If you are prepared to give up your choice, to reconsider it, then you can do *that* under a number of different circumstances. For example:

(a) You may revise your choice arbitrarily (and of course the same questions can be asked of the new choice: e.g., will you stick to your *revised* choice, come what may, or are you prepared to give it up?)

(b) You may revise your choice under the weight of reason. (In which case, where did the reason come from, in case the first choice defined "reason" for you?)

(2) You can stop at a self-evident proposition.

(3) You can stop at a nonself-evident proposition—and then justify *it* nonpropositionally. But there are a number of different "nonpropositional" ways of justifying a proposition. E.g.,

(a) By appealing to "immediate" experience. *Here* is where *psychologism* comes in at last!

(b) By appealing to a decision—which may in turn be arbitrary or otherwise, and revisable or otherwise, or "motivated" by experience or

---

[1] Jacob Friedrich Fries, *Neue oder anthropologische Kritik der Vernunft* (Heidelberg: Christian Friedrich Winter, 1828 [vol. 1], 1831 [vols. 2 and 3]).

otherwise. In which cases . . . And so on.

All of this is a toy, and can be complicated almost *ad libitum*. The point is not to play with the toy, but to see the possibilities more accurately in order to find the way to a solution. To do this we must examine how Popper's account of observation is distorted by the usual reading of Fries's trilemma.

2. The Empirical "Basis"

As we saw in appendix 2, Popper's own view is that observation is used to test—rather than to verify (or justify)—the universal statements of science. "Basic statements" are for him reports of observation asserting that an observable event is occurring in a certain region of space and time; these are statements which are in potential conflict with the theory under consideration; and they are themselves intersubjectively testable by observation.[2]

Popper's statement of his position within the cumbersome and justificationist framework of Fries's "trilemma" has, however, led to great misunderstanding. Consider how Popper has tried to apply his own approach to each horn of Fries's trilemma. First, with regard to the possibility of dogmatism *vis à vis* statements which we desist from justifying, Popper concedes that basic statements are accepted dogmatically. He goes on to explain that the scientist must, through a free act, *decide by agreement* to *accept* basic statements as satisfactory and sufficiently tested. Such a decision is necessary, he argues, for otherwise, unless we reach a statement which we decide to accept, our test will have led nowhere. Thus, "It is our decisions which settle the fate of theories" (p. 108). Popper also concedes a similarity to conventionalism here, as well as a difference, in that the conventionalist tends to accept universal, not singular, statements by agreement—and does so for reasons of aesthetics, not of testability. Yet this dogmatism is, Popper concludes, innocuous since basic statements can always, if need be, be tested further.

Second, as to infinite regress, Popper concedes that the chain of deduction wherein universal statements are tested against testable basic statements is

[2]Popper argues that, in the description of these basic statements, reference to observation is not essential. One could instead refer to "an event involving position and movement of macroscopic physical bodies". As a further step in avoiding any psychologistic overtones, Popper stresses that basic statements are thus not statements *about* our subjective experiences, or "Protokollsätze", as some positivists had interpreted them to be. For statements about experience are often of reduced testability. Thus "I see that the table here is white", being about me, is less testable than "This table is white", which is about the table.

Popper also states some formal requirements for basic statements which are not necessary to our argument here but may briefly be mentioned. Basic statements must be singular existential statements; they must be able to contradict a universal statement; and they must be *un*derivable from a universal statement alone without initial conditions.

indeed infinite. But this, he contends, is also innocuous since there is no question of proving anything.

Finally, as to psychologism, Popper concedes that basic statements and sense experience are related in that sense experience may motivate a decision to accept a basic statement. Yet such experience, as he emphasizes, in no way justifies the basic statement.

All three of these "concessions" are both unnecessary and extremely misleading. The first step in Popper's reply to Fries sounds suspiciously like the dogmatic justification by decision or commitment which is familiar in fideism and in various forms of irrationalism and existentialism, and which I have challenged throughout this book. This has not escaped Popper's critics.[3] Thus Pannenberg has suggested that Popper's dismissal of the element of dogmatism as "innocuous" is at best an "underestimate of the problem".[4] Sir Alfred Ayer has objected that such decisions may be arbitrary—which possibility, of course, brings back the specter of irrationality.

Popper has on occasion replied to such criticism; but his answers are quite unclear. Take his reply to Ayer as an example.[5] Popper objects (p. 1110) that Ayer's criticism is based on the mistaken assumption that every decision or convention must be arbitrary. Yet, on the next page (p. 1111), Popper concedes that the sorts of decisions he is discussing may be called arbitrary . . . but are far from being "totally arbitrary". Three pages later (p. 1114), he states that the conventional or decisional element in the acceptance or rejection of a proposition generally involves "no element of arbitrariness at all". Two sentences later, he nonetheless states that decisions about the acceptance of basic statements *are* "somewhat arbitrary". In *Logik der Forschung* (p. 74), Popper had written that decisions about basic statements are not justified by our experiences, but are, rather, logically speaking, *arbitrary stipulations* ("willkürliche Festsetzungen").

All this is confusing, and the entire matter needs to be restated.

---

[3]Sir Alfred J. Ayer, "Truth, Verification and Verisimilitude", in P. A. Schilpp, ed., *The Philosophy of Karl Popper* (La Salle: Open Court, 1974), pp. 684–92. For further critical discussions of Popper's theory of basic statements, see Kurt Bayertz and Josef Schliefstein, *Mythologie der "kritischen" Vernunft* (Cologne: Pahl-Rugenstein Verlag, 1977), pp. 34–37.

See also Ernin McMullin, "Philosophy of Science and Its Rational Reconstruction", p. 244; Noretta Koertge, "Towards a New Theory of Scientific Inquiry", p. 254; and Kurt Hübner, "Reply to Watkins", pp. 393–94, in Gerard Radnitsky and Gunnar Andersson, *Progress and Rationality in Science* (Dordrecht: D. Reidel, 1978); also printed as *Fortschritt und Rationalität der Wissenschaft* (Tübingen: J.C.B. Mohr Verlag, 1980). See also Hermann Oetjens, *Sprache, Logik, Wirklichkeit: Der Zusammenhang von Theorie und Erfahrung in K. R. Popper's "Logik der Forschung"* (Stuttgart-Bad Cannstatt: Friedrich Frommann Verlag, 1975), esp. chap. 3; Albrecht Wellmer, *Methodologie als Erkenntnistheorie: Zur Wissenschaftslehre Karl R. Poppers* (Frankfurt: Suhrkamp Verlag, 1967), esp. chap. 5; Karl-Otto Apel, *Transformation der Philosophie* (Frankfurt: Suhrkamp, 1973), vol. 2, pp. 43, 326 ff., 409 ff.; and W. H. Newton-Smith, *The Rationality of Science* (London: Routledge and Kegan Paul, 1981), pp. 62–64. See also Harold I. Brown, *Perception, Theory, and Commitment: The New Philosophy of Science*, pp. 71–76.

[4]Wolfhart Pannenberg, *Theology and the Philosophy of Science* (London: Darton, Longman & Todd, 1976), p. 52.

[5]K. R. Popper, "Replies to My Critics", in Schilpp, ed., pages as indicated.

First, the source of the problem here is the same one that we encountered earlier: namely, Popper's unfortunate tendency to demand convention or irrational decision whenever some point is reached which cannot be justified.

Yet there is no need for such a step from Popper's own wider point of view.[6] Such free and arbitrary postulating and deciding is no more needed with basic statements than with rationality: and the fact that neither basic statements nor rationalism can be justified ought to be irrelevant—provided that they are both subject to criticism.

Thus I propose simply to eliminate as superfluous Popper's requirements relating to decisions, agreements, conventions, acceptance, and justification.

The matter may be restated as follows. On a corrected Popperian approach, there is neither dogmatism nor infinite regress, and thus the dilemma that is basic to the Friesian problem does not arise. Although the *process* of testing is potentially infinite, no infinite regress need arise "since . . . there is no question of trying to prove any statement" (*Logic of Scientific Discovery*, p. 105). This is so since the testing is nonjustificational. Only if Popper's approach is misinterpreted, and it is supposed that one can, with test statements, *prove* a theory to be false, or *justify* the contention that it is false, does one indeed get an infinite regress. The test statements are intended to be hypothetical, and criticizable and revisable, just like everything else in the system; there is no justification, no proof, no fixed point anywhere. There is nothing "basic" about basic statements. And hence no possibility of dogmatism with respect to them.

If such basic statements happen to be incompatible with a theory, then the theory is false *relative to them*; and they are false *relative to the theory*. There is no question of theory proving reports wrong, or reports proving theory wrong. *Both* could be wrong: neither is "basic".

Suppose one wishes to test a particular theory. One will determine what sorts of events involving position and movement of macroscopic physical bodies would be incompatible with the theory, and will then set up an experimental arrangement, if possible, to try to produce such events. One will then make or gather reports concerning the test. And, in order to maximize criticism and provide mutual testing of test reports, one will invite or permit more than one reporter. One does *not* get such additional tests to elicit an agreement.

Suppose these reports go against the theory. Stepping back from this situation, regarding the objective structure of circumstances and statements, one then makes a report on what has happened: that the theory is now

---

[6]Popper is obviously aware of the problem. Thus he often immediately (if not consistently) qualifies his more fideistic statements. On the issue of "acceptance", for instance, he writes in *The Logic of Scientific Discovery*, New Appendix *9, p. 419: "We tentatively '*accept*' this theory—but only in the sense that we select it as worthy to be subjected to further criticism, and to the severest tests we can design."

problematic in that it is false relative to the test reports; and that the test reports are themselves, as may be at the moment, unproblematic.[7]

If the test reports had conflicted among themselves—if *some* of them had gone against the theory and some had failed to go against it—one would have a different situation: then one would more accurately report that, although the theory was rendered problematical by some of the test results, the test was itself also problematical in having produced several conflicting reports.

One contributes nothing to this situation by adding a requirement that one needs to decide by agreement which reports to accept. Moreover, Popper is wrong in claiming that the test will have "led nowhere" without such an agreement: it will have led either to problematical or to unproblematical basic statements. These reports do not need to be backed up by "decisions" and "acceptances". One does not need to accept any of them, or even to consider them (however tentatively) to be true; one needs only to give an account of what is happening, and to state how theory and report stand, hypothetically, in relation to one another. One may go on to conjecture about which of the reports are accurate: but this is a conjecture, not a decision, and may itself be tested accordingly. Hence a theory may be *provisionally* and *conjecturally* rejected because it conflicts with some less problematic view. Any theory is refuted only relative to critical arguments incompatible with it, which are themselves open to criticism by the testing of their own consequences. These in turn are criticizable forever.

This process—in which one steps outside the positionality of the theory to comment on the state of examination of the theory, treating the theory as an object, not as one's own point of view, and oneself coming from beyond the theory—is virtually impossible from within a justificationist metacontext (see appendix 1), in which one is always, willy-nilly, imprisoned within the bounds of one's position.

---

[7]In reading *Die beiden Grundprobleme der Erkenntnistheorie,* pp. 131–32, I notice that Popper introduced the idea of problematicality there in the sense in which I am now using it here. This makes it puzzling that he nonetheless thought that something was *added* by requiring a decision concerning unproblematical cases.

See also Joseph Agassi's remarks in "Sensationalism", *Mind,* vol. 75 (1966), pp. 1–24, and in "When Should We Ignore Evidence in Favour of a Hypothesis?", *Ratio,* vol. 15 (1973), pp. 183–205; both now reprinted in his *Science and Flux* (Dordrecht: D. Reidel, 1975), pp. 92–151.

APPENDIX 4. ON ALLEGED PARADOXES IN PANCRITICAL RATIONALISM

PART I

In several articles, John F. Post and J.W.N. Watkins[1] have, separately, argued that pancritical rationalism (or comprehensively critical rationalism) leads to semantical paradox and other difficulties and is hence refuted.[2] I reply to them in the following.

1. Prospectus. I shall summarize my approach briefly in sixteen points which will then be developed in the remainder of this appendix:

(1) There is a serious distortion running throughout this discussion, the major issue of which is the statement that all statements are open to criticism. In this book, this statement was given a detailed and concrete context in which the notion of "criticism" had a distinctive sense. In much of the discussion, this context has been ripped away, with the consequence that my original statement is deprived of its original meaning, and is having

---

[1]J.W.N. Watkins, "Comprehensively Critical Rationalism", *Philosophy*, vol. 44, no. 167 (January 1969), pp. 57–62; "CCR: A Refutation", *Philosophy*, vol. 46, no. 175 (January 1971), pp. 56–61; and "What Has Become of Comprehensively Critical Rationalism?", *Proceedings of the 11th International Conference on the Unity of the Sciences*, 1983, pp. 1087–1100; John F. Post, "Paradox in Critical Rationalism and Related Theories", *Philosophical Forum*, vol. 3, no. 1 (1972), pp. 27–61; and "A Gödelian Theorem for Theories of Rationality", *Proceedings of the 11th International Conference on the Unity of the Sciences*, 1983, pp. 1071–86. Related papers by Post include: "The Possible Liar", *Nous*, vol. 4 (1970), pp. 405–9; "Shades of the Liar", *Journal of Philosophical Logic*, vol. 2 (1973), pp. 370–86; "Propositions, Possible Languages and the Liar's Revenge", *British Journal for the Philosophy of Science*, vol. 25 (1974), pp. 223–34; "Shades of Possibility", *Journal of Philosophical Logic*, vol. 3 (1974), pp. 155–58; and "Presupposition, Bivalence, and the Possible Liar", in *Philosophia*, vol. 8 (1979), pp. 645–49. Post has also permitted me to read his manuscript, "The Modal Liar: Paradox in Self-Referential Falsifiability".

[2]The term "comprehensively critical rationalism" was my original term, introduced in the original American edition of *The Retreat to Commitment*. I now prefer the term "pancritical rationalism", introduced in the first German translation (*pankritische Rationalismus*) in 1964. My reply to Post and Watkins first appears in "The Alleged Refutation of Pancritical Rationalism", *Proceedings of the 11th International Conference on the Unity of the Sciences*, pp. 1139–79. See also my "Non-Justificationism: Popper *versus* Wittgenstein", *Akten des 7. Internationalen Wittgenstein Symposiums*, pp. 255–61; my "A Popperian Harvest", in Paul Levinson, ed., *In Pursuit of Truth*. See also Popper's discussion in *Realism and the Aim of Science*, ed. W. W. Bartley, III, vol. 1 of the *Postscript to the Logic of Scientific Discovery*, part 1, sec. 2. See also my "Transformation of Philosophical Thought: Recent Contributions", and my "On the Differences between Popperian and Wittgensteinian Approaches", both in the *Proceedings of the 10th International Conference on the Unity of the Sciences* (New York: ICF Press, 1982), pp. 1169–71 and 1289–1304.

other meanings imposed upon it. I discuss this matter in part 2 of this appendix, and again in part 5.

(2) Watkins's arguments seriously distort my position, and are invalid. Moreover, they have been replied to by other writers on several occasions.[3] I shall indicate some additional objections of my own in part 5 below, and shall also refer to Watkins's argument occasionally elsewhere in this appendix.

(3) The bulk of my attention will, however, be on Post's view, which has received less attention.[4]

(4) Post contends that my position—that all positions, including my own, are open to criticism—produces semantical paradox,[5] and generates an *uncriticizable* statement. The argument in which he initially couched this claim relied heavily on assumptions that are both false and foreign to my approach; so that my first reaction was simply to point out the error of these assumptions.[6]

(5) Post has responded by accepting my objections, and then recasting his paradox without those assumptions to which I had objected.

(6) I still have reservations about his revised argument, and about some of his remaining underlying assumptions. But this is irrelevant, since I have myself been able to produce a quite similar paradox (inspired by Post's work), using no assumptions that are not acceptable to me. (But see point 12 below.)

(7) I am, however, neither surprised nor disturbed to find that a *semantical* paradox of this sort can be produced from my statement of

---

[3]Critical reviews of Watkins's work on pancritical rationalism include: Joseph Agassi, I. C. Jarvie, and Tom Settle, "The Grounds of Reason", *Philosophy*, vol. 46, no. 175 (January 1971), pp. 43–49; John Kekes, "Watkins on Rationalism", *Philosophy*, vol. 46, no. 175 (January 1971), pp. 51–53; Sheldon Richmond, "Can a Rationalist Be Rational about His Rationalism?", *Philosophy*, vol. 46, no. 175 (January 1971), pp. 54–55; Tom Settle, I. C. Jarvie, and Joseph Agassi, "Towards a Theory of Openness to Criticism", *Philosophy of the Social Sciences*, vol. 4 (1974), pp. 83–90; Noretta Koertge, "Bartley's Theory of Rationality", *Philosophy of the Social Sciences*, vol. 4 (1974), pp. 75–81; Gerard Radnitzky, "In Defense of Self-Applicable Critical Rationalism", *Proceedings of the 11th International Conference on the Unity of the Sciences*, 1983; W. D. Hudson, "Professor Bartley's Theory of Rationality and Religious Belief", *Religious Studies*, vol. 9 (September 1973), pp. 339–50; N.H.G. Robinson, "The Rationalist and His Critics", *Religious Studies*, vol. 11 (1975), pp. 345–48. See also Michael Martin, "Religious Commitment and Rational Criticism", *Philosophical Forum*, vol. 2 (Fall 1970), pp. 107–21. A debate on these issues is printed in *Proceedings of the 11th International Conference on the Unity of the Sciences*, In addition to those articles cited elsewhere in these footnotes, see Walter B. Weimer, "CCR is not Completely Confused Rhetoric (and There is No Need to 'Pan' it)", pp. 1101–18; Jagdish Hattiangadi, "Bartley's Defense of Reason", pp. 1119–23; and Angelo M. Petroni, "What Has Become of Watkins and Post's Criticism of Self-Applicable Critical Rationalism?", pp. 1125–38.

[4]The only published notices of Post's work of which I know are: Tom Settle, "Concerning the Rationality of Scepticism", *Philosophical Forum*, vol. 4, no. 3, (Spring 1973), pp. 432–37; and A. A. Derksen, "The Failure of Comprehensively Critical Rationalism", *Philosophy of the Social Sciences*, vol. 10 (1980), pp. 51–66.

[5]What is involved is not an antinomy but what Post, following Quine, calls a "veridical paradox". See Post, "Paradox in Critical Rationalism", p. 27; and W. V. Quine, *The Ways of Paradox* (New York: Random House, 1966), pp. 5f, 14, 18.

[6]I did this in a draft manuscript, circulated among the parties to the dispute: "On Alleged Paradoxes in Pancritical Rationalism", sometimes referred to as "Appendix" in the pertinent literature, since it was a draft for the present appendix.

pancritical rationalism. On the contrary, I discussed this possibility at length with Popper in 1961 when I was writing the manuscript of the first edition of *The Retreat to Commitment*.

(8) The situation is rather simple. My position refers to itself as criticizable: i.e., it is "self-referential". Moreover, my position employs, although not exclusively, an interpretation of criticizability in terms of possible falsity—and thus involves the semantical concepts of truth and falsity. Finally, my position has always been expressed in natural language: i.e., it has not been formalized.

Since, as Tarski has shown,[7] any natural language containing semantic terms and the possibility of self-reference may be expected to be inconsistent, and to produce just such paradoxes, such results could, of course, be expected from the expression of pancritical rationalism.

When I was writing this book, I believed—as I continue to believe—that such paradoxes can be dealt with as they arise, through means similar to those that Tarski himself had suggested, through distinctions of levels of language, through the use of the notion of object and metalanguages. Gerard Radnitzky, in his discussion of the controversy among Post, Watkins, and myself, makes a similar suggestion.[8]

(9) Thus, despite appearances, the real issue between Post and me is not the production of a semantical paradox. Rather, the real issue is that (a) Post does not, in general, appear to favor Tarski-type resolutions of semantical paradoxes[9]; and (b) Post believes that such a course—even if it were possible generally—is closed to me by certain other presuppositions of pancritical rationalism.[10]

(10) This appendix is not the place to argue the first point: many ways have been developed for dealing with semantical paradoxes; and I agree with the majority of logicians who believe that there is some acceptable way of dealing with them—whether by type and language-level solutions,

---

[7]See Alfred Tarski, "The Semantic Conception of Truth and the Foundations of Semantics", in Herbert Feigl and Wilfrid Sellars, eds., *Readings in Philosophical Analysis* (New York: Appleton-Century-Crofts, 1949), pp. 52–84, esp. pp. 56–60; and Alfred Tarski, *Logic, Semantics, Metamathematics* (Oxford: Clarendon Press, 1956), chap. 8.

[8]Gerard Radnitzky, "Are Comprehensive Theories of Rationality Self-Referentially Inconsistent?", *Proceedings of the 7th International Wittgenstein Symposium* (Vienna: Hölder-Pichler-Tempsky, 1983); and "In Defense of Self-Applicable Critical Rationalism", in *Proceedings of the 11th International Conference on the Unity of the Sciences*, pp. 1025–69.

[9]For Post's views on these matters, see the essays cited in footnote 1 above, esp. "Propositions, Possible Languages and the Liar's Revenge", "Presupposition, Bivalence, and the Possible Liar", "Shades of the Liar", "The Possible Liar", and "Relative Truth and Semantic Categories". See also Y. Bar-Hillel, "Do Natural Languages Contain Paradoxes?", *Studium Generale*, vol. 19 (1966), pp. 391–97; R. L. Goodstein, "On the Formalization of Indirect Discourse", *Journal of Symbolic Logic*, vol. 23 (1958), pp. 417–19; R. L. Martin: "Toward a Solution of the Liar Paradox", *Philosophical Review*, vol. 76 (1967), pp. 279–311; F. Sommers, "On Concepts of Truth in Natural Languages", *Review of Metaphysics*, vol. 23 (1969), pp. 259–86; Avrum Stroll, "Is Everyday Language Inconsistent?", *Mind*, vol. 63 (1954), pp. 219–25; B. C. van Fraassen: "Presupposition, Implication and Self-Reference", *Journal of Philosophy*, vol. 65 (1968), pp. 136–52; and Tyler Burge, "Semantical Paradox"; *Journal of Philosophy*, vol. 76 (1979), pp. 169–98.

[10]Post, "Paradox in Critical Rationalism" sec. 8.

Zermelo-type solutions, category solutions, radical exclusion of all self-reference, or various other solutions.[11]

(11) I shall, however, show that the presuppositions of pancritical rationalism in no way hinder me—contrary to Post's contentions—from adopting some such escape from these paradoxes.

(12) *This means that Post's "uncriticizable" statement is, after all, criticizable. Accordingly, Post's argument collapses.*

(13) I then argue that Post's own alternative proposals—having to do with what he wrongly supposes to be the approaches of Quine and Lakatos—are unacceptable.

(14) I then contend that even if Post were right—if I had no escape either from the semantical paradoxes generally or from the particular "uncriticizable statement" that he produces—such a result would have no impact on the heart of the position presented in *The Retreat to Commitment*.

(15) Having replied to Post, I then return to some details of Post's presentation; for a discussion of our differences of assumption—although not needed for the final argument—is of methodological interest, and may also help prevent further misunderstanding. This detailed review of Post's assumptions forms part 4 of this appendix; the reply to the Postian argument itself forms part 3.

(16) Finally, I discuss briefly my differences with Watkins, concentrating on some points which have not been covered by previous writers. This is done in part 5.

PART 2

2. The Background of the Debate. Some of my differences with Post rest on misinterpretations of my position; some rest on disagreements of substance between us; and some rest on my own failure to state my position sufficiently clearly and adequately in the first place. Before turning to my reply, I would like to recall the background context of our debate.

---

[11]See K. R. Popper, "Self-Reference and Meaning in Ordinary Language", *Conjectures and Refutations* (London: Routledge & Kegan Paul, 1963), chap. 14; Ernst Zermelo, "Untersuchungen über die Grundlagen der Mengenlehre", *Mathematische Annalen*, vol. 65 (1908), pp. 261–81; Adolf Fraenkel, *Einleitung in die Mengenlehre* (Berlin, 1919); Bertrand Russell, "Mathematical Logic as Based on the Theory of Types", *American Journal of Mathematics*, vol. 30 (1908), pp. 222–62; J. von Neumann, "Eine Axiomatisierung der Mengenlehre", *Journal für reine und angewandte Mathematik*, vol. 154 (1925), pp. 219–40; Paul Bernays, *Axiomatic Set Theory*, with a historical introduction by Abraham A. Fraenkel (Amsterdam: North-Holland Publishing Company, 1958); William and Martha Kneale, *The Development of Logic* (Oxford: Clarendon Press, 1962), esp. chap. 11; Alfred Tarski, *Logic, Semantics, Metamathematics* (Oxford: Clarendon Press, 1956), esp. pp. 152–278; Robert L. Martin, ed., *The Paradox of the Liar* (New Haven: Yale University Press, 1970); Alan Ross Anderson, "St. Paul's Epistle to Titus", in Robert L. Martin, ed., *The Paradox of the Liar*.

My original treatment of these matters was, among other things, an examination of the main rationalist traditions of the West, in the course of which I uncovered and identified certain unconscious and mistaken assumptions about rational argumentation which—so long as they were retained—systematically undermined rationalist goals. I advocated removal of these assumptions for the sake of reconstructing and strengthening the rationalist tradition.

In particular, I was confronting the contention—as ancient as Sextus Empiricus and the Greek skeptics,[12] as contemporary as Wittgenstein, Ayer, Rorty, Karl Barth[13]—that there is an essential logical limitation to rationality: that rational defense and examination of ideas *must*, for *logical* reasons, be terminated by an arbitrary and irrational appeal to what may be called *dogmas* or *absolute presuppositions*. These dogmas or presuppositions earned their names from their characteristics, which included the following: (1) such dogmas and presuppositions, chosen arbitrarily and irrationally, or forced on one by the circumstances of fate or history, marked the limits of rationality; (2) they were not subject to review or criticism; (3) they were incapable of justification; (4) all of one's positions that were rational were justified or defended in terms of these presuppositions or dogmas: that is, any rationality in one's life was rationality *relative to* irrational bases. All of one's rational positions could be derived or induced from, or were somehow warranted by, such dogmas and presuppositions.

To rebut this cluster of contentions, I argued: (1) that *nothing* of any interest can be justified in the way required: the demand for justification is a red herring which has nothing whatever to do with the demands of logic or science, but is rather a piece of ancient methodology carried forward uncritically into modern discussion; (2) criticism is nonetheless possible provided one first *unfuses* justification and criticism (all traditional and most modern accounts of criticism are justificationist); (3) there are no limits to rationality in the sense that one *must* postulate dogmas or presuppositions that must be held exempt from review in order to conduct an argument at all; (4) it is false that those of one's positions that are held rationally are those that are deduced, induced, warranted, or otherwise defended in terms of dogmatically held presuppositions.

Post concentrates on one particular element of my discussion to which I myself happened to give some importance—namely, the claim that "Everything is open to criticism". The remainder of my argument, and the problems I was confronting, are not discussed, and are barely alluded to. Now, even if Post were right about the single conclusion that he does discuss

---

[12]Sextus Empiricus, *Works*, Harvard-Loeb Library edition.
[13]Wittgenstein, *On Certainty* (Oxford: Blackwell, 1969); A. J. Ayer, *The Problem of Knowledge* (New York: Penguin Books, 1956); Richard Rorty, *Philosophy and the Mirror of Nature* (Princeton: Princeton University Press, 1979); Karl Barth, *Church Dogmatics*. See my "Non-Justificationism: Popper *versus* Wittgenstein", *Proceedings of the 7th International Wittgenstein Symposium*.

(and I shall argue that he is *not* right even here), this would leave the remainder of my argument, and my solutions, conclusions, and suggestions (including all those just rehearsed) completely unaffected. I shall return to this point in section 7 below; but it should be borne in mind throughout.

3. What Did I Mean in Declaring That Everything Is Open to Criticism?

Just as the background just reviewed has been ignored in most of the discussion, neither has anyone paused to consider carefully what I meant when I declared that everything was open to criticism. What did I have in mind?

The classic account of criticism, which pervades almost all philosophical literature, from the Greeks to the present day, is a *justificationist theory of criticism.* According to this account, the way to examine and criticize an idea is to see whether and how it may be justified. And to justify an idea is to derive it from an authority in terms of which such evaluation and criticism is to be made. In short, such justification combines the following two requirements:

(1) an authority (or authorities), or authoritatively good trait, in terms of which evaluation (i.e., demarcation of the good from the bad ideas) is ultimately to be made;

(2) the idea that the goodness or badness of any idea is to be determined by reducing it to (i.e., deriving it from or combining it out of) the authority (or authorities), or to statements possessing the authoritatively good trait.[14] That which can so be reduced is justified; that which cannot is to be rejected.[15]

To cite again one familiar example of how this works, take the case of Hume. Hume wished to use sense observation as his authority in criticizing and evaluating the controversial issues of his day. Being a freethinker, he was able to show, in short order, that the ideas of God, freedom, and immortality, and of the human soul, could not be reduced to sense observation; and hence he rejected them. But to his surprise and dismay, he also found that scientific laws, the idea of causality, the idea of other minds and an external world, and the statements of history could also not be reduced to sense observation, and hence—by *his* authority and on *his* analysis—should also be rejected.

There are many many difficulties in these justificationist theories of criticism. One problem is the problem of logical strength; the conclusions that their advocates want to draw are almost invariably logically stronger than any available authority;[16] the other difficulty—and the one that

---

[14]See my "Logical Strength and Demarcation", in Gunnar Andersson, ed., *Rationality in Science and Politics* (Boston: D. Reidel, 1983), and appendix 2 of this book.

[15]This is what I call a "justificational strategy of criticism", as explained in the body of this book.

[16]See appendix 2.

concerns us here—is that the authorities themselves are, of course, not justified. It is even inappropriate to ask for justification of them, for that would simply engender an infinite regress. If one could continue to ask: "How do you know?", that line of questioning would never end: it would engender an infinite regress. Thus it is supposed that one must stop with an authority—or dogma, or presupposition—*which acts as justifier.* Since this justifier cannot itself be justified, and since the only way to criticize something is to attempt to justify it, these justifiers cannot be criticized. Dogmas, it is concluded, are *necessary.* The logical structure of argumentation itself appeared to vouch for, even to require, dogmatism.

What I did in *The Retreat to Commitment* was to show that *no authorities or justifiers in this sense were needed in criticism.* I separated the notions of justification and criticism (for the first time explicitly) and showed that criticism can be carried out successfully and satisfactorily without engendering any infinite regress, and hence without requiring any resort to justification whatever: that is, without any resort to dogmas or authorities. That is, when I declare that all statements are criticizable, I mean that it is not necessary, in criticism, in order to avoid infinite regress, to declare a dogma that cannot be criticized (since it is unjustifiable); I mean that it is not necessary to mark off a special class of statements, the justifiers, which *do* the justifying and criticizing but are not open to criticism; I mean that there is not some point in every argument which is exempted from criticism; I mean that the criticizers—the statements in terms of which criticism is conducted—are themselves open to review.

I doubt very much that Watkins would want to contest what I have just written, and I rather doubt that Post would either. That is, had they kept the statement that all statements are open to criticism in its original context, I do not think that they would have raised or would have wanted to raise their objections. *But they have dropped this context. They take "criticism" outside this context and use it in a very wide, uncontrolled sense; and they have thus pursued a discussion which, however interesting in its own terms, is irrelevant to the problems that I have been facing in this book.* Neither Post nor Watkins has ever even tried to show that the process of argumentation itself requires that I reserve some core of doctrine from risk; that I must either accept this core dogmatically or else accept infinite regress, circularity, or some other logical difficulty. But they would need to do just this to refute my argument.

Having made this statement about the background of my argument, and thereby protested against the procedure adopted by Post and Watkins, I shall drop this point, and attempt to answer their arguments *on their own terms.* For they are wrong on *their* terms too.

PART 3

4. *A Postian Paradox.*   In part 4 below, I give a detailed review of Post's original and revised statements of his paradox in critical rationalism. As I indicate there, I disagree with many of the particulars, and with many of the presuppositions, of his discussion.

In this part, I present a modified argument of my own devising, which involves no appeal to presuppositions which I reject, in order to create the same kind of objection to my own position that Post himself is aiming for. My own argument is thoroughly inspired by Post's, but perhaps simpler.

The argument revolves around my contention, set forth in this book, that all positions are open to criticism—including the position that all positions are open to criticism. (We may neglect here the question of whether it is a necessary or sufficient condition for being a rationalist that one so hold all one's positions. This question is discussed in section 13 below, but is not needed for the argument.)

Take the following two claims:

(A) All positions are open to criticism.

(B) A is open to criticism.

Since (B) is implied by (A), any criticism of (B) will constitute a criticism of (A), and thus show that (A) is open to criticism. Assuming that a criticism of (B) argues that (B) is false, we may argue: if (B) is false, then (A) is false; but an argument showing (A) to be false (and thus criticizing it) shows (B) to be true. Thus, if (B) is false, then (B) is true. Any attempt to criticize (B) demonstrates (B); thus (B) is uncriticizable, and (A) is false. And hence, so Post would contend, my position is refuted.

5. *An Argument against Post.*   Post says he was surprised by such a result; and he is evidently disturbed by it. I am neither surprised nor disturbed, for, I have assumed ever since I wrote this book that some such result would turn up. No doubt other such examples could also be constructed.

Such a result was virtually inevitable. My statement of pancritical rationalism, in claiming that all positions are criticizable, including this very claim, is obviously self-referential. And although my understanding of criticism and criticizability is not restricted to interpreting them in terms of possible falsity, such possible falsity is assumed in a large part of my discussion—and thus the semantical concepts of truth and falsity are drawn in. Finally, I have never tried to formalize my position, but have always expressed it in natural language. Yet Tarski has shown that any natural language that contains semantic terms and thus the possibility of generating self-reference may be expected to be inconsistent and will produce just such paradoxes. Thus I, a pancritical or comprehensively critical rationalist, almost *predictably* have on my hands something like the result that the statement that my position is open to criticism is uncriticizable; and that the statement that all positions are criticizable is false.

But what is really the impact of this apparently damaging result? Am I, for instance, now *committed* to this uncriticizable statement? *Hardly.* I would give it up in an instant. I don't *like* it at all; I don't *believe in* it; I don't take it as a *presupposition or dogma;* I have no *faith* in it.

Now is my *lack of faith* blind? Is my complacency foolish? Or do I have some reason to suppose that there may be some way of avoiding such conclusions? In fact, there is plenty of reason for supposing that this problem in self-reference—along with most of the other self-referential paradoxes—may be avoided.

Remember: our statement (B) is uncriticizable only in terms of the (Postian) argument in which it was cast. That argument, however, is certainly criticizable; and there is good reason to suppose that the whole line of argumentation may be avoidable, and with it, these paradoxical conclusions.

I believe that such paradoxes can be dealt with, as they arise, through means similar to those that Tarski himself suggested, through the use of the notion of object- and metalanguages and distinctions of levels of language. But one is not limited to Tarski's approach. There is a rich literature, reaching from Russell's discovery of the paradoxes in Frege's work, through Russell's theory of types, through Tarski's distinction between object and metalanguage, to the present day. This literature suggests various ways for avoiding semantical paradoxes: type and language-level solutions, Zermelo-type solutions, category solutions, radical solutions that exclude all self-reference, and others.[17]

In fact, if we assume that some such means might be devised to avoid Post-type arguments, then the criticizability of (B) can be restored. *The mere possibility of such a solution to the semantical paradoxes makes (B) criticizable after all: it suggests a potential means for invalidating the argument that produces the conclusion that (B) is uncriticizable.* And thus Post is refuted!

I believe that Post anticipated that I might reply in this way, for he constructs an argument to show that I *ought not* to make any such attempt since it would go contrary to the other goals of pancritical rationalism. And here, I believe, we reach the heart of the true substantive difference between us. (The production of the semantical paradox is not the real issue.)

Post argues that if I were to take such an approach, I

---

[17]See footnotes 7 and 11 above.

would avoid the refutation, but at the expense of decreasing the content of the theory, thus making it less criticizable. For *a theory about all theories including itself obviously has greater content than a theory about all other theories, and obviously takes the greater risk of refutation . . .* this sort of revision . . . is inconsistent with the aims of CR . . . The critical rationalist, therefore, is not free to object that his principle *A* really ought not to be construed self-referentially. He is not free to object that *A* is really an inexplicit, elliptical way of expressing the view, say, that at each language-level *n,* every rational, non-inferential statement is criticizable$_{n + 1}$.[18]

But this argument is unacceptable. An argument about content cannot be used to eliminate in advance any language-level route out of the paradoxes. High content (used here by Post in Popper's sense) is indeed an important desideratum in any theory, but obviously does not possess overriding force. To take an example, the hypothesis that all orbits of heavenly bodies are circles has greater content than Kepler's hypothesis that all orbits of heavenly bodies are ellipses. Yet in view of the refutation of the circular hypothesis, it would be absurd to demand that any hypothesis that resorts to ellipses be rejected *a priori* on the grounds that it has less content than the circular hypothesis!

Similarly, if Tarski is right in maintaining that *no* consistent language can possibly contain, within itself, the means for speaking about the meaning or the truth of its own expressions, it is absurd to demand unlimited self-reference in natural language (and to foist this demand on the pancritical rationalist) simply on the grounds that such a theory would have greater content. An inconsistent statement does indeed have "great content", being incompatible with everything!

Thus I assumed from the outset—critically, on the basis of the information available—that any statement of pancritical rationalism in natural language may produce semantical paradoxes—at least to the extent to which criticizability is interpreted in terms of possible truth. And I also took for granted that some formal metalinguistic or other tampering would be necessary whenever such semantical paradoxes appeared.[19]

I am aware, from his other publications, that Post not only objects to my taking this route, but also in general opposes language-level and category solutions to the paradoxes, and particularly to those paradoxes that are related to the possible-liar paradoxes.[20] Yet, notwithstanding his arguments, I do not believe that Post would contend that he has *shown* that none of the language-level or other more traditional approaches to semantical paradoxes can possibly work; in which case the work of the majority of contemporary logicians, who believe that such an approach

---

[18]Post, "Paradox in Critical Rationalism", pp. 52–53.

[19]See Quine, *Ways of Paradox*; Popper, "Self-Reference and Meaning in Ordinary Language"; and the other works cited in footnotes 7 and 11.

[20]See the works by Post cited in notes 1 and 9 above.

to such paradoxes generally can be successful, stands in criticism of the line of argument that produced the Post-like paradoxes in the first place. *And this renders (B) criticizable after all. And thus Post's argument collapses.*

6. *Post's Own Alternative.* Lurking behind my disagreement with Post about how to approach the paradoxes, there is a more serious disagreement. I shall refer to it only briefly; for Post's own statements about it have been troublingly programmatic, and he would need to spell out his ideas before one could properly respond.

I am referring to his suggestion that the way to escape semantical paradoxes in critical rationalism is to adopt the philosophy either of W. V. Quine or of Imre Lakatos.

First, as to Quine. Post reports that Quine rejects the "analytic-synthetic distinction" and thus is able to abandon the rules of logic—including the law of the retransmission of falsity.[21] But this would enable him, so Post alleges, to deny that any criticism of (B) is a criticism of (A), and thus avoid the Post-type semantical paradox. Hence Post appears to suggest that the "lesson" of his paper may be that pancritical rationalism (and related theories) had better abandon the analytic-synthetic distinction, and do so *just* to avoid semantical paradoxes.[22]

This line of argumentation is thoroughly untenable.

The confusion begins with two errors of reporting. Post misrepresents Quine's own position with regard to the paradoxes. For in his own extensive treatments of the semantical and other paradoxes, Quine has not suggested that they should be avoided by giving up the fundamental principles of logic. Rather, he has suggested the same sorts of repair measures that I listed above: Zermelo's method, the method of subscripts, and others.[23] By such procedures, Quine maintains, such paradoxes may be "inactivated". Post also misreports my own position. I do not, contrary to what he says, hold to the analytic-synthetic distinction.[24] I have explicitly repudiated it (and I shall return to this point later, when I discuss Watkins's criticisms).[25] I have also argued that *all* positions—including what are often called "analytic truths" as well as the fundamental laws of logic—are criticizable. Thus the escape route that Post suggests—if it were such a route—would be as open to me as it might be to Quine.

(What Post is referring to in supposing that Quine and I are in

---

[21]Post, "Paradox in Critical Rationalism", pp. 53–56.

[22]Ibid, pp. 54, 56.

[23]See notes 7 and 11 above.

[24]See my "Limits of Rationality: A Critical Study of Some Logical Problems of Contemporary Pragmatism and Related Movements", Ph.D. dissertation, University of London, 1962; my "Rationality, Criticism, and Logic", esp. pp. 174–86; my "On the Criticizability of Logic"; and appendix 5.

[25]See my "Limits of Rationality"; my "On the Criticizability of Logic"; the text of this book, chap. 5, sec. 4, and appendix 5.

disagreement here is my distinction between *criticism* and what I call *revision* within the Quinean argument situation.[26] I suggest that certain limits are imposed on Quine, willy-nilly, by his own characterization of an argument situation; and I argue that such an argument situation presupposes deducibility and retransmission of falsity, which hence cannot be revised within that situation, and can be given up only by stepping outside that situation. (I have also indicated several circumstances in which one might, indeed, be led to step outside that situation.) This in turn led me to suggest a "revisability criterion" which can provide a clear demarcation in an area where Quine said no clear demarcation was possible. All this is discussed in appendix 5, as well as, very briefly, in chapter 5 above.)

Whatever the real positions taken by Quine and myself on these matters may be, it is Post's own argument which is at stake here. His argument seems to me: (1) if we abandon logic, then the paradoxes do not arise; (2) hence we should abandon logic in order to avoid the paradoxes.

But such a proposal is quite odd. The whole interest of the paradoxes is that they are reached in the course of *rigorously logical argument*. Therein lies their importance, their telling power, and their threatening character: using logic, and presupposing logic, one reaches illogic. The whole point of the mathematical investigation of paradoxes conducted so vigorously during the past eighty years or so has been to avoid the paradoxes *without endangering logical argument*. If the paradoxes could not be avoided, then one might be led deeply to mistrust logic and rational argumentation. Indeed, one might well be led to abandon logical argumentation altogether.

But what can Post even mean to suggest in claiming that we might "*consistently* deny the retransmission of falsity", or that we could or should abandon logic *in order to* avoid the paradoxes? True, we would not have any such paradoxes after such moves. But we also would no longer have rational argumentation either.

No one previously, to my knowledge, has advocated such a means for resolving the paradoxes—*and certainly not Quine*. It will not do simply to appeal to Quine as if Quine had provided an example of what Post may have in mind. If Post really wants to advocate such a course as part of a superior "theory of rationality", he must spell out its character in detail, stating what sort of "rationality" would be left.

This brings me to Post's brief declaration of faith in Imre Lakatos's highly schematic theory of research programs.[27] Post reports that "in view of the irrefutability or uncriticizability of the 'core' of a research program", Lakatos's position presents an "improved, self-applicable theory of rationality" which succeeds whenever pancritical rationalism does, but which

[26]See appendix 5.
[27]Post, "Paradox in Critical Rationalism", p. 57, n. 17.

enjoys full self-referential success as well. This suggestion is also odd. For there is no intrinsic connection between self-reference and uncritizability.

One could not escape semantical paradox by making the "core" of one's research program irrefutable and uncriticizable *unless,* say, the core of one's research program *happened* to be an uncriticizable statement produced by a semantical paradox (as Post wrongly alleges is so of the core of my own view). And that alone would not provide an *improved* theory of rationality, or indeed a theory of *rationality* at all. For every dogmatist irrationalist makes his position uncriticizable and irrefutable.

In sum, Post appears to believe that—instead of "inactivating" the semantical paradoxes in one of the more usual ways advocated by the majority of contemporary logicians (ways which, however clumsy and unnatural, do render them harmless)—it would be preferable, part of a "better theory of rationality", to give up logic (retransmission of falsity) and deliberately to render the "core" of one's "research program" irrefutable and uncriticizable. Neither Quine, who was my teacher, nor Lakatos, who was my colleague and for many years my friend,[28] would be well-disposed to such an approach.

Such an approach is all the harder to comprehend in that Post declares that he is *not* an irrationalist, and that it is *not* his aim to show that irrational commitment is necessary or to find a rational excuse for irrationalism, and that nothing in his paper should be construed as entailing a retreat to some form of irrationalism.

7. What if Post Were Right about the Paradoxes?

It should be clear that, and why, I reject Post's argument. But what if Post were right? What if it were indeed *impossible* to avoid semantical paradoxes in the statement of pancritical rationalism? How would that affect the argument of *The Retreat to Commitment?* Although the question is worth asking, it should be emphasized that this section is entirely hypothetical, since I do believe that the semantical paradoxes can be inactivated.

(1) I would not have to abandon the claim that all positions are criticizable, but would have to stress more emphatically than I did originally the way in which this claim is meant (see section 3 above), i.e., to deny the logical necessity for a dogma. I should also note, again for clarity, that some statements that are produced by semantical paradox—e.g., (B)—are, in a very different and very attenuated sense, not criticizable.

(2) My characterization of the rationalist would remain essentially intact. He would remain one who holds all his positions, including his most fundamental standards and his basic philosophical position itself, open to

---

[28]See my "On Imre Lakatos", in Paul K. Feyerabend and Marx Wartofsky, eds., *Essays in Memory of Imre Lakatos* (Dordrecht: Reidel, 1976), pp. 37–38.

criticism in the intended sense that he does not, and logically need not, declare a dogma. The only "uncriticizable" statements he would harbor would be "uncriticizable" in a different sense: those forced on him by semantical paradox in the course of *rational* argument using natural language; and he would neither be committed to these nor have been led to them by faith. Nor would they have been forced on him by the need to stem an infinite regress. (It would also continue to be possible for the pancritical rationalist to argue himself out of his position in the other ways that I have described.)[29]

(3) All my other claims, my analysis of the problem-situation, and my solution to the problems of fideism and scepticism, would remain intact. In particular:

(4) My crucial distinction between justificational and critical argument would remain intact.

(5) It would remain impossible, within a justificational or authoritarian theory of knowledge, to resolve the dilemma of ultimate commitment. My critique of justificational argumentation would remain intact.

(6) Thus our historical observations about the Western justificationist tradition would be unaffected (e.g., it would remain authoritarian in structure; within it, justification and criticism would remain fused; within it, the assumption that tokens of intellectual legitimacy are logically transmitted would be retained).[30]

(7) An alternative, nonjustificational, nonauthoritarian approach to philosophy, using nonjustificational criticism, would remain open.

(8) Within such a nonjustificational approach, it would still be possible to resolve the dilemma of ultimate commitment. For the case for arbitrary commitment rested on the claim that rationality was so limited logically that such commitment was inescapable. But *nothing in the semantical paradoxes invokes limits to rationality or requires ultimate commitment—not even to the statement (B) that is "uncriticizable"*.

(9) Thus my refutation of the *tu quoque* argument would also remain intact. The uncriticizability of (B) would in no way show that the rationalist must be committed to it, or that he must make a dogma out of it, or that he could use it to cut off argument about some contested position.

For with regard to the semantical paradoxes, the justificationist and nonjustificationist approaches—*both* being self-referential, *both* being expressed in natural language—appear to be symmetrical. Semantical paradoxes could be produced as easily in justificational approaches as they can evidently be produced in nonjustificational critical approaches. The problems in earlier theories of rationality had nothing to do with pos-

---

[29]See appendix 5.

[30]See my "Rationality, Criticism, and Logic", sec. 10, and my "Rationality versus the Theory of Rationality", pp. 24–29; and appendix 6.

sible semantical paradox but arose from much more serious logical difficulties. The justificationist program, for instance, led to the unwelcome
choice between infinite regress and dogmatism. *Its difficulties arose not
from inconsistencies that appear in, and are intrinsic to, all natural languages in which there is self-reference, but from particular philosophical
and methodological errors and assumptions of the justificationist tradition.*

The two approaches are, however, crucially *asymmetrical* in that one
(justificationism) forces this choice between infinite regress and dogmatism,
whereas for the other (nonjustificationism), such a choice does not arise.
Within a nonjustificational approach, there is no occasion or need to stem
infinite regress or circular argument; and thus the twin difficulties on which
justificational approaches foundered do not arise.

It is this crucial difference, this asymmetry, that permits a solution to the
problem, and an escape from the *tu quoque.* Previously, the question was
whether something had to be accepted as uncriticizable *in order to* stem
infinite regress and avoid circular argument. Whereas the kind of uncriticizable statement that is forced on one by the semantical paradoxes is of
no use in stemming infinite regress and circular argument.

(10) Even if someone did make an article of faith or dogma out of (B),
there is virtually nothing he could do with it. (B) has insufficient content to
be used to justify other claims. Similarly, those semantical paradoxes that
arose within the justificationist approach have never been turned into
dogmas: they are useless for that purpose.

PART 4

8. A Review of Post's Earlier Formulations.   The previous seven sections of
this appendix contain a full answer to Post, and most of what is needed to
answer Watkins as well. In this section, I review some of the details of Post's
arguments. Although this review is not necessary for the argument, some of
the points that arise are intrinsically interesting. And by reviewing these
matters I may also help to prevent further misunderstanding of my
positions.

While Post's first reference to my work appeared earlier,[31] his first detailed
discussion of it was his "Paradox in Critical Rationalism and Related
Theories".[32]

There he claims that pancritical rationalism rests on this principle:

[31]See Post, "The Possible Liar".
[32]Op. cit.

A. *Every rational, noninferential statement is criticizable and has survived criticism.*[33]

From *A*, there immediately follows, as Post argues:

B. *Every rational noninferential statement is criticizable.*

All this can readily be formalized. Post suggests that '*PSX*' stand for '*S* is a potential criticizer of *X*'. Thus *X* will be criticizable just in case $(\exists S)PSX$. '*RX*' stands for '*X* is rational and noninferential in the present problem-context *K*'. Thus *B* becomes:

B. $(X)\ (RX \rightarrow (\exists S)PSX)$.

Since *B* itself is supposed to be criticizable, there follows:

C. $(\exists S)PSB$.

To elicit a paradox from these, Post needs two additional premises:

(1) $(S)\ (PSC \rightarrow PSB)$

(2) $(S)\ (PSB \rightarrow -PSC)$.

(Post introduces these two premises as if they were just two additional premises, and neglects to mention the quite extraordinary role they play. For these premises, taken together, prove that $PSC \rightarrow -PSC$; or $-C \rightarrow C$. And thus *C* is always proved, no matter what *A*, *B*, and *C* may happen to be. Thus the two premises are themselves a *recipe* for paradox. Presumably Post intended to say that these two premises are forced on me by my position.)

Premise (1) means that every potential criticizer of *C* is a potential criticizer of *B*. (2), on the other hand, means that no potential criticizer of *B* is a potential criticizer of *C*. If a statement *S* were specified which, if accepted, would count as a criticism of *B*, then that would also show the truth of *C*, and thus could not count against *C*. That is, any criticism of the statement that *B* is criticizable would be a criticism of *B*; and any criticism of *B* would provide an example of, and hence confirm, the criticizability of *B*—i.e., *C*, the statement that *B* is criticizable.

But from premises (1) and (2) together, there follows:

(3) $-(\exists S)PSC$.

That is, *C* is not criticizable.

If we assume that *C* is rational and noninferential, however, it follows that *B* is false. And thus—so Post argues—pancritical rationalism is refuted. The claim that all rational statements can be criticized is incorrect, for the claim that this claim can be criticized itself cannot be criticized.

Post goes on to argue that *C*, although uncriticizable, is demonstrably true; that *B*, which is criticizable, is self-referentially consistent but invalid;

[33]Post adds that any given statement *X* is a rational statement if and only if a rational man is entitled to accept it—that is, if and only if *X* is "rationally acceptable". Hence *A* could presumably be rewritten:

A₁. *Every noninferential statement that a rational man is entitled to accept is criticizable and has survived criticism.*

Presumably *A* could also be rewritten, as Post interprets it, as follows:

A₂. *Every rationally acceptable noninferential statement is criticizable and has survived criticism.*

and that *A*, which is also criticizable, is invalid and self-referentially inconsistent. *B* could be restored to validity, and *A* to self-referential consistency, only by withdrawing the claim that *C* is rational. But in that case *A* would be incomplete, contrary to the comprehensive aims and claims of pancritical rationalism. This leads Post to his "Gödelian theorem" that all rationality theories in a certain class that includes my own (and also Popper's)[34] are either self-referentially inconsistent or inherently incomplete.

9. The Rationality of Statements vs. the Rationality of People. Post's argument, which is directly derived from his work on possible-liar paradoxes, does not accurately interpret the core of my own position; and thus my own position is not subject to or refuted by his arguments and is not encompassed by his theorem.

Post's argument is, in its original form, a discussion of what makes a *statement* rational; and what makes a statement rational, on his account, is an alleged *semantic* (or partly semantic) *property* of statements called *criticizability*. It is, however, one of the merits of pancritical rationalism, and of this book, that it presents a theory about people, not statements. It is, quite explicitly (pp. 35, 76, 84–85, and especially p. 86), an account of the *essence of being a rationalist*. It is an account of how a rationalist or critical person might behave. It is not an account—although it may have some relevance to an account—of rational statements or of rational belief. As I wrote (p. 86): "emphasis on the criteria for rational *belief* is suitable only for the history of panrationalism and critical rationalism. The important structural shift to pancritical rationalism involves a change of emphasis to the problem of how to tell a genuine from a nongenuine rationalist." One certainly does not tell a rationalist from an irrationalist simply by looking at the beliefs or the statements which he holds.[35]

I doubt the merit of discussing the problem of rationality in terms of the rationality of statements ("rationality" being taken as a semantic or "partly semantic" predicate). For statements are intrinsically neither rational nor irrational. The *rationality* of a claim, as expressed by a statement, is much more dependent on time and place and historical context than is the *truth* of a statement. The claim that the earth is flat would not, in most of Europe, in the twelfth century, have been irrational for most people. The rationality of a statement has more to do with the way that it is *held* than it does with its content. Thus, while I happen to believe that the Christian God does not exist, I tend to be embarrassed when I meet the "village atheist", one who

---

[34]See Post, "The Possible Liar", p. 408, and "Paradox in Critical Rationalism", p. 27. Post also demands that any criticizable statement must meet certain other requirements. These additional requirements do not concern me here. In correspondence, Post has told me that he now wishes to construe criticizability not as semantic but only as "partly semantic". See also his "A Gödelian Theorem for Theories of Rationality".

[35]On whether a belief can be rational, see Joseph Agassi and I. C. Jarvie, "Magic and Rationality Again", *British Journal of Sociology*, vol. 24 (June 1973), esp. p. 236.

makes this claim dogmatically—and irrationally. One could, of course, say that he holds a rational claim irrationally. But why not speak more clearly and say that he holds an accurate statement in an irrational or rigid way? As this last remark indicates, *rationality is really very different from truth*. The truth of a statement does depend importantly on the statement: it depends on whether it corresponds with the facts; whereas rationality is not a property of statements but is a matter of the way in which a statement is held, and also of the *history* of that statement, of the way in which the statement has been examined.[36]

10. The Problem of the Specification of Criticism.

Thus pancritical rationalism does not involve, and I have never developed, a theory of rationality as a property of statements.

Yet if I were to develop such a theory, it would differ from Post's. For essential to Post's discussion, as he has pointed out, is his claim that criticizability is a semantic property of statements in the sense that for a statement to be criticizable we must be able to *specify* its "potential criticizer".[37] For any statement to be criticizable, Post requires that we be able to *present* a syntactically well-formed sentence, together with its semantic interpretation, which expresses a statement that, if correct, would render the statement under examination false, or unsatisfactory in some other way (e.g., unfruitful, inappropriate, irrelevant, etc.).

What Post means by "specification" and "presentation" is unclear—as is the way in which the criticizable statements would be demarcated from the uncriticizable statements in terms of this requirement. In so far as I understand this requirement, it seems to me to be unreasonable. It is no part of pancritical rationalism to insist that one must be holding a statement irrationally and uncritically unless one can immediately produce a statement which would, if accepted, constitute a rebuttal.[38] Momentary inability to specify a potential criticism may mark a failure of imagination, or may simply indicate that one has not yet sufficiently investigated the theory in question in its relation to its problem situation and to other theories. *Lack of interest* in potential criticism, or *hostility* to potential criticism, would be quite another thing: that would indeed probably mark a dogmatic or at least uncurious attitude. What I had in mind when writing of a pancritical rationalist was one who holds his claims open to review even when—and particularly when—he is unable to imagine, let alone specify, what would count against them.

Post's demand acquires what plausibility it may have from his insistence

---

[36]See my "Rationality, Criticism, and Logic", secs. 4, 20.

[37]Post, "Paradox in Critical Rationalism", esp. sec. 3.

[38]For a review of the issue of specifiability and rationality, see Walter B. Weimer, "For and Against Method", *Pre/Text*, vol. 1, nos. 1–2 (Spring-Fall 1980), pp. 161–203, esp. p. 185.

that to deny it would be to go against the spirit of Popper's philosophy; thus he quotes Popper's remark that "criteria of refutation have to be laid down beforehand". But Post misconstrues Popper. First, this remark has to do with science, not with criticism in general; second, the remark comes from a *footnote* explaining under what circumstances an observation counts in support of a theory, not from an account of what Popper means by "criticizability". (Popper gives no such account.) Again, Popper speaks here of specifying *criteria* of refutation in advance, *not* of specifying a refuting statement or counterexample. Thus one might say that if a theory were found to be inconsistent, that would suffice for its rejection; or that if it were found to be contradicted by empirical observation, that would suffice for its rejection. But one would not be able to specify specific inconsistencies or contrary evidence in advance!

It is, of course, valuable and important, *whenever possible*, to specify in advance what sorts of things would count against a theory. It is also characteristic of the evaluation of scientific theories that one can quite often make such specifications in advance—and that one can indeed not only specify the *sorts* of things that would countermand a theory but can also sometimes point to specific counterexamples. Popper himself notes how Einstein was able to specify in advance what would count against relativity theory, whereas Freudians and Marxists (despite their claims to scientific status for their theories) are unable (and perhaps also unwilling) to specify what would count against their views.

But I was in no way restricting myself to science when I wrote of criticizability: I was concerned with a broad range of ideas, with religion, ethics, theory of value, and metaphysics, as well as with science. In this broader domain there is not the slightest reasonable hope of always being able to specify potential criticisms in advance, although one may try even here to specify the *sorts* of things that would be critically effective.[39] Yet there is all the more reason, in such circumstances, to continue to hold such theories as open to criticism.

Moreover, Post's account seems to involve justificationism at this point (elsewhere he declares himself a nonjustificationist). To demand for every putatively criticizable statement a specification or presentation of a potential criticizer is in effect *to demand a justification of the claim that that statement is criticizable and to refuse to hold that claim hypothetically* (which is to say, critically).

Post had intended his demand to be in the spirit of Popper's critical philosophy. In fact, it runs against that spirit. I am thinking, in particular, of

---

[39]I make an attempt to specify some of the sorts of things that count as criticism in chap. 5, sec. 4, of this book. See also "Rationality, Criticism, and Logic", secs. 13–19.

Popper's strong reminder that *we never know what we are talking about.*[40] Thus, there is an infinity of unforeseeable and nontrivial statements belonging to the informative content of any theory—as well as an exactly corresponding infinity of statements belonging to its logical content. Hence it is impossible to know the full implications or significance of any theory. It is thus impossible to know what will refute it. We cannot specify (or predict) today what we shall know only tomorrow.[41]

The way in which one criticizes a theory will depend on how one understands it. One gets to understand a theory through working on it: through criticizing it. An important part of this process is to discover its logical relations to the existing network of theories, problems, and evidence in the relevant field: that is, its relation to what Popper calls the objective "problem situation". But there is no way to know or specify in advance how this process will go, or what sorts of potential objections to the theory under investigation will emerge during the course of this enterprise. Thus on Popper's account the understanding of a theory—and hence its criticism—is never-ending task, although, in the course of time, the theory may come to be understood better and better.

The informative content of a theory includes any theory incompatible with it—and thus any future theory that may supersede it. So the informative content of Newton's theory—and thus its potential criticizers—includes Einstein's theory. But Einstein's theory could not possibly have been predicted when Newton's theory was put forward. Nor, lacking Einstein's theory, could the relevant sorts of empirical falsifiers have been specified: i.e., those basic statements which clash with Newtonian theory but which could not possibly even have been stated prior to the creation of Einstein's theory. Nor could the statements that could be relevant to a crucial experiment between Newton's and Einstein's theories be specified. And thus the sorts of potential criticizers of Newton's theory that eventually became important historically were unspecifiable during the first several hundred years of life of Newton's theory.

11. The Paradox Reconsidered.   Having mentioned these differences between Post's account and my own—concerning certain assumptions in which his argument is couched, but which I reject—I now wish to turn to his argument itself.

Post's argument purports to make use of the "core statement" of

---

[40]Popper, *Unended Quest* (La Salle and London: Open Court, 1982), sec. 7. See my discussions in my "Wittgenstein and Homosexuality", in Robert Boyers and George Steiner, eds., *Salmagundi*, Fall 1982-Winter 1983, pp. 166–96; and in my "Ein schwieriger Mensch: Eine Porträtskizze von Sir Karl Popper", in Eckhard Nordhofen, ed., *Physiognomien: Philosophen des 20. Jahrhunderts in Portraits* (Königstein: Athenäum Verlag, 1980), pp. 43–69. See also the discussion by Renée Bouveresse in *Karl Popper* (Paris: J. Vrin, 1981), pp. 59–63. See also my "Knowledge Is a Product Not Fully Known to Its Producer".

[41]See Popper's discussion in *The Open Universe: An Argument for Indeterminism*, vol. 2 of the *Postscript to the Logic of Scientific Discovery*, esp. chapters 2 and 3.

pancritical rationalism. In fact, it makes use of something rather different. Take his statement A:

> A. *Every rational, noninferential statement is criticizable and has survived criticism.*

Post means this as a report of my remark (p. 119) that a "position may be held rationally without needing justification—*provided that it can be and is held open to criticism and survives severe examination*". That is,

> A'. *Every position which is held open to criticism and survives severe examination may be held rationally.* (And there is no need to go into the question of its justification.)

A and A' are, however, very different. Even if we allow my "position" to be interpreted by his "statement", Post's A reverses and crucially alters A'. Post's B does not follow from my A'. Nor does a reversed version of B follow from A'.[42] Thus someone who holds A' need not hold B':

> B'. *Every criticizable statement is rational and noninferential.*

Nor does Post's C follow from my A'. Thus his paradox, *as originally constructed*, does not capture pancritical rationalism.

12. The Paradox Reformulated.

In "A Gödelian Theorem for Theories of Rationality", Post takes account of some of the objections that I have just stated.[43] He insists that he does not demand justification of pancritical rationalism; he abandons his requirement of specifiability as a necessary condition for a potential criticism; and he is willing to drop the suggestion that criticizability is an intrinsic or semantic property of statements, and instead to try to formulate the matter in terms of the ways in which people hold statements.

Having conceded the correctness of most of my objections to his views, Post then immediately produces a new formulation of his argument which, he believes, overcomes my objections.

His reformulated first premise, *A1*, now reads as follows:

> *A1.* Consider a person P, a context K, a time t, and an attitude, belief, or position X (expressible or not) which is problematic (or up for possible revision) for P in K at t. Then P holds X rationally in K at t only if: P holds X open to criticism at t, and (so far as P can then tell or guess) X has at t so far survived criticism.

From *A1* there follows *B1*:

> *B1.* P holds X rationally at t only if P holds X open to criticism at t.

We also obtain *C1*:

---

[42]The first critic to misrepresent pancritical rationalism in this way, and who may be responsible for Post's error, is J.W.N. Watkins, in his "CCR: A Refutation" (see note 1 above and the discussion below), p. 57. See Watkins's statement (1).

[43]Post's new paper is printed in the *Proceedings of the 11th International Conference on the Unity of the Sciences*. My objections to his earlier work were communicated privately, especially in the unpublished draft manuscript: "On Alleged Paradoxes in Pancritical Rationalism".

C1. There is a (potential) criticism of *B1*, which might someday be produced and be seen to be successful.

Go through a similar line of argument as before—stated in full in Post's paper—and his alleged refutation of my claim is restored.

13. Necessary or Sufficient? While attempting to take *most* of my objections into account, Post ignores the objections in section 11 above. And thus his paradox, as reformulated, also does not capture the core of my position.

Our difference here concerns the question whether criticizability and survival of criticism are necessary or sufficient conditions of rationality. I intended them as sufficient conditions and usually expressed them as such in *The Retreat to Commitment*. But I was careless in my expression, and occasionally I stated them as if they were necessary conditions or requirements. Thus it is fair for Post to read them in this way.

But how *should* it be? Am I correct to construe them as sufficient conditions? Or is Post correct not only that I sometimes expressed them as necessary conditions, but also that they *should,* from my point of view, be so construed?

The answer to this question emerges directly from the argument of *The Retreat to Commitment* itself. My characterization of pancritical rationalism stemmed from a critical examination of the panrationalist (or comprehensive rationalist) account, according to which *comprehensive* justification was a *necessary* condition of rationality. (The traditional account was indeed put as a necessary condition.) Since such justification was impossible, it followed that a rationalist was impossible, and thus the question with which I began my book: "Is it possible to remain a rationalist?" (p. xxvi, pp. 83 ff., and passim).

My answer—after discovering the existence of nonjustificational criticism —was that the sort of justification that had traditionally been required is not only impossible but also quite unnecessary. Rather, nonjustificational criticizability was a *sufficient* condition for rationality. Since this can readily be obtained, it is possible to be a rationalist.

The question whether these criteria are necessary or sufficient could be argued at length. I do not propose to do so here. For, as I have shown in section 4 above, a similar paradox can be generated without reference to this question.

14. Criticizability Is Not Captured by Possible Falsity Alone. As indicated above, the chief claim Post attributes to me—that every rational, noninferential statement is criticizable and has survived criticism—is weaker than the one I really hold. My view is that *all* statements are criticizable— not just the rational and noninferential ones, whatever they may be.[44]

---

[44]See my "On the Criticizability of Logic", pp. 67–77; and footnote 2; and appendix 5 of this book.

With this claim alone, as I have shown, a similar paradox can be created, and the question of necessary versus sufficient conditions for rationality, as discussed in the last section, loses most of its importance in the present context.

Post's line of argumentation, however, seems to rest on (or at any rate to stem from) the assumption (so far unexamined) that *for a statement to be criticizable is for it to be possibly false.* If I were to accept this assumption, I would be forced to maintain that all positions are possibly false.

But this position—that all positions are possibly false—is, so it seems to me, obviously false. And it is so quite apart from Post's paradoxes. For if all statements are possibly false, then there are no necessary truths (*and* is it a necessary truth, then, that there are no necessary truths?).

I believe not only that not all positions are possibly false, but also that there are indeed necessary truths.[45] And since I also have been maintaining that all positions (including necessary truths) are criticizable, I hardly suppose that criticizability and possible falsity are so closely linked as Post has assumed throughout his discussion—including, especially, his early articles on the paradoxes of the possible liar.

To indicate what I have in mind here, it may be helpful to say something about the background in which *The Retreat to Commitment* was conceived. I had begun to work on the problems underlying it in 1956, when I was at Harvard, being thoroughly indoctrinated at that time by my teachers W. V. Quine and Morton White in the inadequacies of the distinction between analytic and synthetic statements. Although it was only after beginning to study with Popper in London that I found a way to solve my problems, I never abandoned the approach taken by Quine and White on this matter (although I later, see section 6 above and appendix 5 below, set a limit on the applicability of Quine's argument). My doctoral dissertation (1962), which incorporated part of this book, was entitled: "Limits of Rationality: A Critical Study of Some Logical Problems of Contemporary Pragmatism and Related Movements", referring to the pragmatist connections of Quine and White. The thesis was concerned chiefly with the controversy over the analytic-synthetic distinction. My view that the analytic-synthetic distinction is not viable was very much confirmed and enriched by my seven-year association with Imre Lakatos. I watched closely as *Proofs and Refutations,* his brilliant essay on the logic of mathematical discovery, was conceived and written. Lakatos emphatically rejected what he called "the logicist demarcation between science and mathematics".[46] One way to describe his book would be as a rich historical study of the ways in which demonstrable and

---

[45]See Popper's discussion of natural necessity in *The Logic of Scientific Discovery* (London: Hutchinson, 10th impression, 1980), Appendix *x, "Universals, Dispositions, and Natural or Physical Necessity", pp. 420–41, including the new Addendum to p. 441.

[46]Imre Lakatos, *Mathematics, Science and Epistemology, Philosophical Papers* (London Cambridge University Press, 1978), vol. 2, p. 91.

necessary truths which could not possibly be false are in fact revised and rejected in the course of mathematical discovery, *in the course of being examined and criticized.*

In view of this, it is surprising that Post would state that my position "presupposes analyticity", or that Watkins (to whom we shall turn in Part IV) takes the analytic-synthetic distinction for granted throughout his discussion and in his very formulation of what he supposes to be my position.[47]

I do, of course, agree that for a large range of statements one main thing that one does in criticism is indeed to attempt to show falsity, and that one therein usually does assume possible falsity. That is, for a large class of statements, to hold a statement open to criticism is to conjecture or guess that the statement may be wrong and that some day some effective criticism, the nature of which we cannot even imagine today, may be produced against it. But that is not all there is to criticism.

This is not the place to rehearse the elaborate arguments of Quine and White, or the historical examples of Lakatos, to show how necessary truths, statements that cannot possibly be false, may be criticized, revised, rejected in the course of argument.[48] Although I disagree with Lakatos about many matters, I agree completely with his statement: "But whatever the solution may be, the naïve school concepts of static rationality like *apriori-aposteriori, analytic-synthetic* will only hinder its emergence."[49] This corrigibility of "necessary" truths is sometimes also a matter of possible falsity. Often, however, it may be a matter of the revision, the narrowing or stretching and adjustment of concepts. In this process, one may come to revise those conditions which serve to render a certain statement impossible to be false. It is not so much a question of truth and possible falsity as a question of context and of how to arrange and order. Or it may be argued that someone did not prove what he set out to prove—not that what was proved was false or possibly false. Or that the statement of an argument or proposition is inelegant or uneconomical. And so on. The idea that "necessary" truths cannot be revised is probably due to a failure of imagination and a lack of knowledge of the history of mathematics and of science. For our intellectual history contains many examples of ardently and most sincerely believed claims that have been declared to be demonstrable,

---

[47]Another critic of my position, A. A. Derksen, realizes that I do not hold to the analytic-synthetic distinction. See his "The Failure of Comprehensively Critical Rationalism", pp. 51–66, esp. note 1.

[48]See Imre Lakatos: *Proofs and Refutations: The Logic of Mathematical Discovery* (London: Cambridge University Press, 1976); and *Mathematics, Science and Epistemology*, esp. chaps, 1, 2, 4, 5, 7. See also W. V. Quine, *From a Logical Point of View*, esp. chaps. 2 and 3; *Word and Paradox* (New York: John Wiley & Sons, 1960); *The Ways of Paradox and Other Essays* (New York: Random House, 1966); and W. V. Quine and J. S. Ullian, *The Web of Belief* (New York: Random House, 1978). See also Morton White, *Toward Reunion in Philosophy*; and *Religion, Politics and the Higher Learning* (Cambridge, Mass.: Harvard University Press, 1959).

[49]Lakatos, *Mathematics, Science and Epistemology*, pp. 40–41.

or necessary truths, synthetic *a priori* true, self-evident, and such like. In Kant's philosophy, for instance, Newtonian physics, Euclidean geometry, and Aristotelian logic were given such a privileged position. But all three have since been displaced—by Einsteinian physics, by non-Euclidean geometries, and by modern logic.

In attempting to hold such "necessary" truths open to revision, the issue is really not one of sincerity, but one of intellectual policy when one is considering the scope of criticism, and when one has the maximization of criticism as one of one's aims.

PART IV

15. On Watkins

> For any proposition there is always some sufficiently narrow interpretation of its terms, such that it turns out true, and some sufficiently wide interpretation such that it turns out false . . . concept-stretching will refute *any* statement, and will leave no true statement whatsoever.
>
> —IMRE LAKATOS[50]

Watkins's papers have been replied to by a number of writers,[51] but he has ignored most of these criticisms. I shall not rehearse the objections of other writers here, although I think that most of them are sound, but will add only a few points that others have not mentioned.

Watkins's first argument against pancritical rationalism was similar to Post's; but instead of developing it in terms of serious (if irrelevant) problems of semantical paradox, he chose to use it as obvious evidence that I had developed a "dictatorial strategy". That is, Watkins claims that pancritical rationalism was a perfect example of a dictatorial strategy in the sense that it permits me to win however the argument may go: a defender of pancritical rationalism, he contends, is *assured* victory over his critics however good their criticisms, for his position is never at risk.

---

[50]Lakatos, *Proofs and Refutations*, p. 99.
[51]For replies to Watkins, see references in footnote 3, above. For a reply to Derksen, see my "On the Criticizability of Logic", pp. 67–77.

Watkins's argument went like this: suppose a critic of pancritical rational-ism produces a cogent argument showing that pancritical rationalism is *not* open to genuine criticism. This would *be* a damaging criticism; hence it would be impossible for a critic ever to show that pancritical rationalism is uncriticizable. To show that pancritical rationalism is *un*criticizable is to criticize it, and hence to prove that it is criticizable after all.

Outside the context of semantical paradox—and there is no such context in Watkins's work—this is a deplorable argument. If someone were to come forward with a cogent argument against pancritical rationalism; and if I were then to reply: "Oh, you see, *that just goes to show* that I was right in saying that my position is open to criticism", I would be laughed at. And we all know from Charlie Chaplin that one thing that dictators cannot stand is to be laughed at.

Popper teaches that we should take systems of thought as a whole and appraise them (metalinguistically, of course) as connoisseurs, as it were, searching to identify components within them that could possibly be used to deflect criticism or to immunize those systems in any way against criticism and thereby to turn them into what he calls "reinforced dogmas". Popper's own favorite examples included Freudian and Marxist theory, and also, to a lesser extent, positivism and the Copenhagen interpretation of quantum mechanics. Ernest Gellner did the same sort of thing with Wittgensteinian and Oxford philosophy.[52] In *The Retreat to Commitment,* and also in *Morality and Religion,* I tried to do this sort of thing with various contemporary theological systems. The "game" here was to identify criticism-deflecting strategies (such as the theory of resistances in Freudian theory), *ad hoc* changes in definitions of key terms, *ad hoc* adoption of auxiliary hypotheses (e.g., epicycles), and such like. Another whole context that served to immunize almost all systems from criticism was, I argued, justificationism as such: justificationism explicitly called for uncriticizable dogmas which were off-limits from the outset, and which also *rendered* off-limits anything that could be derived from them.

Let us suppose that some critic of pancritical rationalism, in the course of an appraisal of the position as a whole, finds it guilty in his judgment of all the devices and ploys I have just mentioned, and also gives concrete examples of how these work in the actual practice of the position. Now, if the proponent of such a system—our hypothetical pancritical rationalist—is indeed, working within his sytem, already entangled in, ensnared in, such devices, then maybe he *would* interpret the outsider's criticism as confirma-tion of his own (evidently dogmatic) contention that his position is open to criticism. As Popper has argued, anyone who is ensnared by such criticism-reducing strategems *will* tend to interpret all his or her experience as being

[52]Ernest Gellner, *Words and Things.*

confirmatory of, rather than threatening to, his or her position: everything will verify it; nothing will falsify it.

Someone *could*, in the name of pancritical rationalism, behave in such a way: he could declare as his fundamental position that everything he held was criticizable; and then, whenever he was criticized, he could take that as evidence of the truth of his statement.

Anything may be misused. Only by putting an argument in its context can one gauge whether it is being used in a critical or uncritical way. Let us take a look again at the appropriate context for our own discussion. A number of things need to be noticed.

First, such behavior on the part of this hypothetical individual who has declared himself a pancritical rationalist *will in no way invalidate the critic's contentions.* Watkins misses the fact that there is no such thing as "uncriticizability" in general, or uncriticizability in a vacuum, as it were. A system that is uncriticizable is uncriticizable in some *particular, specific,* respects. That is, it must use a *particular* criticism-deflecting strategem; it must use a *particular ad hoc* device; and so on. And the critic will, of course, identify these. Although the fact of this particular criticism will show that the system is in *some* respect criticizable, it won't make those of its features which diminish its criticizability, or which even render it virtually uncriticizable in particular circumstances, disappear.

Second, any such behavior on the part of Watkins's hypothetical pancritical rationalist would in fact be self-defeating. For it would strengthen the hand of the critic, who could now add to his previous indictment. The critic would now say that, in addition to having all those criticism-reducing stratagems *at his disposal,* the pancritical rationalist was also putting them *into practice* to the extent of using any criticism of his position as evidence of the correctness of his position. Worse, the poor man was even ignoring all the laughter.

Moreover, the whole situation becomes more complicated when we take account of the different possible points of view in this hypothetical situation, and look at the whole situation more realistically than Watkins's one-dimensional approach allows.

The fact that a system of thought has been criticized *by an outsider* in one particular respect does not make of it a system that is held *by its proponents* in a way that exposes it to criticism generally. This only shows that it is able to be criticized by an outsider; it does not show that it functions in such a way as to permit an insider to be affected by that very criticism. The fact that a criticism has been raised and noted (by outsider or insider) does not make that point of view criticizable in the sense of making criticisms *effective* against the holder of such a viewpoint.

The issue is not whether there are criticisms available: the issue is whether these criticisms can be and are used in such a way as to be effective in regenerating the system and transforming those who hold it. Any system that encouraged the kind of behavior that Watkins suggested—i.e., using criticism as evidence of criticizability at the expense of not taking criticism seriously—would be grossly defective with regard to the very possibility of regeneration.

But there is no evidence that pancritical rationalism ever has been or very effectively could be held in such a way. Pancritical rationalism *explicitly* aims to create a way of life that would be exposed to *optimum* effective criticism with optimum effect on those who hold it (see above, p. 113); and it undertakes this aim in the spirit of Popper's statement that we must decide that "if our system is threatened we will never save it by any kind of . . . *stratagem*".[53]

Watkins fails to take this into account. He juggles with the words "criticizable" and "rational" and ignores a systems and contextual approach. Above all, he ignores the context in which the theory was put forward.

This brings me to Watkins's second line of criticism, which is to produce trivial examples of true statements that are "obviously" uncriticizable. This is a commonsense "know-nothing" approach, reminiscent of Johnson's "refutation" of Berkeley.

To show its irrelevance, I want to state again the two contexts in which I claimed that all positions are criticizable.

The *first,* which I reviewed in section 3 above, is that all positions are criticizable in the sense that: (1) it is not necessary, in criticism, in order to avoid infinite regress, to declare a dogma that could not be criticized (since it was unjustifiable); (2) it is not necessary to mark off a special class of statements, the justifiers, which *did* the justifying and criticizing but was not open to criticism; (3) there is not a point in all argument, the *terms,* which is exempted from criticism; (4) the criticizers—the statements in terms of which criticism is conducted—are themselves open to review.

In this first sense, all Watkins's examples are irrelevant: his examples could hardly serve as examples of dogmas or terms of argument or justifiers; they will hardly interest the commitment merchant; they lend no credence to the supposition that such dogmas or justifiers are ever necessary; they are in no way parallel to the "unjustifiable" positions of earlier theories of rationality. Such examples of "uncriticizable" statements are not, for instance, needed *in order to criticize*; whereas, in justificationist philosophies, unjustifiable statements are needed in order to justify. These examples do not unravel the crucial distinction between justification and

[53]*The Logic of Scientific Discovery,* p. 82.

criticism; they do not affect the rebuttal of the *tu quoque*; they are truly irrelevant to the problem of irrationality. In such a discussion, the problem of rationality is forgotten. The problem has shifted—and degenerated.

But I also had a *second* sense of "criticizability" in mind, a sense which is largely independent of the first. I have already alluded to this sense in section 6, and written of it in section 14. This second sense in which I advocated that all positions are criticizable was in no way intended to be an original claim on my part and also is not really needed to refute the sceptical and fideistic positions against which I have been contending in this book. In this sense, when I said that all positions are open to criticism I meant that statement in the sense in which Quine (and White, Lakatos, and others) had argued against the analytic-synthetic distinction, claiming the revisability of all statements (including "analytic statements" and "necessary truths"), and also in the sense in which Popper had insisted on the theory-impregnation (and hence revisability) of even the most obvious observation statements.[54]

Thus, in bringing forth his examples of an incontestably true nineteen-word sentence, and other examples, such as: "I am more than three years old", and "During 1969 Mr. Nixon was President of the U.S.A.", Watkins is not just taking me on, but is combatting a very well-developed position in contemporary philosophy to which I happen to adhere. But even if Watkins should be right in rejecting this position (if he does reject it), that would not affect my argument. I like this position, and find it congenial to the pancritical rationalist's goal of maximizing criticism. But my refutation of scepticism and fideism, and of justificationism, and my treatment of the limits of rationality, do not depend on this second sense of "criticizability".

This is hardly the place to review the controversy over the analytic-synthetic distinction or the issue of the revisability of observation statements. I would, however, like to conclude with a brief remark on Watkins's "obviously true" nineteen-word sentence

(S) There exists at least one sentence written in English prior to nineteen eighty that consists of precisely nineteen words.

Watkins says that this is *"certainly true* and hence uncriticizable".

But this statement *is* criticizable or revisable in my sense—and in the senses of Quine, White, and Lakatos that I had in mind. Nor is it even far-fetched to suppose how it might be revised: although I have recently heard that it is no longer possible to send an inland telegram in Britain, Watkins could find that, in many countries, for the purpose of costing

[54]Ibid., chap. 5.

telegrams by the "word", certain sorts of words are grouped together in ways that differ from the *principles of counting* on which the truth of his statement depends: many would, for instance, take "nineteen eighty" to be "nineteen-eighty" and one word, not two.[55]

---

[55]See Lakatos, *Mathematics, Science and Epistemology*, p. 14, where he writes: " *'Class'* and *'membership-relation'* turned out to be obscure, ambiguous, anything but 'perfectly well known'. There even emerged the completely un-Euclidean need for a consistency proof to ensure that the 'trivially true axioms' should not contradict one another. All this and what followed must strike any student of the seventeenth century as *déjà vu*: proof had to give way to explanation, perfectly well known concepts to theoretical concepts, triviality to sophistication, infallibility to fallibility."

APPENDIX 5. THE CRITICIZABILITY OF LOGIC

1. What Are the Presuppositions of Argument?

In this appendix I shall return to a question discussed briefly in chapter 5, section 4; and also in the preceding appendix; namely, whether and to what extent logic is open to criticism and revision.[1]

The starting point in any contemporary discussion of the dispensability, revisability, and criticizability of logic is the views of W. V. Quine, as expressed in his treatment of the traditional distinction between analytic and synthetic. According to Quine, when a body of belief is brought to the test of criticism, any part of it may be revised. No segment of it, such as the set of analytically true statements, including logic, is so insulated that we could say in advance that "the mistake could not be here".

Quine's influential position has important antecedents. His predecessor as Edgar Pierce Professor at Harvard, C. I. Lewis, for instance, wrote as follows:[2]

> The difference between . . . the decision of relativity versus absolute space and time, and those more permanent attitudes such as are vested in the laws of logic, . . . is only a difference of degree. . . . Conceptions, such as those of logic, which are least likely to be affected by the opening of new ranges of experience, represent the most stable of our categories; but none of them is beyond the possibility of alteration.

Such a conclusion—that everything, including logic, is open to revision— may appear to be identical to pancritical rationalism. Hence, in writing this book I stressed how importantly these views differ from mine.

There are, admittedly, a number of senses in which logic not only is open to revision but has indeed been revised. As an example, the traditional

---

[1]My views on logic have been badly garbled in several German publications, due in part to serious errors in the original German translation (1964) of *Flucht ins Engagement*, where I am translated as writing of the presuppositions of "das Denken als solches", and of "eine absolute Voraussetzung des Denkens". In the original English there is no reference to the presuppositions of *Denken*, but there is a reference to those of *Argument*. See also Karl-Otto Apel, *Transformation der Philosophie* (Frankfurt: Suhrkamp, 1976), vol. 2, p. 412. Jürgen Habermas gives a garbled criticism of my views on logic in *Der Positivismusstreit in der deutschen Soziologie*, ed. Maus und Fürstenberg (Neuwied und Berlin: Luchterhand, 1969), pp. 252 ff. See Hans Albert's excellent reply to Habermas on these points in the same volume, pp. 291 ff.

[2]C. I. Lewis, "A Pragmatic Conception of the A Priori", *Journal of Philosophy*, 20 (1924); and "Logic and Pragmatism", *Contemporary American Philosophy* (New York: Macmillan, 1930), vol. 2, pp. 31–51. See also Morton White, *Age of Analysis* (New York: Mentor Books, 1955), chap. 11, p. 175.

Aristotelian logic of categorical propositions has been largely abandoned because it is too clumsy and restricted to enable one to formulate in it and defend the validity of many rules of inference which are valid in ordinary discourse, not to mention the inferences of physics and mathematics. In addition, various artificialities are introduced into logical systems to avoid the logical paradoxes of Grelling, Richard, Russell, and others.[3]

No doubt our logical theories may be similarly repaired and revised far more than anyone supposes at present, and it is impossible to foresee when such repairs will be necessary. Nonetheless, however much alternative systems of logical rules of inference may differ among themselves, they have an important feature in common: whenever these rules are observed and, starting from true premises, the argument is conducted in accordance with them, we arrive at a true conclusion. The question arises whether logic can be revised in the sense of denying that true premises always must lead, in any valid inference, to true conclusions.

Certain of Quine's comments suggest that he does regard such radical revision as in principle possible. In "Two Dogmas of Empiricism", Quine mentioned only the possibility of revising the law of excluded middle. But in *Word and Object* he explicitly adds the law of contradiction.[4]

Quine seems to envision matters something like this. Let the circle below represent the "man-made fabric" of knowledge of which he writes:

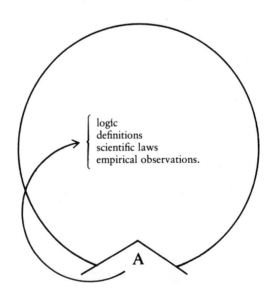

logic
definitions
scientific laws
empirical observations.

A

---

[3]See my *Lewis Carroll's Symbolic Logic* (New York: Clarkson N. Potter, 1977), pp. 16–19.
[4]See W. V. Quine, *Word and Object* (New York: The Technology Press of the Massachusetts Institute of Technology, 1960), p. 59. See W. V. Quine, "Two Dogmas of Empiricism", in *From a Logical Point of View*.

At "A", imagine what Quine calls a "recalcitrant experience", something that does not fit into the system and forces one to make some revision within it. To bring the system into equilibrium, that reconciling arrow may light anywhere: on a scientific theory, on a definition—or on logic.

But what about that arrow?

I contend that the workings of the arrow are outside of, and are presupposed by, Quine's "argument situation". The idea of *revising* in the light of tests presupposes the notion of *deducibility,* i.e., the idea of the *retransmission of falsity* from conclusions to premises and, *ipso facto*, of the *transmission of truth* from premises to conclusion. Deducibility appears to presuppose a *minimal logic,* in the sense of "logic" that refers to the general theory of derivation, demonstration, and refutation.

If so, the idea that a system might abandon even this minimal logic must be mistaken: so much logic would be needed to argue and learn—to bring the rest of our theories into closer correspondence with reality. Hence *not all of* logic can be part of the totality that is under test. There is an absolute difference in principle between what is under revision and what is presupposed by the revision or argument situation. Contrary to what Lewis says, this marks a difference *in kind,* not only in degree; contrary to both Lewis and Quine, there is a difference in kind between a fundamental alteration in logic and the replacement of other views such as (to take Quine's examples) Ptolemy's with Kepler's, or Newton's with Einstein's.

But *how much* of logic is presupposed by deducibility?

In 1959, when I first thought this problem through, I supposed the notion of deducibility to be far richer in this connection than I now do. I was influenced at that time by G. Gentzen, and also, especially, by a series of articles on logic which Popper published in 1947 and 1948.[5]

Popper's work on logic was in part inspired by Tarski's "On the Concept of Logical Consequence" (1936), where Tarski showed that the concept of logical consequence could be readily elucidated once one had a list of the

---

[5]K. R. Popper, "New Foundations for Logic", *Mind*, vol. 56 (1947); and "Corrections", *Mind*, vol. 57 (1948), pp. 69 ff.; "Logic without Assumptions", *Proceedings of the Aristotelian Society*, vol. 47 (1947), pp. 251–92; "Functional Logic without Axioms or Primitive Rules of Inference", *Proceedings Koninklijke Nederlandsche Akademie van Wetenschappen*, vol. 50, no. 9 (1947), pp. 1214 ff.; "On the Theory of Deduction: Part I, Derivation and Its Generalizations", *Proceedings Koninklijke Nederlandsche Akademie van Wetenschappen*, vol. 51, no. 2 (1947), pp. 173 ff.; "On the Theory of Deduction: Part II, The Definitions of Classical and Intuitionist Negation", ibid., vol. 3 (1947), p. 322 ff.; "The Trivialization of Mathematical Logic", *Proceedings of the 10th International Congress of Philosophy* (Amsterdam, 1948), vol. 1, pp. 722 ff.; "Why Are the Calculi of Logic and Arithmetic Applicable to Reality?", *Conjectures and Refutations*, pp. 201–14. See also J. O. Wisdom, "Overlooked Aspects of Popper's Contributions to Philosophy, Logic, and Scientific Method", in Mario Bunge, ed., *The Critical Approach to Science and Philosophy* (New York: Free Press, 1964), pp. 116–24. See William Kneale, "The Province of Logic", in H. D. Lewis, ed., *Contemporary British Philosophy*, 3d ser. (London: Allen & Unwin, 1956), pp. 237–61. See G. Gentzen, "Untersuchungen über das logische Schliessen", *Mathematische Zeitschrift*, vol. 39 (1934), pp. 176–210 and 405–31. Ian Hacking has also attempted an approach along such lines in his "What Is Logic?", *Journal of Philosophy,* vol. 76, no. 6 (June 1979), pp. 285–319. See also Göran Sundholm: "Hacking's Logic", *Journal of Philosophy*, vol. 78, no. 3 (March 1981), pp. 160–68; and Christopher Peacocke: "Hacking on Logic: Two Comments", *Journal of Philosophy*, ibid., pp. 168–75.

formative signs.[6] Popper turned this around. He began not with the formative signs but with the concept of logical consequence. Taking that—understood as the transitive and reflexive relation of deducibility—as primitive (together with some general primitive rules of inference not referring to formative signs), he tried to show that all the formative signs could be defined in terms of it. He wished to show this even for quantification and identity, neither of which had been definable by the truth-table method. From these "inferential definitions", and with "trivial inferences", the whole of mathematical logic would be derived (i.e., classical Aristotelian logic, Boolean algebra, propositional logic, the lower functional logic).

By this means Popper hoped to do something Tarski had doubted was possible: to provide a firm demarcation between formative and descriptive signs. More important, he would thereby attain the old goal of "trivializing" mathematical logic—in the same sense in which it had earlier been hoped to trivialize logic through the truth-table method: logic would be obtained entirely from definitions of formative signs—without employing axioms or primitive rules of inference for the formative signs.[7]

This approach relates importantly to my disagreement with Quine. If the situation Quine describes does presuppose the idea of deducibility (as I maintain), and if, from the notion of deducibility, a significant part of mathematical logic can be obtained, then much more than a minimal logic is isolated from revision in Quine's argument situation.

Some recent work by Czesław Lejewski seems to weaken this possibility. Lejewski reconstructs Popper's theory of deductive inference and Tarski's theory of logical consequence in the language of S. Leśniewski, showing that Popper's and Tarski's theories are inferentially equivalent. In the course of doing this, he elicits and makes explicit the unstated presuppositions of Popper's theory. These turn out to amount to an axiom system; and, as Lejewski shows, cannot be reduced to a set of inferential definitions. Popper's system assumes certain postulates which are independent and prior to definitions. Thus he has failed to construct a logic without assumptions

---

[6]Alfred Tarski: "On the Concept of Logical Consequence", chap. 16, *Logic, Semantics, Mathematics* (Oxford: Oxford University Press, 1956).

[7]Popper's work in logic was indifferently received, partly due to several blunders in it; yet even one of the most unfavorable reviewers remarked that "Presumably [Popper's] ideas can be carried through, at least in principle". (H. B. Curry, *Mathematical Reviews*, vol. 9, no. 7 [July-August 1948], p. 321; and also reviews in *Journal of Symbolic Logic*, vols. 13 and 14.) A number of logicians were influenced by Popper's work—notably W. C. Kneale and Bruce Brooke-Wavell. (W. C. Kneale, "The Province of Logic", and W. C. and Mary Kneale, *The Development of Logic* [Oxford: Oxford University Press, 1962], p. 563. See also Bruce Brooke-Wavell, "A Generalization of the Truth-Table Method", Ph.D. dissertation, University of London, 1958. Brooke-Wavell argues that "deducibility" is definable in terms of general tabular predicates. Together with Popper's derivation of logic from the single undefined concept of "deducibility", this would yield the derivability of logic from basic tabular rules supported by the truth-table algebra.) Evert Beth said that Popper's work had partly inspired him to build his own well-known method of "semantic tableaux". (See his comment, quoted in the Schilpp volume for Popper, p. 1096.)

or axioms, and cannot by his method obtain logic through inferential definitions alone.[8]

Replying to Lejewski, Popper accepted this criticism, acknowledging that his papers were, as an attempt to build up a simple system of natural deduction, "just a failure".[9] Popper also now states that he has come to accept Tarski's scepticism about the possibility of demarcating clearly formative and descriptive signs.

If Lejewski's work stands, our original insight about the presuppositions of the deducibility or argument situation may still be true, but it has much less support. We can no longer appeal to Popper's "New Foundations" to specify what part of logic is involved in the argument situation. But the basic insight remains correct: there *is* still a minimal logic presupposed in that situation. So we need to return to the question asked above: what is this minimal logic? How much logic does deducibility involve? What part of logic, if any, is unrevisable (within the argument situation) under any circumstances whatever?

2. Toward a Revisability Criterion

I do not know what the full answer to this question may be, but I think it to be rather different from what one might expect.[10]

The key to the answer relates to the whole ecological purpose of arguing and of using logic as conceived in *The Retreat to Commitment*: to heighten criticism, to expose views to maximum review, to "make things difficult" for our positions.

Some components of ordinary or "standard" logic always contribute to this goal; and others do not. Ordinary logic includes both the law of noncontradiction and the law of excluded middle. Of the two, our minimal logic would have to retain the law of noncontradiction as a metalinguistic rule governing the argument situation: for if contradictions were permitted, falsity could not be retransmitted and criticism in the sense intended would be impossible. The law of noncontradiction always works to heighten criticism. Any abandonment of it leads not simply to

---

[8]Czesław Lejewski: "Popper's Theory of Formal or Deductive Inference", in P. A. Schilpp, ed., *The Philosophy of Karl Popper*, vol. 1, pp. 632–70.

[9]See Popper, "Replies to My Critics", in Schilpp, ibid., vol. 2, p. 1096. Peter Schroeder-Heister has provided a reconstruction of Popper's approach: see his "Popper's Theory of Deductive Inference and the Concept of a Logical Constant", *History and Philosophy of Science*, vol. 5 (1984), pp. 79–110.

[10]See my exchange with Derksen in *Philosophy of the Social Sciences*, pp. 67–77. See also Alfred Tarski, "The Semantic Conception of Truth and the Foundations of Semantics", *Philosophy and Phenomenological Research*, vol. 4 (1944), reprinted in *Readings in Philosophical Analysis*, ed. Herbert Feigl and Wilfrid Sellars (New York: Appleton-Century-Crofts, 1949), p. 59, where Tarski suggests that the "ordinary laws of logic" must be retained in the presence of the liar paradox.

a weakening but to a minimization of criticism.[11]

With regard to the law of excluded middle, the situation is surprisingly—and importantly—different. For there are some circumstances in critical argument where the law of excluded middle may be dispensed with precisely for the purpose of heightening criticism. That is, there are circumstances wherein the law of excluded middle can weaken criticism.

An example is intuitionist logic, as developed and advocated by L.E.J. Brouwer, one well-known feature of which is to abandon the law of excluded middle (which, although a well-formed formula of the system, is not demonstrable within it). Thus the theorems of intuitionist logic must be proved by weaker means than are available in classical logic. In this particular case, the weaker logic serves to set up restrictions on the admissibility of certain kinds of proof. Indirect proof is ruled out. No statement may be admitted unless it can be *directly* proved by producing an instance in a finite determinate number of steps. In introducing such requirements, and ruling out indirect proof, proof is made more difficult, and criticism is, in this context, for this limited purpose, consequently strengthened.[12]

This hardly means that the law of excluded middle may always or even often be abandoned to the betterment of criticism. Quite the contrary. One must distinguish between the different critical aims of constructing or demonstrating or proving, on the one hand, and of nondemonstrative testing, on the other.[13] Intuitionist logic is constructive, whereas in most situations in science we are faced not with a construction task, but with one of testing, in which not all legitimate statements are decidable. This may be seen by recalling the controversy over indeterminacy in quantum physics.

Several philosophers and scientists, including Quine, Werner Heisenberg, Friedrich Waismann, and others, have suggested that indeterminacy may force abandonment of the law of excluded middle. The argument can be summed up thus: it is impossible to determine both the position and the momentum of a particle at a particular time. Hence some statements about particles seem to be neither true nor false but undecidable. Only the law of

---

[11]I do not mean by this that we must hang on to some particular object-linguistic form of the law of noncontradiction: e.g.,—(p.p̄). One would, however, as Hans Lenk suggests, need to maintain a functional equivalent or analogue, which might be achieved object-linguistically with Sheffer's stroke or Pierce's operator, or metalinguistically with predications of truth and falsity, or in a variety of other ways.

[12]L.E.J. Brouwer; "Mathematik, Wissenschaft und Sprache", *Monatshefte für Mathematik und Physik*, vol. 36 (1929), pp. 153–64; and "Consciousness, Philosophy, and Mathematics", in *Proceedings of the Tenth International Congress of Philosophy* (Amsterdam: North-Holland Publishing Co., 1949), vol. 1, pp. 1235–49. The interpretation of Brouwer given here was presented in my "Limits of Rationality: A Critical Study of Some Logical Problems of Contemporary Pragmatism and Related Movements", pp. 304–9. Popper includes a closely similar interpretation of Brouwer in *Objective Knowledge*, pp. 139–40.

[13]One might informally develop a number of related distinctions: there would be *argument for*, *argument against*, *argument about the truth of*, *argument about the conditions under which a particular statement would be false*. *Argument about*, as meant here, requires basic Logic I with retransmission of falsity. In *argument for*, on the other hand, one might have almost any transmission rules: one might have transmission of truth, for instance, without retransmission of falsity.

excluded middle forces us to say that these must be either true or false. Therefore abandon the law of excluded middle. The argument is simply incorrect. For it is not only the law of excluded middle that provokes the trouble here. Another assumption, unmentioned in the argument just sketched, is the old logical-positivist principle of verification: that there is something wrong with a statement in science that cannot be decided or verified—that it is meaningless. Insisting upon this untenable principle leads to the rejection of the law of excluded middle, and to a consequent reduction of testability within quantum mechanics. By retaining the principle of verification, one distracts attention from the possibility of solving this problem by distinguishing ontological and epistemological levels, and noting that from the fact that a certain thing cannot be determined it does not follow that that thing does not exist or that anything said about it is meaningless. From the fact that, given a particle's momentum, we cannot determine its position, it does not follow that a statement about its real position is not true in fact, let alone that such a statement is meaningless—unless one is assuming something like the verification principle. Thus it is the verification principle, rather than the law of excluded middle, which may be dropped here.

In sum, Brouwerian "positivism" in constructive mathematics increases criticism, while logical positivism in quantum physics decreases criticism. In physics, a stronger logic, retaining the law of excluded middle, serves to increase testability. For purposes of criticism, as opposed to proof, one will ordinarily wish to use a stronger logic.

Something can be done with these results.

We can put forward informally a sort of "revisability criterion".[14] A position would be unrevisable (in argument) if and only if there are no circumstances under which it can be abandoned without weakening the exposure of the system as a whole to criticism. Such unrevisable positions, if any, would mark the absolute presupposition of critical argument.

This gives a fairly clear line which, although not corresponding to the traditional "analytic-synthetic" dichotomy, does mark off one portion of the class of truths traditionally known as analytic. This in turn rebuts Quine's claim that no sharp boundary line between analytic and synthetic truths may be drawn.

If we take Popper's falsifiability criterion as a way of marking off scientific from nonscientific statements, and our revisability criterion as a way to demarcate what is revisable within the situation of critical argument from what is not, the spectrum of types of statement falls into at least three relatively clear categories. Various other categories are not so clearly demarcated. What I have in mind is suggested by the chart on the next page.

---

[14]See chap. 5 above.

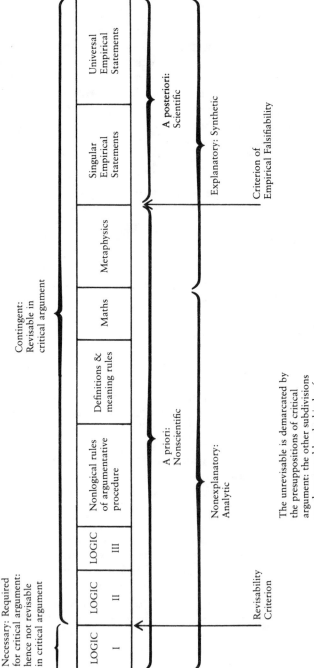

Necessary: Required for critical argument; hence not revisable in critical argument

Contingent: Revisable in critical argument

| LOGIC I | LOGIC II | LOGIC III | Nonlogical rules of argumentative procedure | Definitions & meaning rules | Maths | Metaphysics | Singular Empirical Statements | Universal Empirical Statements |

Revisability Criterion

A priori: Nonscientific

A posteriori: Scientific

Nonexplanatory: Analytic

Explanatory: Synthetic

Criterion of Empirical Falsifiability

The unrevisable is demarcated by the presuppositions of critical argument: the other subdivisions are demarcated by the kinds of arguments that may be used to defeat their components.

The chart is offered in a spirit of amusement, and should be thrown away—like a ladder . . . or a banana peel—once it has served its purpose. In a small area on the left is located our minimal sense of logic: this is referred to as "Logic I". In an area on the right are the theories of empirical science. Between, in a larger section, are some statements that have traditionally been called analytic and others that have traditionally been called synthetic, but which are neither empirically refutable (and hence scientific in Popper's sense) nor presupposed in all critical argument (as in Logic I). This middle area would presumably contain all of metaphysics, most of mathematics, and most of that class of statements like "All brothers are male siblings" around which much of the analytic-synthetic controversy has revolved. Accordingly, a number of classifications are distinguished on the chart:

> analytic/synthetic
> nonscientific/scientific
> nonexplanatory/explanatory
> necessary/contingent
> a priori/a posteriori.

These various categories have uses, despite their often vague and almost always overlapping character, most having been proposed to deal with some problem that none of the others quite fitted. Since the original problems overlap, the categories and distinctions do, too, and remain a source of some confusion. If at least two ends of the spectrum are pinned down, it may be easier to salvage what is useful in the remaining categories, and also to see how varied is the spectrum that they cover.

The chart may help suggest, for instance, why some philosophers prefer to identify metaphysics and definitions, or lump them together vaguely even when they do not identify them. For these fit none of the restrictive *logical or else empirical* dichotomies that are so common. They have, however, under the influence of Aristotelianism, tended to be definitionalized rather than empiricized. For Aristotle, the ultimate presuppositions of argument are definitions of essences, presupposed necessarily in order to terminate infinite regress.[15] On such an account, metaphysics, definitions, and necessary propositions tend to become identified. Moreover, philosophies that stress verifiability rather than falsifiability as a criterion for science inevitably encourage attempts to reduce those large parts of science which cannot be verified to definitional or rule status, and thus tend to become essentialist or instrumentalist.

Only two reasonably definite criteria are then indicated on the chart. I can

[15]See *The Open Society*, chap. 11.

state no such criteria for demarcating the traditional analytic-synthetic divisions. Had Quine said only that there is a good bit of shifting back and forth, and that the classification of some statements will be uncertain, there would be no disagreeing with him.[16]

I have made a separate space, Logic II, in this middle area, to contain elements of logic, such as the law of excluded middle, which are not presupposed in all critical argument. Another "catch all" category, Logic III, is indicated, which will vary with the logical and descriptive terms of various languages. Distinguishing these three different levels of logic (in a way that is hardly intended to be exact or exhaustive) may help to suggest why logic has at some times seemed entirely a matter of convention, and at other times, to the same or different thinkers, seemed necessary.

Logic in the first sense, Logic I, is required in order to have a critical argument at all. Whatever "necessity" logic in these further senses may have arises only within a certain domain and for particular purposes—not for the sake of critical argument itself. Thus in Brouwer's ideal world of mathematics, one in which all legitimate statements are decidable at any time, one drops the law of excluded middle in order to maximize criticism, in order to make as difficult as possible the discovery of the population of that world, and to insure as much as possible against error in specifying that population. The situation differs in the world of experience, where all legitimate statements are not in fact so decidable. Thus, the combination of a particular task dependency and a particular domain dependency produced the need in intuitionism to proscribe the law of excluded middle. Yet even here there is no relativization of logic in respect to the fundamental aim of maximizing criticism, of stacking the cards, as it were, against our conjectures.

In insisting that a minimal sense of logic is presupposed by the critical argument situation itself, I have thus identified an absolute presupposition of argument. Philosophers have long sought to specify what was absolutely presupposed in intellectual activity and what was not. This particular answer is, of course, not the one anticipated, since it is neither a principle from which all else can be derived nor a category to which all else need conform. Most categories and principles, along with much else traditionally regarded as *a priori*, necessary, analytic, unrevisable, indispensable, I see as revisable and dispensable within the argument situation.

---

[16]On the other hand, Quine links the problem of the analytic-synthetic with an untenable empiricist distinction between logical or formative signs and descriptive signs, a distinction in terms of which descriptive signs gain meaning only on the basis of observations or sense data. Such a view requires a sharp and definite distinction between formative and descriptive signs; and if the view is abandoned, as Quine thinks it should be, it seems that the importance of the analytic-synthetic distinction diminishes too. But if descriptive words do not acquire meaning in this way, if they are *all* theoretical, all theory-impregnated, then they may or may not be used in a conventionalist way depending upon whether we wish to stick to the theories in question or to subject them to severe test. Viewed in this way, the problem does not even arise in the way suggested by Quine.

3. The Despair of Reason

Despite what has been said here about how some minimal logic is presupposed by the argument situation, a reader who noted the apparent similarity, alluded to above—between Quine's view that everything (including logic) is open to revision and my account of pancritical rationalism in which everything (including the practice of arguing and revising and using logic) is open to criticism—may wonder whether I am not backing out of pancritical rationalism—or simply contradicting myself.[17] It might seem as if I were now insisting that we are committed to logic.

Some support for such a response to my argument is to be found in work by Jonathan Bennett concerning the analytic-synthetic controversy.[18] A look at his views serves to bring out the relationship and the difference between the problem of the limits of rationality and the problem of the analytic and synthetic.

For Bennett, to call a sentence "analytic" is to register the conviction that it is highly indispensable for establishing or justifying, in providing answers to "How do you know?" questions. Bennett attempts to refute Quine's views about the possibility of revising anything in argument by citing the argument about the limits of rationality; by arguing that, in any argument, the infinite regress of justification has to be stopped by referring to something that is *not* open to revision; that in *every* argument situation at least one sentence is not up for revision, on which the rest of the argument depends; and that such is necessary if one is to be able to construct an argument at all. For such terminal sentences, Bennett writes: "the question of their possible falsification" is *ruled out*. Such "terminal sentences are put off the cards for possible revision"; once one works back to them, "there is nothing more to say".

Claiming that such an unrevisable statement would be "traditionally analytic" (in the sense Quine was attacking), in that the difference between such a statement and other statements was a difference not in degree but in kind, Bennett concluded that Quine's views should be rejected.[19]

Bennett's approach is justificationist, and makes use of the argument

---

[17]See my exchange with Derksen in *Philosophy of the Social Sciences*. See also Hans Lenk, "Philosophische Logikbegründung und Rationaler Kritizismus", *Zeitschrift für Philosophische Forschung*, vol. 24 (1970), pp. 183–205.

[18]Jonathan Bennett, "Analytic-Synthetic", *Proceedings of the Aristotelian Society* (1958–59); and "On Being Forced to a Conclusion", *Aristotelian Society Supplementary Volume 35* (1961). Interestingly, in the first paper Bennett cites Carroll's story of Achilles and the Tortoise in order to support his argument. See my critique of Carroll's tale, and of its use in this connection, in my "Achilles, the Tortoise, and Explanation in Science and in History", *British Journal for the Philosophy of Science* (1963). See also my *Lewis Carroll's Symbolic Logic*, pp. 466–70.

[19]Quine basically accepted Bennett's *exposition* of his position. See his reference to Bennett's work in *Word and Object*, p. 68n. Another follower of Quine who writes in a way similar to Bennett is Morton White. In his *Toward Reunion in Philosophy* (Cambridge, Mass.: Harvard University Press, 1956), p. 288, White maintains that an *a priori* statement is one that we believe quite firmly and therefore "make immune"

concerning the limits of rationality which was refuted above. Outside a justificationist context his argument has no force. Apart from this, he fails to demarcate analytic statements in one important traditional sense. One steady element in the changing philosophical conceptions of analyticity has been the hope thereby to specify something that is common to, presupposed in, *all argument whatever*—such as Logic I, as explained above. Bennett argues only that something is presupposed, regarded as unrevisable, as ultimate, in *each* (justificational) argument. He does not claim that this something that is presupposed in *each* argument must be presupposed in *all* arguments: different arguments can have different unrevisable principles. With the traditional notion of analytic-as-unrevisable, it was hoped that disputes could be limited—by showing that something necessarily had to be accepted *in common* as unrevisable by experience. Yet Bennett appeals, as a defense of the "traditional" notion, to the "fact" that the dilemma of ultimate commitment—the main source of ultimate relativism—cannot be avoided. His argument, therefore, even if it were correct, hardly speaks to that aspect of the problem.[20]

My claim that all critical argument depends on Logic I (and that Logic I is hence unrevisable in argument)—in the sense that such logic defines the space in which argument takes place—differs, then, from Bennett's contention that every argument depends on some particular unrevisable ultimate premise.

Even after such clarifications and distinctions are made, an explanation may still be demanded of how I could *argue* myself out of the practice of argument and using logic while at the same time, necessarily, in that argument, presupposing logic. I cannot mean simply that I could be *forced* (by brainwashing, nervous collapse, etc.) to abandon the practice of argument and using logic.

I see no difficulty in satisfying this demand. A large part of the philosophical tradition testifies to the possibility of being argued logically out of the practice of argument and using logic. "It may seem a very extravagant attempt of the sceptics to destroy *reason* by argument and ratiocination", as Hume puts it in *An Enquiry Concerning Human Understanding,* but this is, as he adds, "the grand scope of all their enquiries and disputes".[21] What I have in mind is indeed the *despair of reason and truth* to

---

to overthrow. "It is, in short, a sentence of which we say, 'This is pinned down . . . calling S an a priori statement is another way of uttering 'I accept' followed by S, followed by 'without attention to experience'." Such an approach is deeply subjectivist, in the sense discussed by Popper in *Objective Knowledge*, chap. 3, whereas the approach I took to presuppositions of argument was objectivist.

[20]When a philosopher attempts to defend some traditional notion, as does Bennett, with an argument that implies that the traditional notion *cannot* solve the problem it was intended to solve, what has probably happened is that the philosophical problem in question has been forgotten while the philosopher's attention has been diverted to a subordinate issue, one that is, as in this case, of a technical character, and only important philosophically in the broader connection. I am criticizing Bennett here in terms of what I have called the "check of the problem".

[21]David Hume, *An Enquiry Concerning Human Understanding*, sec. 12.

which Nietzsche referred when he wrote of "gnawing and crumbling scepticism and relativism".[22]

Consider several examples.

First, there are the logical paradoxes (the liar, Richard, Grelling, etc.). The paradoxes are reached in the course of rigorously logical argument. Therein lies their telling power: using logic, and presupposing logic, one reaches illogic. If the paradoxes could not be avoided, then one would have grounds for deeply distrusting logic and rational argumentation. Of course one might say that in rejecting logic because it led to illogic, one is presupposing logic and is hence inconsistent. But the irrationalist makes no claim to be consistent. And would it be *more* consistent to *accept* logic that led to illogic?

If the example of the paradoxes seems unconvincing—perhaps from the perspective that ways have now been found to avoid them—take as another example or set of examples a line of argumentation which is particularly pertinent to *The Retreat to Commitment,* which is concerned, after all, to build an argument against fideism, relativism, and scepticism.

(1) Relativism, fideism, and scepticism contend, on the basis of arguments about the limits of rationality widely thought to be rational, logical, and indestructible, that serious argumentation is futile in the sense that, from a rational or logical viewpoint, one position is as good as another. Their basic contention is that there is a *rational excuse for irrationalism.*

(2) The upshot of determinism—another position reached by many on the basis of reason and logic—is that all argument is *illusory.* If the doctrine of determinism, often championed in the name of reason and science, is true, then reason and science are illusory. It would not just be *some* things that are fixed from all eternity: everything is so fixed, including the results of any particular scientific argument. Even the result of any argument about determinism is determined: that one person shall become a determinist is fixed—without any regard to the weight of the argument; and that another shall become an indeterminist is similarly fixed. If one's views are fully determined by natural laws and boundary conditions, then they do not depend on the force of argument or on the weighing of evidence.[23] If scientific determinism is true, we may believe or reject it; but we do so not because we judge the argument in its favor to be sound or unsound, but because facts and laws determine that we shall so believe or fail to believe. If determinism is true, then the distinction between being *forced* to reject logic and being argued out of logic loses its meaning.

If one were, by argument and logic, to reason oneself into the relativist,

[22]See Nietzsche's untimely meditation on *Schopenhauer as Educator.*

[23]See my discussion of determinism in "The Philosophy of Karl Popper; Part 2: Consciousness and Physics: Quantum Mechanics, Probability, Indeterminism, The Body-Mind Problem", *Philosophia,* 7, nos. 3–4, (July 1978), pp. 675–716. See also my *Werner Erhard: The Transformation of a Man,* pp. 99–105. On the important related thesis that no causal physical theory of the descriptive and argumentative functions of language is possible, see Popper: "Language and the Body-Mind Problem", *Conjectures and Refutations,* pp. 293–98.

fideist, and sceptical positions—or into the determinist position—and at the same time were to notice these implications—one might well conclude, through apparent reason and logic, that reason and logic are to be rejected as guides to life. Using argument, and presupposing argumentation, we destroy argumentation.

I am not a determinist, and I believe determinism has been refuted.[24] Moreover, I believe that the argument of this book defeats the only powerful argument on behalf of scepticism, fideism, and relativism. Yet I want to hold myself open to the despair of reason, in case the argument should lead somewhere different tomorrow. Thus the pancritical rationalist may hold his practice of reasoning and obeying logic—just like everything else—open to comprehensive criticism and rejection.

The fact that argument presupposes a minimal logic as unrevisable in no way identifies a *commitment* on the part of a pancritical rationalist. To be sure, the practice of critical argument and logic are bound up together. One can no more argue without a minimal logic than one can live without breathing or speak without language. None of these three—living, speaking, arguing—require irrational commitment to a dogma. Nor for that matter are logic and arguing even peculiar to or identificatory of a pancritical rationalist—any more than breathing or speaking is. To the extent to which he wishes to employ arguments, *any ir*rationalist must use a minimal logic too. The strength of the irrationalist's *tu quoque* was indeed that it defeated the rationalist *logically and rationally,* on the rationalist's own terms: it defeated the rationalist with an *internal* criticism. If one wanted to argue that anyone who *uses* logic is *committed* to logic, then one would have to claim that the irrationalist, too, is committed to logic![25] In which case the *tu quoque* would, once again, vanish.

---

[24]See *The Open Universe.*

[25]Of course any good irrationalist recognizes, rightly, that use of logic and commitment to logic are separate matters. All these matters are confused in Anthony O'Hear's *Karl Popper* (London: Routledge and Kegan Paul, 1980), a book whose presentation and interpretation often show little understanding of the issues. As one example, O'Hear writes (p. 150): "the irrationalist who is logically superior to the rationalist cannot, without self-contradiction, engage in argument, even so far as to point out the logical superiority of his position." This statement is misconceived from beginning to end, and a few of the errors may be noted: (1) Self-contradiction—even if it were present here, and it is not—would not, in itself, worry an irrationalist who acknowledges no allegiance to logic. (2) The irrationalist's logical superiority to justificationist rationalists has been to note that the rationalist, *from his own point of view,* cannot do what he claims to do—i.e., that the rationalist has failed to acknowledge the limitations of reason and argumentation. (3) The irrationalist can, of course, use these, and other arguments, against the rationalist. *Use of* argument needs to be carefully distinguished from *belief in* argument. The irrationalist can use these arguments, not because he himself takes argument seriously, but because he knows that the rationalist does. The irrationalist uses argument because he knows that argument is effective against rationalists. The *rationalist* may be impressed by arguments showing the logical superiority of irrationalism; and the irrationalist may find it amusing to see the rationalist defeated on his own terms even if he himself does not take those terms seriously. The irrationalist may, of course, also take argument seriously—and may even do so consistently—in any area which, in his opinion, does not run up against the alleged limits of reason. The irrationalist, with no need to be consistent, may invoke reason frequently or not at all. One must remember that, for him, *reason is a whore.*

APPENDIX 6. THE TRANSMISSIBILITY ASSUMPTION

In chapter 5 of this book, I asked why an authoritarian structure has been retained—had even gone unnoticed—in modern philosophies that were intentionally anti-authoritarian and critical in spirit. I found an answer to this question in the fact that in almost all traditional and modern philosophies—those that called themselves critical as well as those that did not—the idea of criticism was fused with the idea of justification.[1]

It is time now to ask a somewhat deeper question, whose answer will be a little more technical. What I have in mind is: *Why are justification and criticism fused in the ways we have described?*

Consider again what occurs during justificational criticism. In justificational criticism, the view to be criticized or evaluated is examined with regard to the question whether it can be *derived from* (justified by) the authority. Thus it is supposed to inherit logically whatever merit it possesses from the justifying authority whence it is derived. Thus if the justifying authority is true, the view being examined, if derivable from it, is true; if the justifying authority is probable, it is at least as probable; if the justifying authority is empirical, it is empirical. And so on. Without all this, there would be no justification.

This whole procedure is held in place by yet another hidden philosophical dogma: *Most philosophical views take for granted that all properties, measures, and tokens of intellectual value or merit are transmitted from premises to conclusion, in the same manner as truth, through the relationship of logical derivability or deducibility.*[2] I call this the "transmissibili-

---

[1]The insight that the Western philosophical tradition is authoritarian in structure is due to Popper (1960), as is the critique of the transmissibility assumption in its application to empirical science (1934). The explicit unfusing of justification and criticism is due to me (1960), as is the application of the transmissibility assumption to the problem of rationality (1960). See Popper, "On the Sources of Knowledge and of Ignorance", 1960, reprinted in *Conjectures and Refutations*; and *The Logic of Scientific Discovery*, secs. 36 and 83. See also my "Limits of Rationality", 1962, and "Rationality versus the Theory of Rationality", 1964, both cited above; and my "A Note on Barker's Discussion of Popper's Theory of Corroboration", *Philosophical Studies*, January-February 1961, pp. 5–10.

[2]Several philosophers of science, including Carnap, Hempel, and Goodman, have argued the place of a similar assumption in theories of confirmation in the natural sciences, referring to this assumption by names

ty assumption". It is also called the "content condition", the "consequence condition", and other names as well.

Thus theories about the evaluation and criticism of competing views include (1) some more or less well-defined notion about the character of whatever property (e.g., truth, probability, empirical character) is to be used in evaluating and criticizing; and (2) the assumption that this property, whatever its character, must be fully transmissible logically—like truth and unlike falsity (which is retransmitted). Thus logical derivates inherit the quality and degree of merit of the premises whence they are derived. This "common feature", writes Adolf Grünbaum, "should be an ingredient of any theory of corroboration or rational credibility".[3]

This assumption is held with ferocious, if usually unexamined, tenacity— a tenacity which can only be explained historically. The earliest attempted criteria of evaluation were criteria of truth, demarcating good ideas from bad ones coincident with the demarcation between the true and the false. (See appendix 2.) But criteria of truth proved to be either unattainable or practically inapplicable to the issues for which they were needed; and the search for criteria of truth was displaced by a search for weaker but more attainable measures. Probability (in the sense of the probability calculus) is most often used for this purpose. (Prior to the development of modern probability theory several different senses of "probability" were used in this connection; but probability in the sense of the probability calculus is now almost invariably meant in such connections.)

Truth and *probability* do happen to be transmissible from premises to conclusion through the deducibility relationship: the derivates of a statement are true if the statement is true; and they are *at least as probable* as the statement whence they are derived. But most other evaluational properties are not like this. And various other properties of statements which have little if anything to do with evaluation are also not transmissible. One example of the latter would be the property of "being written in English". Truth and probability are indeed two of the *very few* characteristics which are transmissible.

My historical conjecture is that these two concepts exerted such a determining influence over early developments within the justificationist

---

like "consequence condition", "entailment condition", and "content condition". My remarks here are not intended to apply only to scientific matters. For an example of the misunderstandings created by misapplying the transmissibility assumption or consequence condition, see my "A Note on Barker's Criticism of Popper's Theory of Corroboration".

[3] Adolf Grünbaum; "Falsifiability and Rationality", mimeographed. Read at the International Colloquium on Issues in Contemporary Physics and Philosophy of Science, September 2, 1971; See also Grünbaum's "Is Falsifiability the Touchstone of Scientific Rationality? Karl Popper versus Inductivism", in R. S. Cohen, P. K. Feyerabend, and M. W. Wartofsky, *Essays in Memory of Imre Lakatos* (Dordrecht: D. Reidel, 1976), pp. 213–52; and "Is the Method of Bold Conjectures and Attempted Refutations *Justifiably* the Method of Science?", *British Journal for the Philosophy of Science*, June 1976, pp. 105–36.

metacontext that it is now unquestioningly assumed that other putative properties, however they might differ from truth and probability, nevertheless automatically share their logical transmissibility. Indeed, the demand for justification makes undesirable any property unable to justify its derivates by lending them its own respectability.

If the ability of truth and probability to be transmitted led, historically, to the general assumption that *any* indicator of merit or intellectual respectability is transmissible, the situation is now ironically also reversed: some measures, such as probability, are retained *because* they are logically transmissible. The transmissibility requirement itself is taken for granted. The self-reinforcing structure of the Western justificationist metacontext so protects this assumption that today, when criteria of truth remain unavailable, and when probability measures are unable to arbitrate rationally among competing scientific hypotheses, not to mention less precise ideas, logical transmissibility is still expected of other evaluatory properties and tokens without regard to their real logical capabilities; and it is also demanded that evaluations be made in terms of probability without regard to *its* evaluational capabilities. Hence the heroic yet futile attempts to retain probability as a positive evaluational property.

Take contemporary empiricist philosophy of science as an example. To comprehend it and its quandaries, it is important to notice that most theories relying on probability as an evaluatory measure also include "empirical character" as a further requirement for any acceptable theory. Legitimate statements must be reducible to something like individual "basic statements" reporting sense experience; and the logical derivates of a legitimate statement inherit not only its degree of probability but also its empirical character. Empirical character, however, is *not* transmissible. From every basic empirical statement both nonempirical metaphysical statements and all tautologies follow logically—not to mention the problem of induction: that legitimate universal scientific hypotheses cannot be reduced to truth functions of a finite class of basic observation statements. Out of this conflict (between the transmissibility of probability and the nontransmissibility of empirical character) are produced several of the well-known "paradoxes" of induction and confirmation. When transmissible probability is mixed with the nontransmissible property of "empirical character", the results are indeed bizarre. Nonempirical consequences of empirical statements inherit the probability of the original empirical statement, consequently becoming respectable from the point of view of the probability standard. Yet, lacking empirical character, they remain disreputable from *that* standpoint. If meaning criteria are added as still further criteria of respectability, still more anomalies can appear.

Yet it is simply not necessary to be bound by this transmissibility assumption. Alternative approaches to evaluation and criticism are possible which not only do not contain the transmissibility assumption but which are incompatible with it. One example is the theory of testability or corroborability. It provides an example of nonjustificational evaluation and criticism in broad terms.

Testability or corroborability assesses not the degree to which a theory is probabilified or confirmed or justified, but the degree to which it is *testable* or *corroborable*. This provides an indication of progress, expressing *relative potential satisfactoriness* of a theory, applicable in evaluating a theory even before that theory has been tested empirically.

The measure of degree of testability, unlike truth and probability, is, however, not logically transmissible. Quite the contrary.

The difference between this theory and those referred to above can be defined thus. Whereas evaluational measures like probability and (Carnapian) degree of confirmation are transmitted in the same direction as truth, degree of testability, which is a measure of content, is, like falsity, *retransmitted* from conclusion to premises. The difference between testability theory and various probabilistic theories of confirmation may be defined by reference to this irreducible difference in the ways the two properties are logically transmitted.[4] (Other evaluational measures and properties—such as explanatory power—are also not transmitted.)

The point may be explained as follows. If the theory of testability did share the transmissibility assumption, then any consequence of a hypothesis would have to be as highly testable as the original. But no such thing happens: since a hypothesis is testable (in the syntactical sense) by its consequents, the hypothesis must possess at least as high a degree of testability (and thus corroborability) as any of its consequents. But it *may* (and if logically stronger almost invariably *will*) possess a higher degree of testability. If a hypothesis can possess a higher degree of testability than its consequents, then a consequent does not *inherit* this particular property through the deducibility relationship. A theory does not bequeath its degree of testability to those theories it entails, its necessary conditions, which traditional accounts would represent it as justifying.

This point might be illustrated trivially by examining the testability relations of these three hypotheses:

(1) All who dwell in London are English.
(2) All who dwell in Hampstead are English.
(3) All who dwell in Bloomsbury are English.

Assuming, correctly, that Bloomsbury and Hampstead are both in London, and that both the second and the third statements follow from the first, let

---

[4]That there should be any doubt about the transmissibility of degree of testability is odd. For the idea of logically deriving one statement from another not identical to it involves the notion that various statements differ in logical strength. Yet the statement which is stronger is *ipso facto* more testable—which means that its degree of testability is no more transmissible to its implicates than is its logical strength.

us suppose that the second statement is falsified. By *modus tollens,* the rule of retransmission of falsity, the first statement is falsified too.

But suppose that the second statement has not been falsified, and that another of the first statement's consequents, the third statement, has never been tested. Clearly, the first statement will be falsified by the third just in case the third is subsequently tested and found false. But the second statement will not be falsified thereby, since it is logically unrelated to the third. Thus the first statement is more testable or falsifiable than the second, since the first is falsifiable by something that does not falsify the second. And the second cannot be more falsifiable than the first, since anything that falsifies the second falsifies the first.

This example, and similar ones, bring into relief not only the absence of any assumption that a measure of intellectual respectability or rationality (in this case "degree of testability") is logically transmissible from premises to conclusion, but also the nonjustificational character of the theory of criticism involved.

(To avoid confusion, the reader should refer again to appendix 3, where it is shown that in the theory of testability the falsity of a view is not *established* in a refutation thereof. Rather, the view is provisionally rejected because it conflicts with some other better tested, less problematic view. But the view that occasions the refutation is itself open to criticism by the testing of its own consequences. And these in turn are criticizable; and so on forever. This *process* of testing is, of course, in principle infinite; but there is no infinite *regress,* because the aim of justifying or establishing has been abandoned.)

If all measures of intellectual respectability resembled truth and probability in being transmissible, all criticism would perforce be justificational. Since degree of corroborability and testability are not transmissible, not all criticism need be justificational. Hence a nonjustificational, nonauthoritarian theory of knowledge and rationality is indeed possible.

INDICES

ABOUT THE AUTHOR

WILLIAM WARREN BARTLEY, III is engaged in research at the Hoover Institution, Stanford University, where he is writing the biographies of Sir Karl Popper and F. A. von Hayek. In 1979 he was named "Outstanding Professor" in the 19-campus California State University system.

Born in Pittsburgh, Professor Bartley prepared at Harvard College and at the London School of Economics and Political Science, where he wrote his doctoral dissertation under Popper's supervision.

His previous appointments include the Warburg Institute of the University of London; the London School of Economics and Political Science; the University of California (Berkeley and San Diego); and Gonville and Caius College, Cambridge University. From 1967 to 1973, he taught at the University of Pittsburgh, where he was Professor of Philosophy and of History and Philosophy of Science.

Professor Bartley is the author of *Lewis Carroll's Symbolic Logic*; *Wittgenstein,* a biography that has been translated into six languages; *Morality and Religion*; *Werner Erhard: the Transformation of a Man,* the best-selling biography of the founder of *est*; as well as of *The Retreat to Commitment.* He has contributed to many journals, and is also the editor of Sir Karl Popper's *Postscript to the Logic of Scientific Discovery.*

He has held fellowships from the United States Educational Commissions in the United Kingdom and in New Zealand; the American Council of Learned Societies, the American Philosophical Society, the Deutscher Akademischer Austauschdienst, the University of California Institute for the Humanities, the *est* Foundation , the Danforth Foundation, the Walter and Vera Morris Foundation, the Wincott Foundation, the Institute for Humane Studies, the Thyssen Foundation, and other bodies. He has lectured widely in the United States, Europe and the Orient.